Don't miss ... ern Journey into Danger.

SAIYUKI RELOAD

KAZUYA MINEKURA

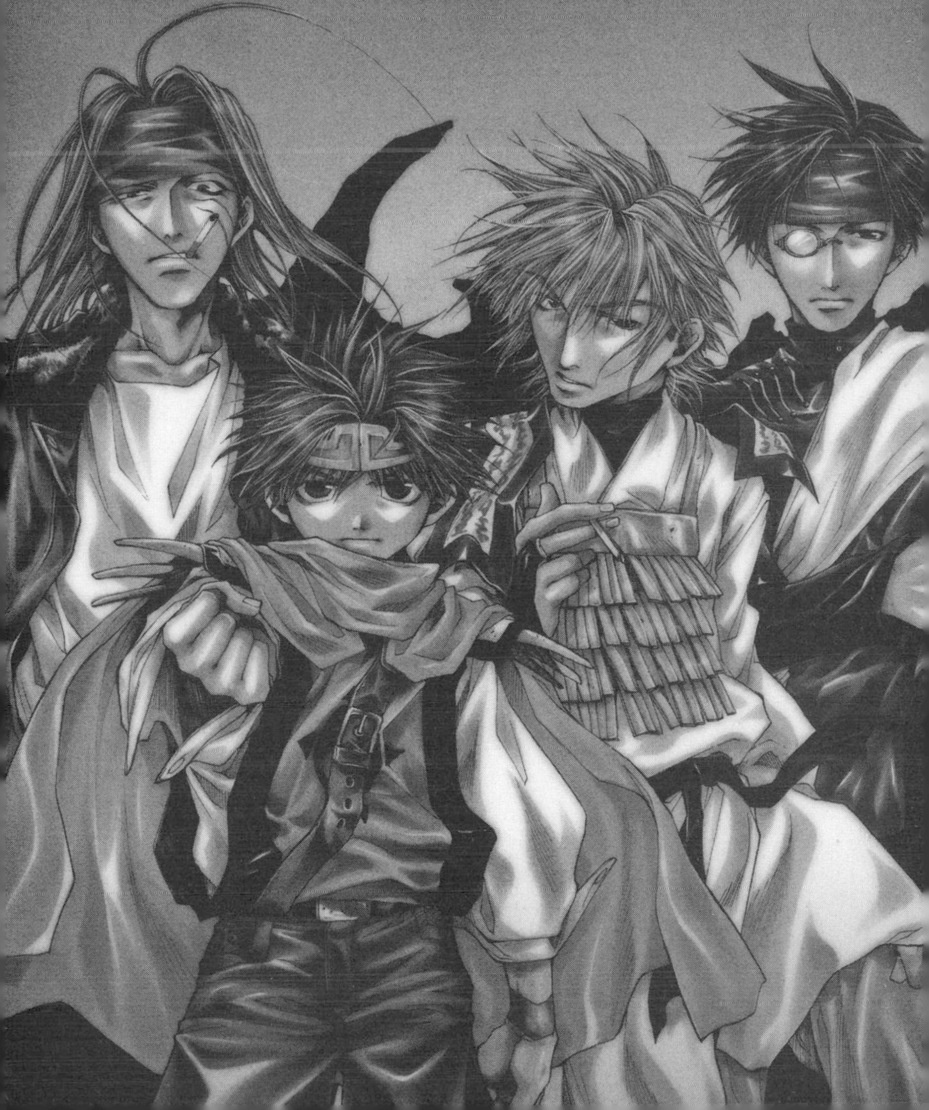

SAIYUKI RELOAD

Don't miss Saiyuki: The Legend of the Western Journey into Danger.

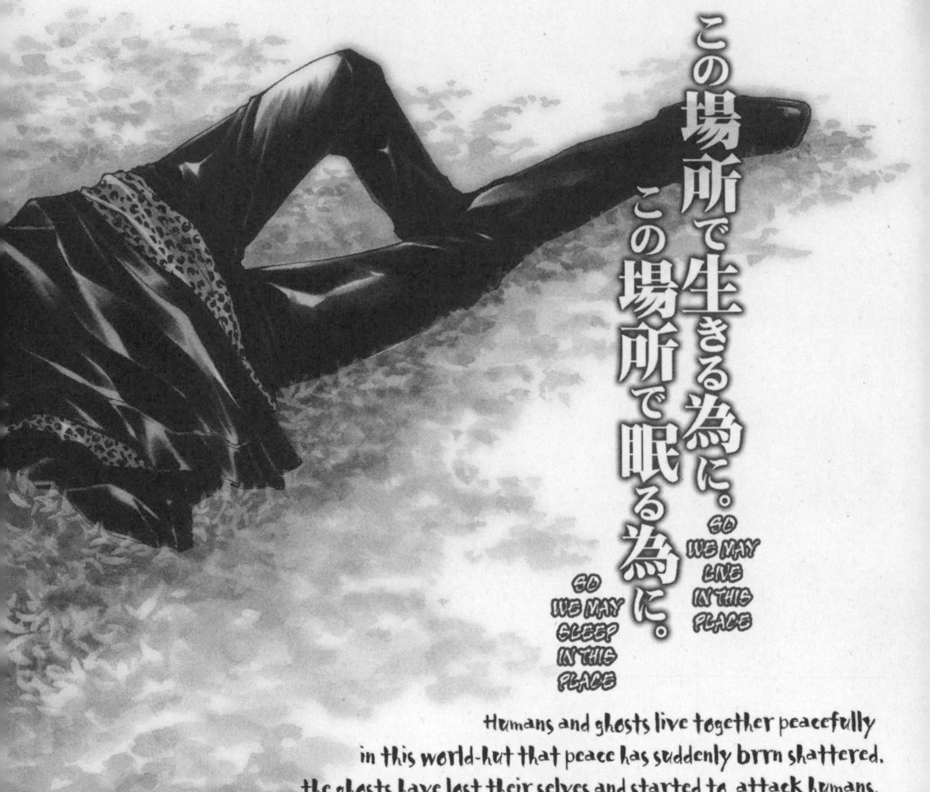
この場所で生きる為に。
この場所で眠る為に。
SO WE MAY LIVE IN THIS PLACE
SO WE MAY SLEEP IN THIS PLACE

Humans and ghosts live together peacefully in this world-but that peace has suddenly brrn shattered. the ghosts have lost their selves and started to attack humans. It all seems related to an evil experiment aimed at reviving Gyumao, a powerful ghost who has been sraled in a tomb for 500 years. Genjo Sanzo has been ordered to stop the experiment. Together with his three friends-Son Goku, Sha Gojo, and Cho Hakkai-begins a journey to the western region of India.

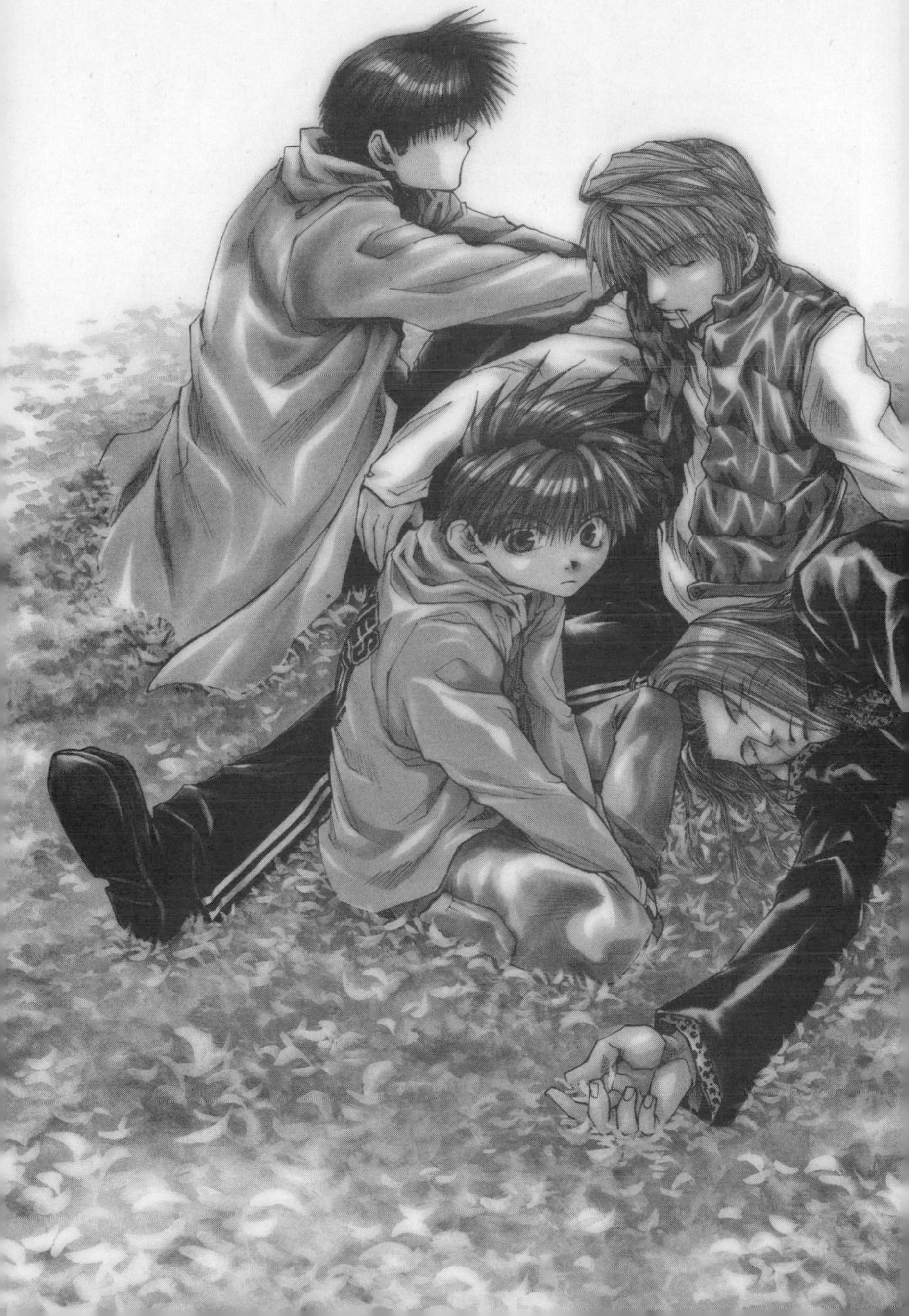

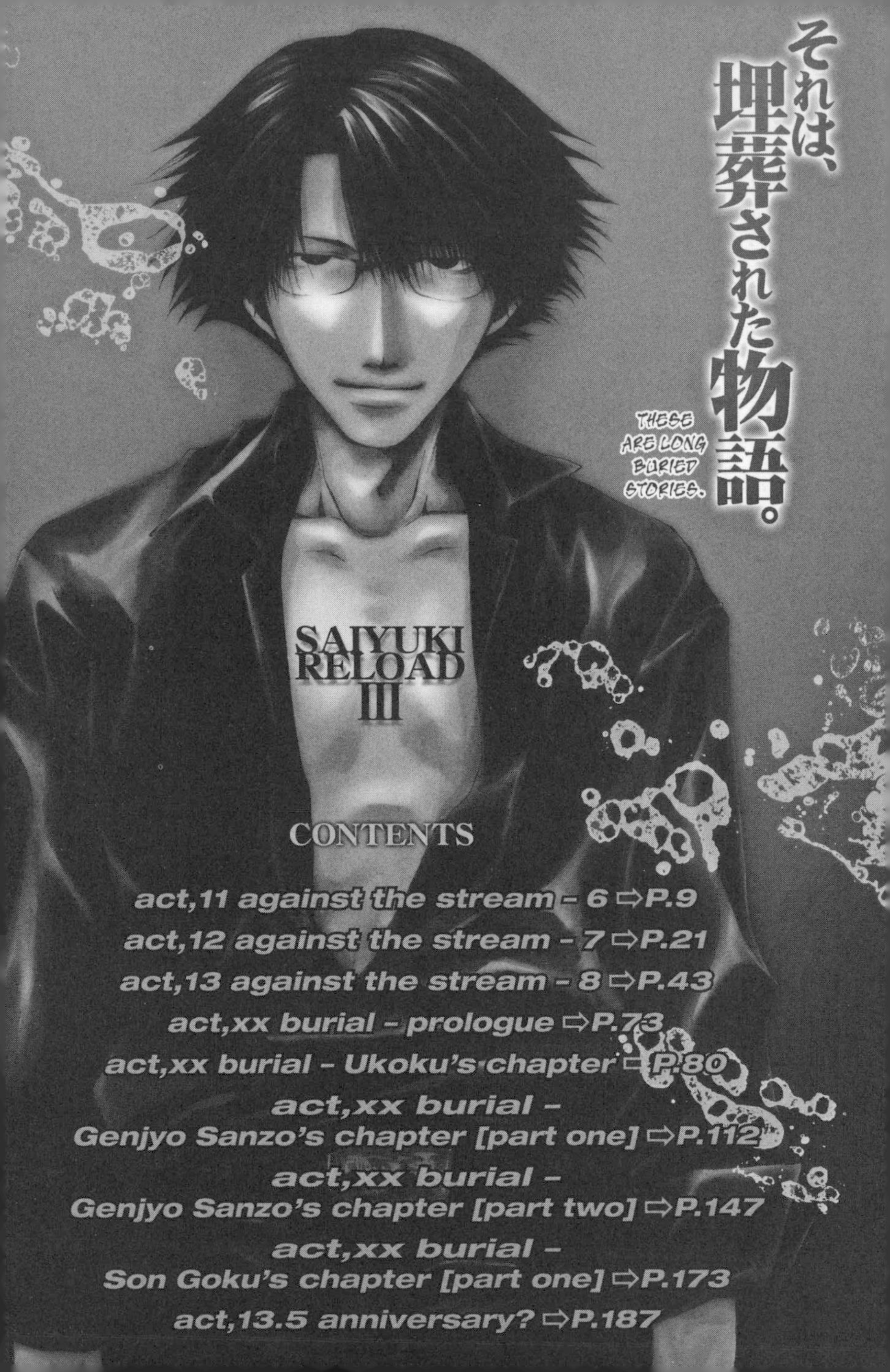
それは、埋葬された物語。
THESE ARE LONG BURIED STORIES.

SAIYUKI RELOAD III

CONTENTS

最遊記 RELOAD

峰倉かずや

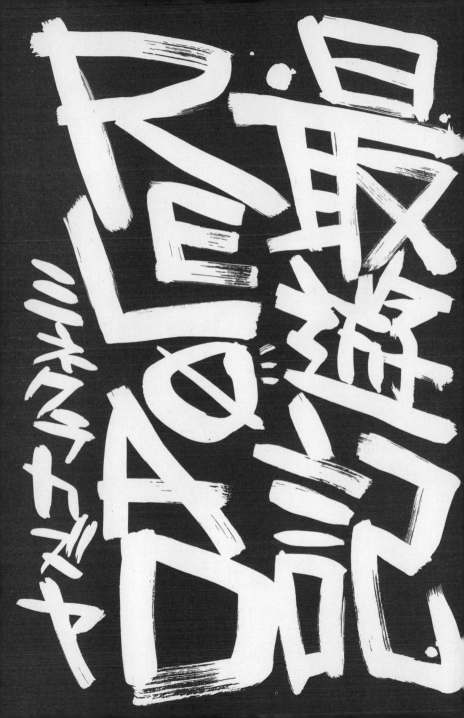

Saiyuki Reload Vol. 3
Created by Kazuya Minekura

Translation - Athena Nibley and Alethea Nibley
English Adaptation - Lianne Sentar
Associate Editor - Peter Ahlstrom
Retouch and Lettering - Jason Milligan
Production Artist - Lucas Rivera
Cover Artist - Kyle Plummer

Editor - Lillian Diaz-Przybyl
Digital Imaging Manager - Chris Buford
Production Managers - Jennifer Miller and Mutsumi Miyazaki
Managing Editor - Lindsey Johnston
VP of Production - Ron Klamert
Publisher and E.I.C. - Mike Kiley
President and C.O.O. - John Parker
C.E.O. and Chief Creative Officer - Stuart Levy

A  Manga

TOKYOPOP Inc.
5900 Wilshire Blvd. Suite 2000
Los Angeles, CA 90036

E-mail: info@TOKYOPOP.com
Come visit us online at www.TOKYOPOP.com

ISBN: 1-59816-027-3

First TOKYOPOP printing: March 2006
10 9 8 7 6 5 4 3 2
Printed in USA

Genjyo Sanzo –

A very brutal, worldly priest. He drinks, smokes, gambles and even carries a gun. He's looking for the sacred scripture of his late master, Sanzo Houshi. He's egotistical, haughty and has zero sense of humor, but this handsome 23-year-old hero also has calm judgment and charisma. His favorite phrases are "Die" and "I'll kill you." His main weapons are the Maten Sutra, a handgun, and a paper fan for idiots. He's 177cm tall (approx. 5'10"), and is often noted for his drooping purple eyes.

Son Goku –

The brave, cheerful Monkey King of legend; an unholy child born from the rocks where the aura of the Earth was gathered. His brain is full of thoughts of food and games. To pay for crimes he committed when he was young, he was imprisoned in the rocks for five hundred years without aging. Because of his optimistic personality, he's become the mascot character of the group; this 18-year-old of superior health is made fun of by Gojyo, yelled at by Sanzo and watched over by Hakkai. He's 162cm tall (approx. 5'4"). His main weapon is the Nyoi-Bo, a magical cudgel that can extend into a sansekkon staff.

Sha Gojyo –

Gojyo is a lecherous kappa (water youkai). His behavior might seem vulgar and rough at first glance (and it is), but to his friends, he's like a dependable older brother. He and Goku are sparring partners, he and Hakkai are best friends and he and Sanzo are bad friends (ha ha!). Sometimes his love for the ladies gets him into trouble. Because of his unusual heritage, he doesn't need a limiter to blend in with the humans. His favorite way of fighting is to use a shakujou, a staff with a crescent-shaped blade connected by a chain; it's quite messy. He's 184cm tall (approx. 6'), has scarlet hair and eyes and is a 22-year-old chain smoker.

Cho Hakkai –

A pleasant, rather absent-minded young man with a kind smile that suits him nicely. It's sometimes hard to tell whether he's serious or laughing to himself at his friends' expense. His darker side comes through from time to time in the form of a sharp, penetrating gaze, a symbol of a dark past. As he's Hakuryu's (the white dragon) owner, he gets to drive the Jeep. Because he uses kikou jutsu (Chi manipulation) in battle, his "weapon" is his smile (ha ha!). He's 22 years old, 181cm tall (approx. 5'11") and his eyes are deep green (his right eye is nearly blind). The cuffs he wears on his left ear are Youkai power limiters.

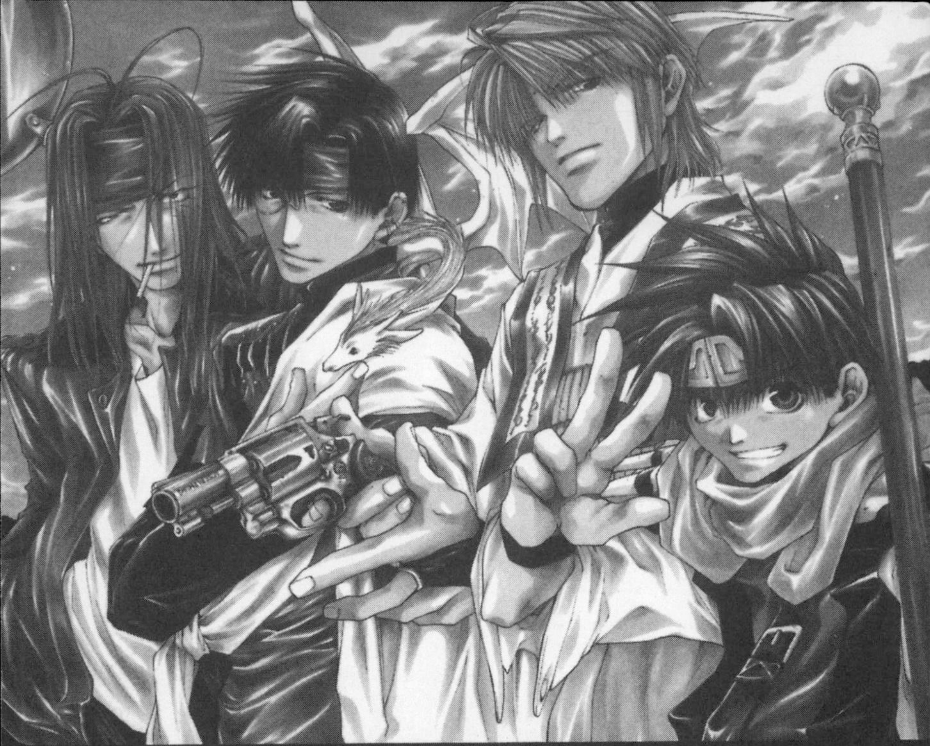

The Story So Far

Chaos has ravaged Shangri-La. During an attempt by dark forces to revive the Ox King Gyumaoh, the combination of science and youkai magic sent a Minus Wave surging through the land, driving all youkai berserk, thus causing mass violence and upsetting the peaceful balance between the races. Now it's up to four companions--the youkai Son Goku, Sha Gojyo, and Cho Hakkai, and the human Priest Genjyo Sanzo--to travel West and stop the experiment that plagues the world. It's an excellent plan...save for the fact that the four companions suffer from "teamwork issues."

After fighting--and defeating--evil yet outdated clones of themselves, Sanzo and co. found their path obstructed by a large river inhabited by youkai. The turbulent trip across the water ended up separating Goku (and his young companion Kon) from the rest of the group, so Sanzo, Gojyo and Hakkai were left to fight the enemy waiting nearby: the illusionist Zakuro. After some blood, swearing, and the usual epiphany-related-to-one's-past, Sanzo sent Zakuro running and the party continued on its way.

Meanwhile, Goku returned Kon to his village, only to find a mob of murderous youkai out for human meat. Goku pounded the youkai soundly and saved the innocent villagers, but a shadow fell over him the instant he paused for breath. Kougaiji has arrived, and he's not the pushover he used to be...

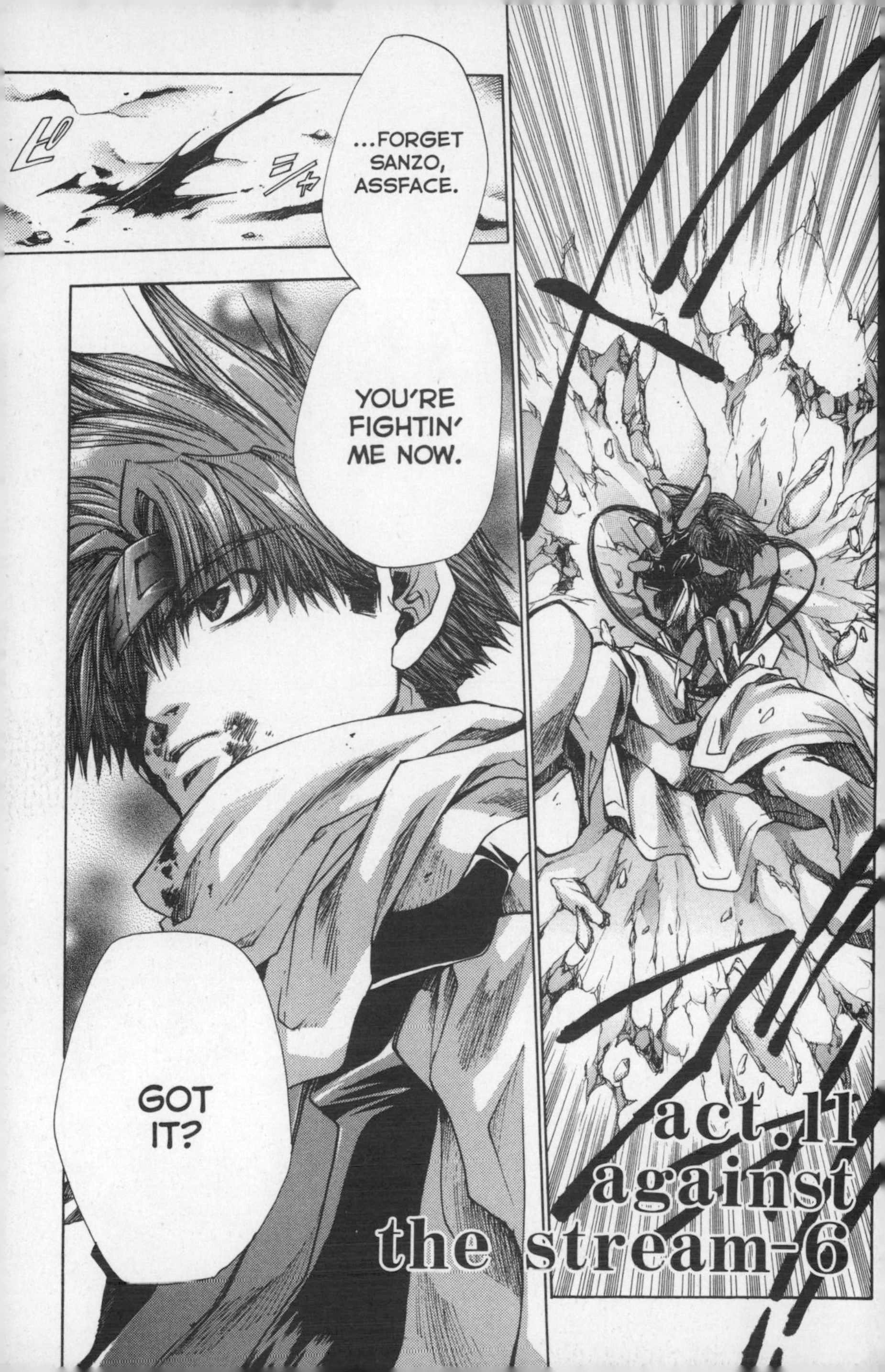
act.11
against
the stream-6
...FORGET SANZO, ASSFACE.
YOU'RE FIGHTIN' ME NOW.
GOT IT?

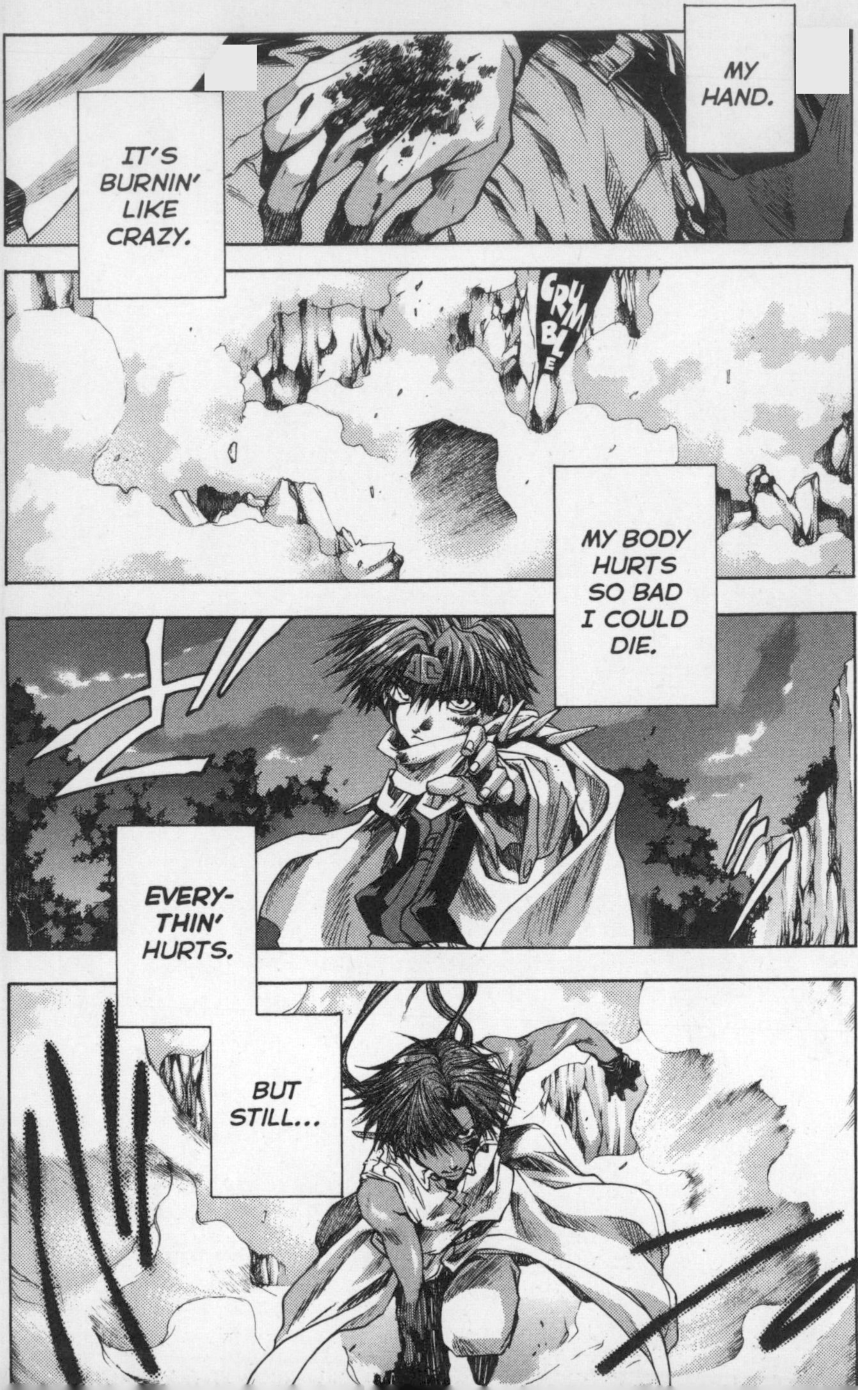
MY HAND.
IT'S BURNIN' LIKE CRAZY.
CRUMBLE
MY BODY HURTS SO BAD I COULD DIE.
EVERY-THIN' HURTS.
BUT STILL...

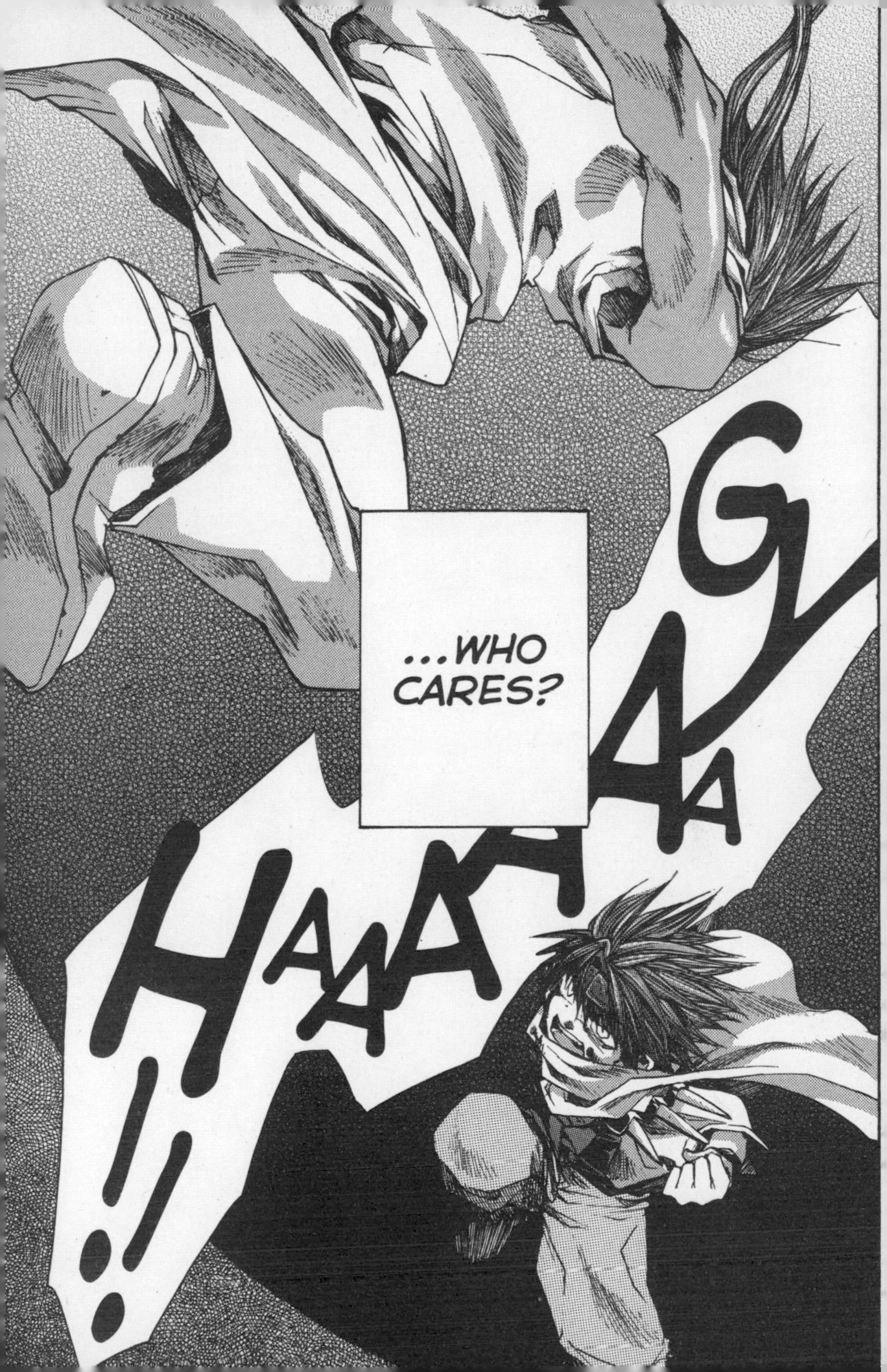
...WHO CARES?
HAAAAAAGH!!!

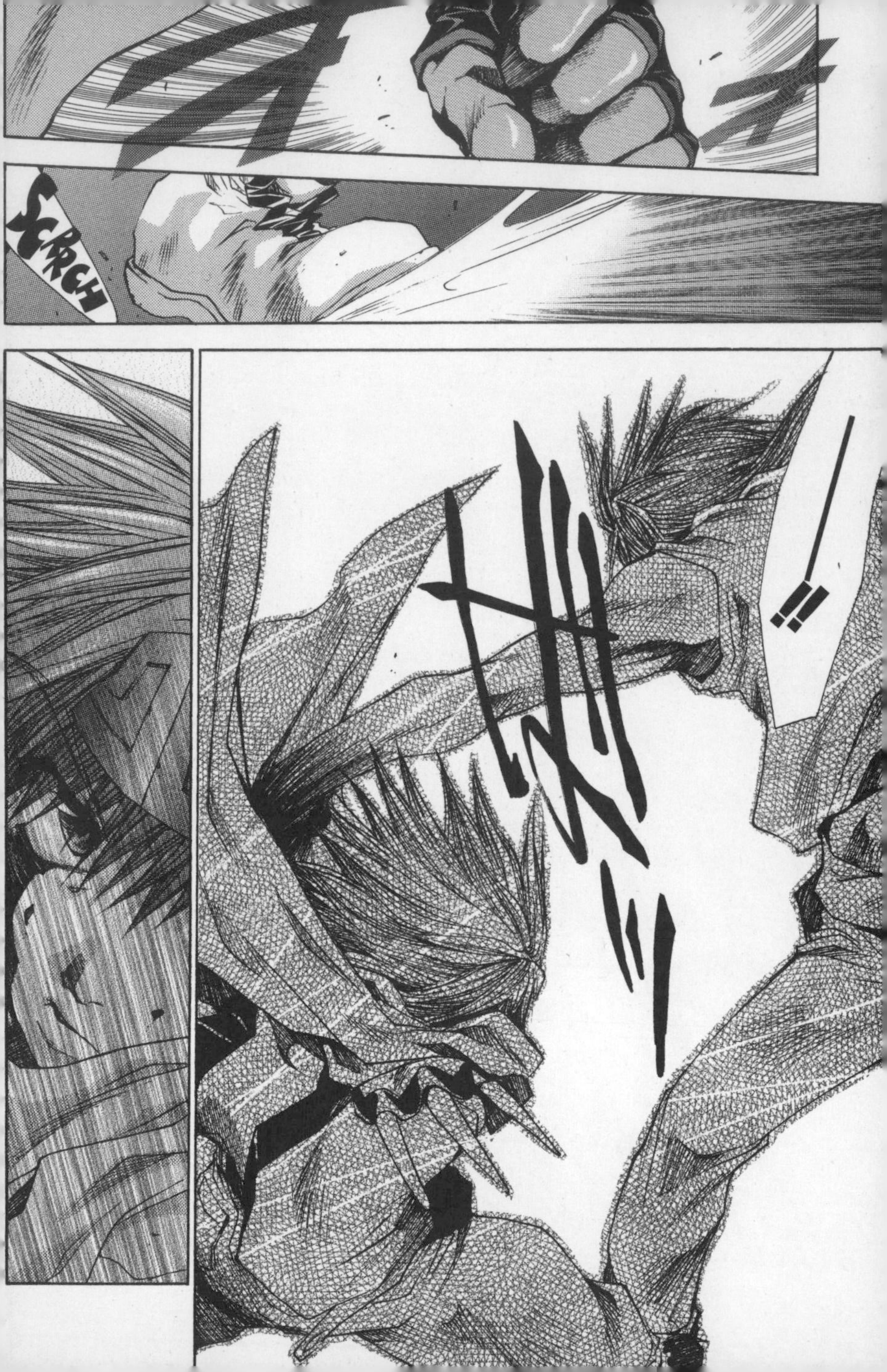
SCRRCH

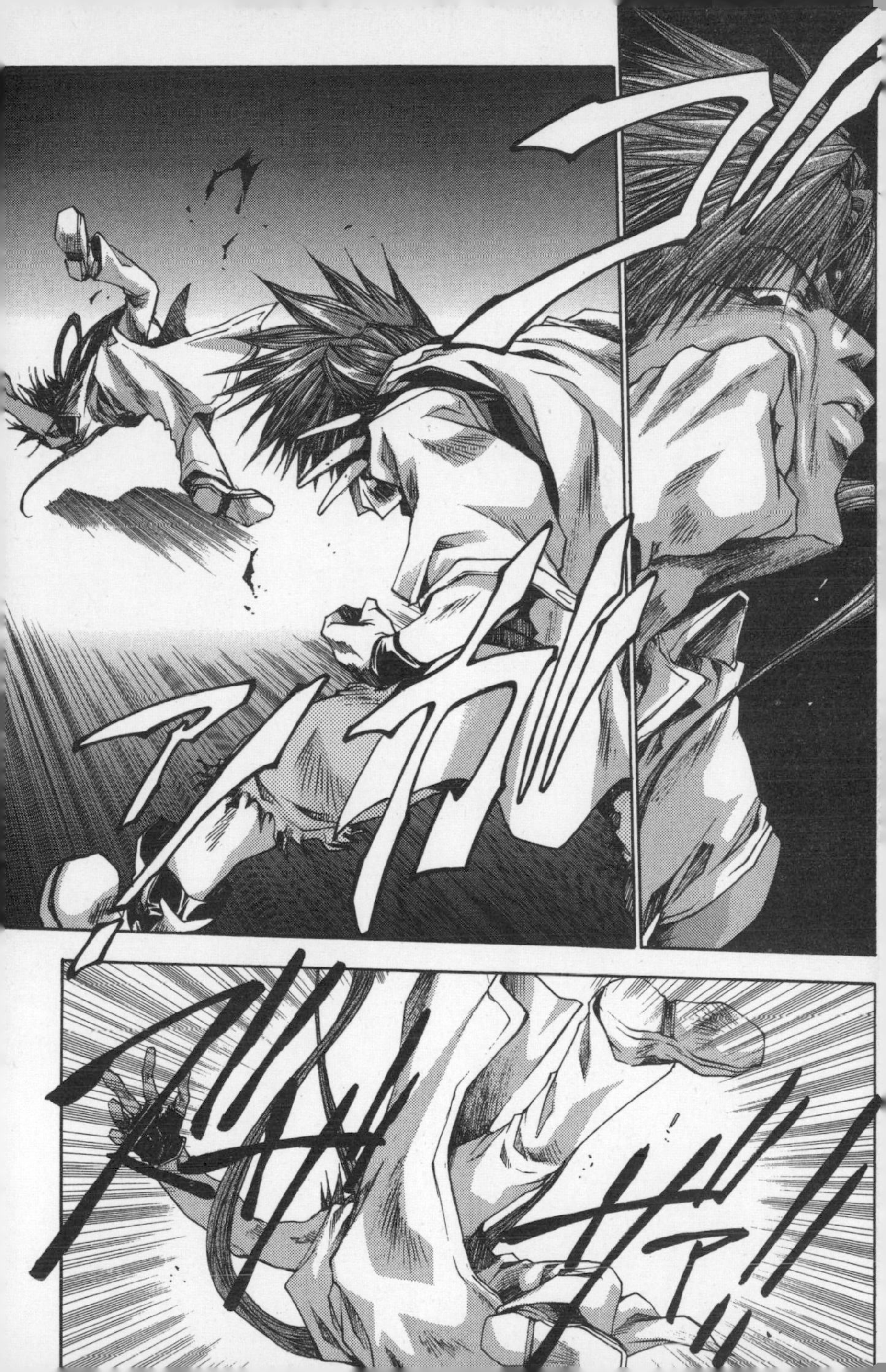

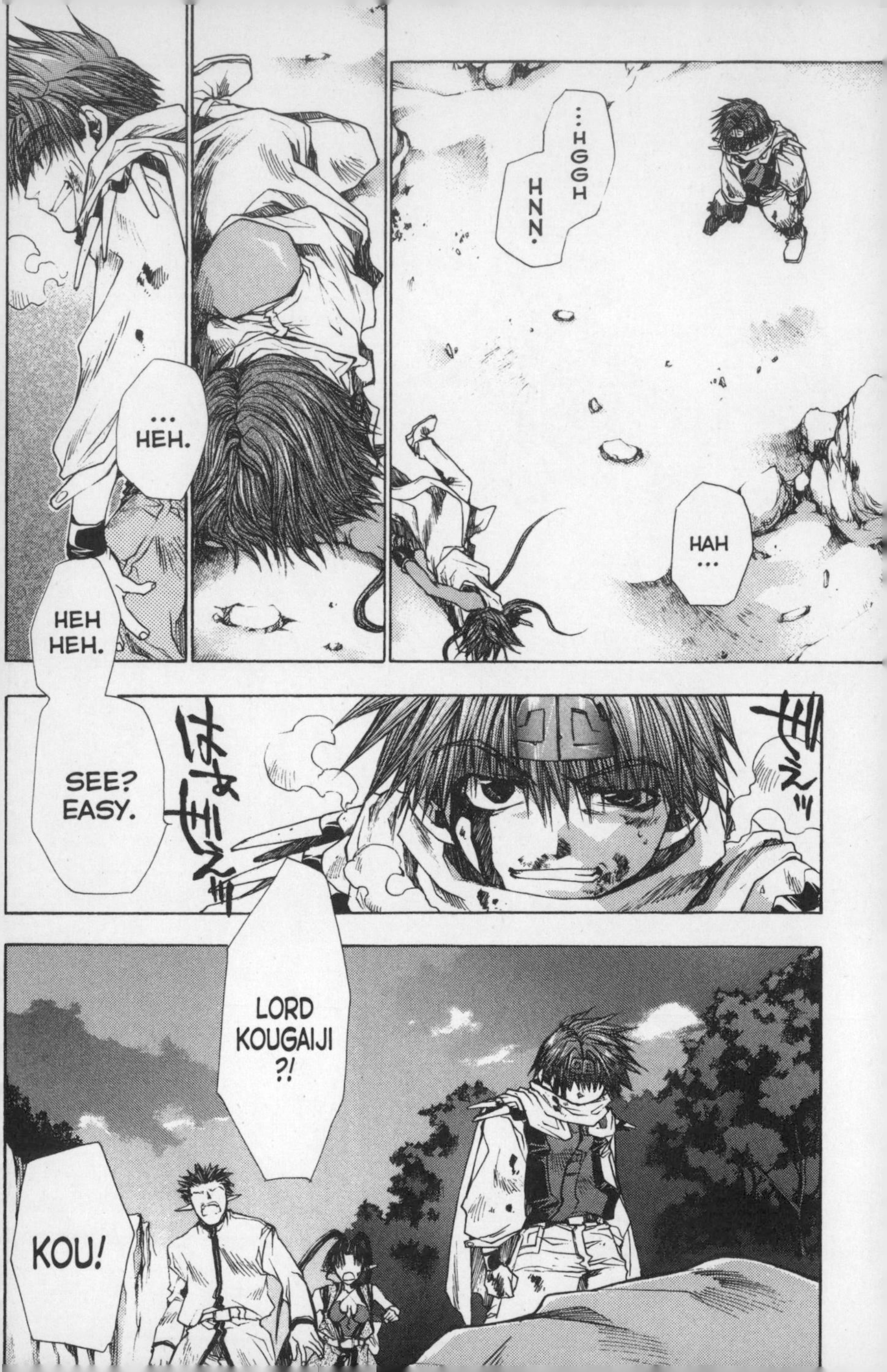
...HGGH
HNN.
HAH ...
... HEH.
HEH HEH.
ぜぇッ
SEE? EASY.
はぁぜぇ
LORD KOUGAIJI ?!
KOU!

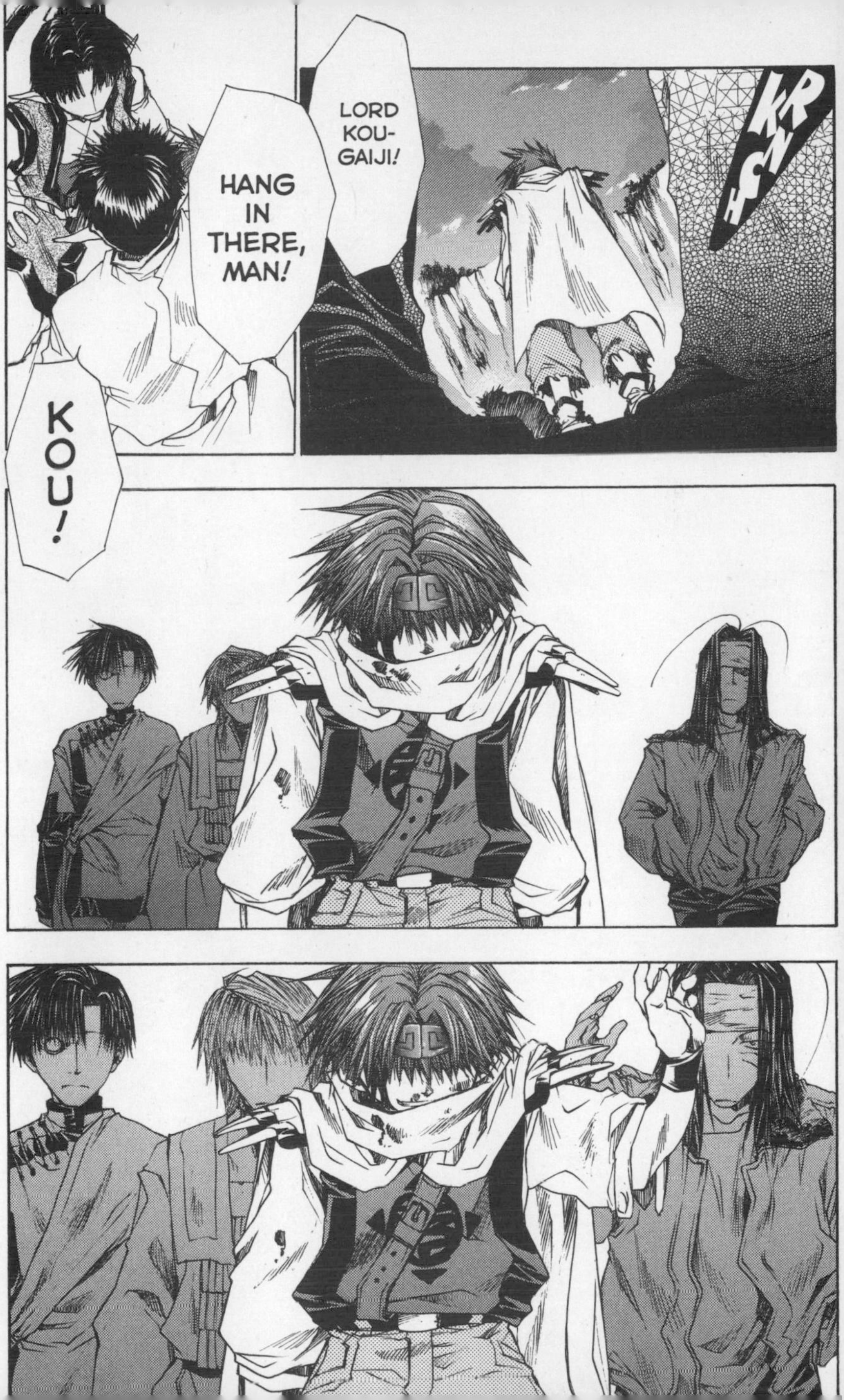
KRNCH
LORD KOU-GAIJI!
HANG IN THERE, MAN!
KOU!

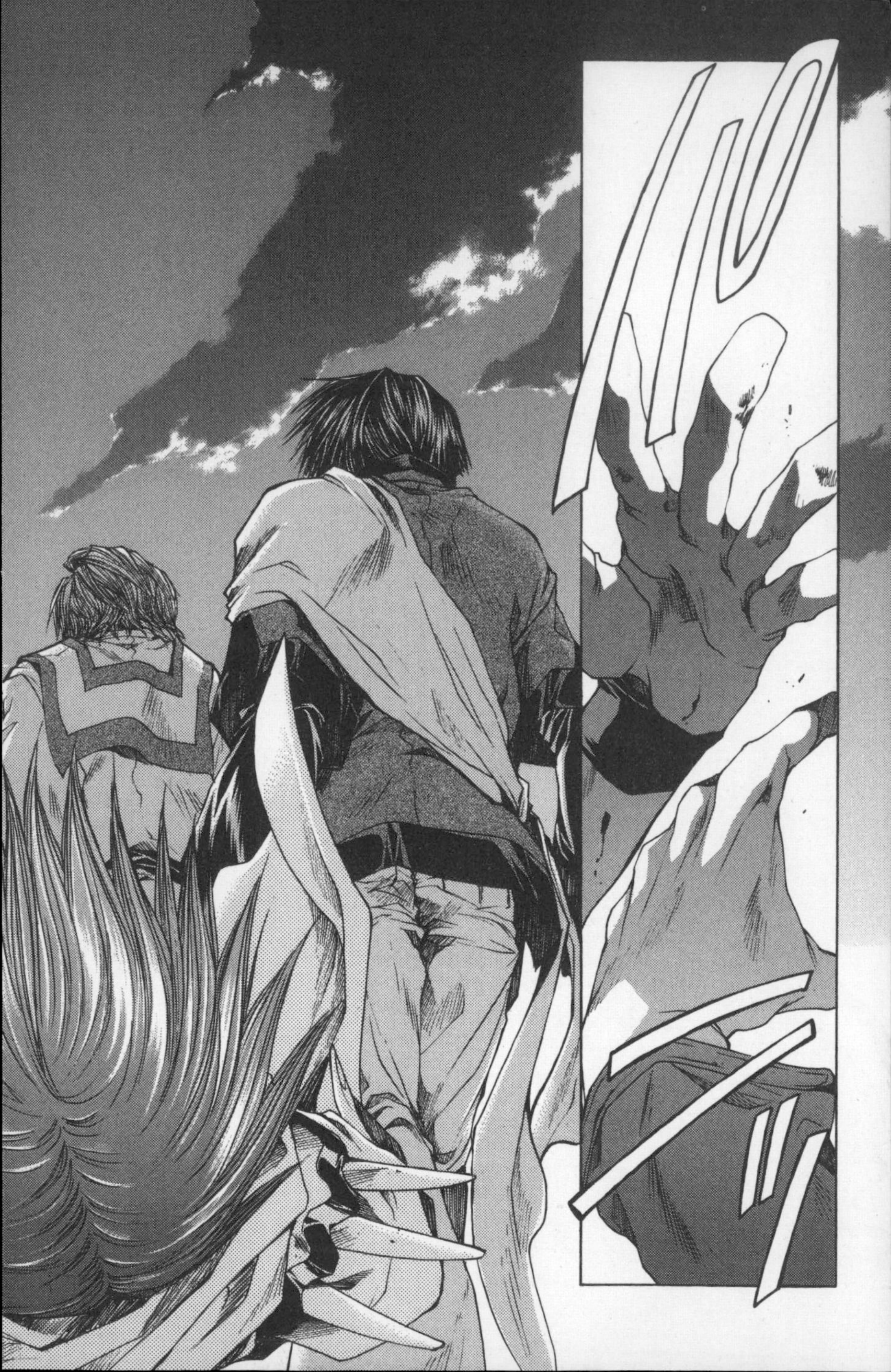

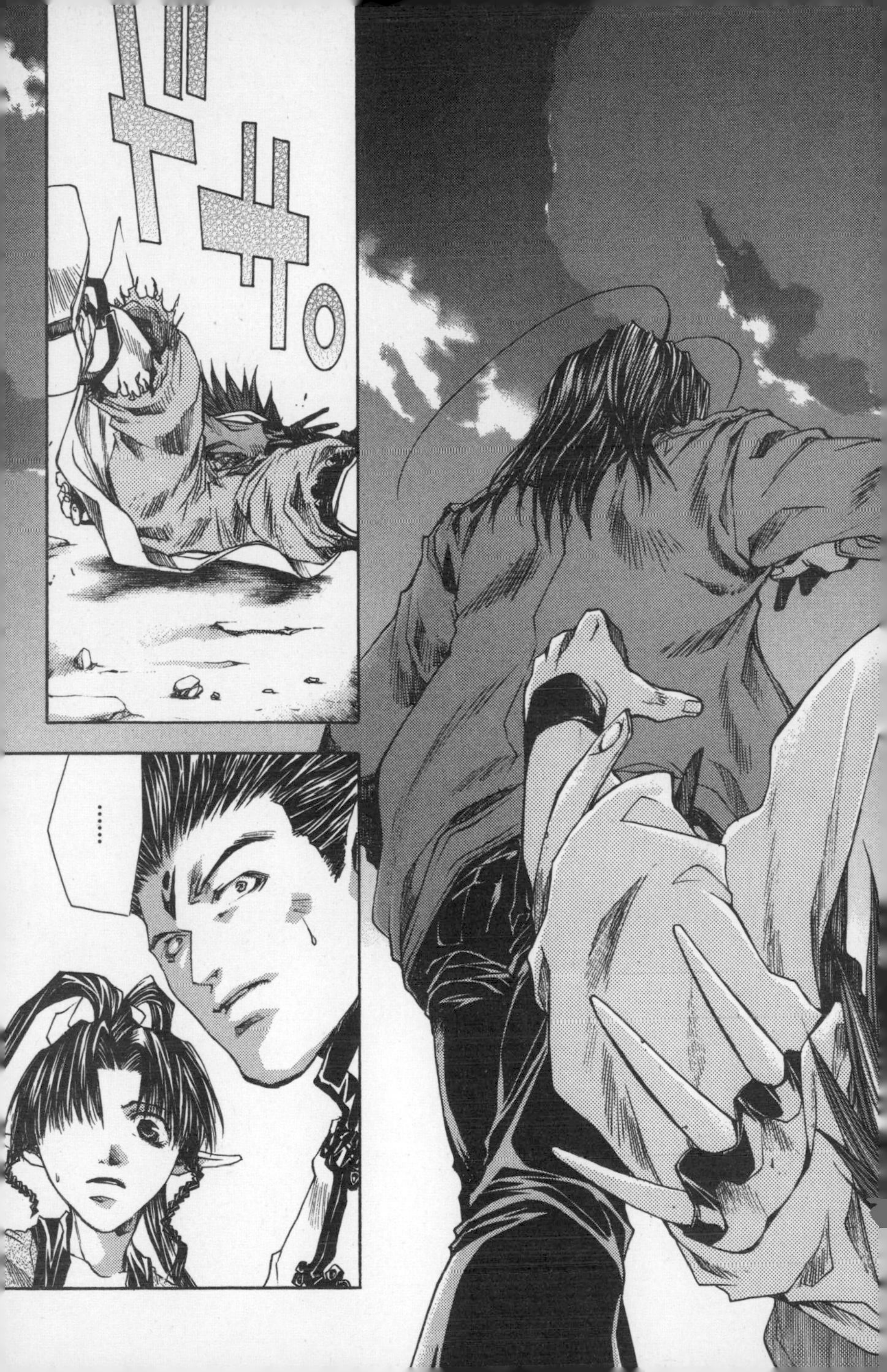
ドサ。
……

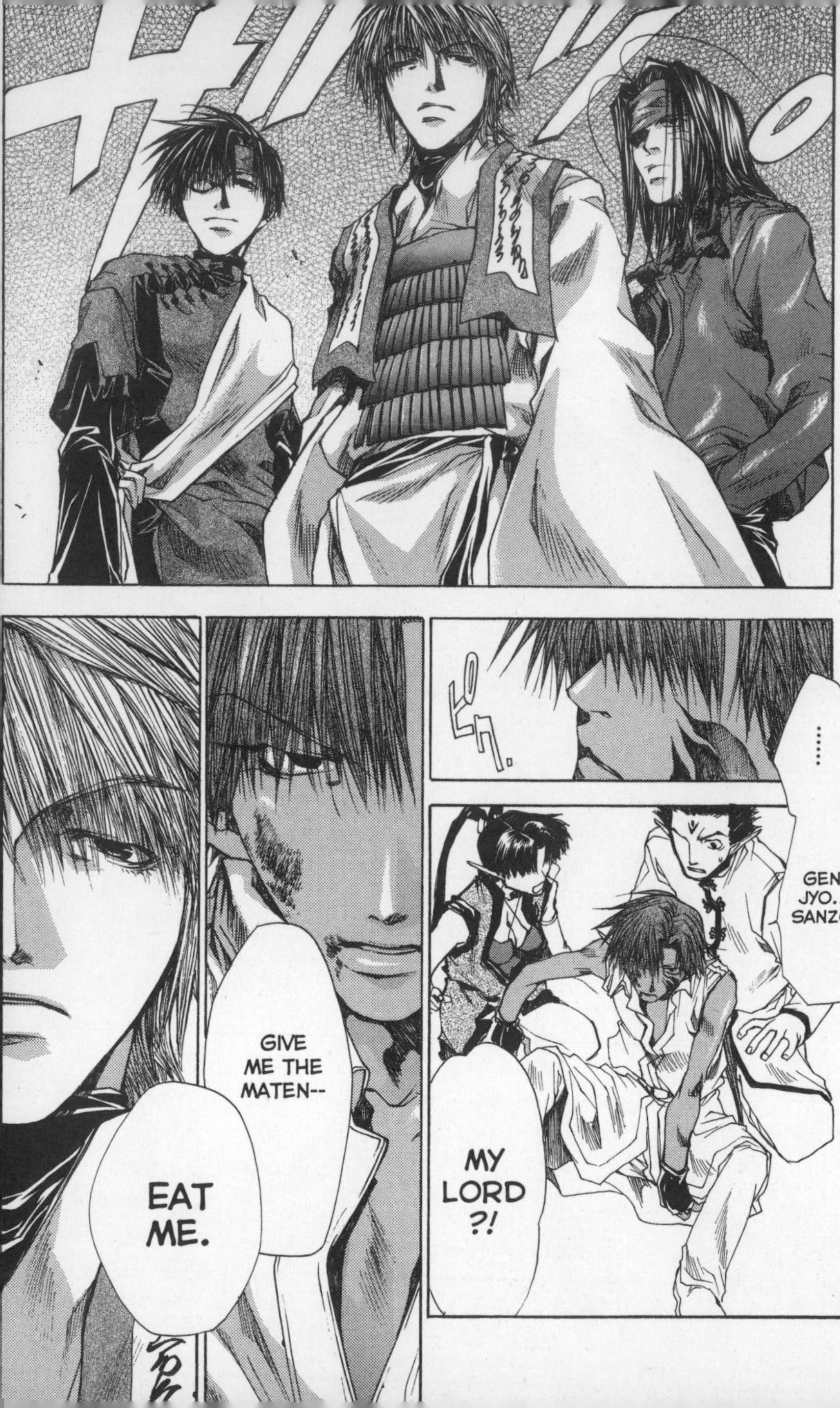
......
GEN-JYO... SANZO.
MY LORD?!
GIVE ME THE MATEN--
EAT ME.

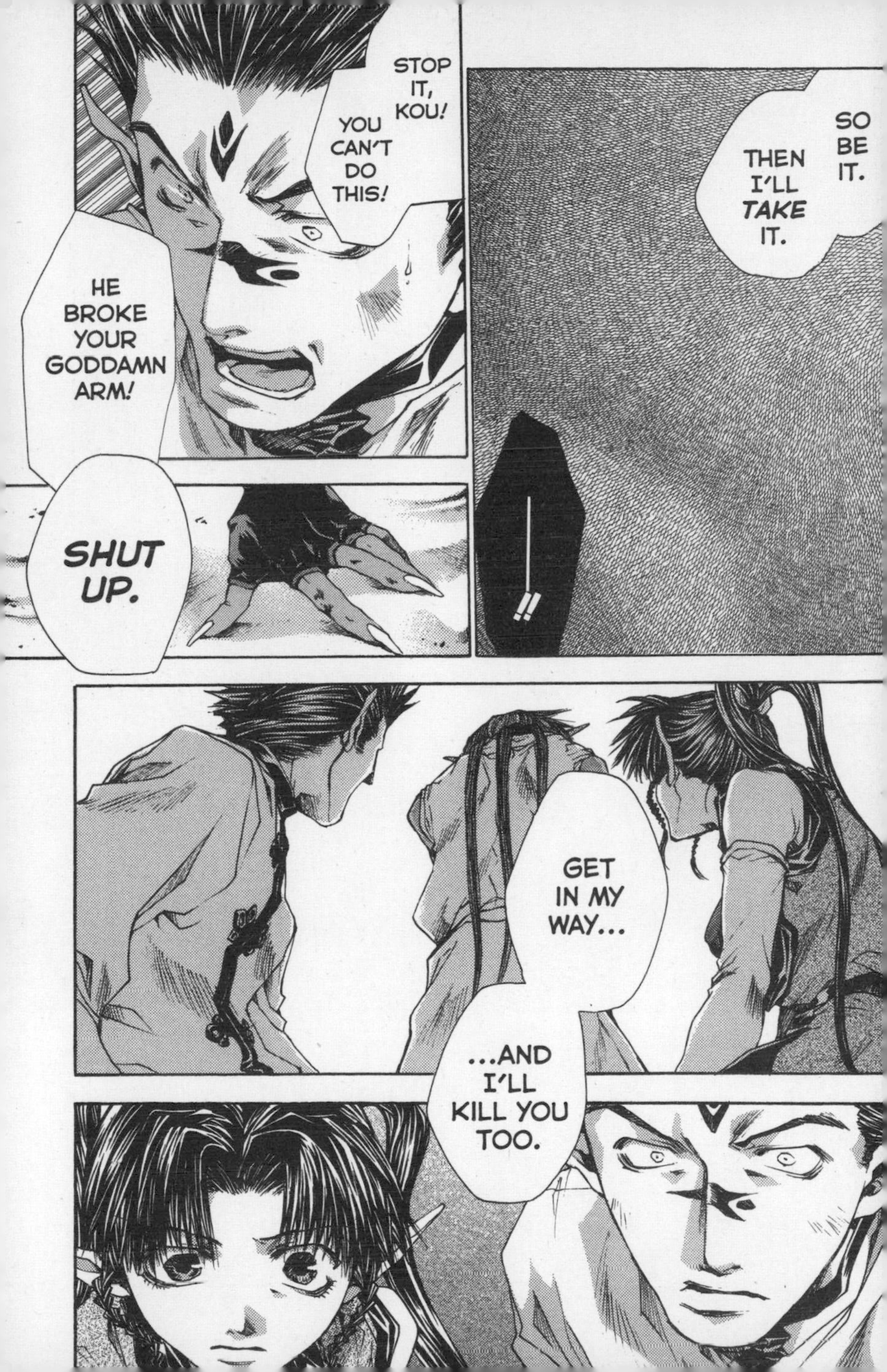
SO BE IT.
THEN I'LL *TAKE* IT.
!!
STOP IT, KOU!
YOU CAN'T DO THIS!
HE BROKE YOUR GODDAMN ARM!
SHUT UP.
GET IN MY WAY...
...AND I'LL KILL YOU TOO.

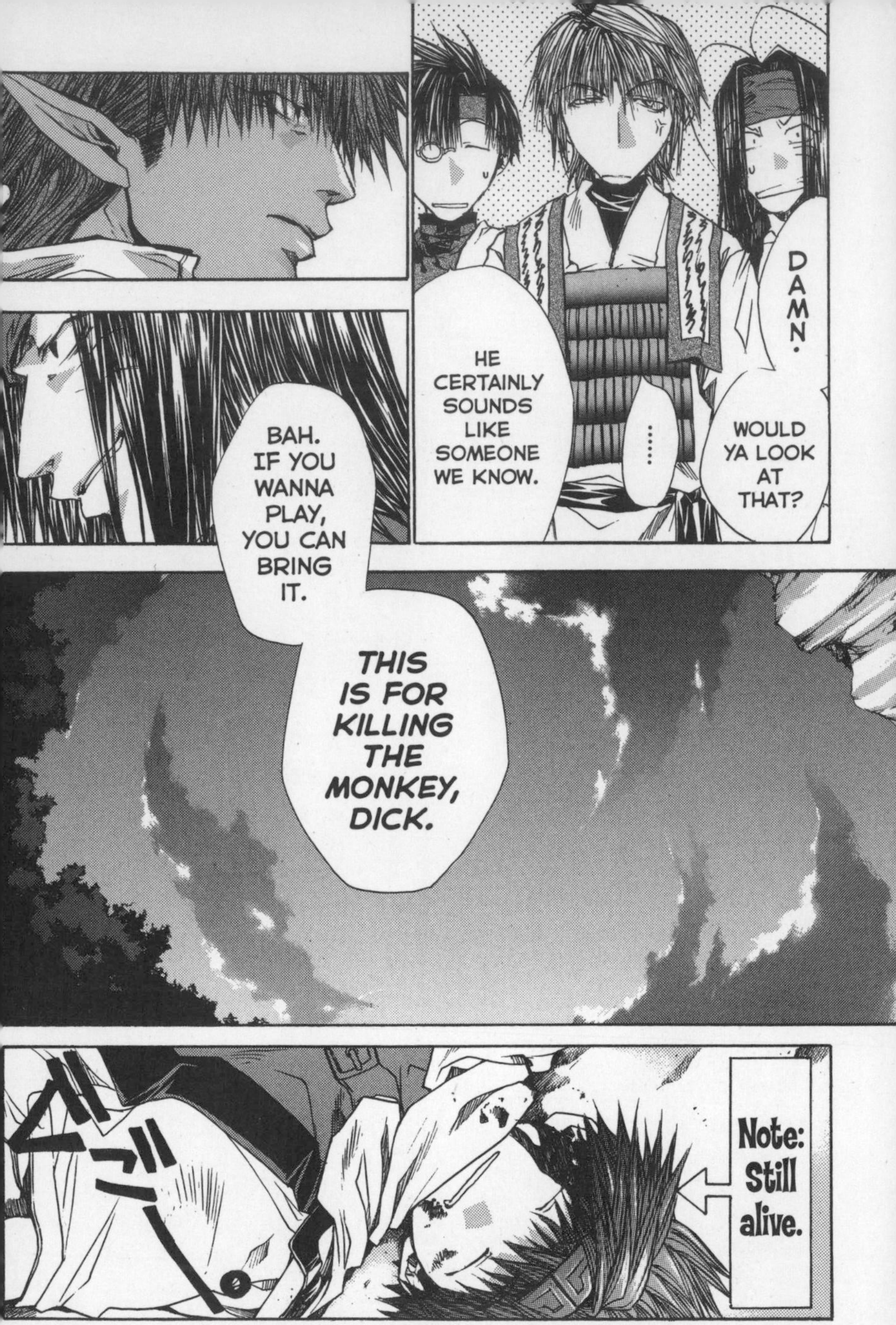
DAMN.
WOULD YA LOOK AT THAT?
......
HE CERTAINLY SOUNDS LIKE SOMEONE WE KNOW.
BAH. IF YOU WANNA PLAY, YOU CAN BRING IT.
THIS IS FOR KILLING THE MONKEY, DICK.
Note: Still alive.

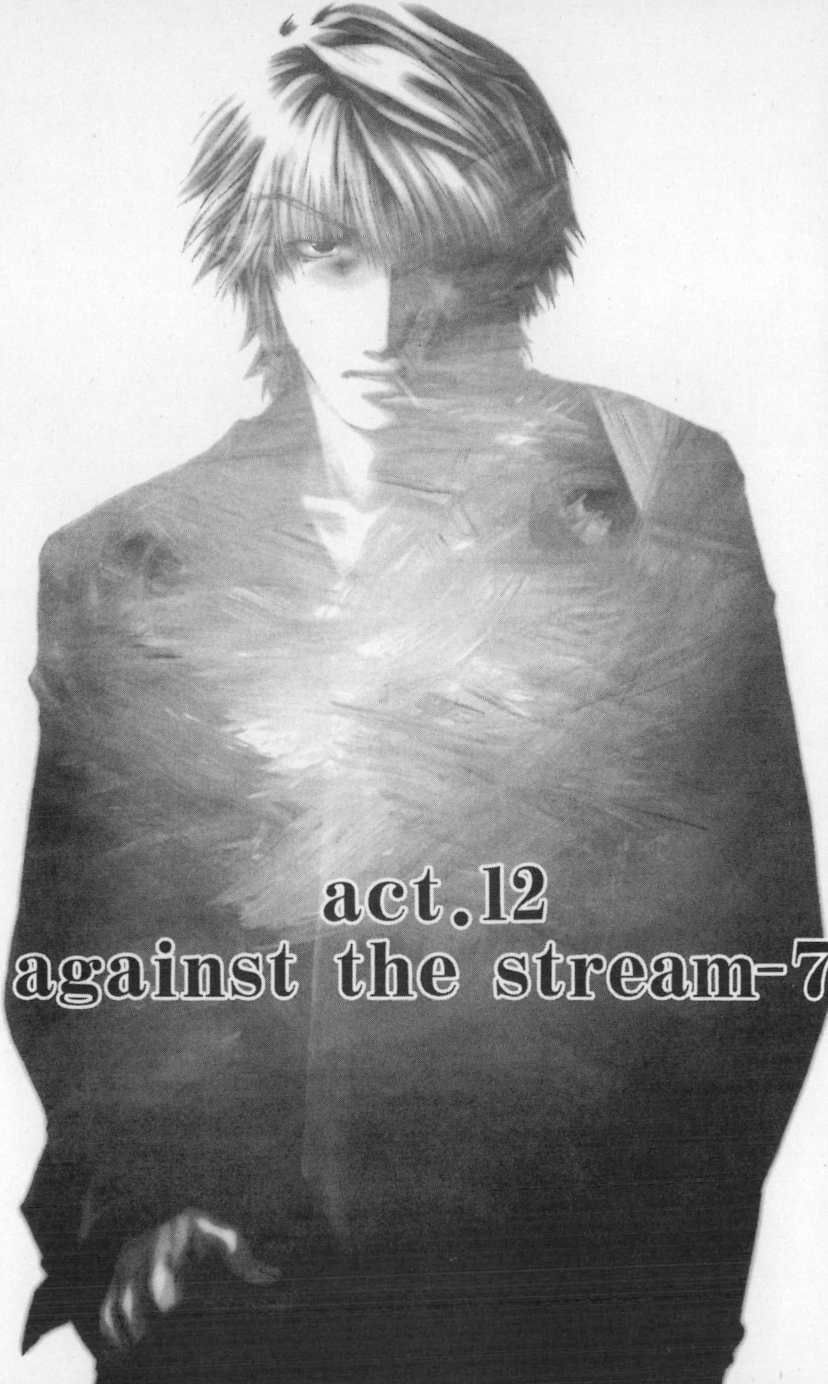

act.12
against the stream-7

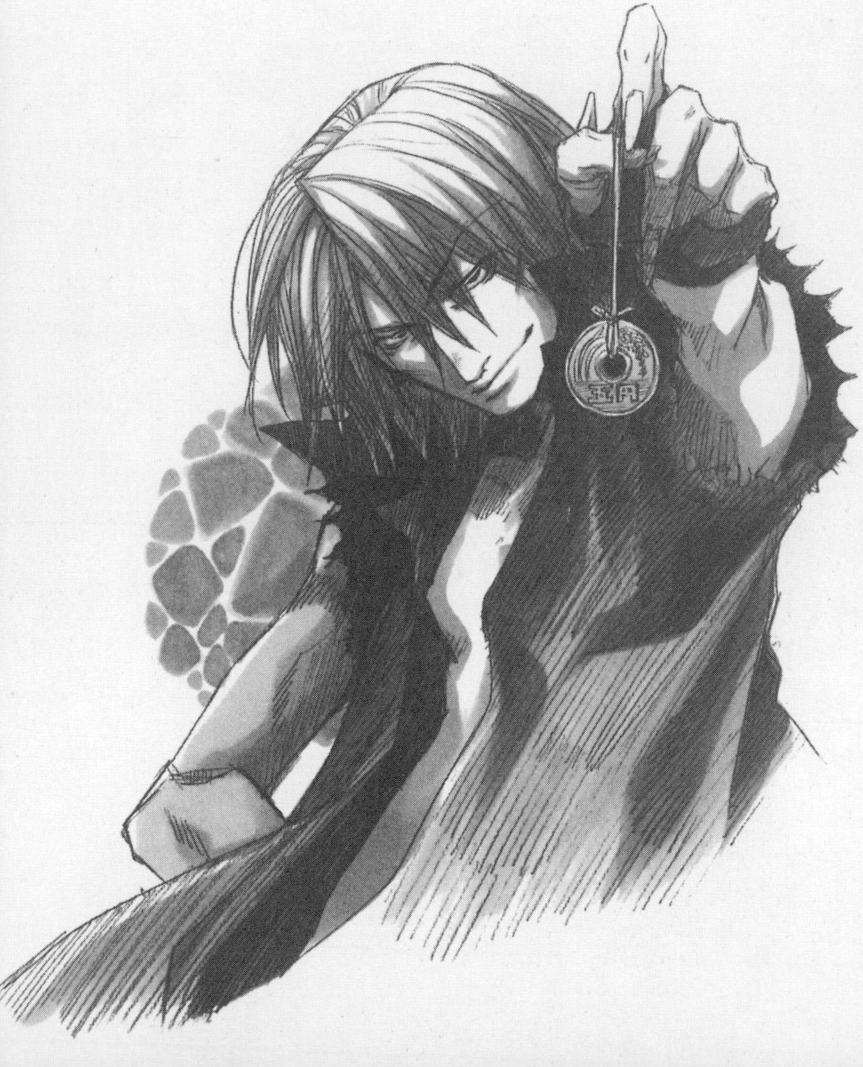

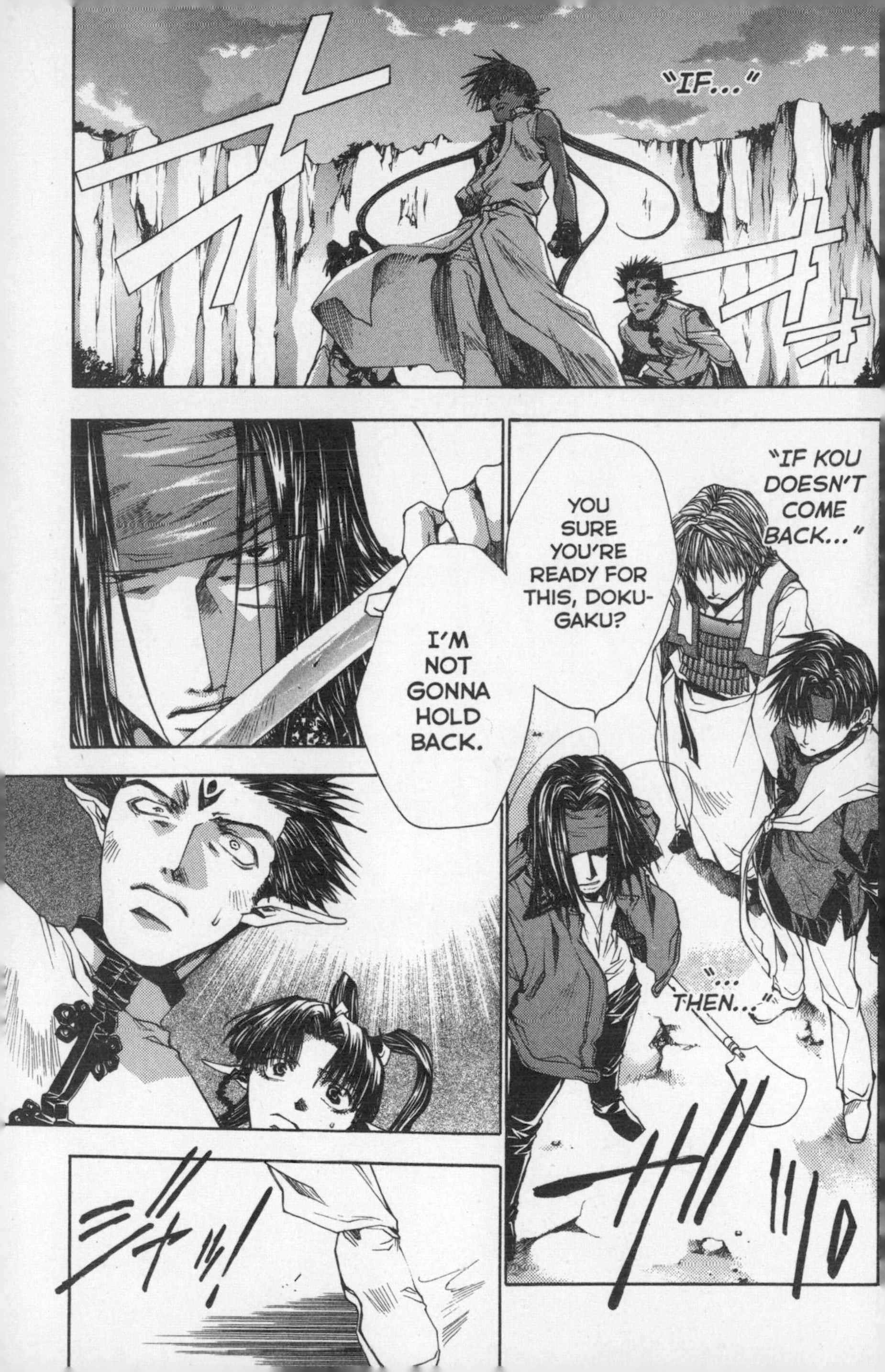
"IF..."
"IF KOU DOESN'T COME BACK..."
YOU SURE YOU'RE READY FOR THIS, DOKU-GAKU?
"...THEN..."
I'M NOT GONNA HOLD BACK.

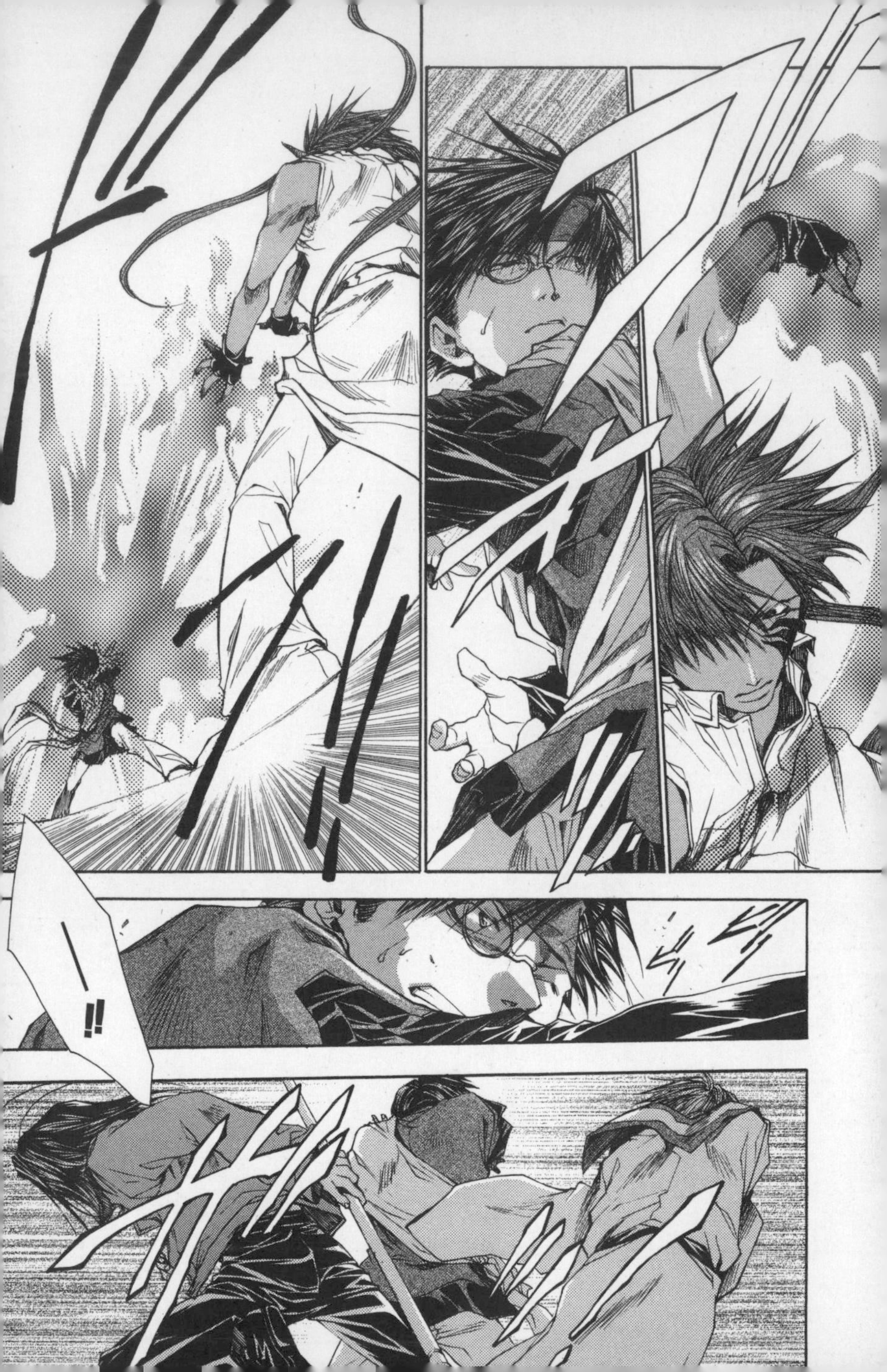
—!!

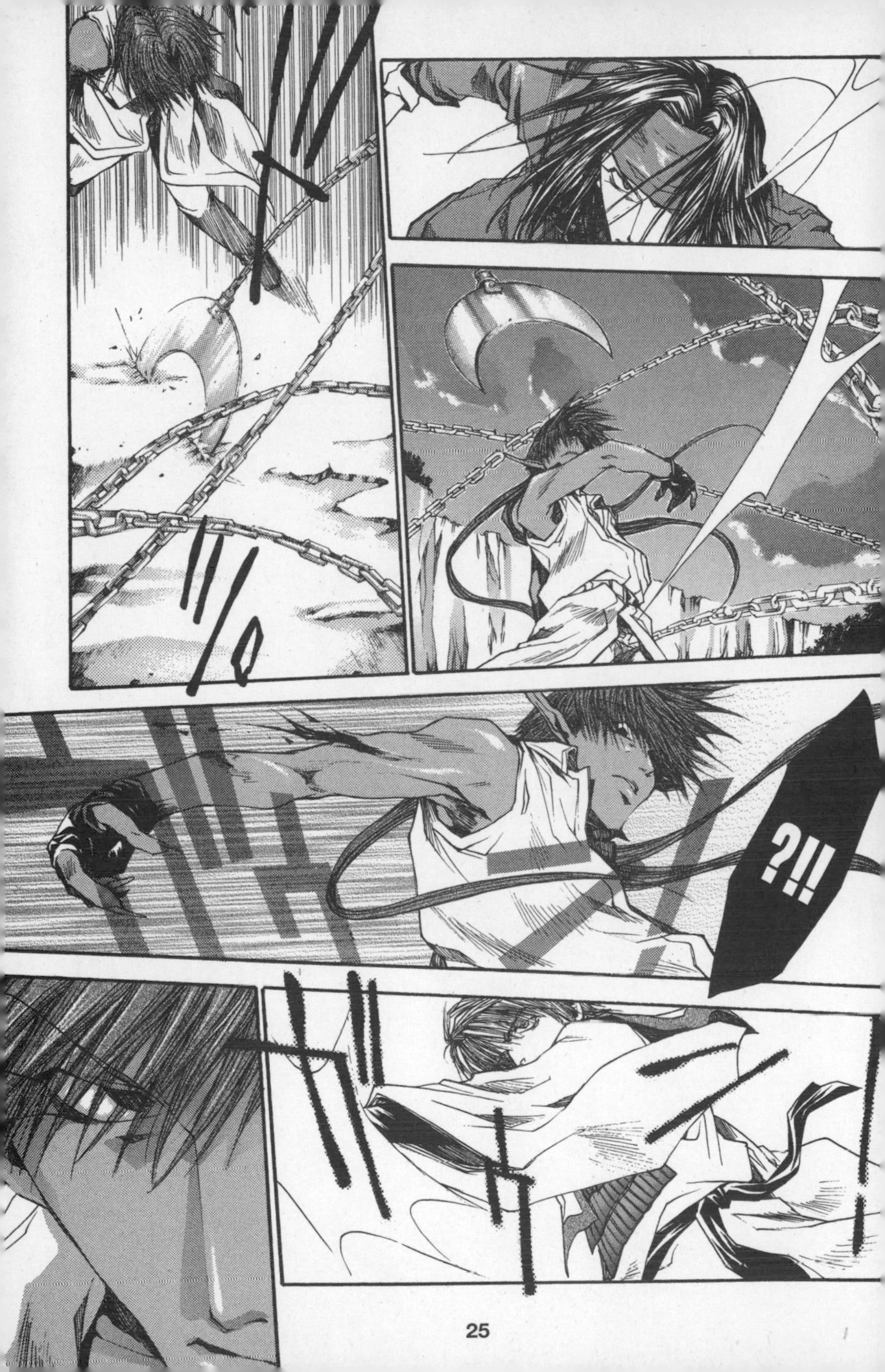
?!!

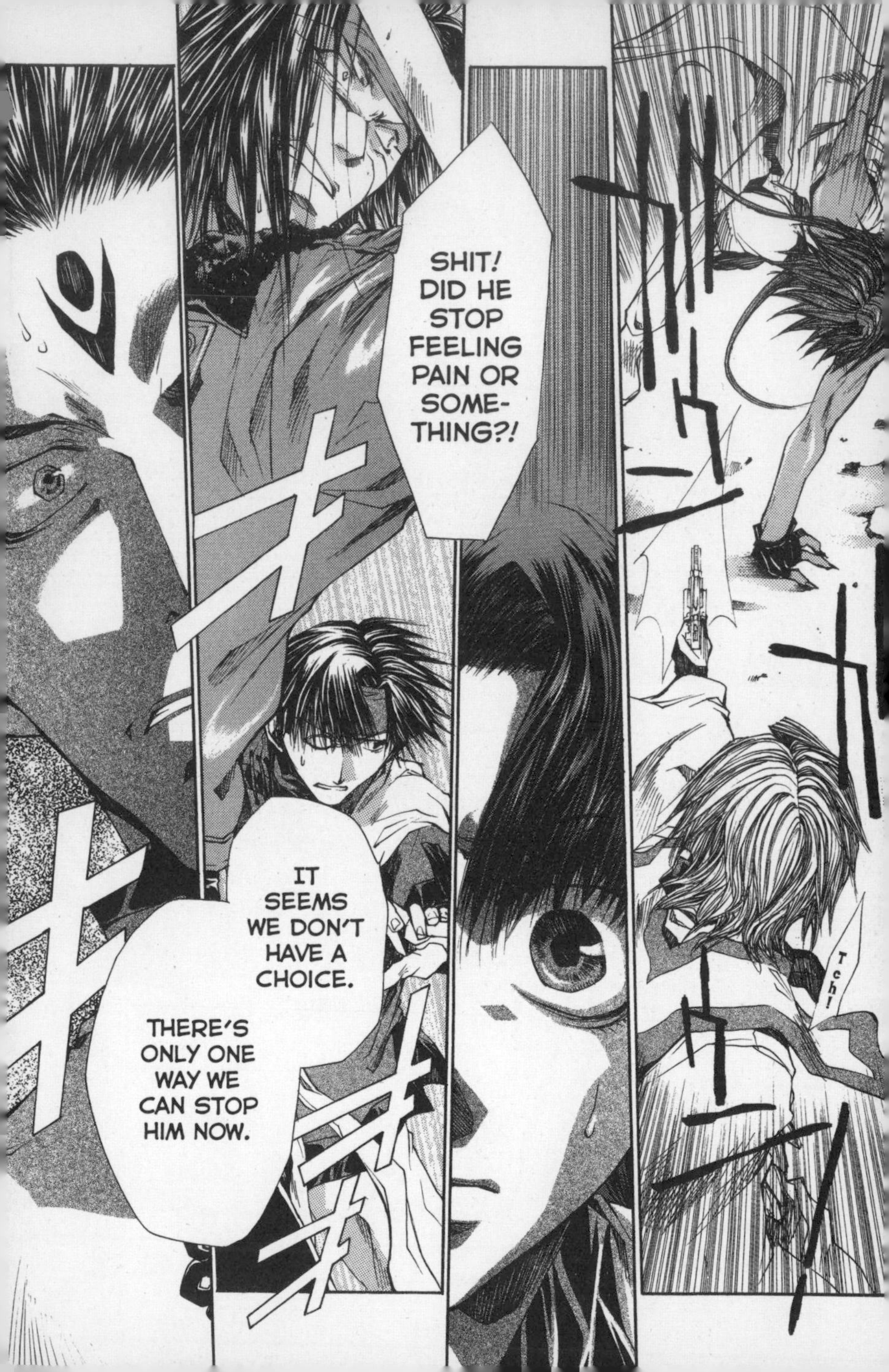
Tch!
SHIT! DID HE STOP FEELING PAIN OR SOME-THING?!
IT SEEMS WE DON'T HAVE A CHOICE.
THERE'S ONLY ONE WAY WE CAN STOP HIM NOW.

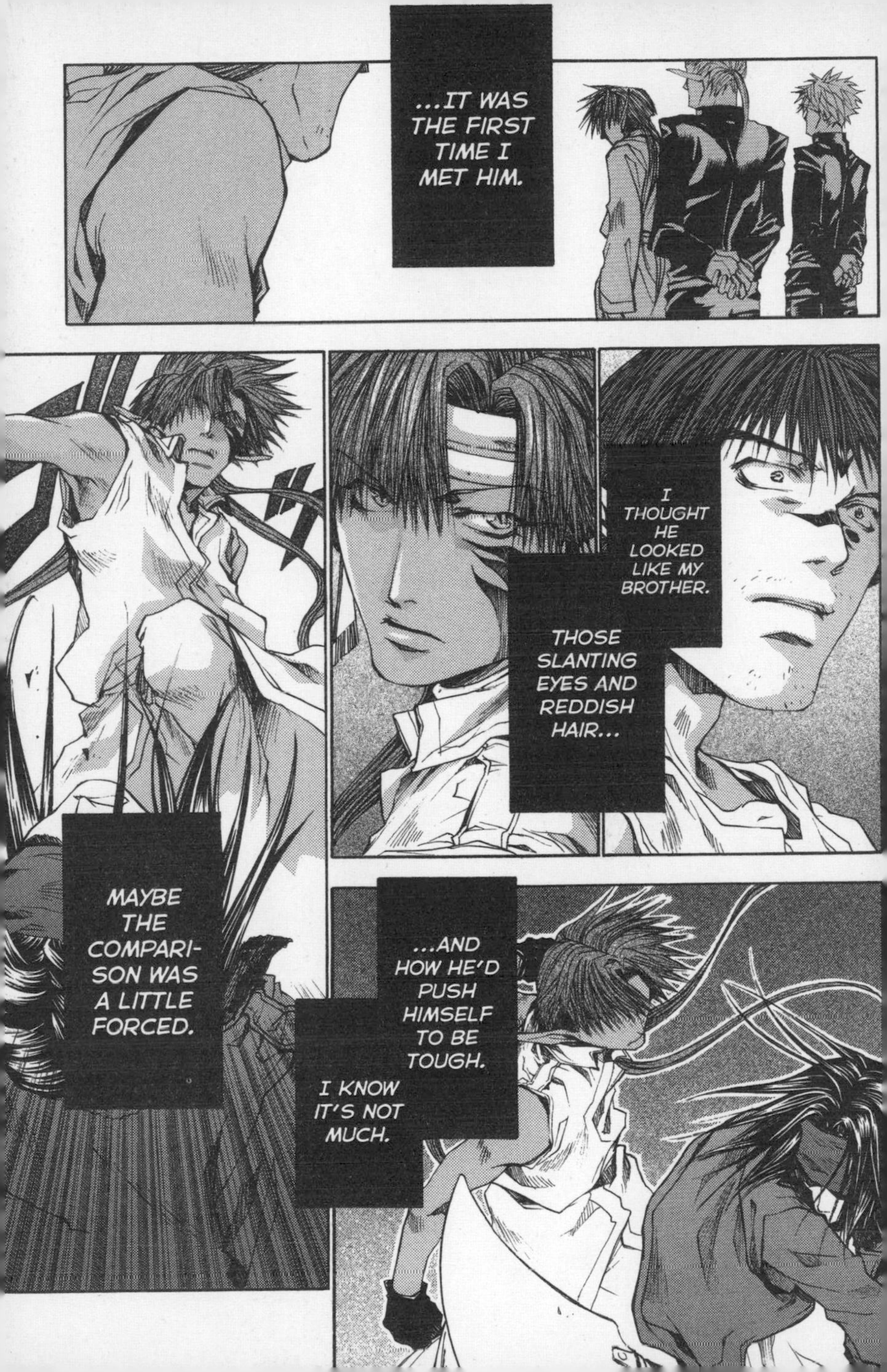
...IT WAS THE FIRST TIME I MET HIM.
I THOUGHT HE LOOKED LIKE MY BROTHER.
THOSE SLANTING EYES AND REDDISH HAIR...
...AND HOW HE'D PUSH HIMSELF TO BE TOUGH.
I KNOW IT'S NOT MUCH.
MAYBE THE COMPARI-SON WAS A LITTLE FORCED.

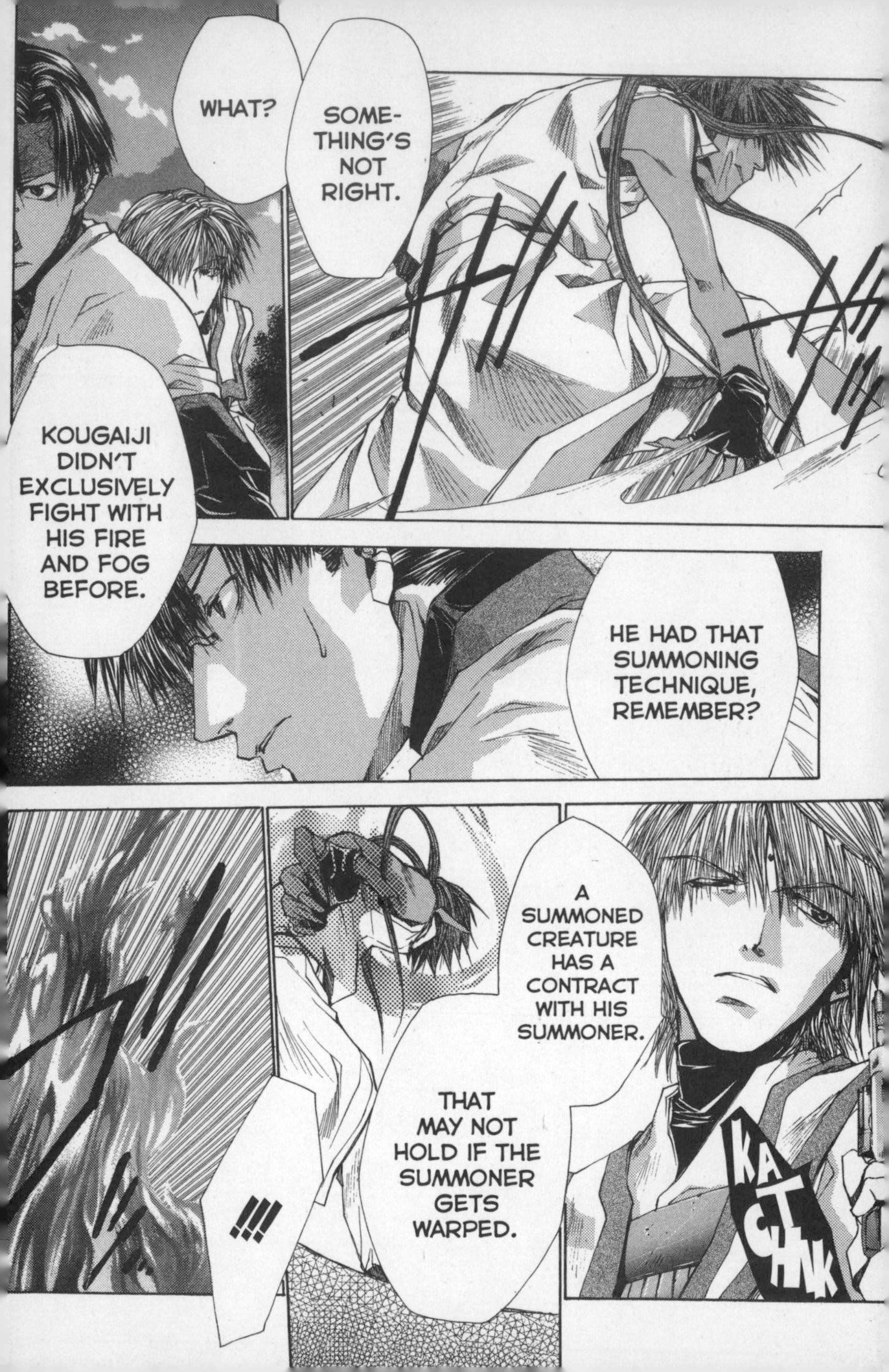
SOME-THING'S NOT RIGHT.
WHAT?
KOUGAIJI DIDN'T EXCLUSIVELY FIGHT WITH HIS FIRE AND FOG BEFORE.
HE HAD THAT SUMMONING TECHNIQUE, REMEMBER?
A SUMMONED CREATURE HAS A CONTRACT WITH HIS SUMMONER.
THAT MAY NOT HOLD IF THE SUMMONER GETS WARPED.
KATCHNK
!!!

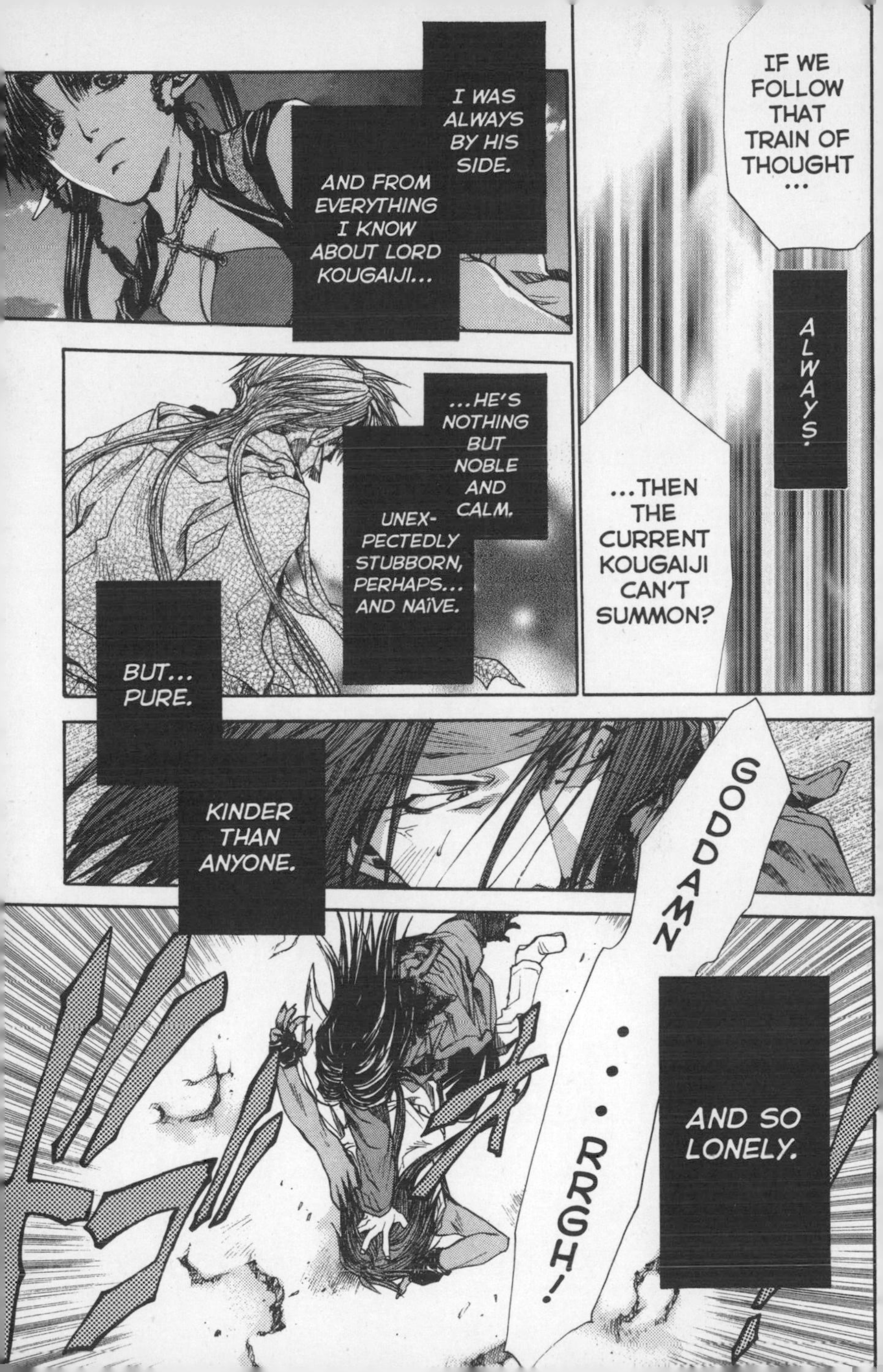

IF WE FOLLOW THAT TRAIN OF THOUGHT...
ALWAYS.
...THEN THE CURRENT KOUGAIJI CAN'T SUMMON?
I WAS ALWAYS BY HIS SIDE.
AND FROM EVERYTHING I KNOW ABOUT LORD KOUGAIJI...
...HE'S NOTHING BUT NOBLE AND CALM.
UNEX-PECTEDLY STUBBORN, PERHAPS... AND NAÏVE.
BUT... PURE.
KINDER THAN ANYONE.
GODDAMN...RRGH!
AND SO LONELY.

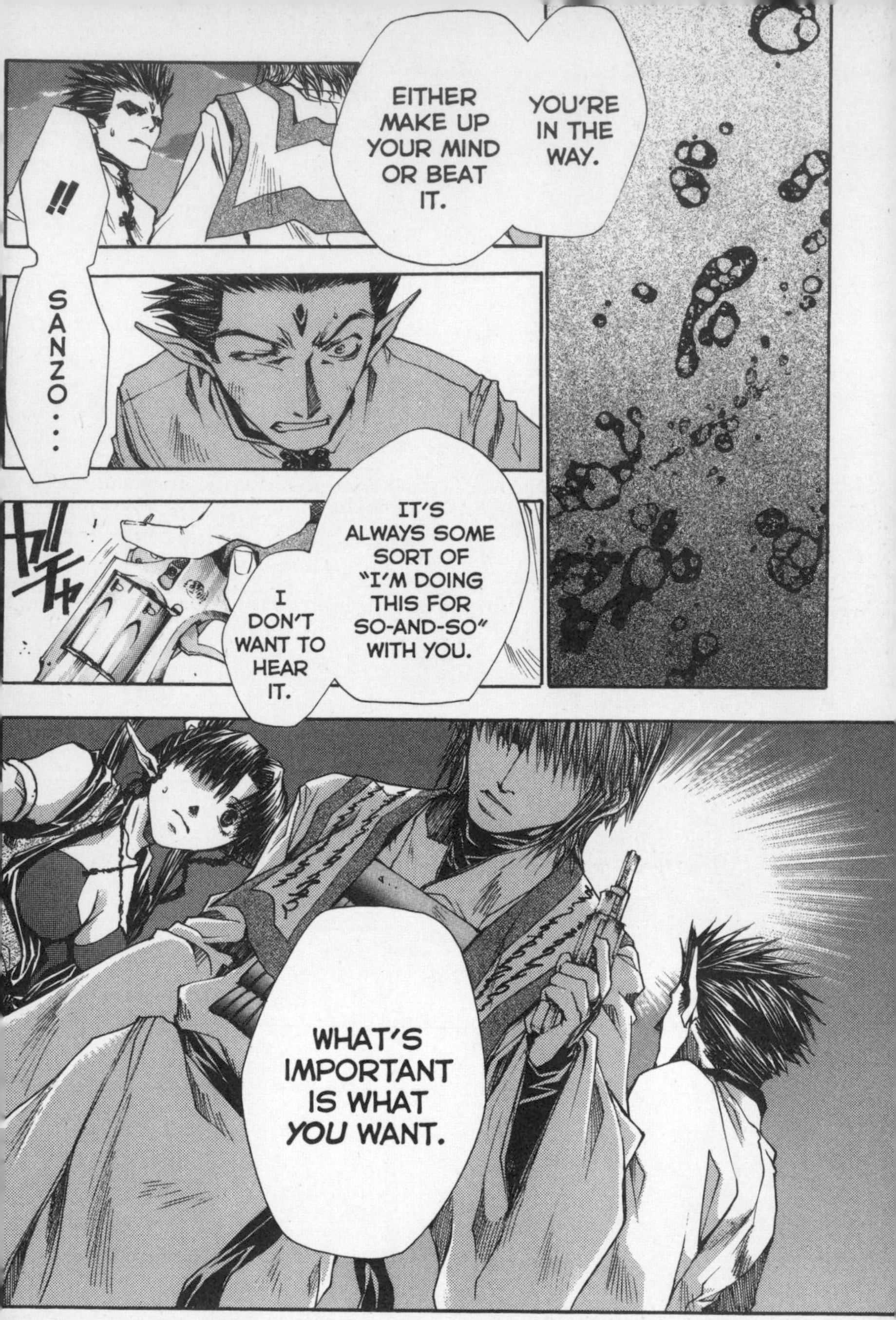
YOU'RE IN THE WAY.
EITHER MAKE UP YOUR MIND OR BEAT IT.
!!
SANZO...
IT'S ALWAYS SOME SORT OF "I'M DOING THIS FOR SO-AND-SO" WITH YOU.
I DON'T WANT TO HEAR IT.
WHAT'S IMPORTANT IS WHAT *YOU* WANT.

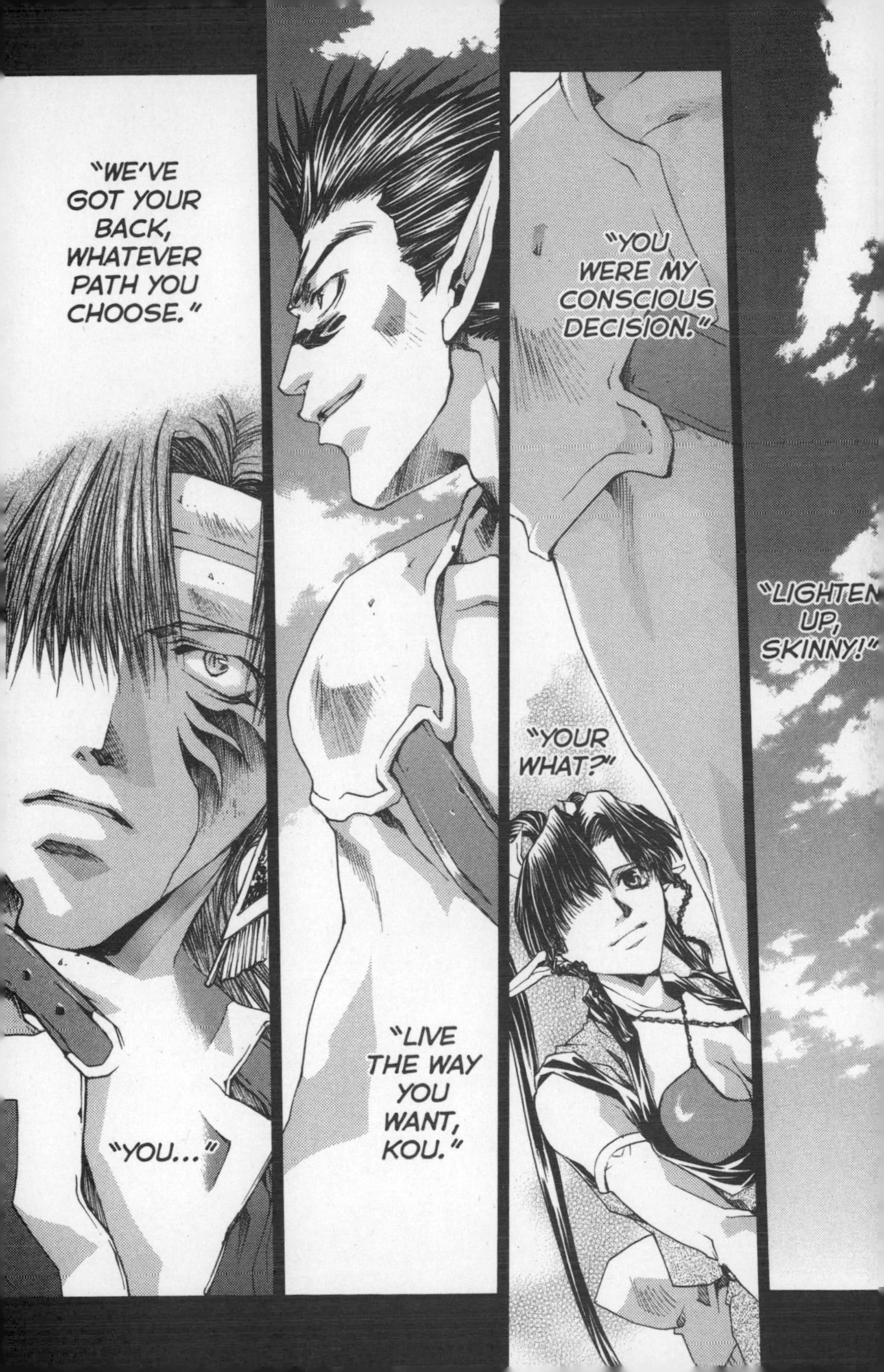
"LIGHTEN UP, SKINNY!"
"YOU WERE MY CONSCIOUS DECISION."
"YOUR WHAT?"
"LIVE THE WAY YOU WANT, KOU."
"WE'VE GOT YOUR BACK, WHATEVER PATH YOU CHOOSE."
"YOU..."

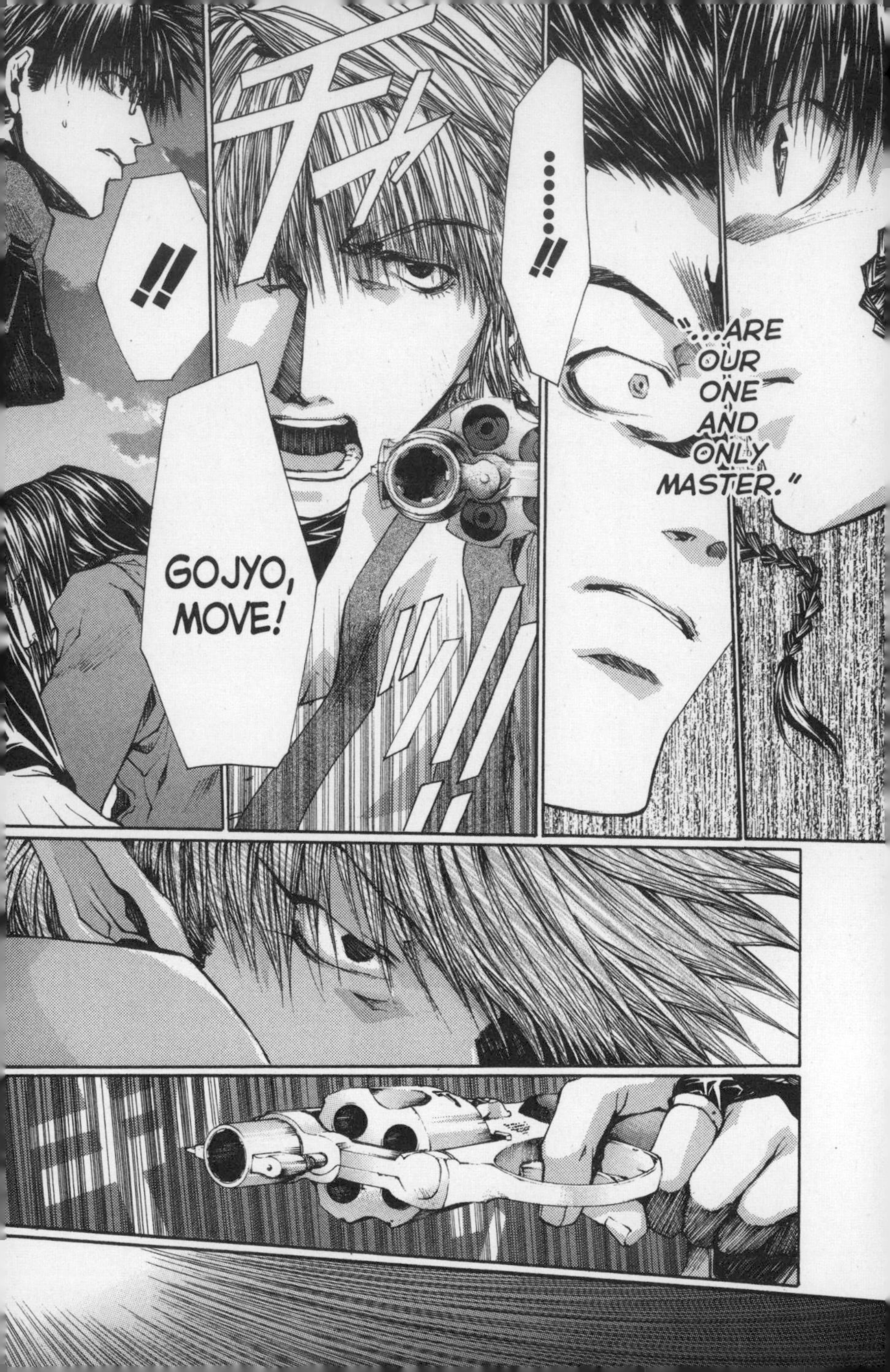
"...ARE OUR ONE AND ONLY MASTER."
......!!
GOJYO, MOVE!
!!

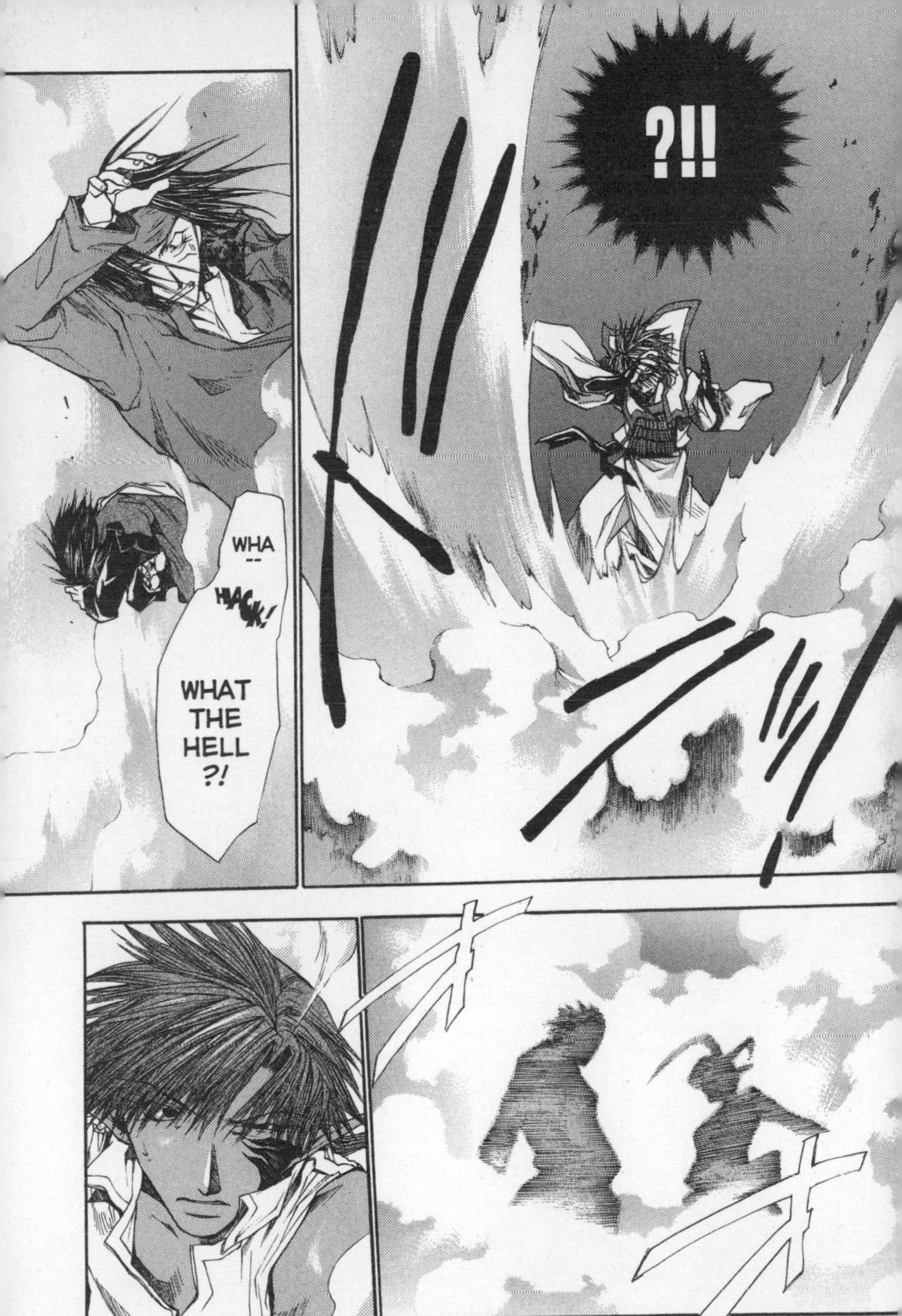
?!!
WHA --
HACK!
WHAT THE HELL ?!

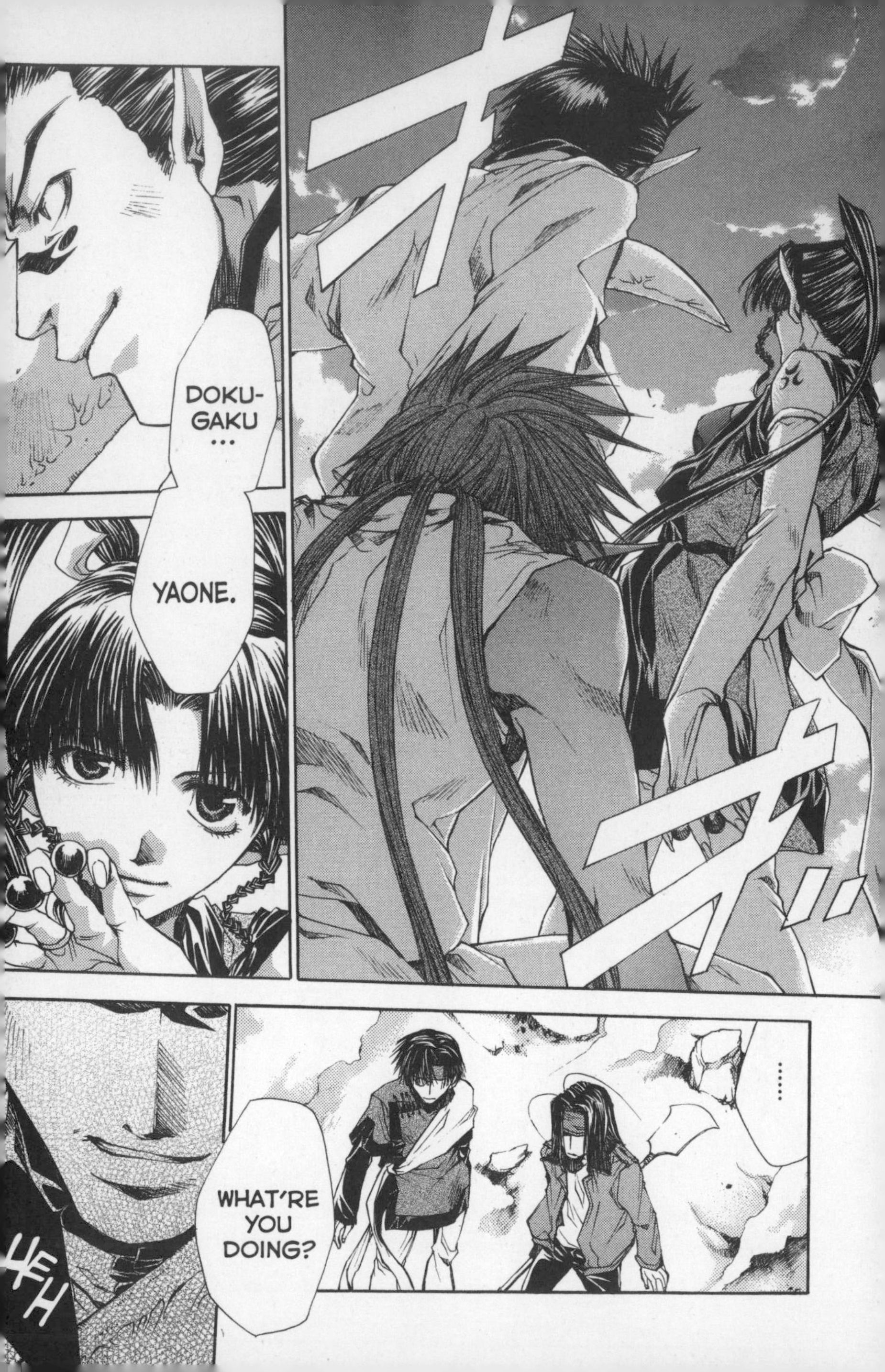
DOKU-GAKU...
YAONE.
......
WHAT'RE YOU DOING?
HEH

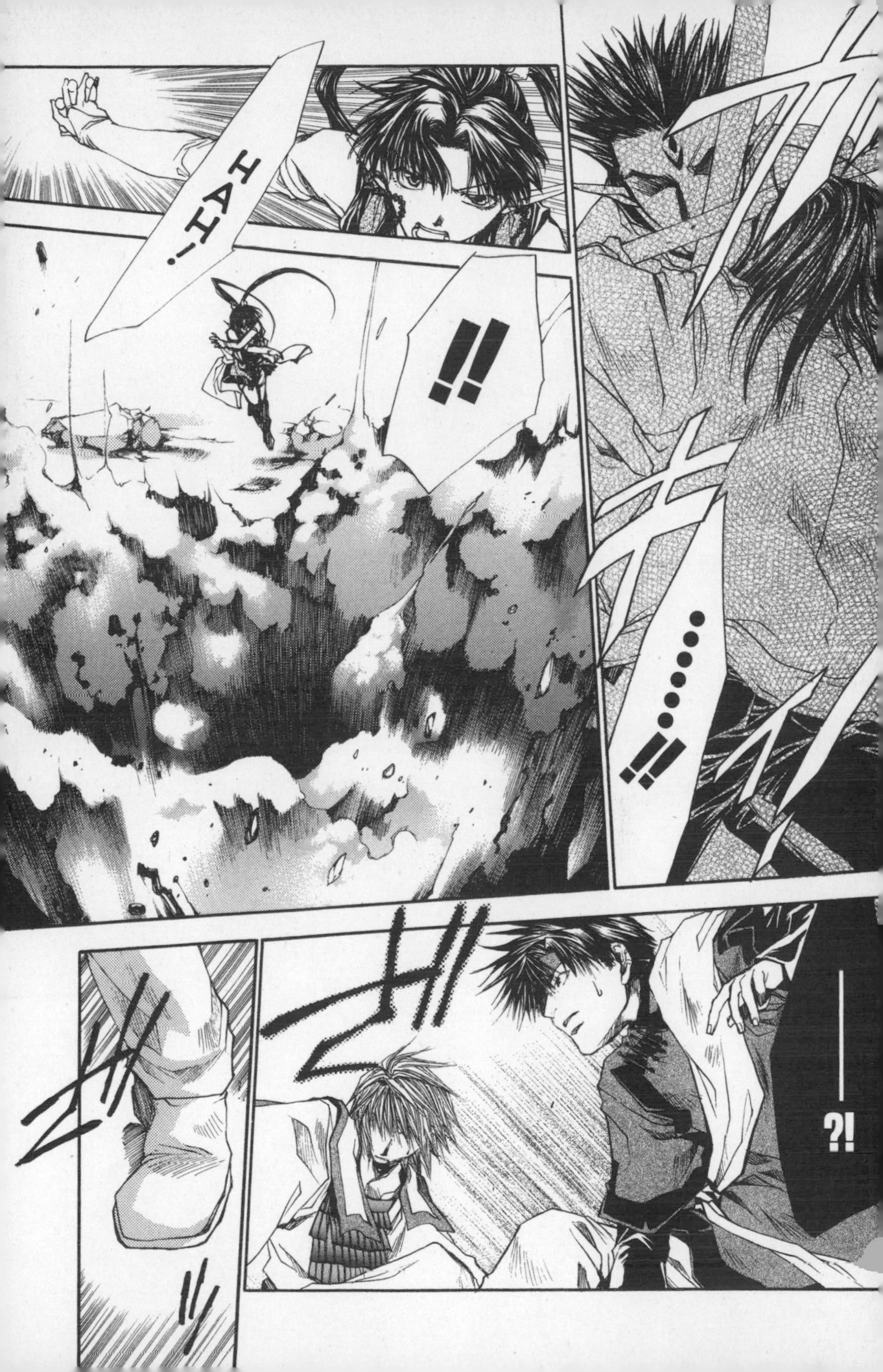
......!!
HAH!
!!
——?!

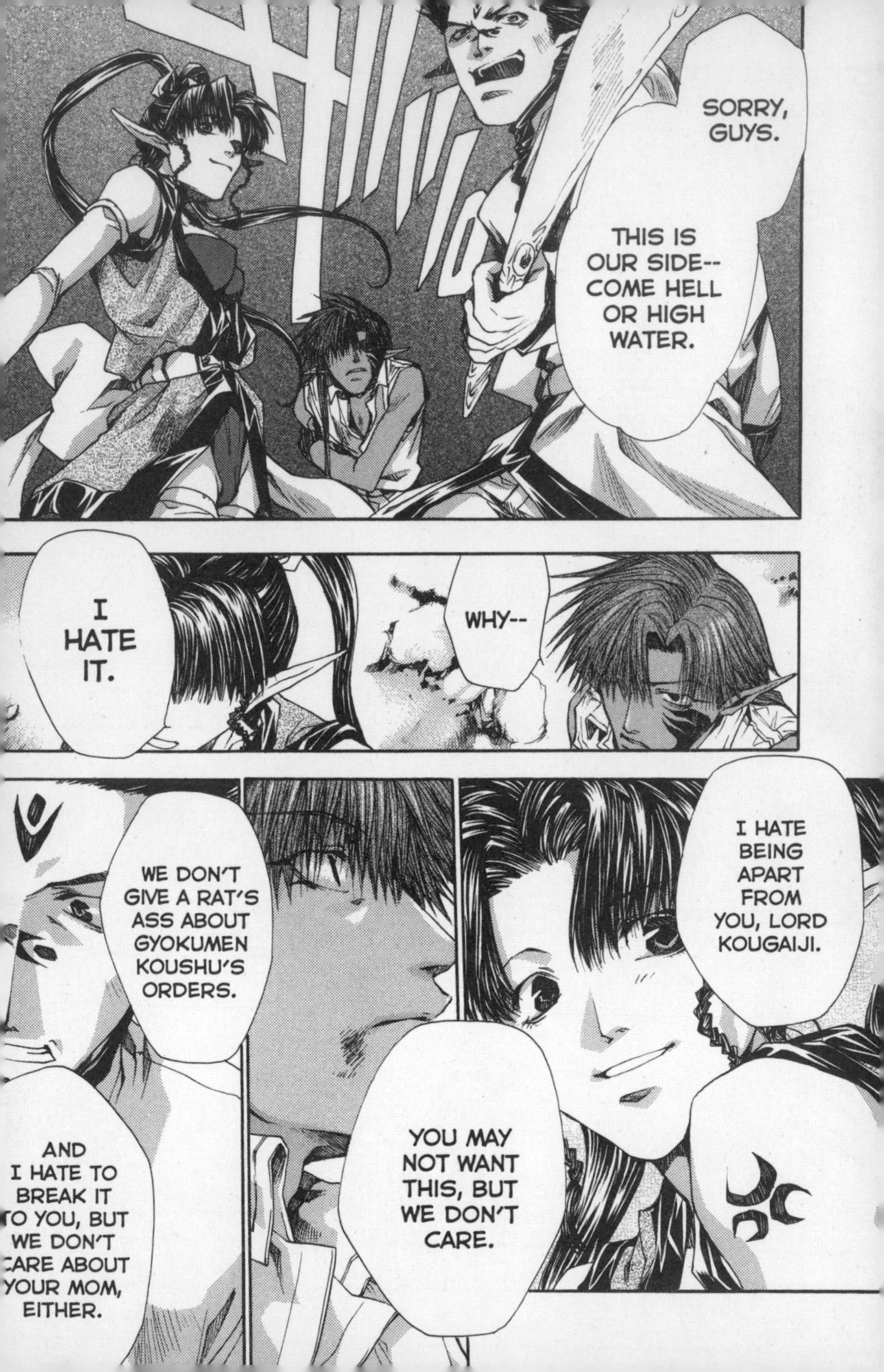
SORRY, GUYS.
THIS IS OUR SIDE-- COME HELL OR HIGH WATER.
WHY--
I HATE IT.
I HATE BEING APART FROM YOU, LORD KOUGAIJI.
YOU MAY NOT WANT THIS, BUT WE DON'T CARE.
WE DON'T GIVE A RAT'S ASS ABOUT GYOKUMEN KOUSHU'S ORDERS.
AND I HATE TO BREAK IT TO YOU, BUT WE DON'T CARE ABOUT YOUR MOM, EITHER.

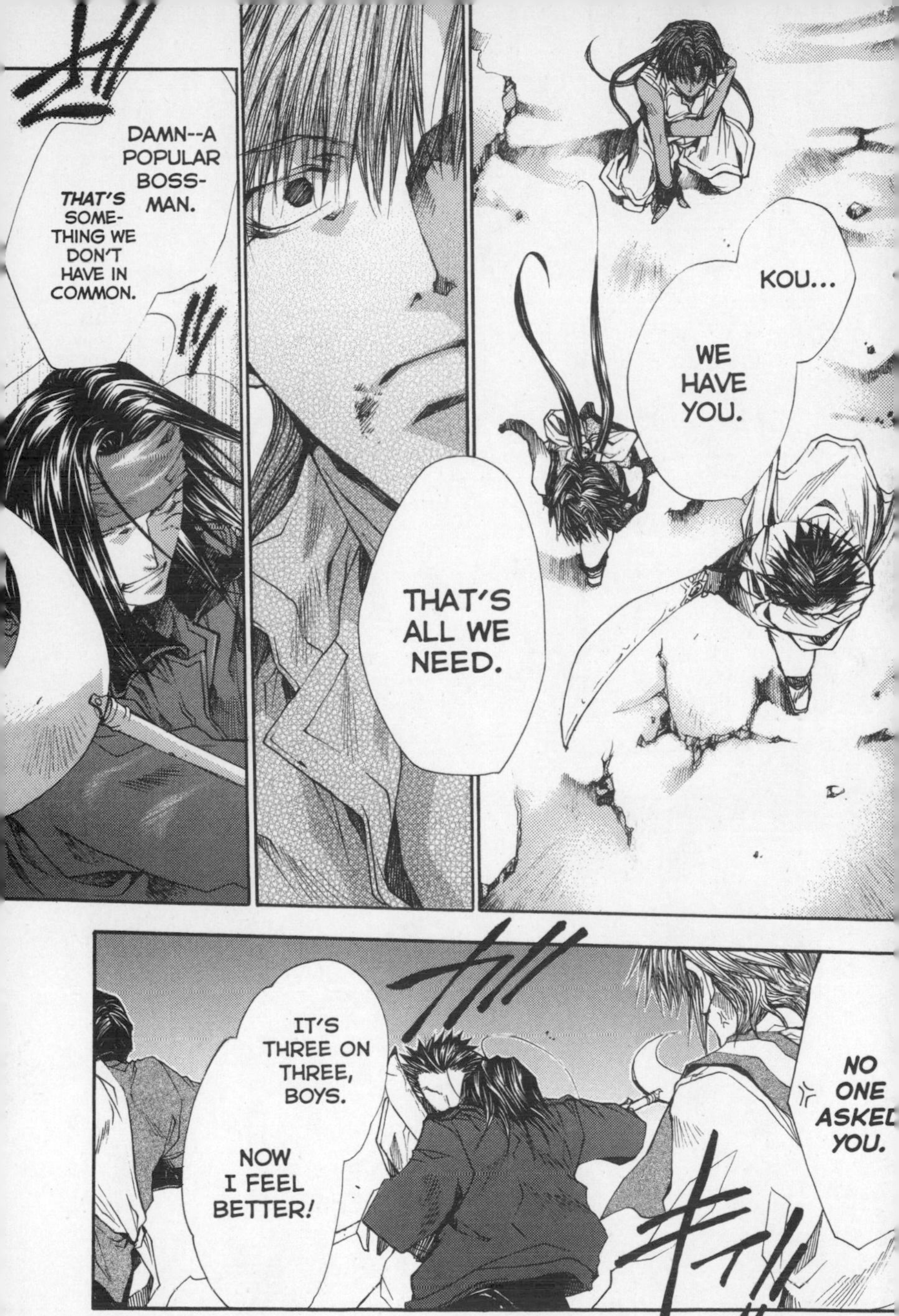
KOU...
WE HAVE YOU.
THAT'S ALL WE NEED.
DAMN--A POPULAR BOSS-MAN.
THAT'S SOMETHING WE DON'T HAVE IN COMMON.
NO ONE ASKED YOU.
IT'S THREE ON THREE, BOYS.
NOW I FEEL BETTER!

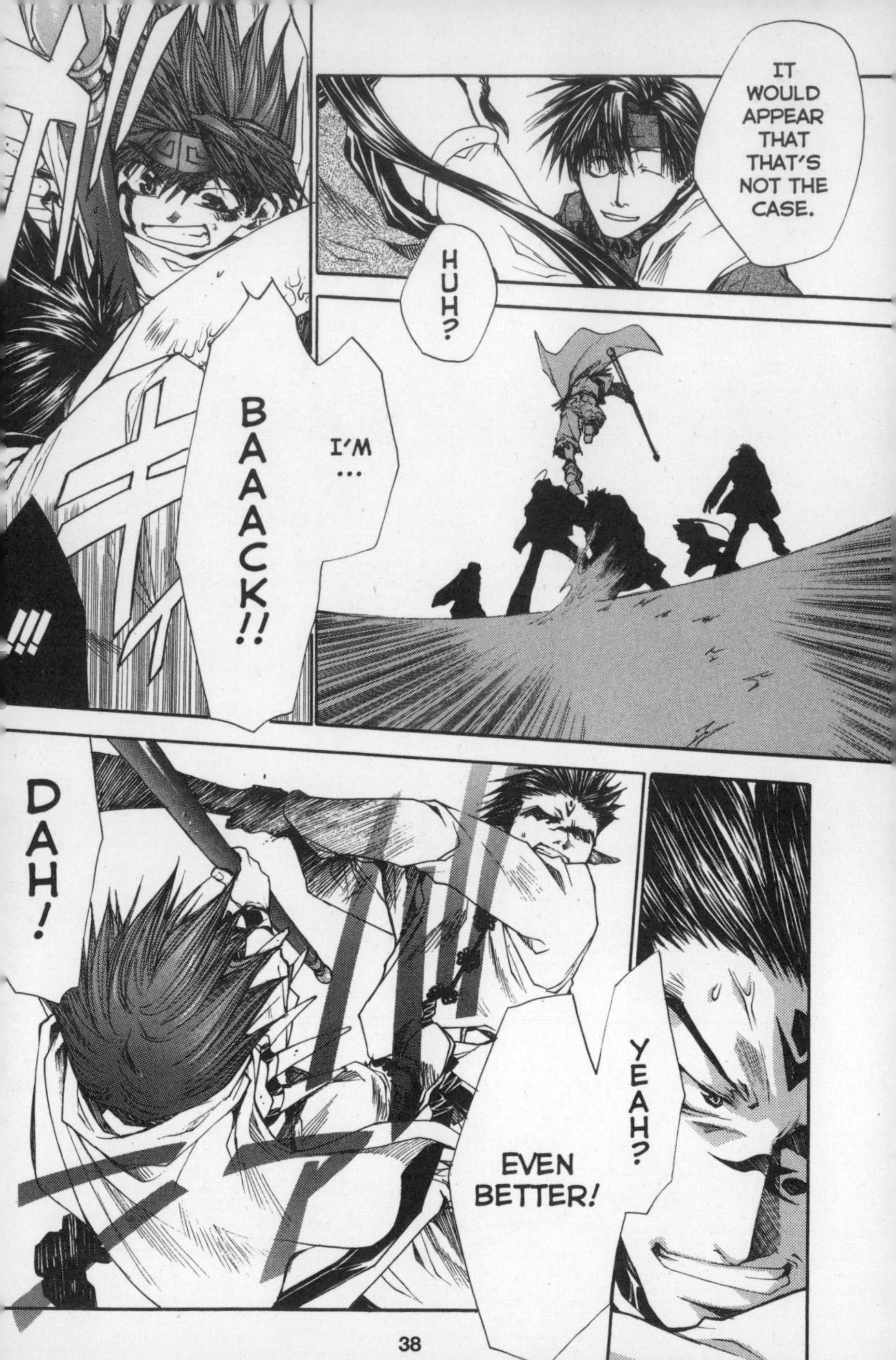
IT WOULD APPEAR THAT THAT'S NOT THE CASE.
HUH?
I'M ...
BAAAACK!!
!!!
YEAH?
EVEN BETTER!
DAH!

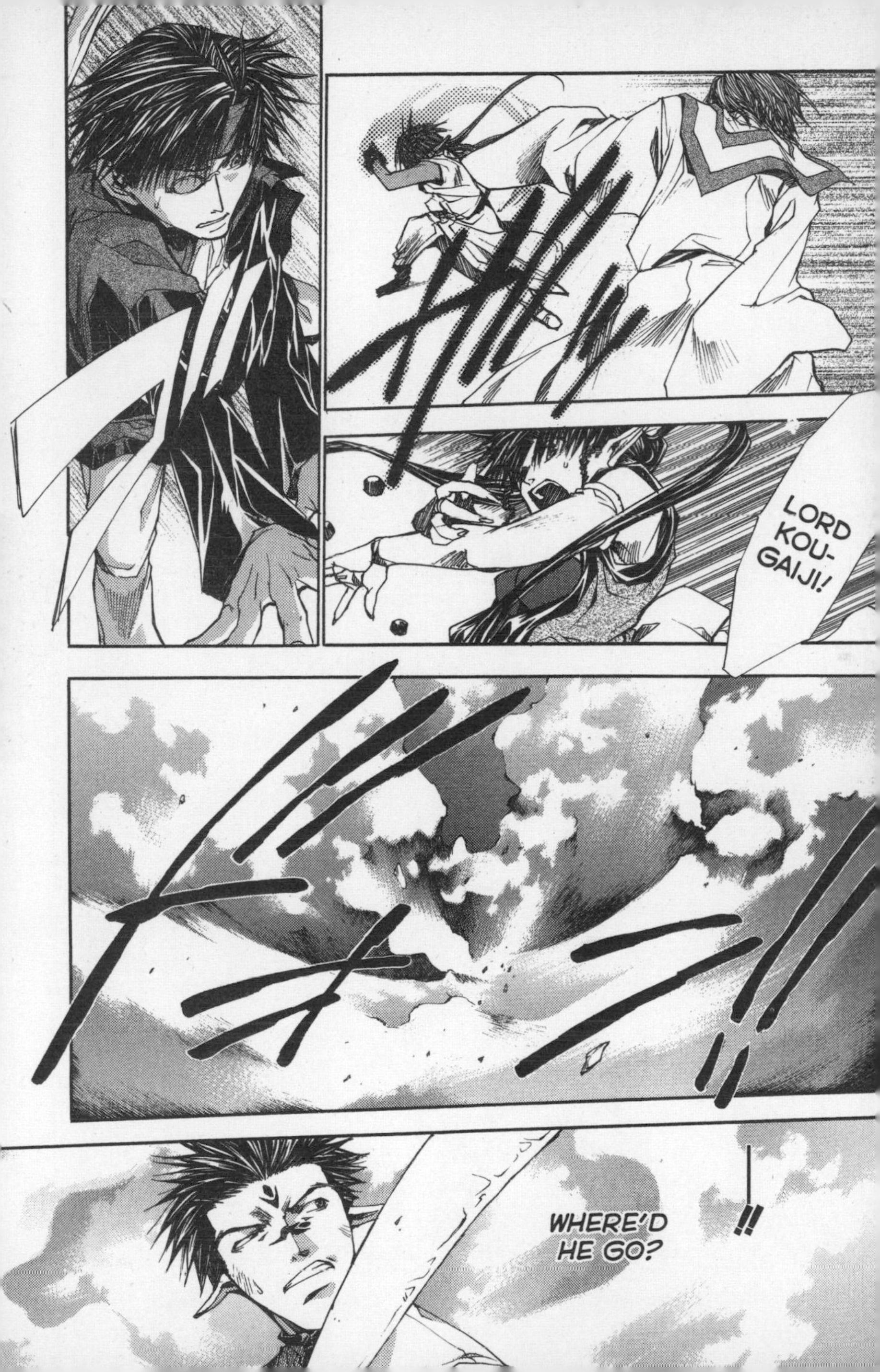
LORD KOU-GAIJI!
!!
WHERE'D HE GO?

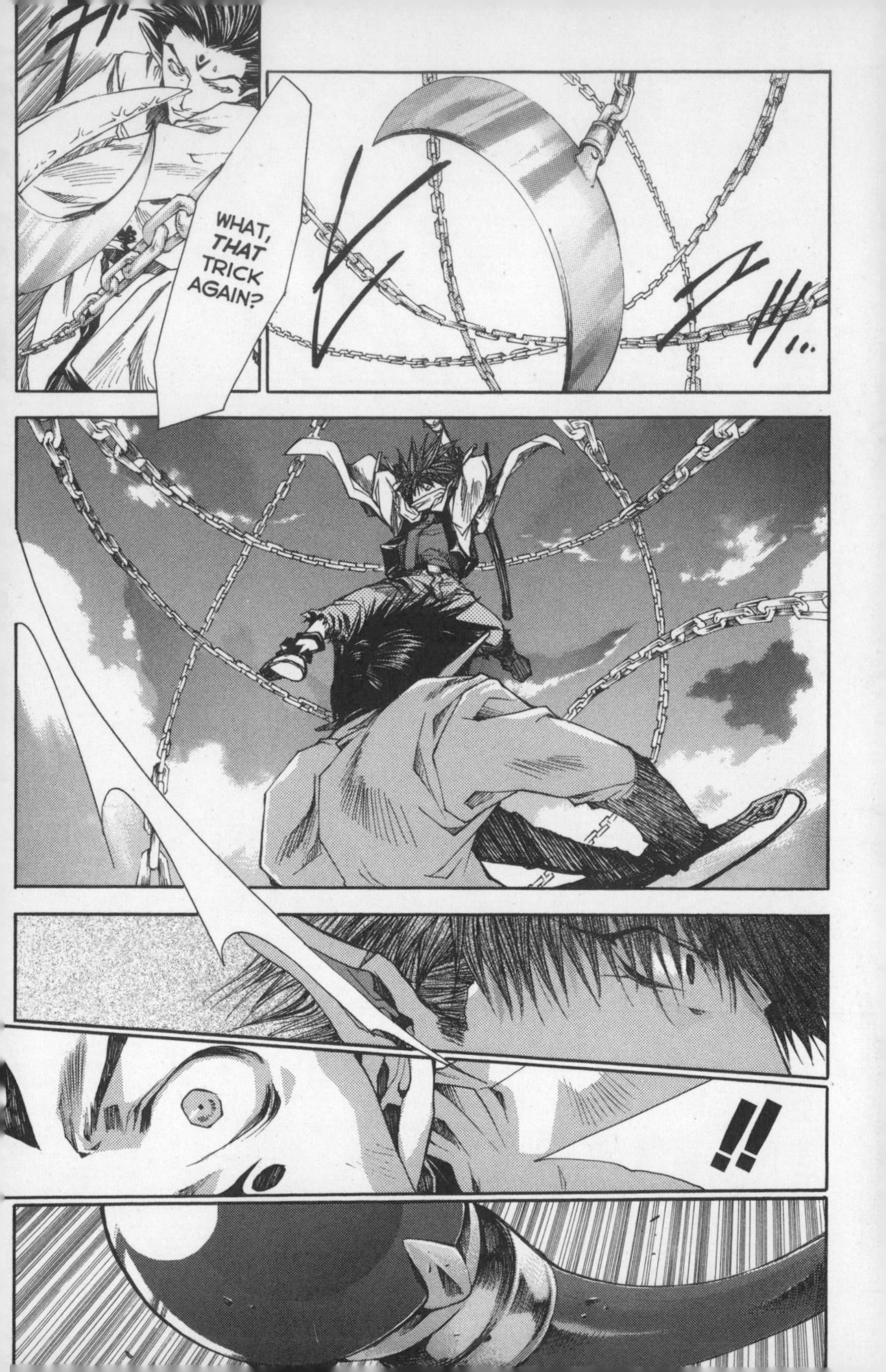
WHAT, THAT TRICK AGAIN?
!!

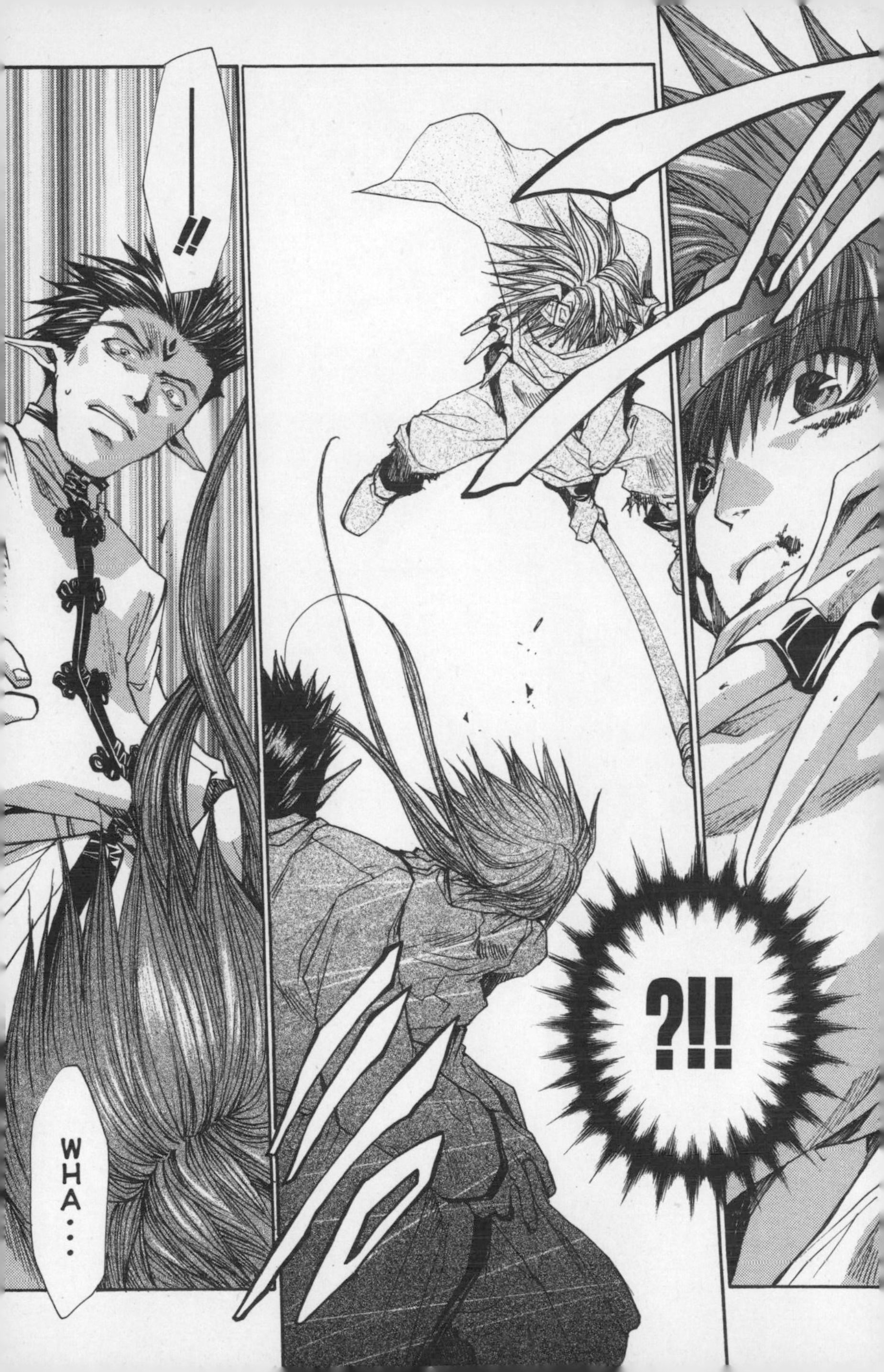
?!!
—!!
WHA...

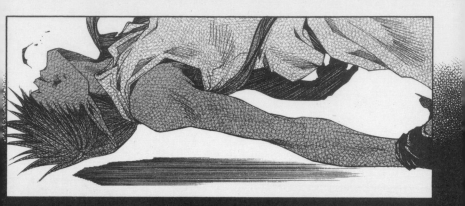

KOU!

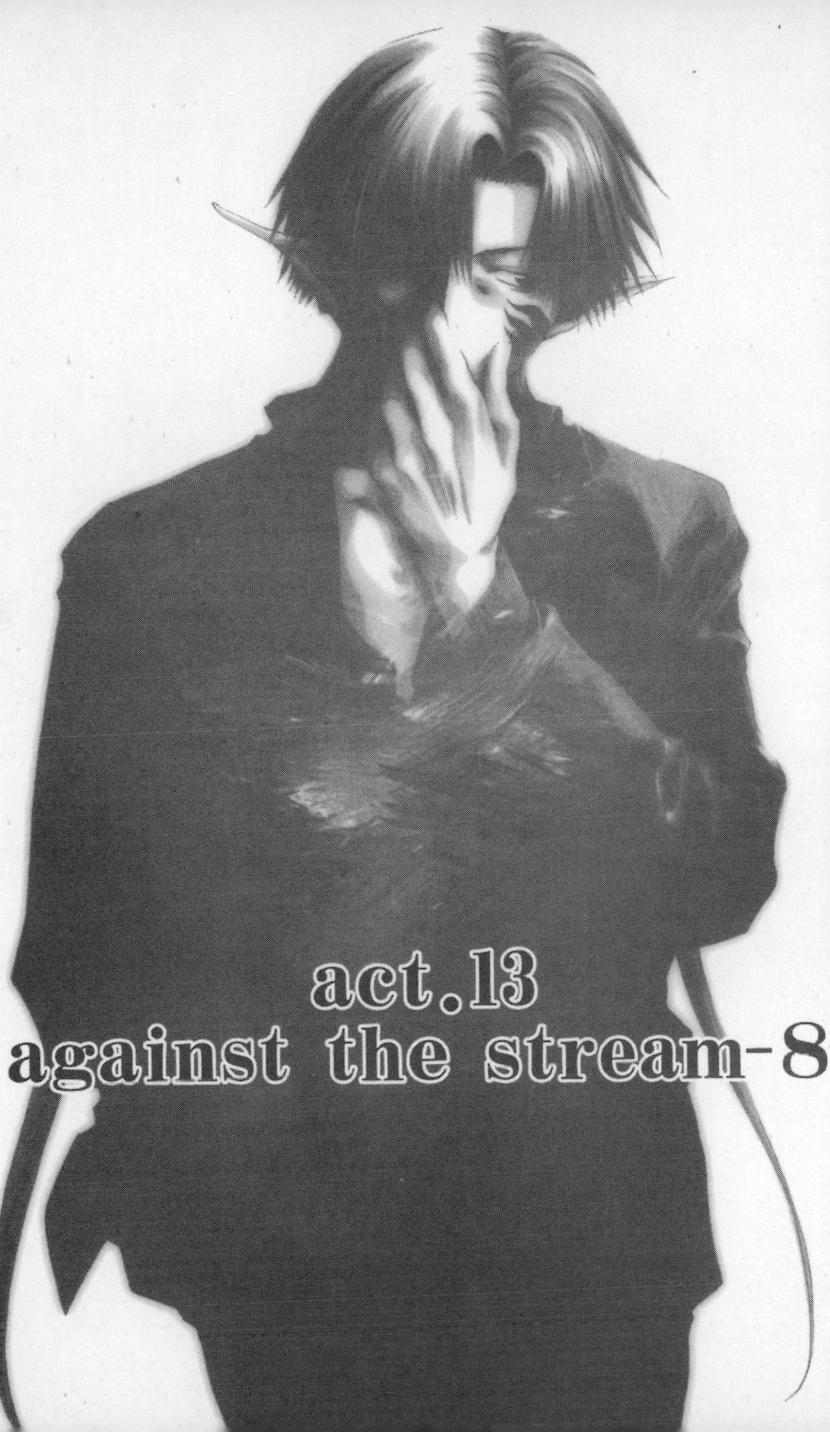

act.13
against the stream-8

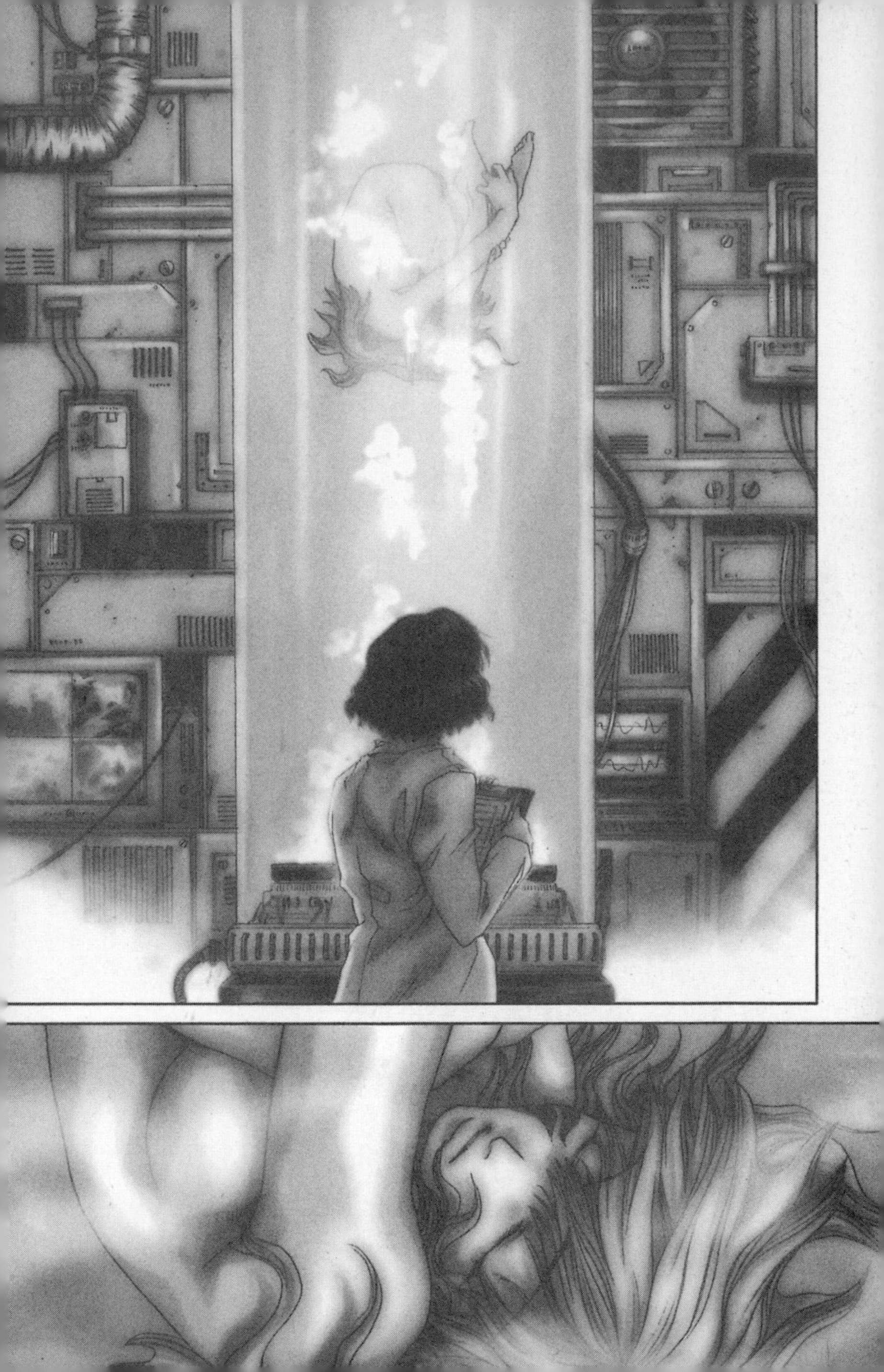

IT'S DARK.
DEEP...
...AND DARK.
VOICES.
WHO IS THAT?
YOU MAY NOT WANT THIS...
...BUT WE DON'T CARE.
KOU.
WE HAVE YOU.
WHO?
THAT'S ALL WE NEED.

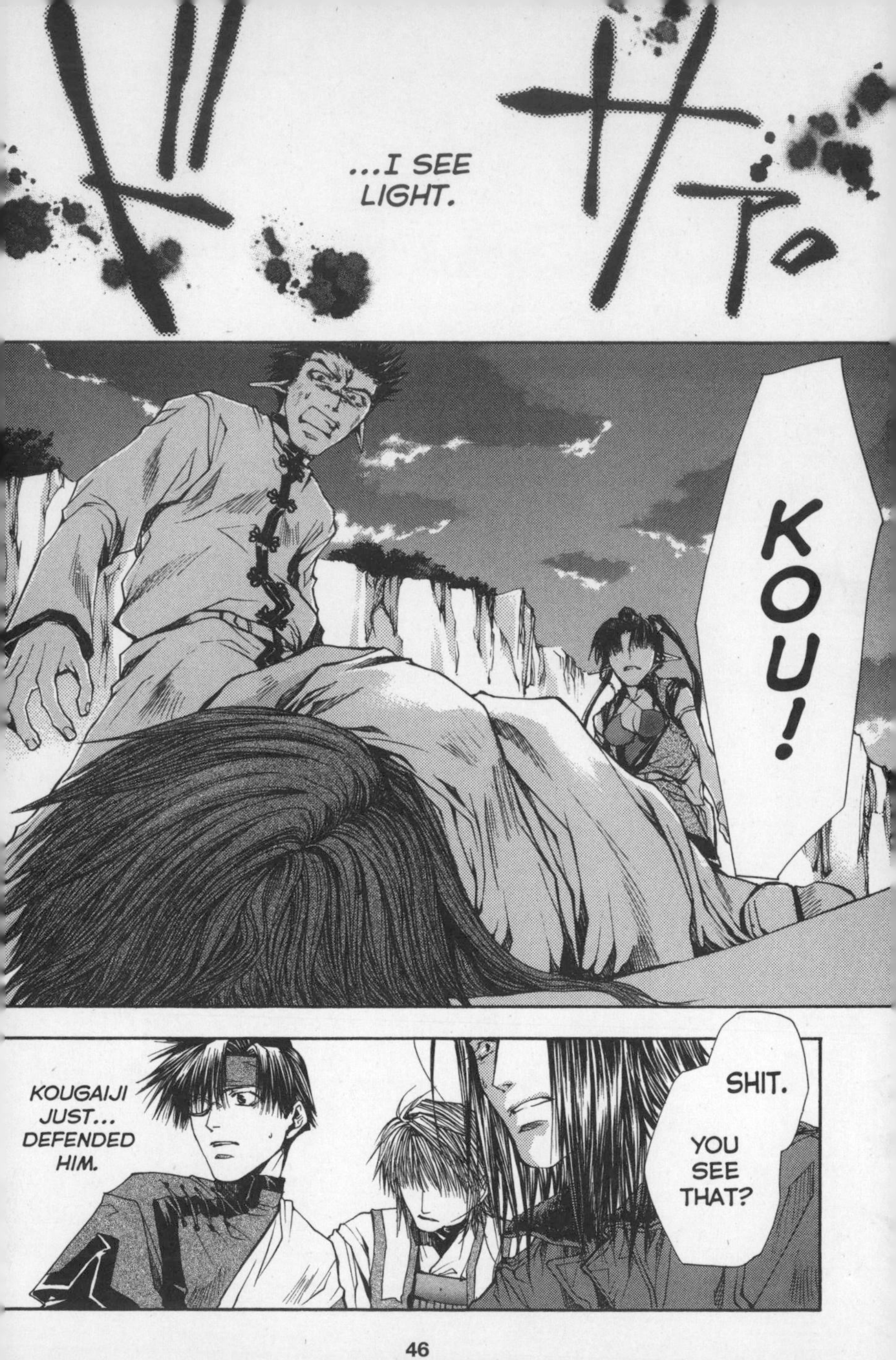
...I SEE LIGHT.
KOU!
SHIT.
YOU SEE THAT?
KOUGAIJI JUST... DEFENDED HIM.

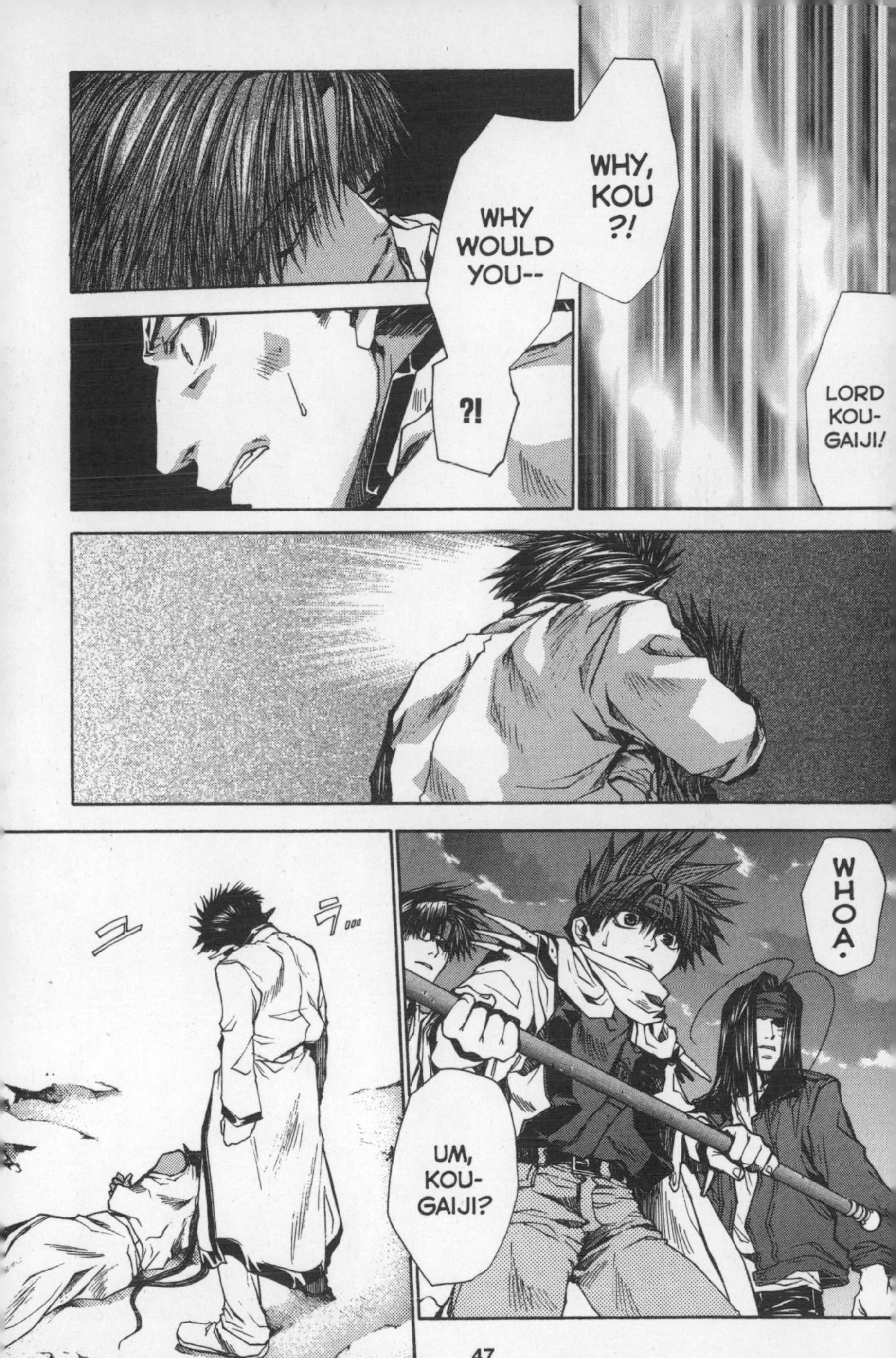
LORD KOU-GAIJI!
WHY, KOU ?! WHY WOULD YOU--
?!
WHOA.
UM, KOU-GAIJI?
ユ ラ...

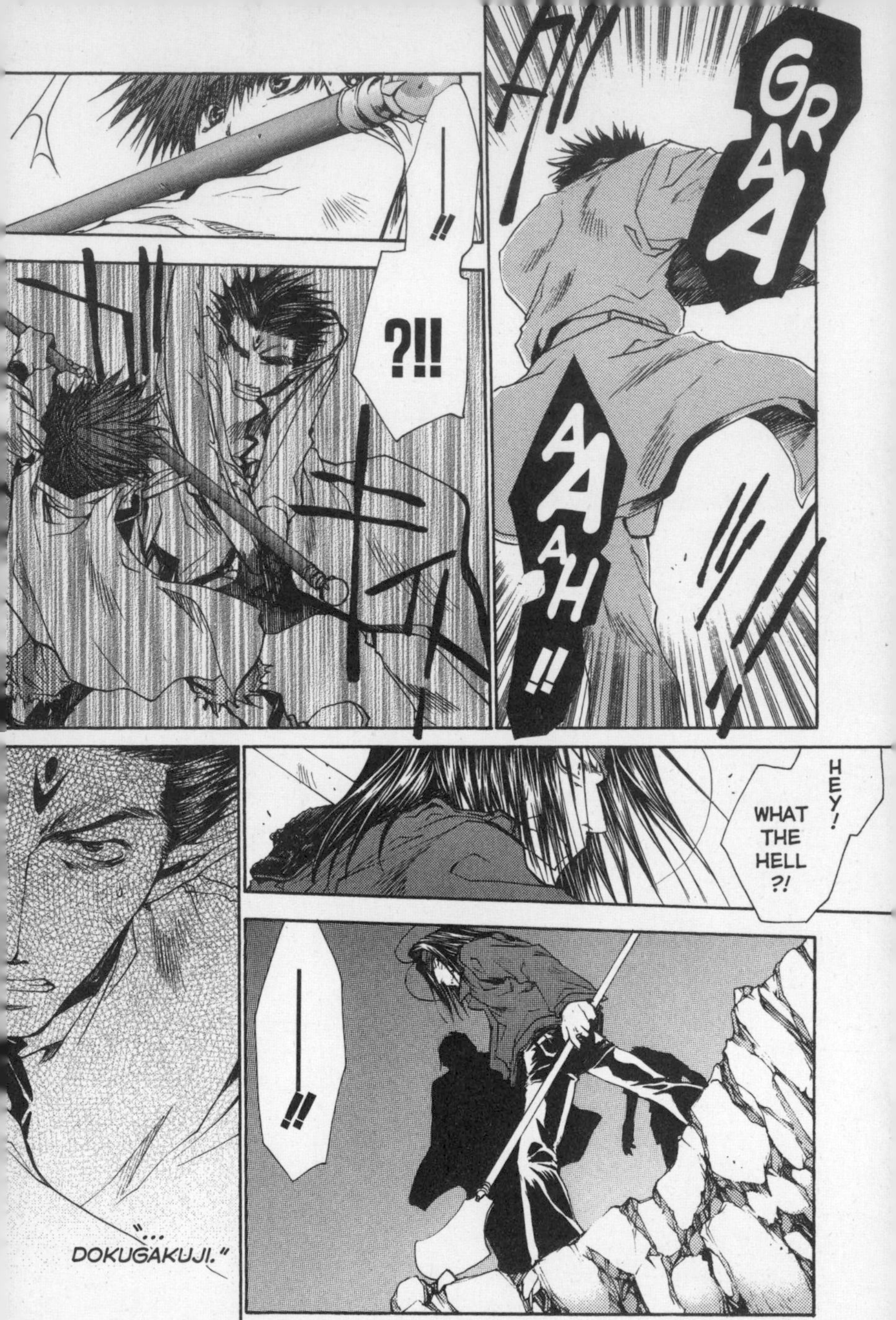
GRAA
AAAH!!
—!!
?!!
HEY! WHAT THE HELL?!
—!!
"... DOKUGAKUJI."

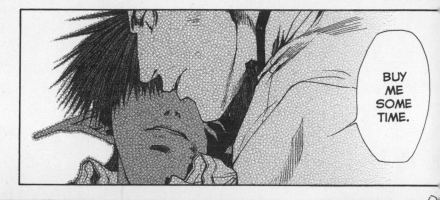

BUY ME SOME TIME.

ON SAN MAYA SATO

MAEI SO-WAKA-ONSHA REI

JAWA-MEI ONHATTA ...

SCATTER!!

IT'S A TRAP!!

開 KA!!
!!

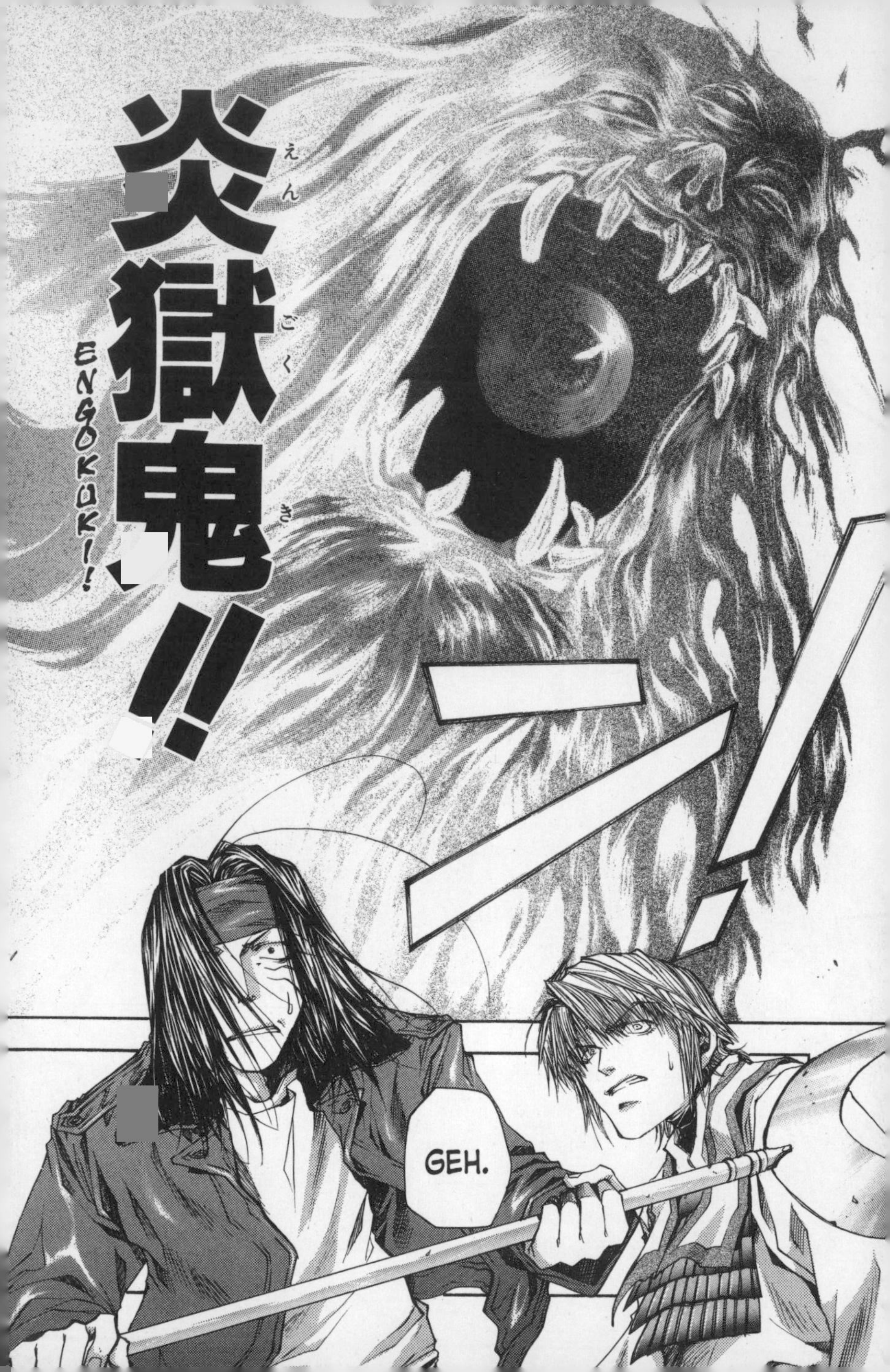
炎獄鬼!!
えんごくき
ENGOKUKI!!
GEH.

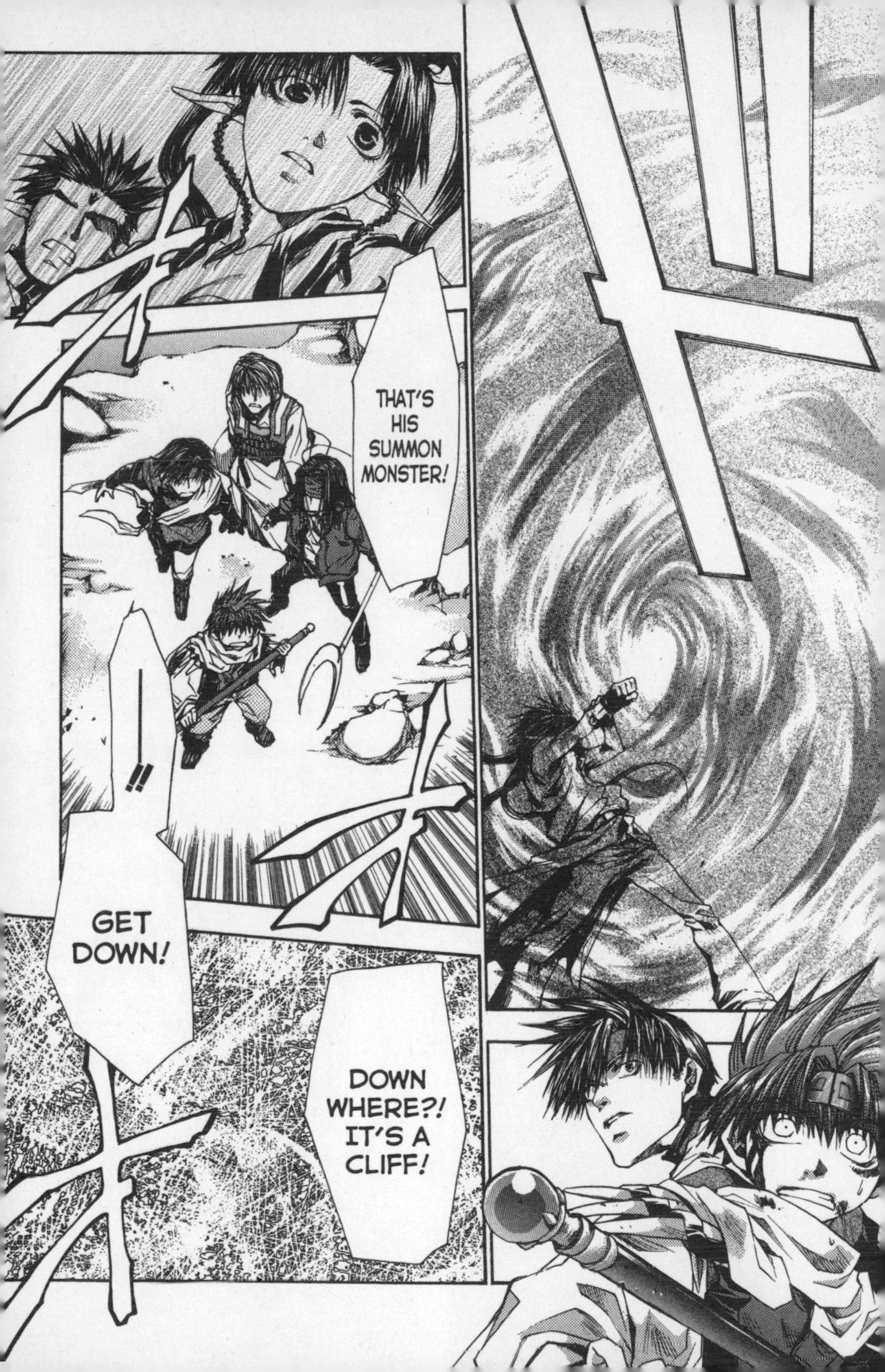
THAT'S HIS SUMMON MONSTER!
!!
GET DOWN!
DOWN WHERE?! IT'S A CLIFF!

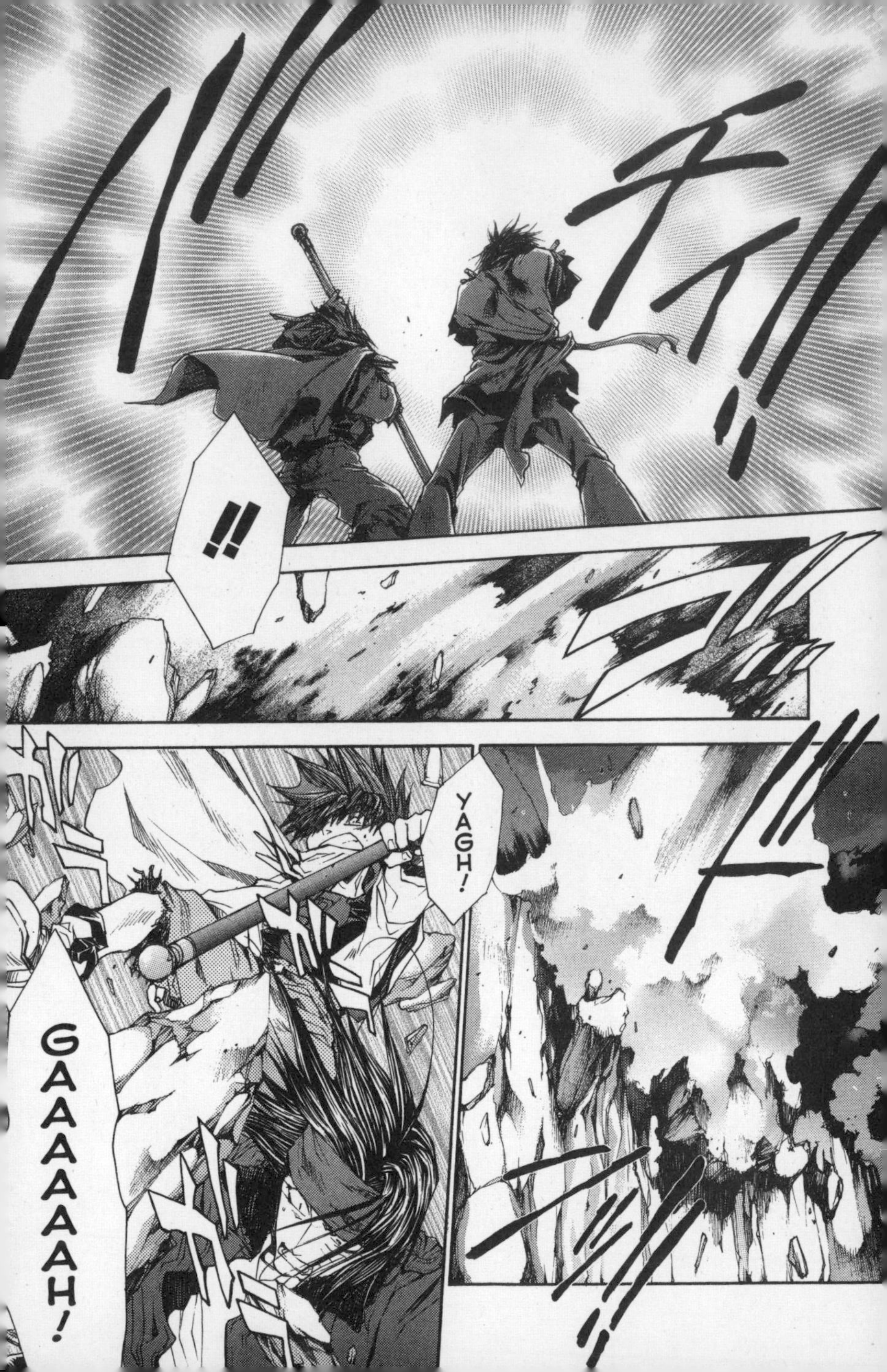
!!
YAGH!
GAAAAAAAH!

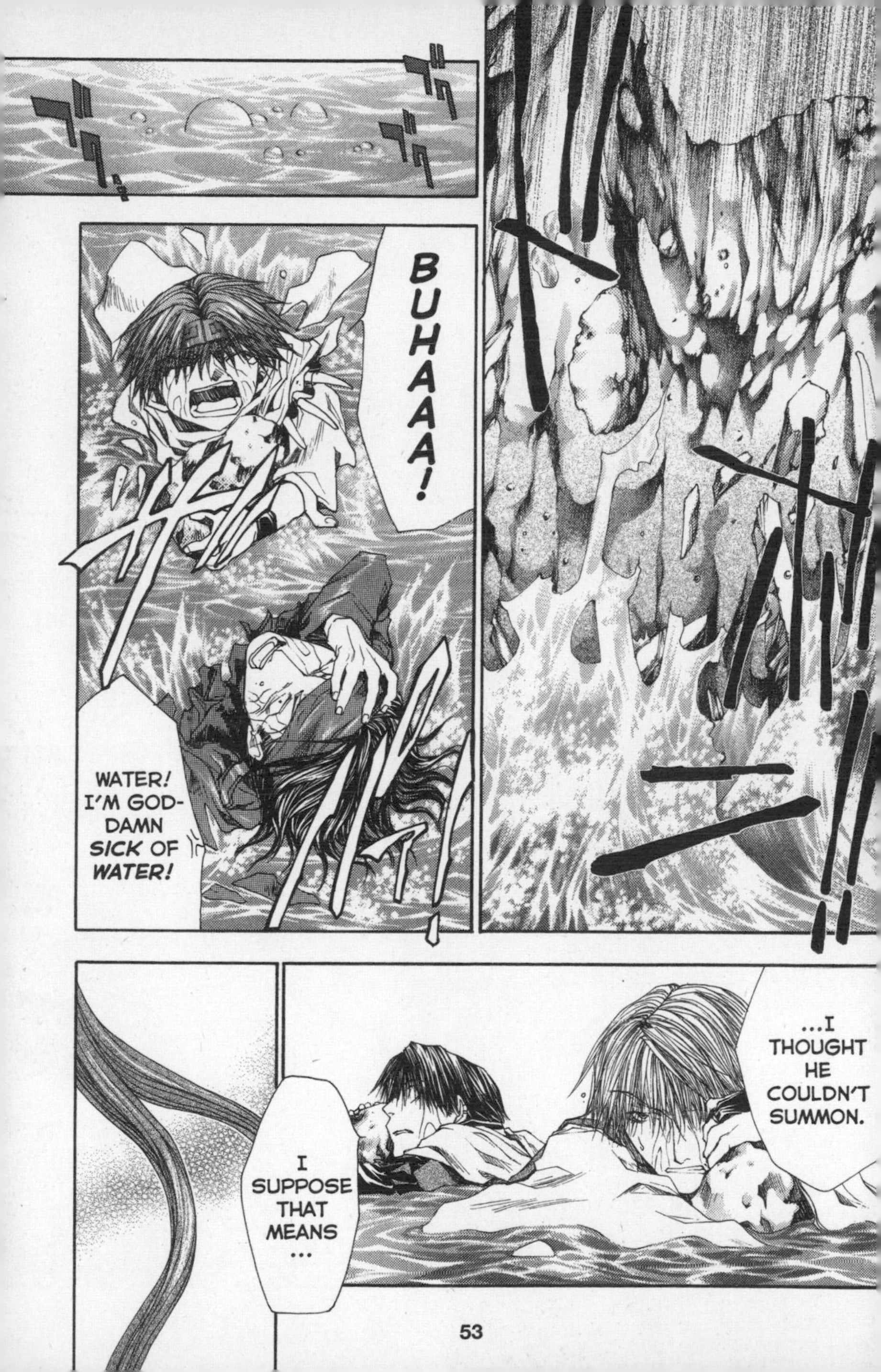
BUHAAAA!
WATER! I'M GOD-DAMN SICK OF WATER!
...I THOUGHT HE COULDN'T SUMMON.
I SUPPOSE THAT MEANS ...

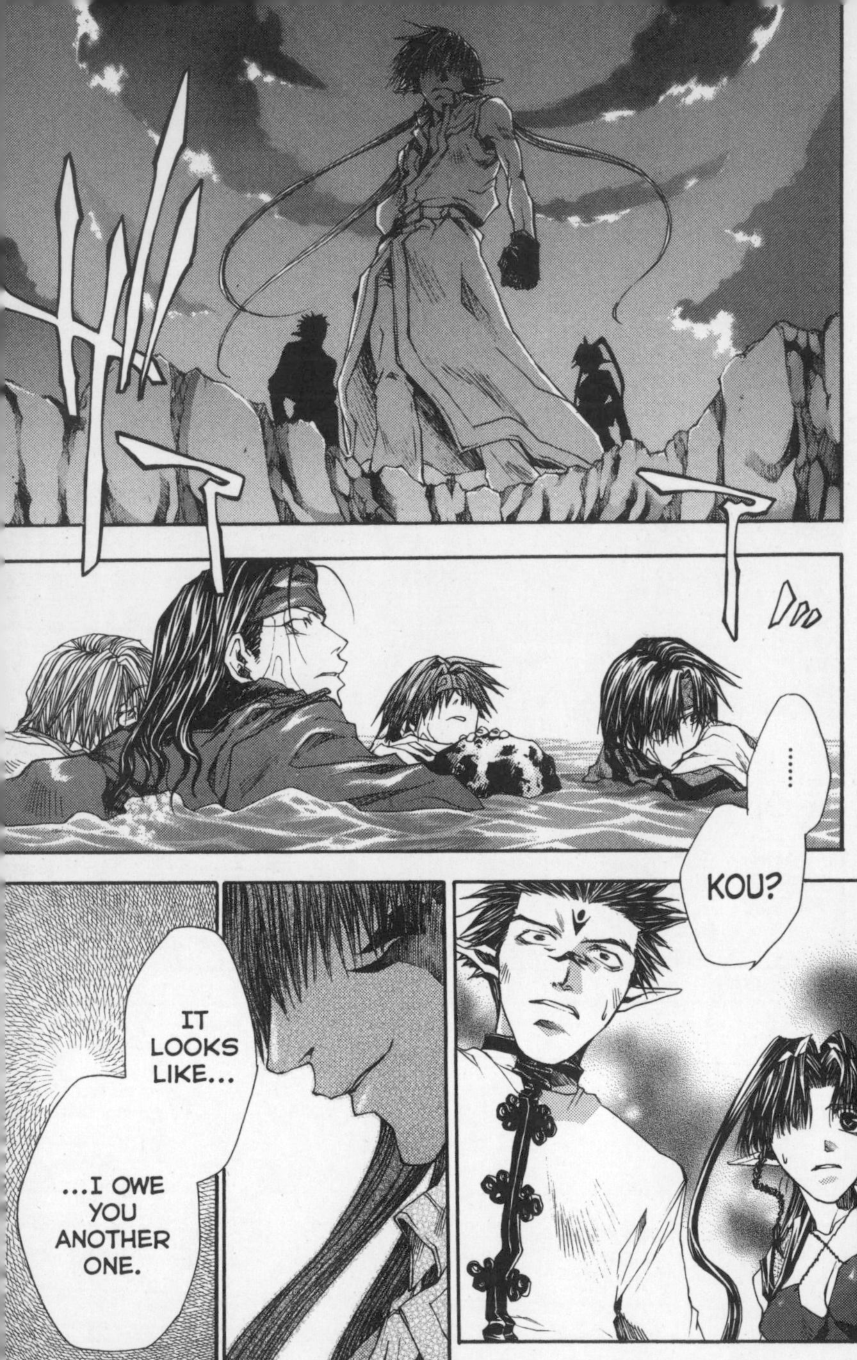
......
KOU?
IT LOOKS LIKE...
...I OWE YOU ANOTHER ONE.

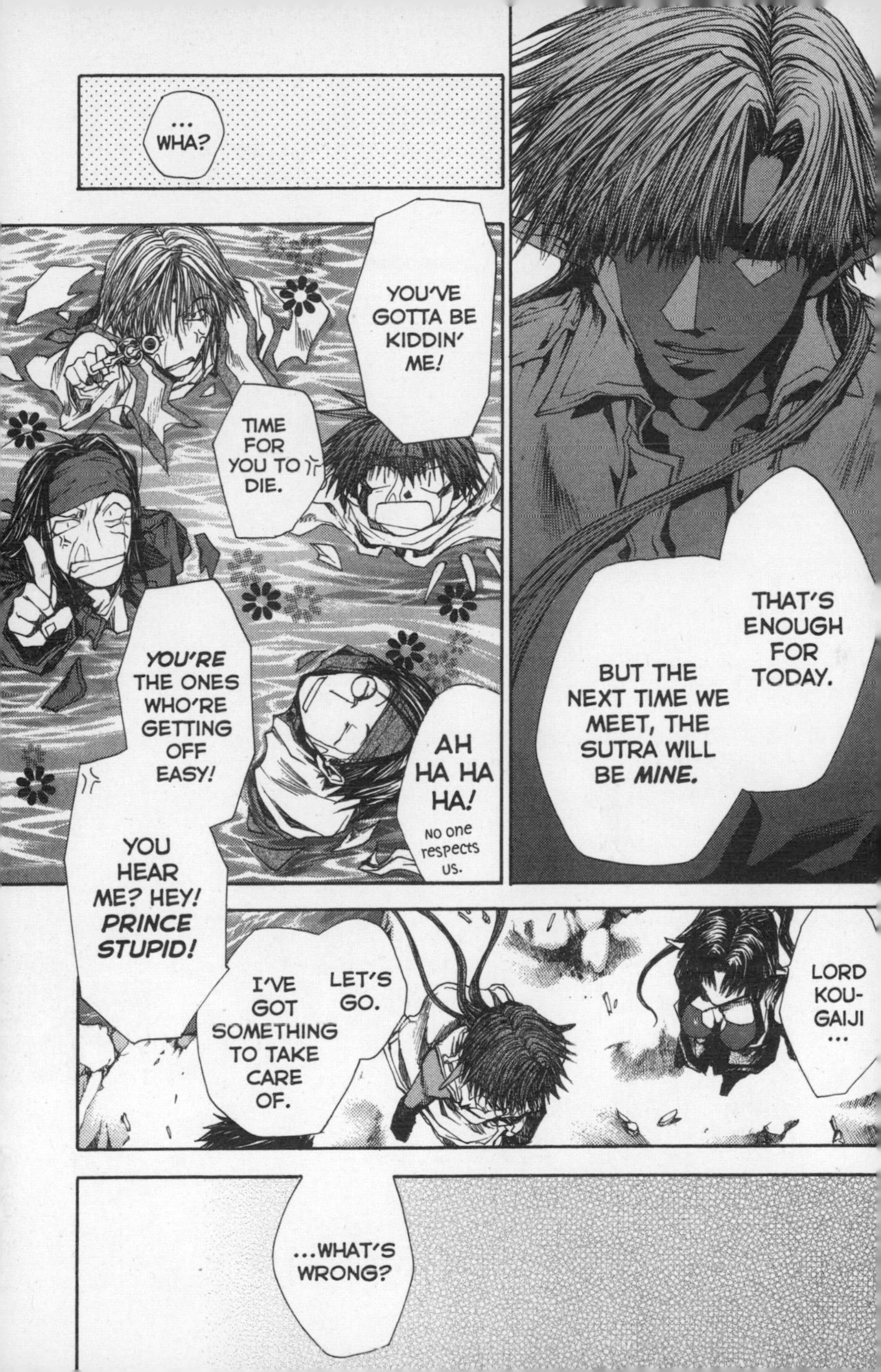
THAT'S ENOUGH FOR TODAY.
BUT THE NEXT TIME WE MEET, THE SUTRA WILL BE *MINE.*
... WHA?
YOU'VE GOTTA BE KIDDIN' ME!
TIME FOR YOU TO DIE.
AH HA HA HA!
No one respects us.
YOU'RE THE ONES WHO'RE GETTING OFF EASY!
YOU HEAR ME? HEY! *PRINCE STUPID!*
LORD KOU-GAIJI ...
LET'S GO.
I'VE GOT SOMETHING TO TAKE CARE OF.
...WHAT'S WRONG?

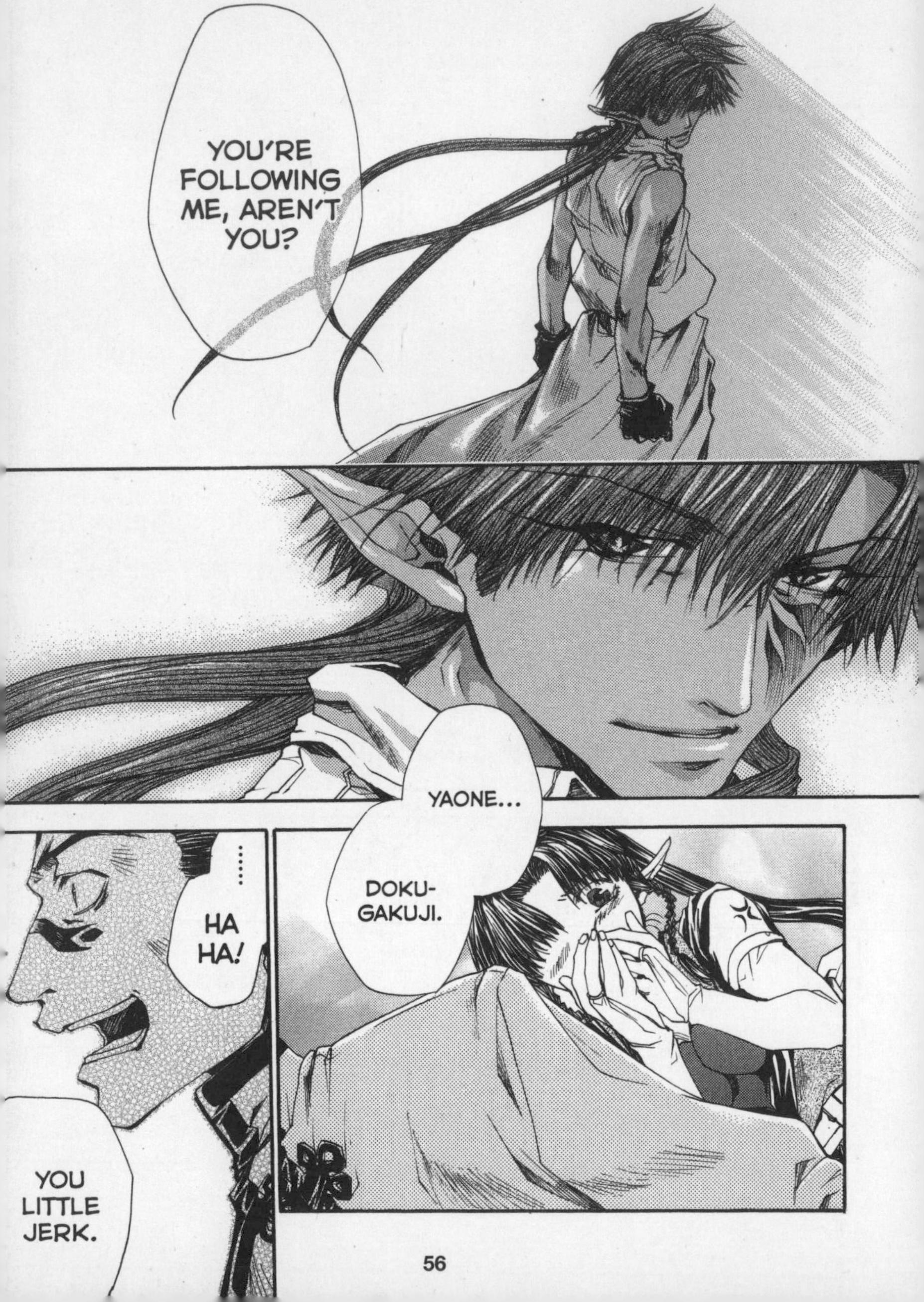
YOU'RE FOLLOWING ME, AREN'T YOU?
YAONE... DOKU-GAKUJI.
......
HA HA!
YOU LITTLE JERK.

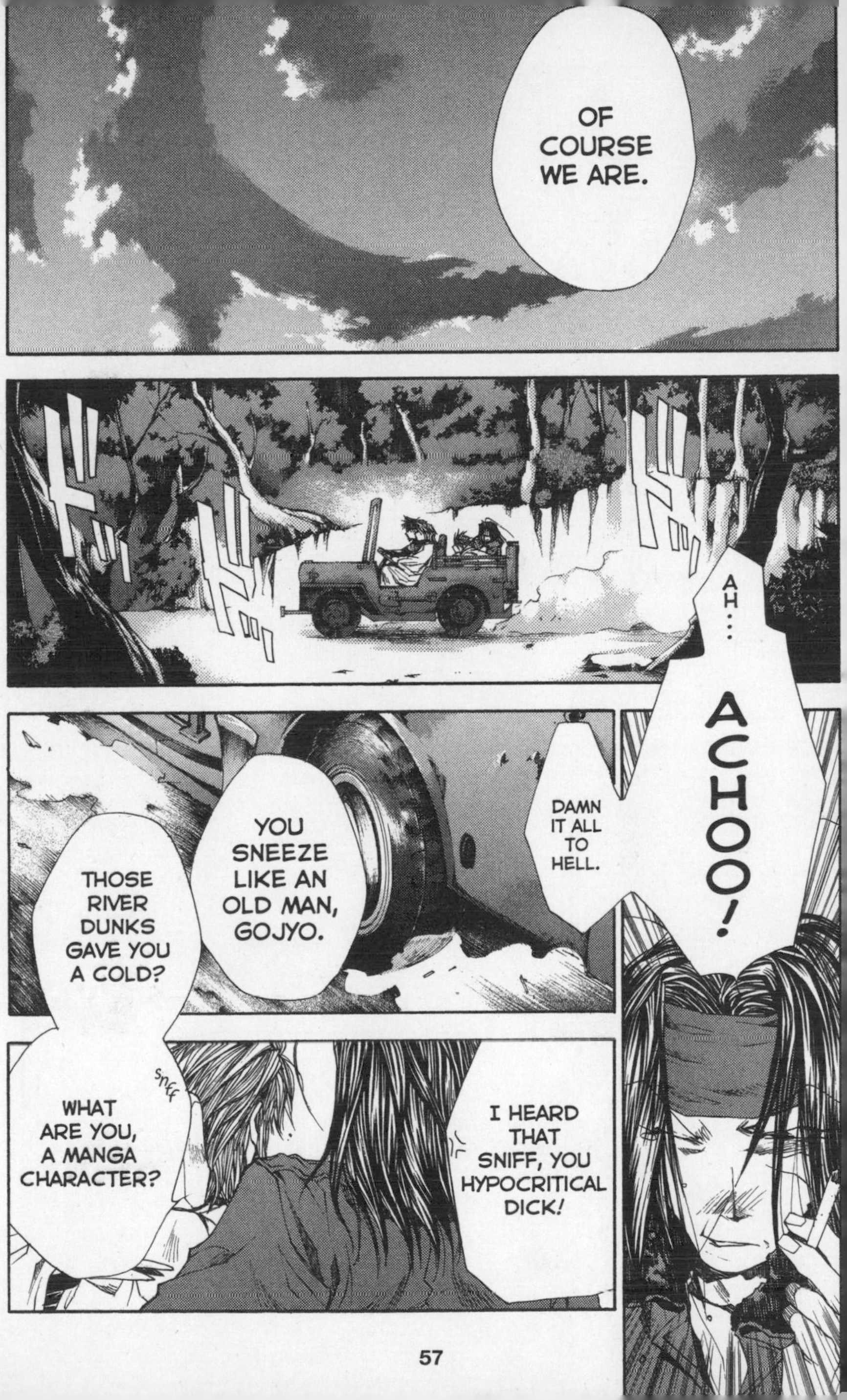
OF COURSE WE ARE.
AH... ACHOO!
DAMN IT ALL TO HELL.
YOU SNEEZE LIKE AN OLD MAN, GOJYO.
THOSE RIVER DUNKS GAVE YOU A COLD?
sniff
WHAT ARE YOU, A MANGA CHARACTER?
I HEARD THAT SNIFF, YOU HYPOCRITICAL DICK!

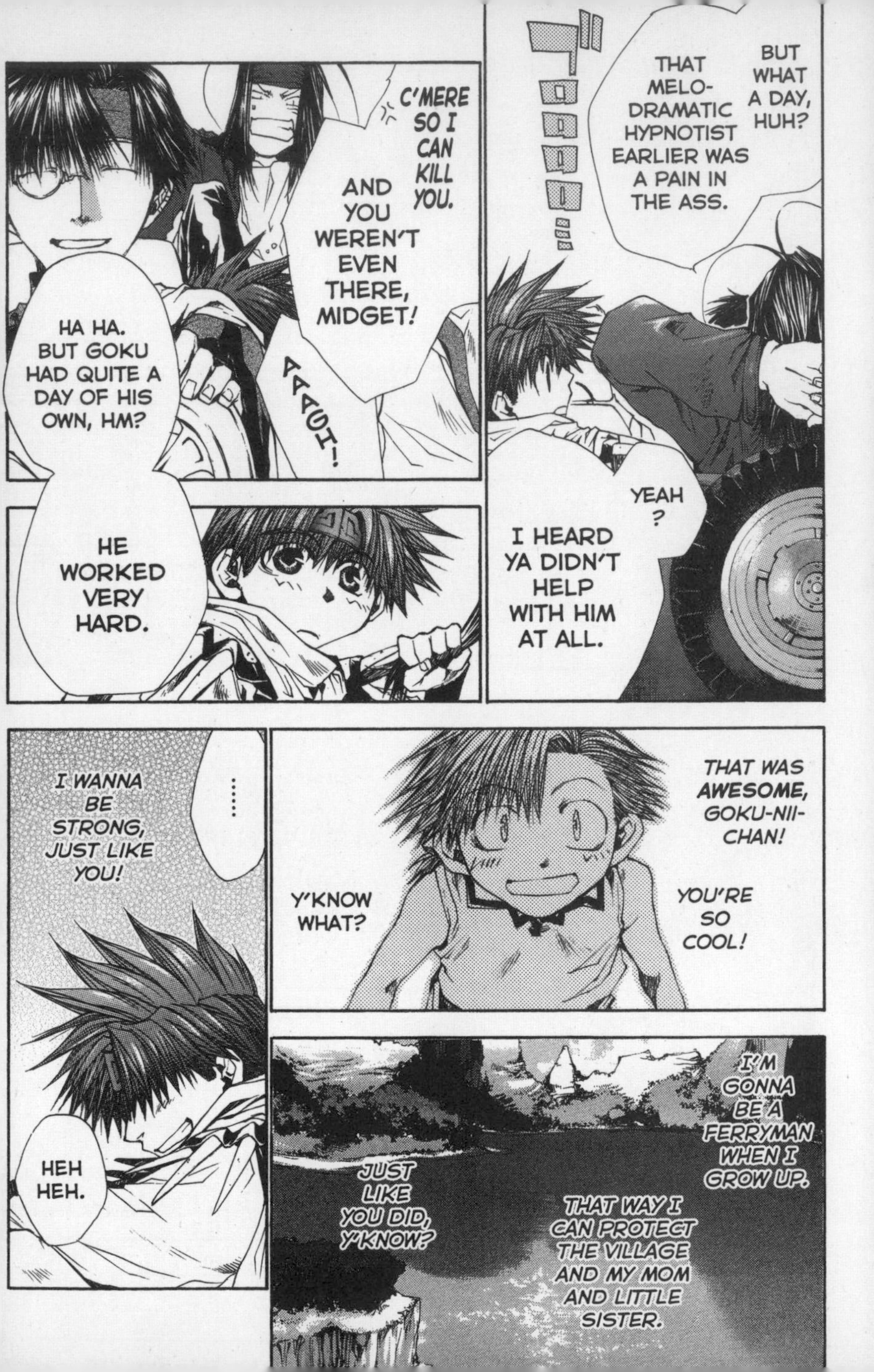
BUT WHAT A DAY, HUH?
THAT MELO-DRAMATIC HYPNOTIST EARLIER WAS A PAIN IN THE ASS.
YEAH?
I HEARD YA DIDN'T HELP WITH HIM AT ALL.
C'MERE SO I CAN KILL YOU.
AND YOU WEREN'T EVEN THERE, MIDGET!
AAAGH!
HA HA. BUT GOKU HAD QUITE A DAY OF HIS OWN, HM?
HE WORKED VERY HARD.
THAT WAS AWESOME, GOKU-NII-CHAN!
YOU'RE SO COOL!
Y'KNOW WHAT?
I'M GONNA BE A FERRYMAN WHEN I GROW UP.
THAT WAY I CAN PROTECT THE VILLAGE AND MY MOM AND LITTLE SISTER.
JUST LIKE YOU DID, Y'KNOW?
I WANNA BE STRONG, JUST LIKE YOU!
......
HEH HEH.

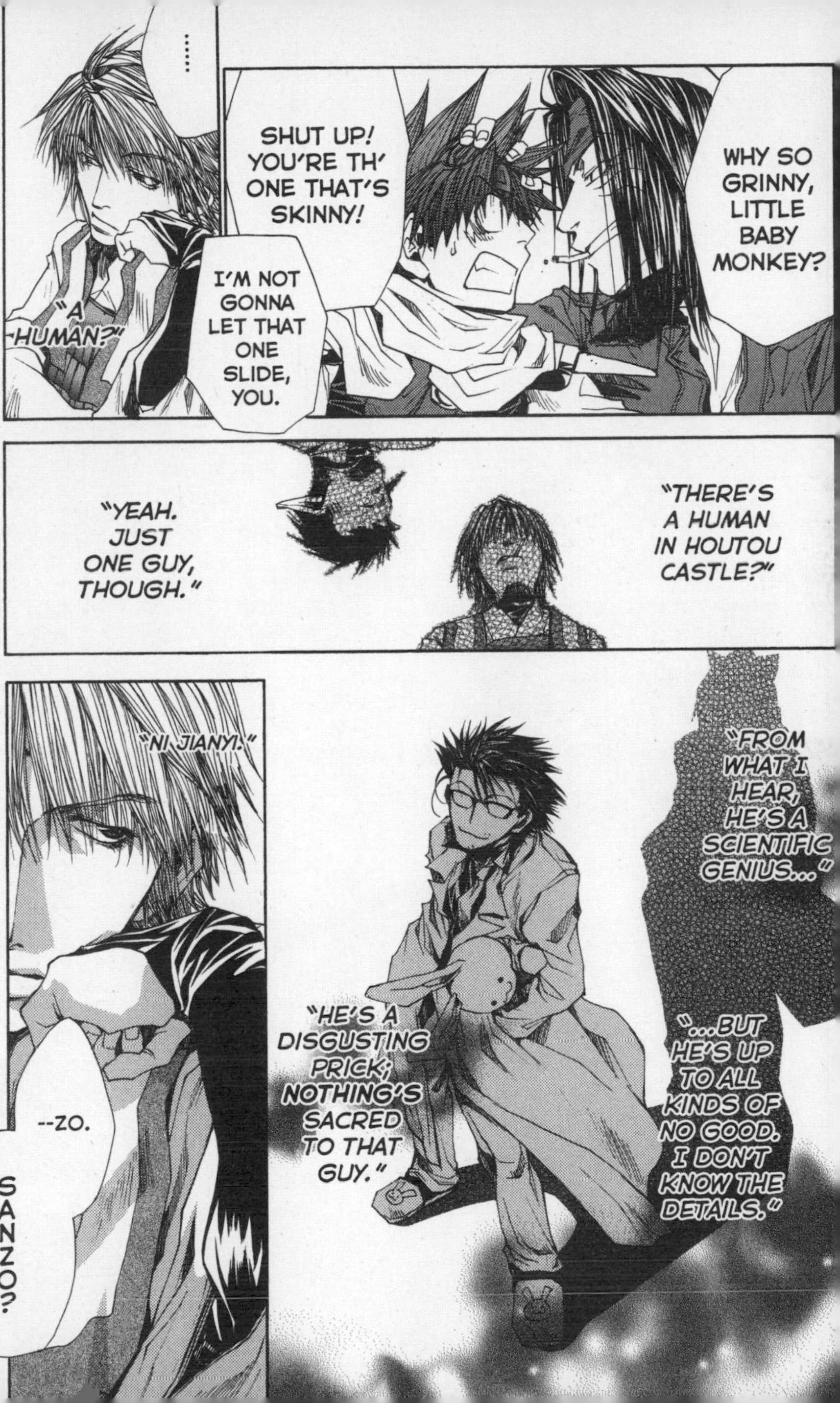
WHY SO GRINNY, LITTLE BABY MONKEY?
SHUT UP! YOU'RE TH' ONE THAT'S SKINNY!
I'M NOT GONNA LET THAT ONE SLIDE, YOU.
......
"A HUMAN?"
"THERE'S A HUMAN IN HOUTOU CASTLE?"
"YEAH. JUST ONE GUY, THOUGH."
"FROM WHAT I HEAR, HE'S A SCIENTIFIC GENIUS..."
"...BUT HE'S UP TO ALL KINDS OF NO GOOD. I DON'T KNOW THE DETAILS."
"HE'S A DISGUSTING PRICK; NOTHING'S SACRED TO THAT GUY."
"NI JIANYI."
--ZO.
SANZO?

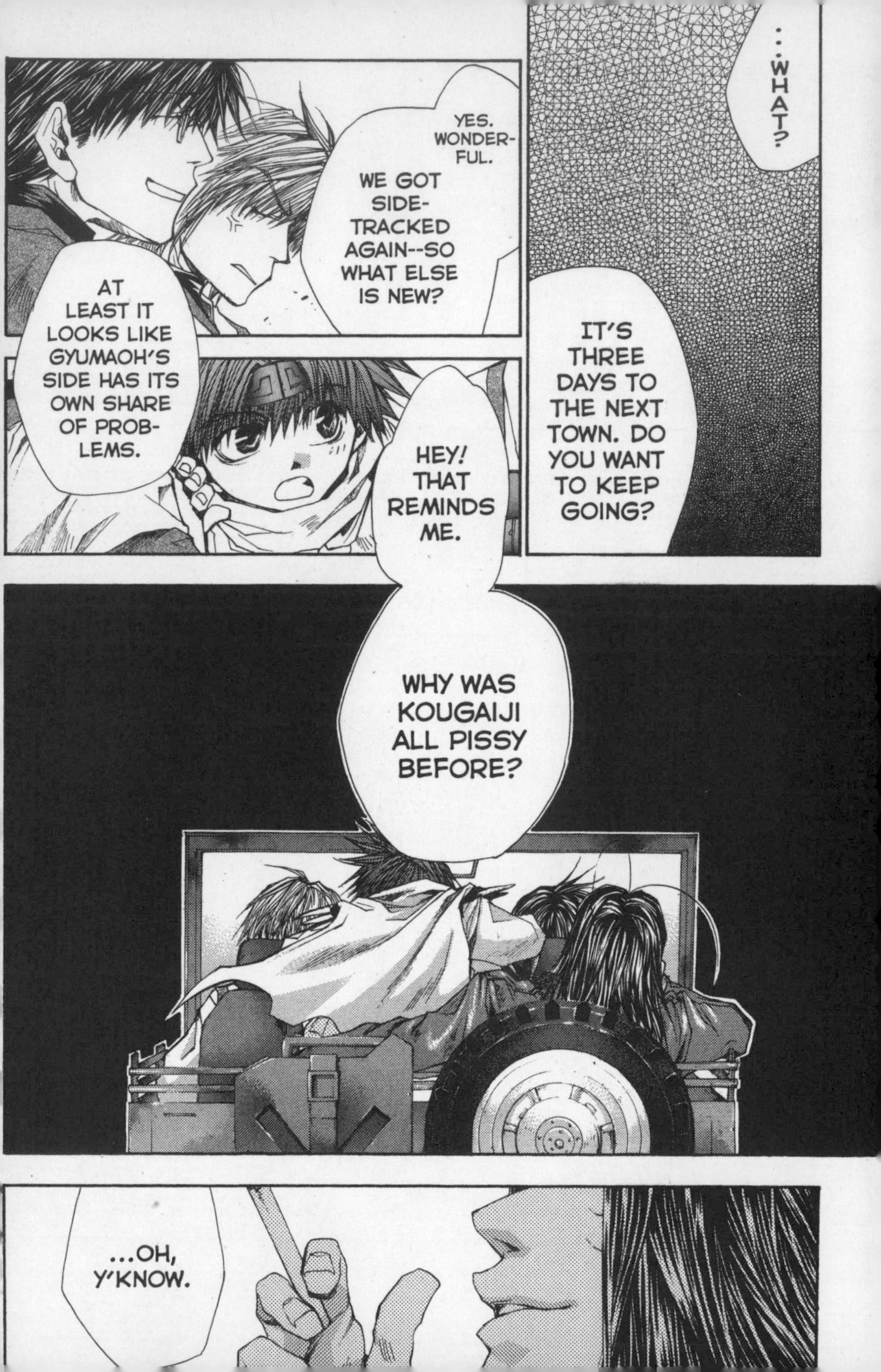
...WHAT?
IT'S THREE DAYS TO THE NEXT TOWN. DO YOU WANT TO KEEP GOING?
YES. WONDERFUL.
WE GOT SIDE-TRACKED AGAIN--SO WHAT ELSE IS NEW?
AT LEAST IT LOOKS LIKE GYUMAOH'S SIDE HAS ITS OWN SHARE OF PROB-LEMS.
HEY! THAT REMINDS ME.
WHY WAS KOUGAIJI ALL PISSY BEFORE?
...OH, Y'KNOW.

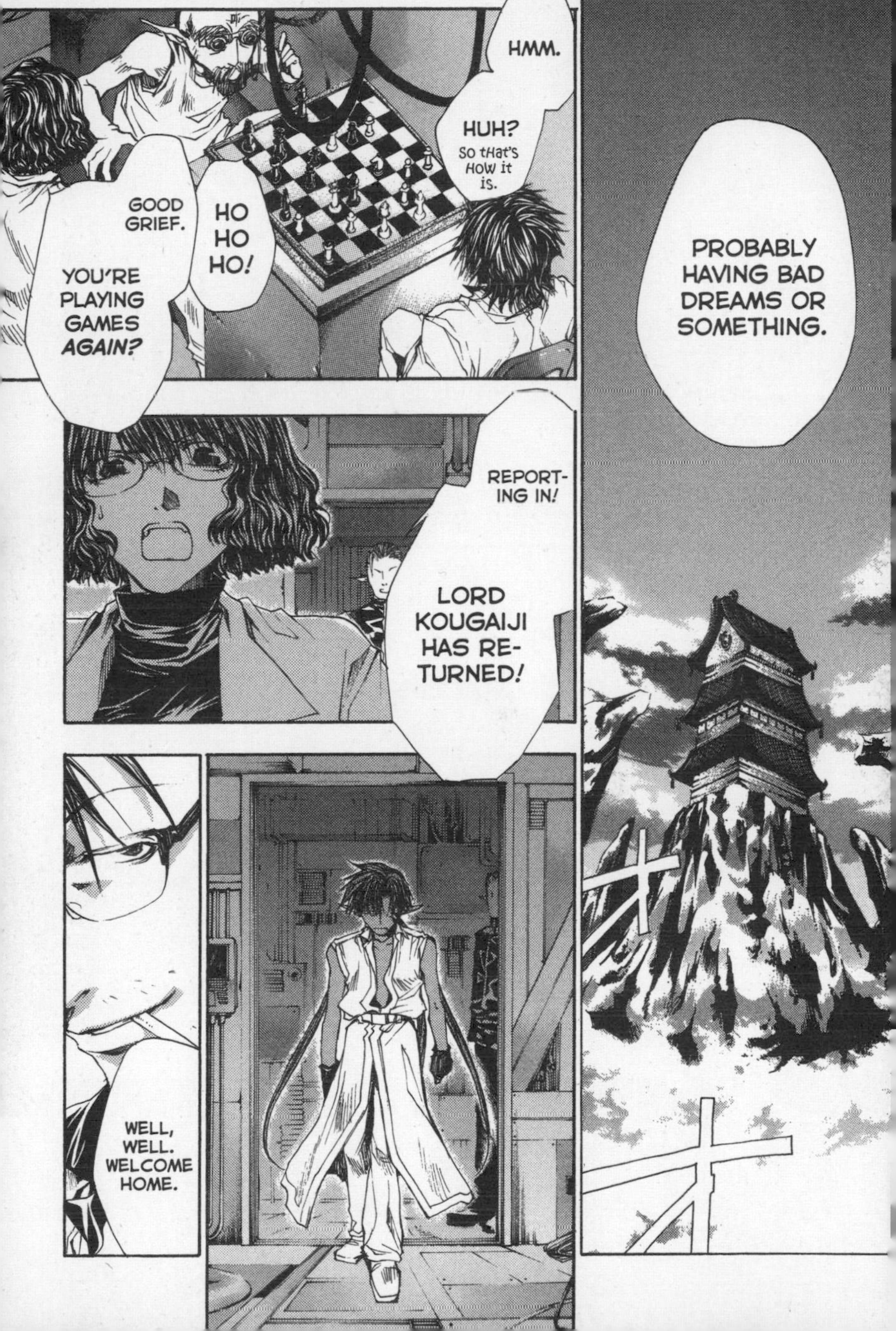
PROBABLY HAVING BAD DREAMS OR SOMETHING.
HMM.
HUH? So that's HOW it is.
HO HO HO!
GOOD GRIEF. YOU'RE PLAYING GAMES *AGAIN?*
REPORT-ING IN!
LORD KOUGAIJI HAS RE-TURNED!
WELL, WELL. WELCOME HOME.

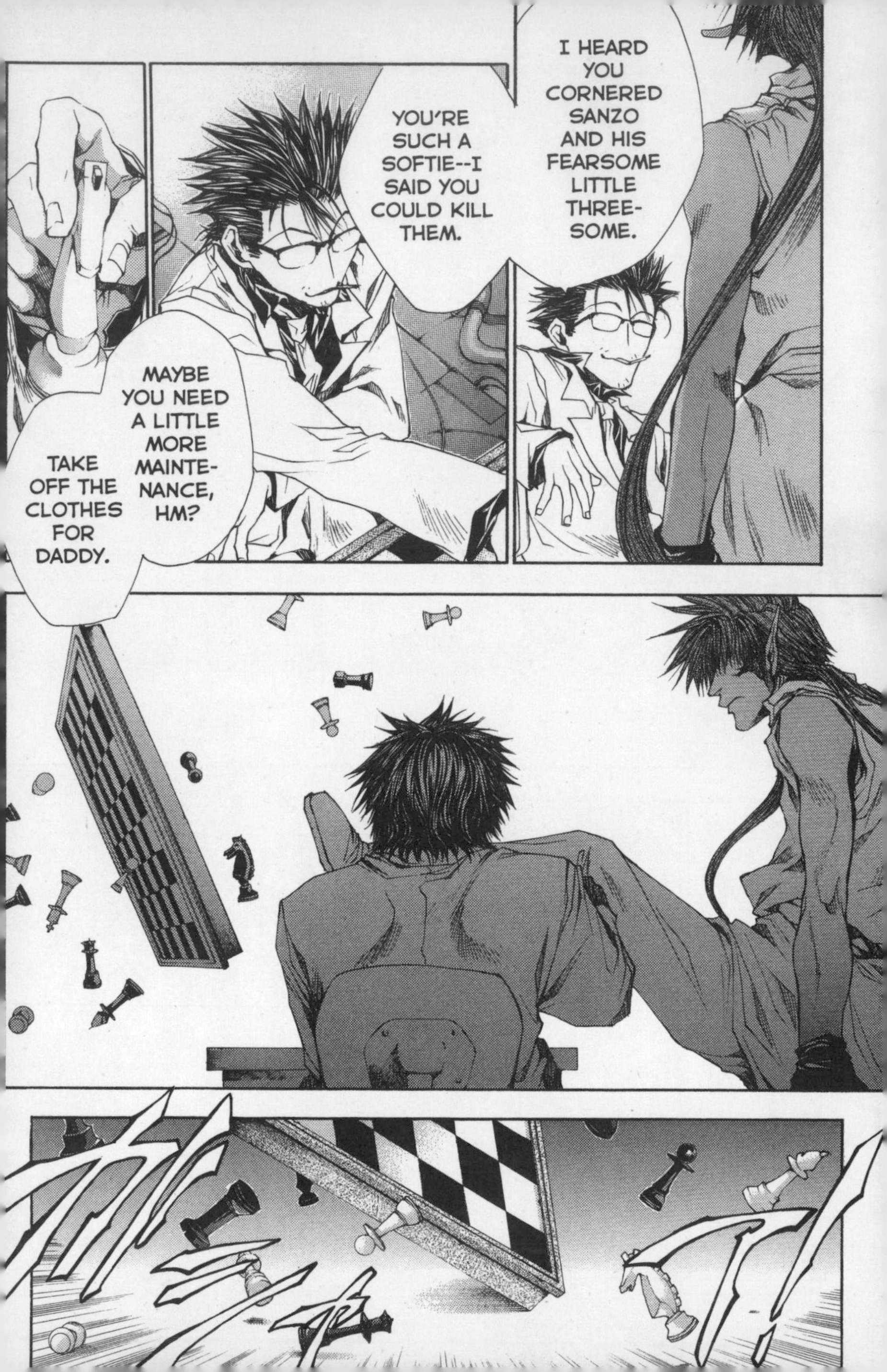
I HEARD YOU CORNERED SANZO AND HIS FEARSOME LITTLE THREE-SOME.
YOU'RE SUCH A SOFTIE--I SAID YOU COULD KILL THEM.
MAYBE YOU NEED A LITTLE MORE MAINTE-NANCE, HM?
TAKE OFF THE CLOTHES FOR DADDY.

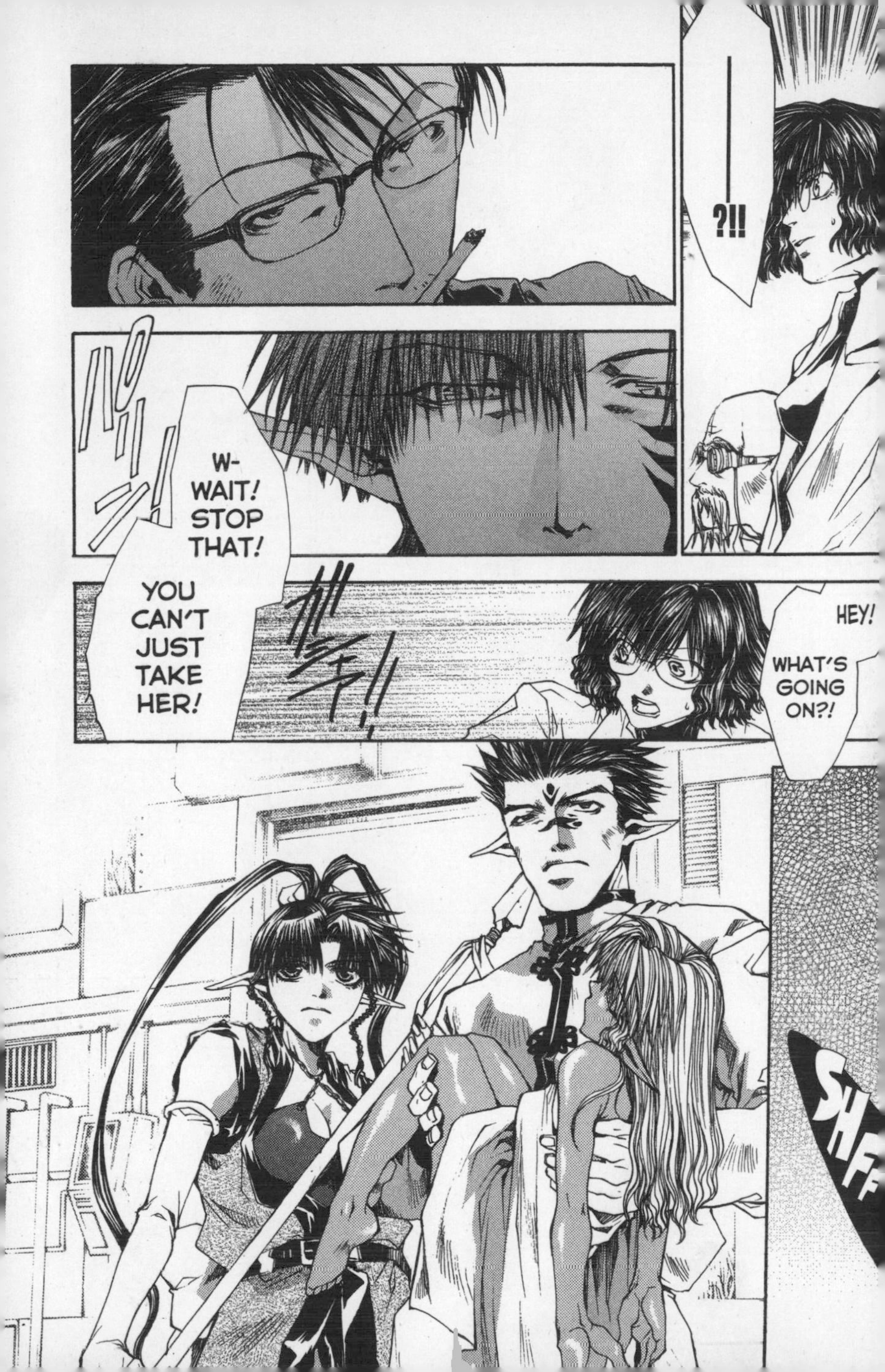
?!!
W- WAIT! STOP THAT!
HEY!
WHAT'S GOING ON?!
YOU CAN'T JUST TAKE HER!
SHFF

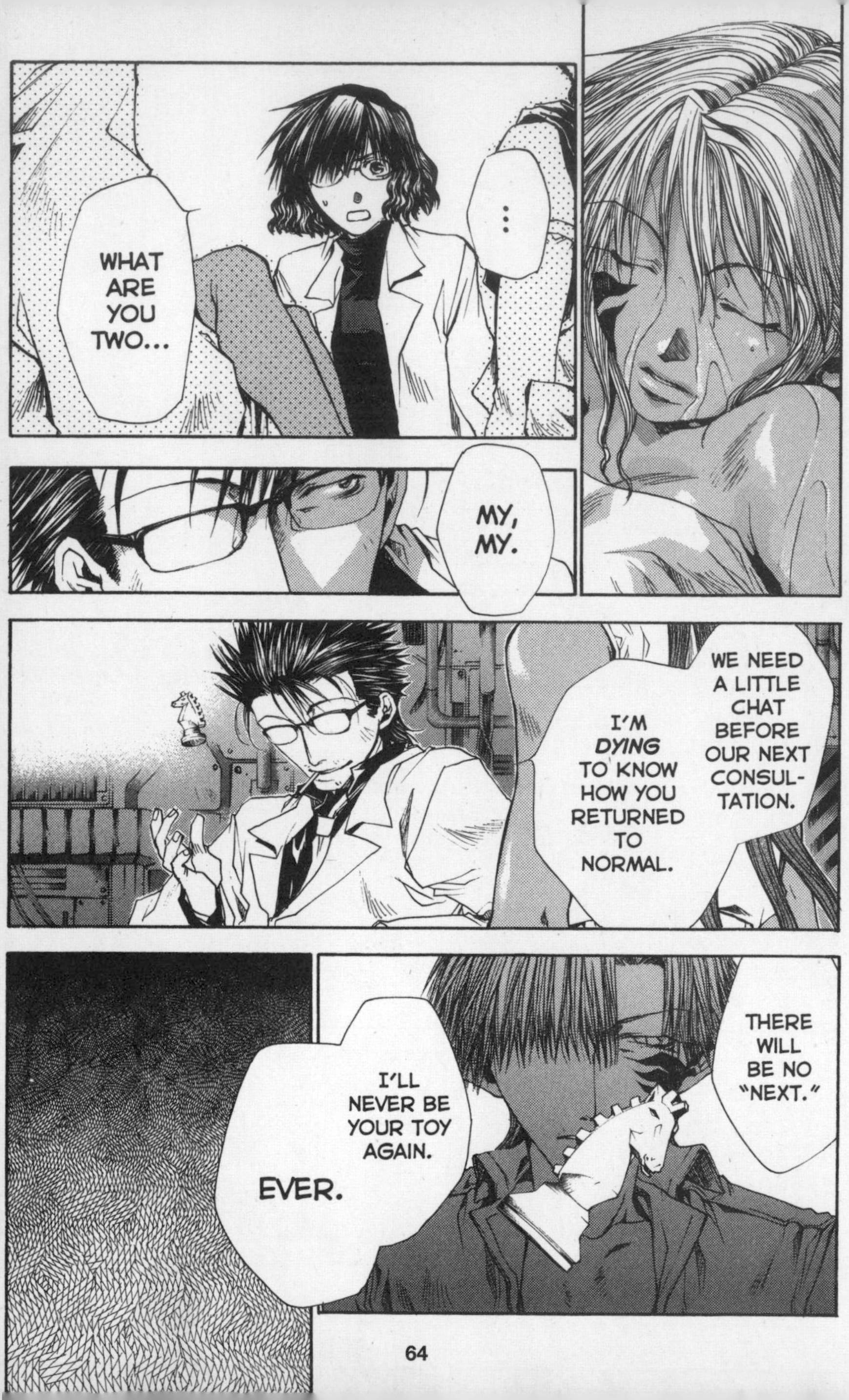
...
WHAT ARE YOU TWO...
MY, MY.
WE NEED A LITTLE CHAT BEFORE OUR NEXT CONSUL-TATION.
I'M *DYING* TO KNOW HOW YOU RETURNED TO NORMAL.
THERE WILL BE NO "NEXT."
I'LL NEVER BE YOUR TOY AGAIN.
EVER.

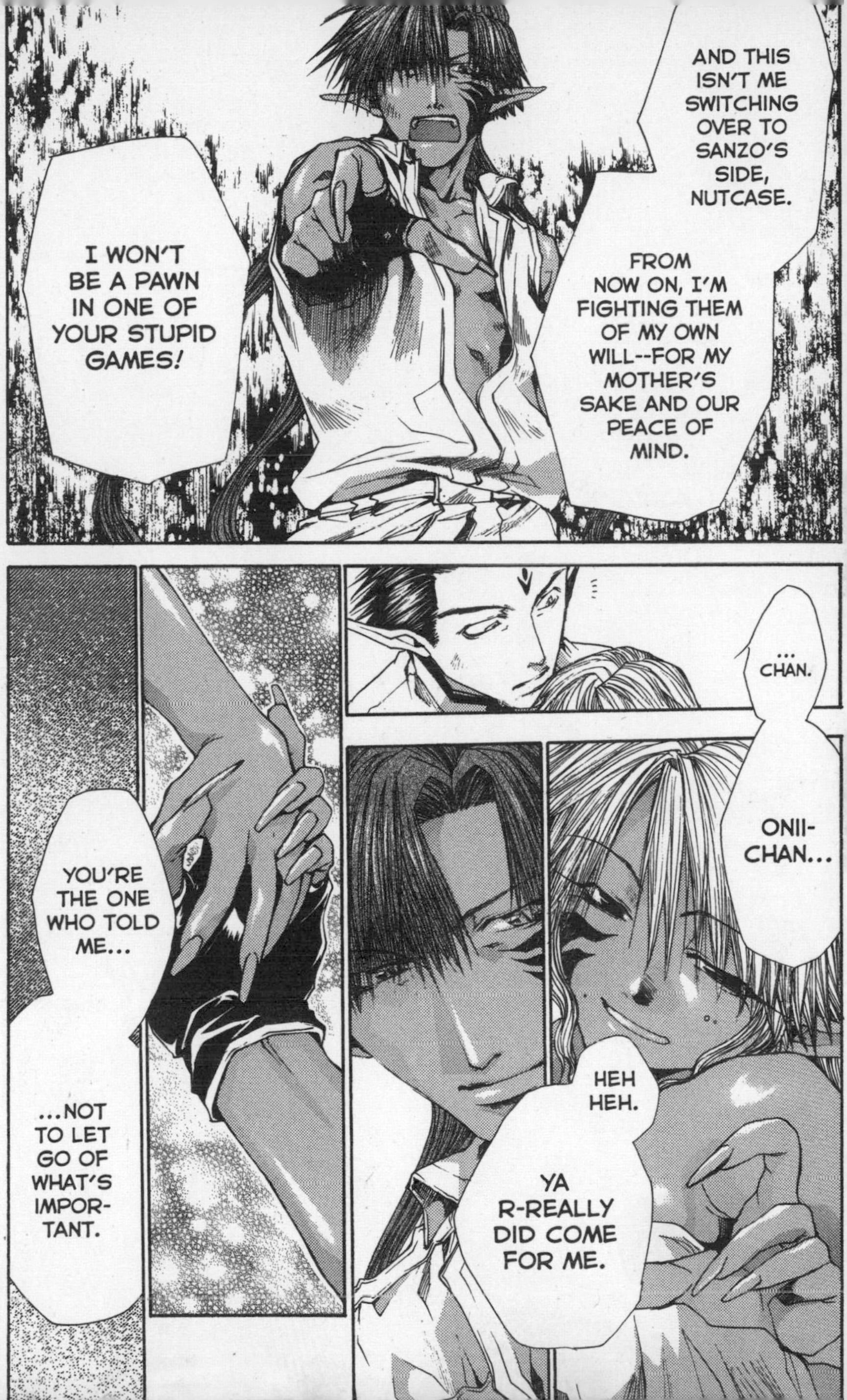
AND THIS ISN'T ME SWITCHING OVER TO SANZO'S SIDE, NUTCASE.
FROM NOW ON, I'M FIGHTING THEM OF MY OWN WILL--FOR MY MOTHER'S SAKE AND OUR PEACE OF MIND.
I WON'T BE A PAWN IN ONE OF YOUR STUPID GAMES!
...CHAN.
ONII-CHAN...
HEH HEH.
YA R-REALLY DID COME FOR ME.
YOU'RE THE ONE WHO TOLD ME...
...NOT TO LET GO OF WHAT'S IMPORTANT.

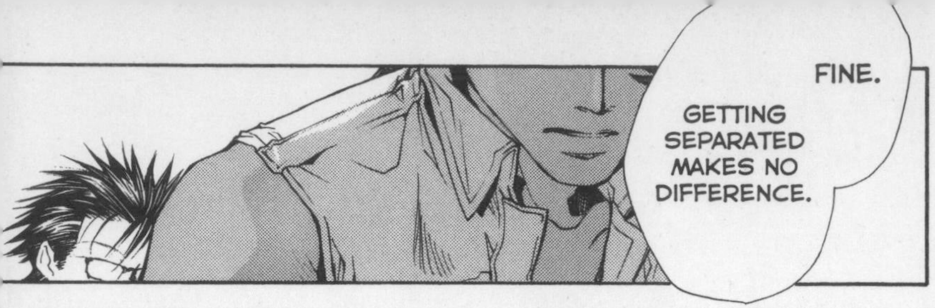
FINE.
GETTING SEPARATED MAKES NO DIFFERENCE.

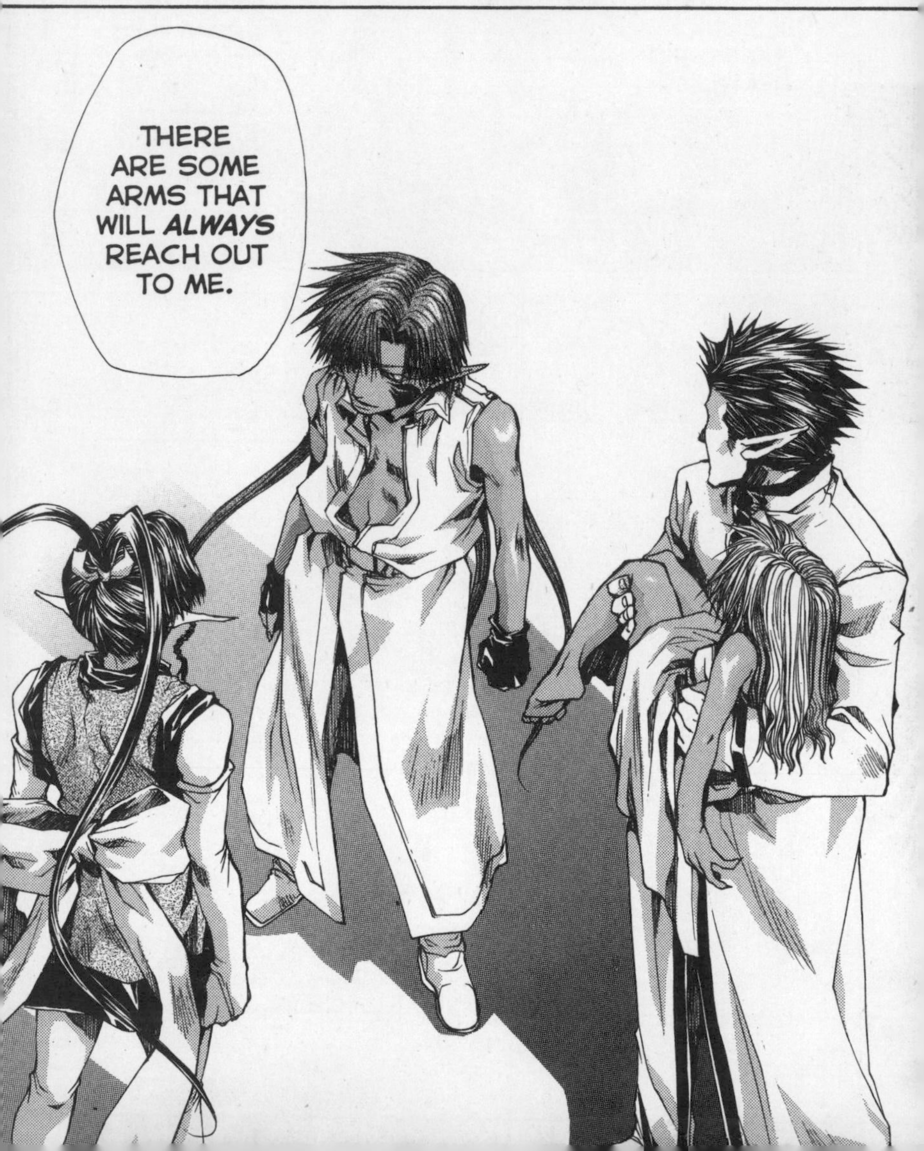
THERE ARE SOME ARMS THAT WILL *ALWAYS* REACH OUT TO ME.

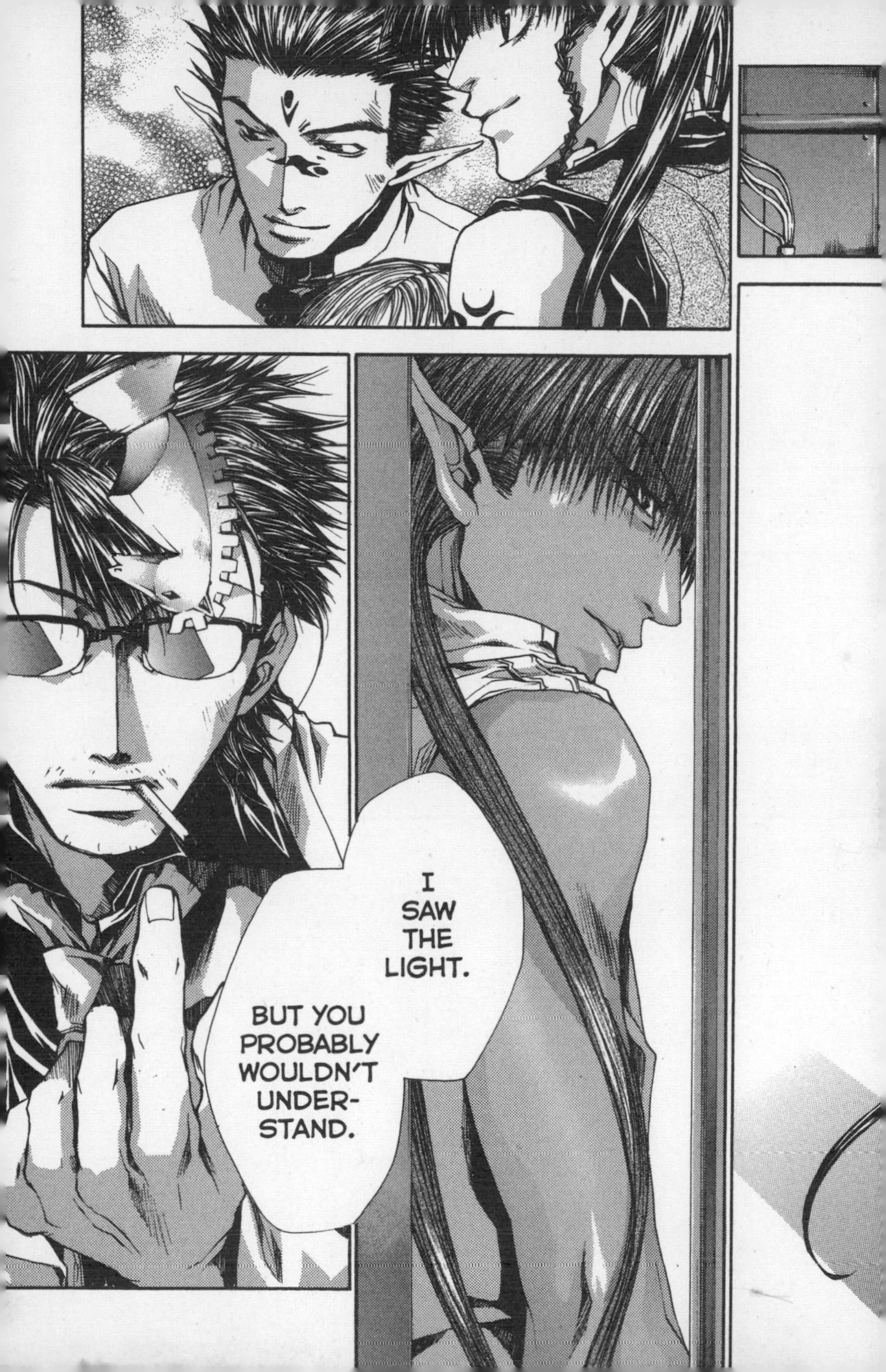
I SAW THE LIGHT.
BUT YOU PROBABLY WOULDN'T UNDER-STAND.

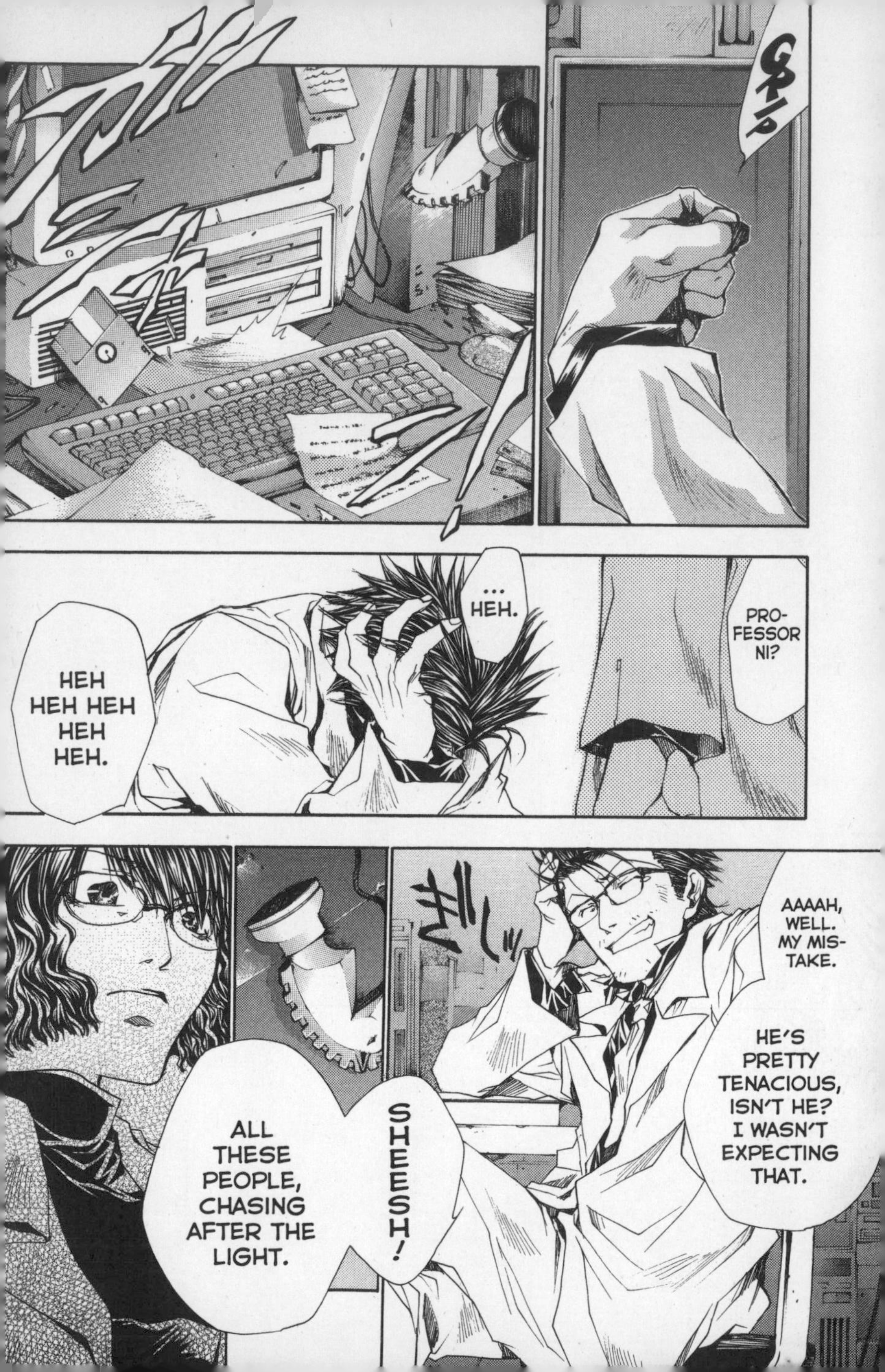
GRIP
PRO-FESSOR NI?
... HEH.
HEH HEH HEH HEH HEH.
AAAAH, WELL. MY MIS-TAKE.
HE'S PRETTY TENACIOUS, ISN'T HE? I WASN'T EXPECTING THAT.
SHEESH!
ALL THESE PEOPLE, CHASING AFTER THE LIGHT.

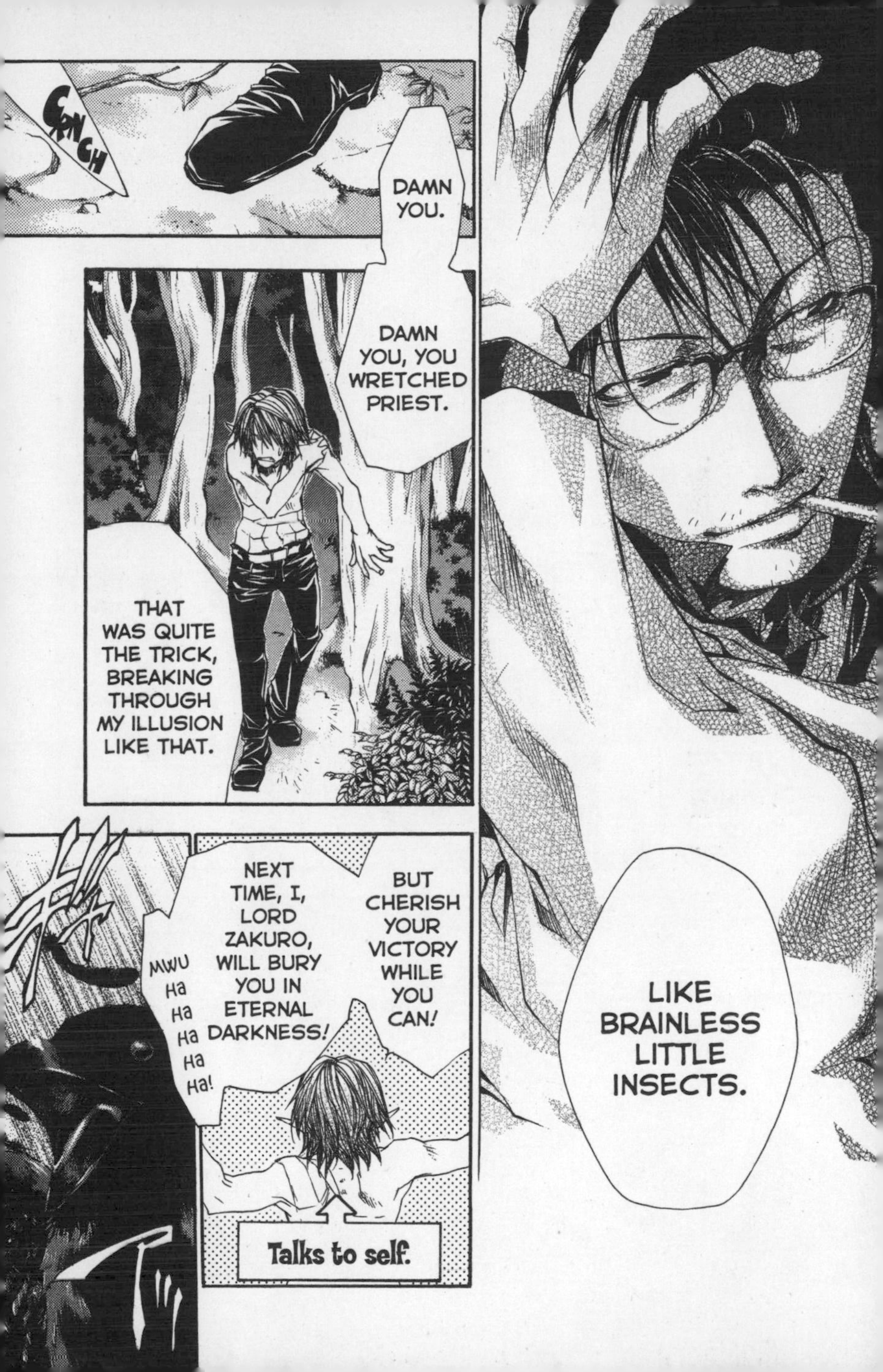
LIKE BRAINLESS LITTLE INSECTS.
DAMN YOU.
CRNCH
DAMN YOU, YOU WRETCHED PRIEST.
THAT WAS QUITE THE TRICK, BREAKING THROUGH MY ILLUSION LIKE THAT.
BUT CHERISH YOUR VICTORY WHILE YOU CAN!
NEXT TIME, I, LORD ZAKURO, WILL BURY YOU IN ETERNAL DARKNESS!
MWU Ha Ha Ha Ha Ha!
Talks to self.

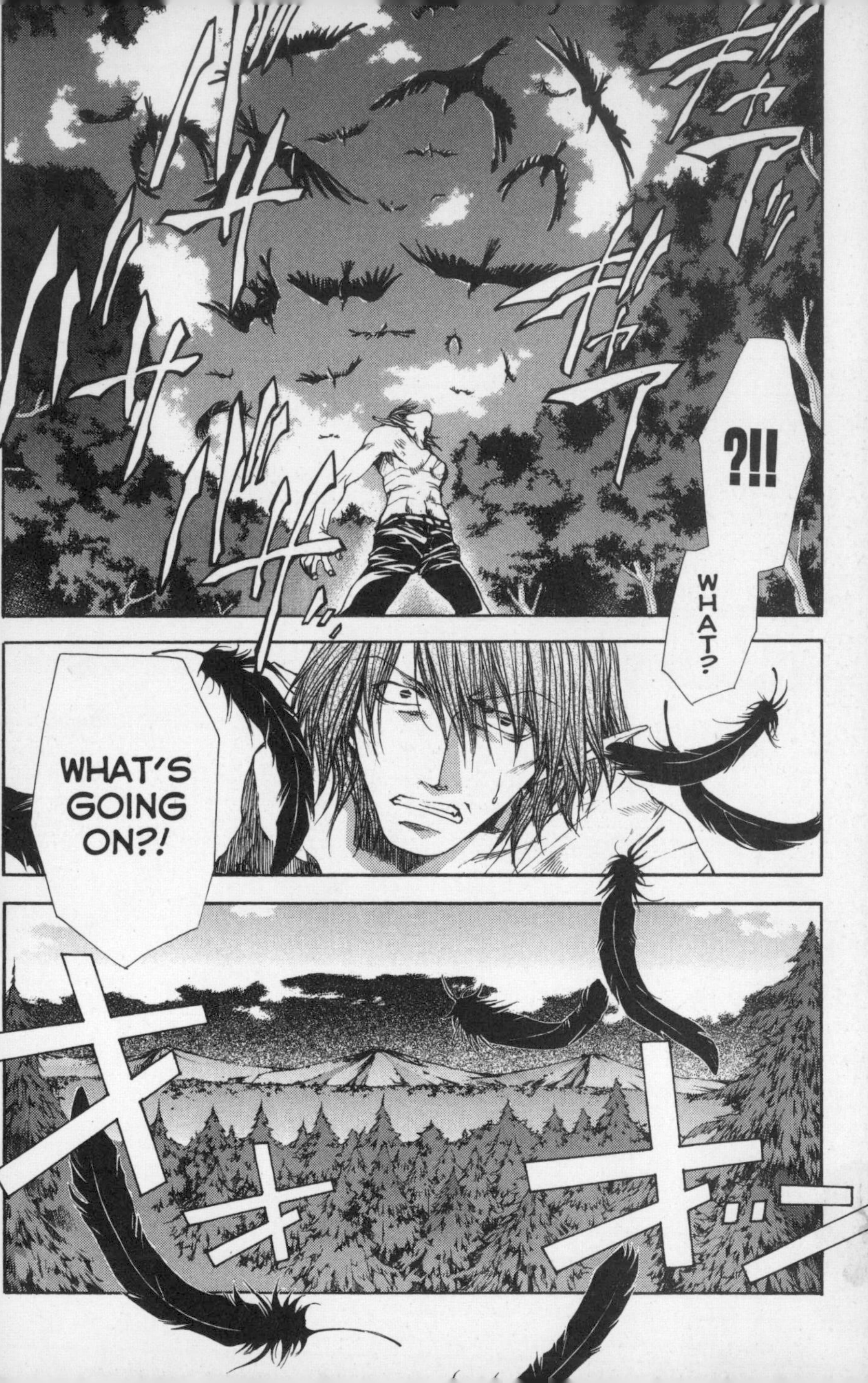
?!!
WHAT?
WHAT'S GOING ON?!

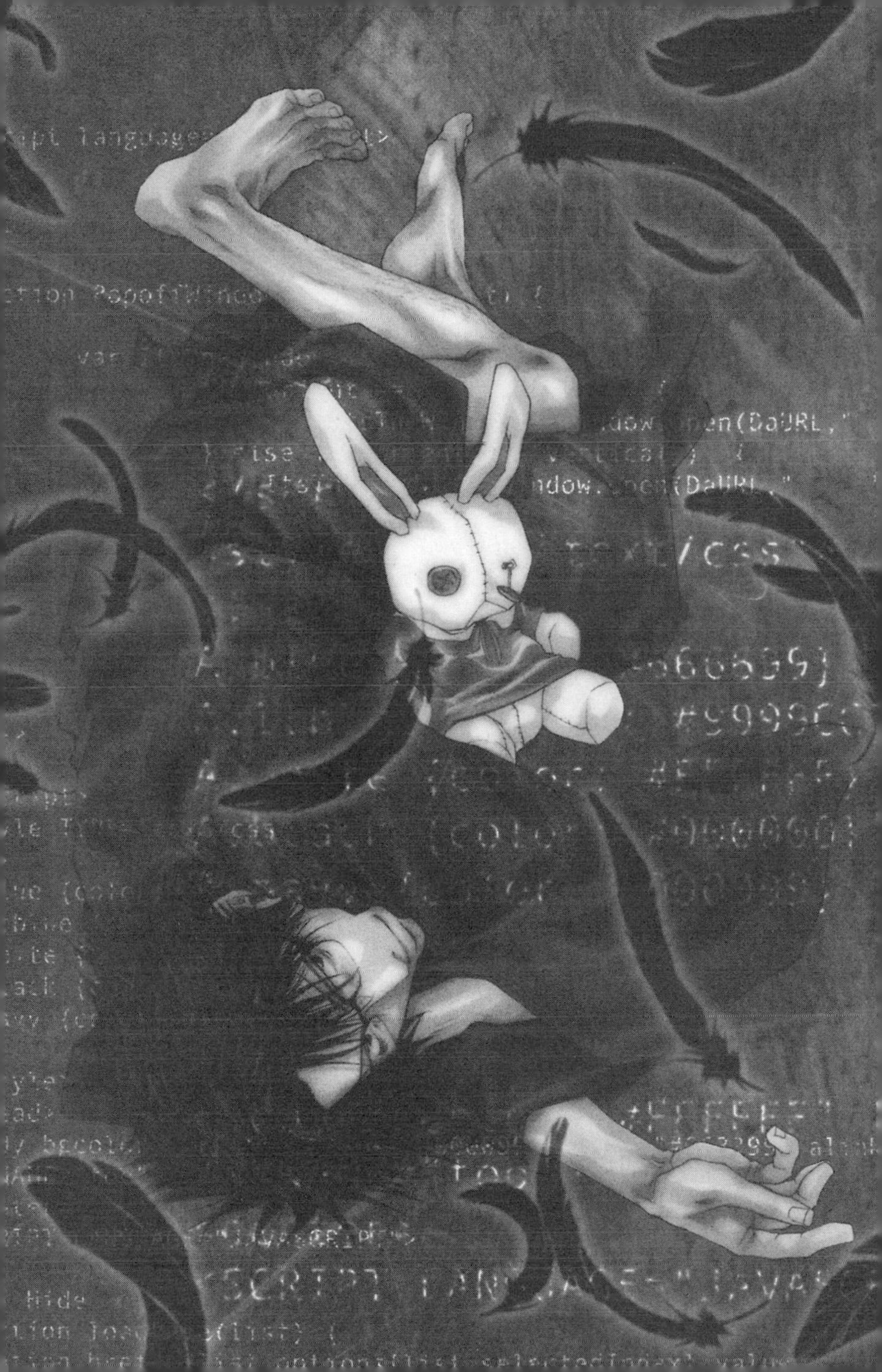

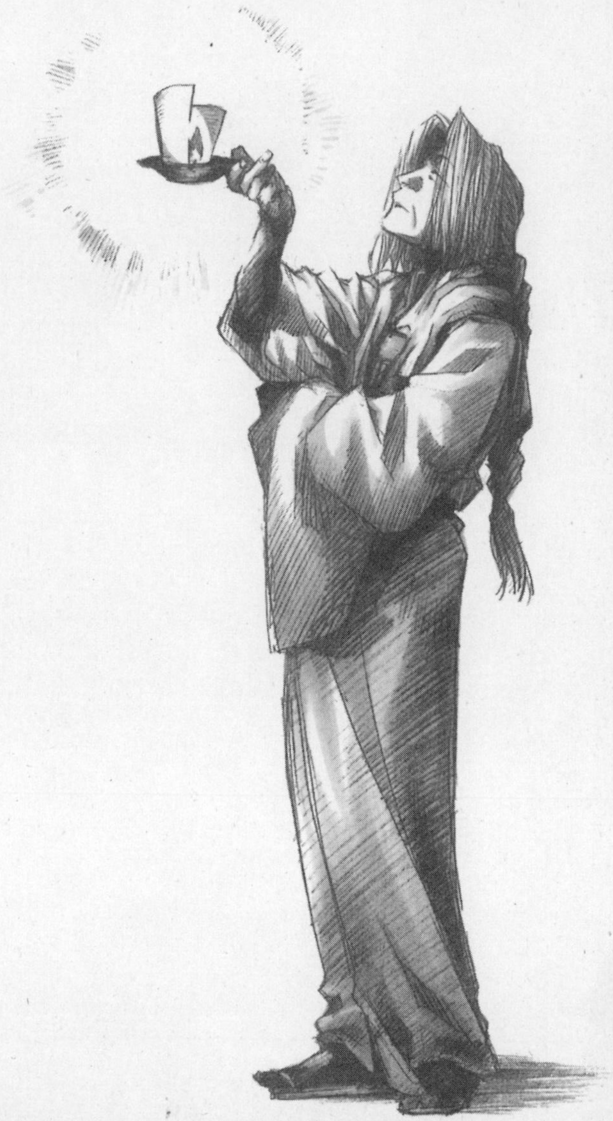

HE TOOK THE FORM OF THE MOONLIGHT.

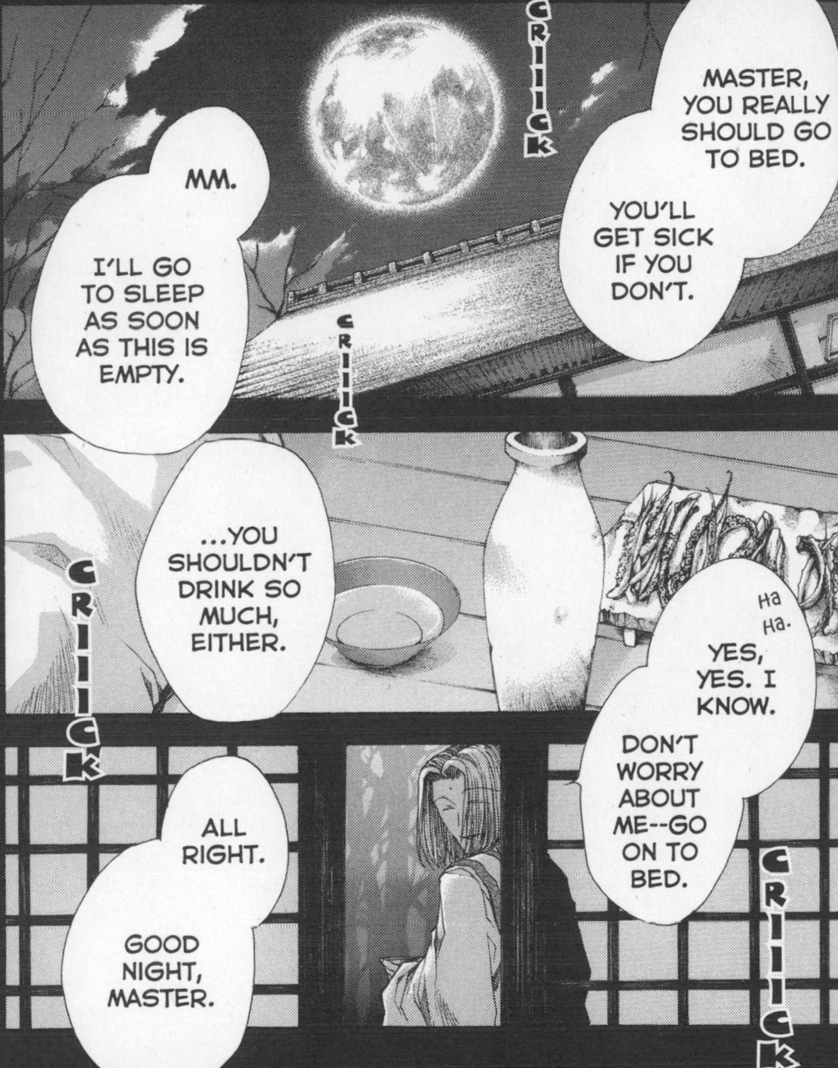
CRIIICK
MASTER, YOU REALLY SHOULD GO TO BED.
YOU'LL GET SICK IF YOU DON'T.
MM.
I'LL GO TO SLEEP AS SOON AS THIS IS EMPTY.
CRIIICK
...YOU SHOULDN'T DRINK SO MUCH, EITHER.
CRIIICK
HA HA.
YES, YES. I KNOW.
DON'T WORRY ABOUT ME--GO ON TO BED.
CRIIICK
ALL RIGHT.
GOOD NIGHT, MASTER.

act.xx
burial - prologue

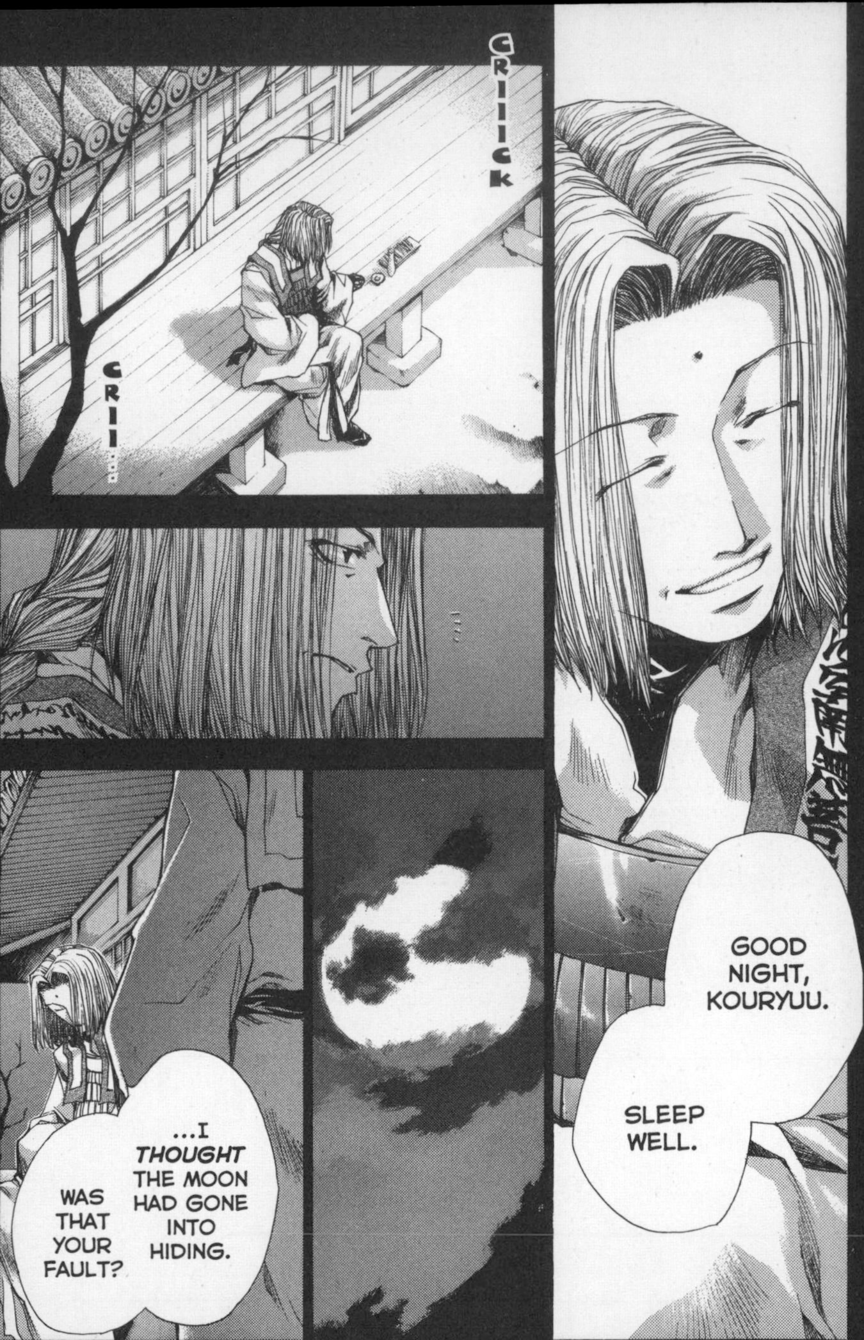
GOOD NIGHT, KOURYUU.
SLEEP WELL.
CRIIICK
CRII...
...I *THOUGHT* THE MOON HAD GONE INTO HIDING.
WAS THAT YOUR FAULT?

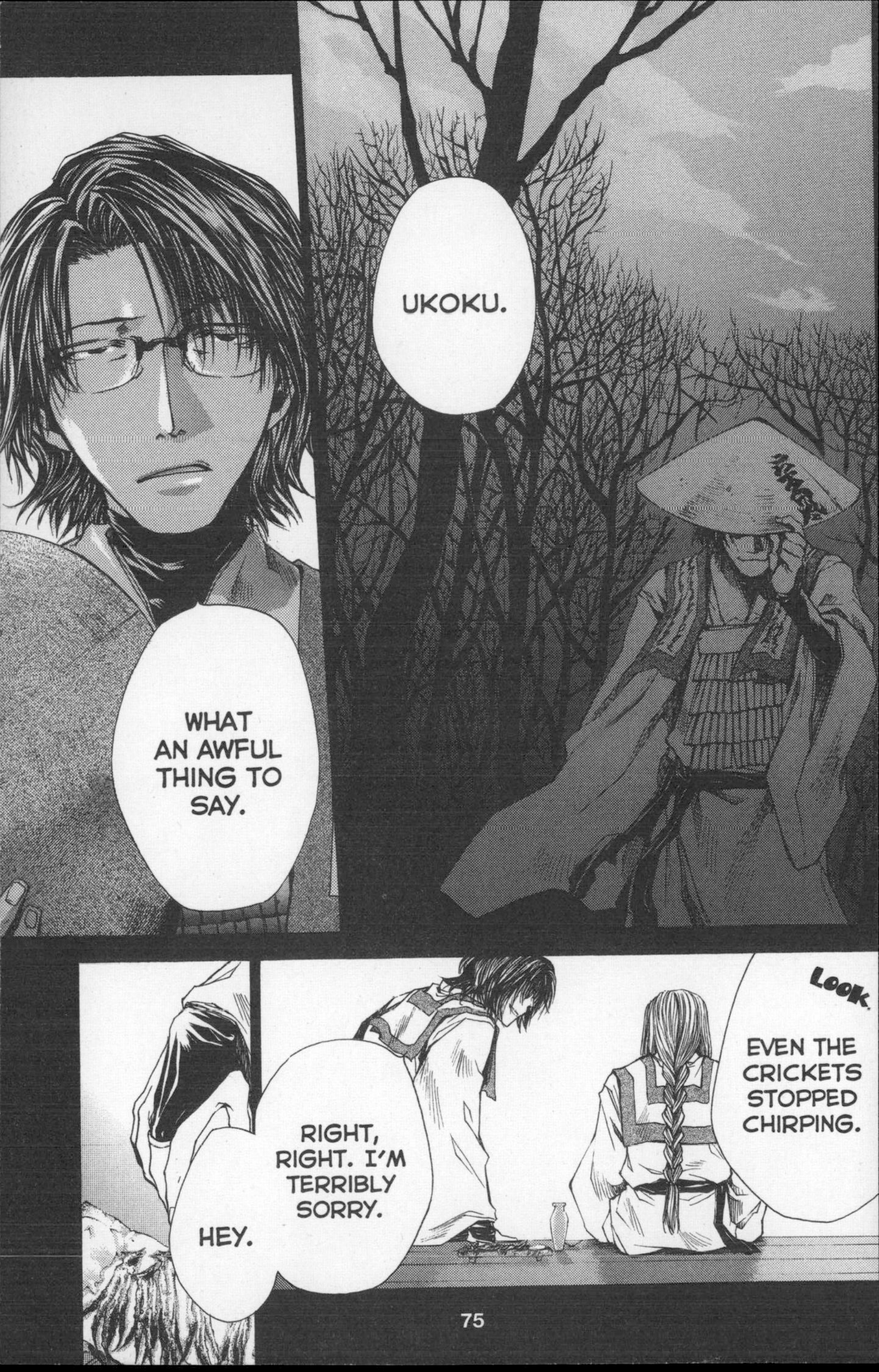
UKOKU.
WHAT AN AWFUL THING TO SAY.
LOOK.
EVEN THE CRICKETS STOPPED CHIRPING.
RIGHT, RIGHT. I'M TERRIBLY SORRY.
HEY.

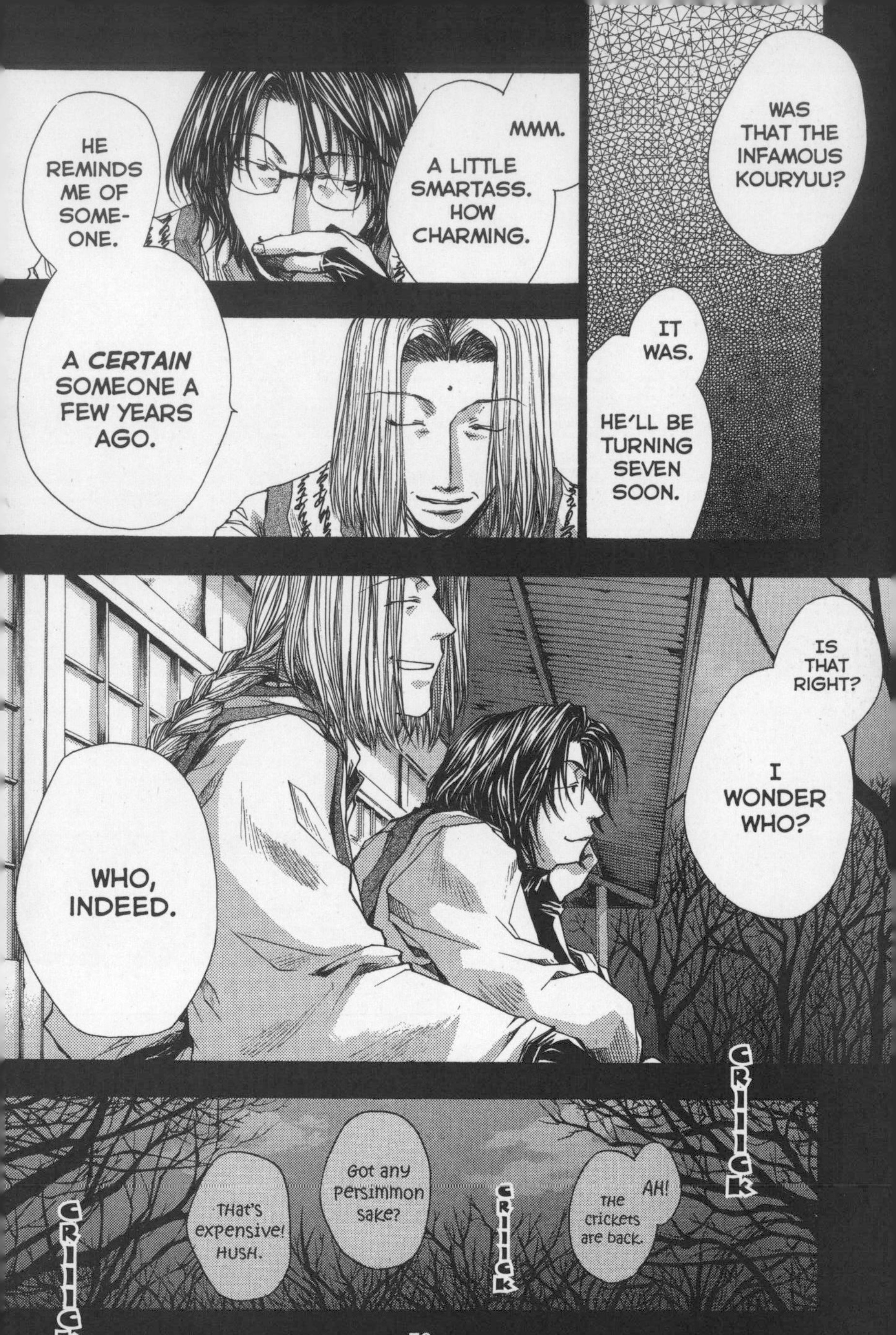
WAS THAT THE INFAMOUS KOURYUU?
IT WAS.
HE'LL BE TURNING SEVEN SOON.
MMM.
A LITTLE SMARTASS. HOW CHARMING.
HE REMINDS ME OF SOME-ONE.
A *CERTAIN* SOMEONE A FEW YEARS AGO.
IS THAT RIGHT?
I WONDER WHO?
WHO, INDEED.
CRIIICK
AH!
THE crickets are back.
CRIIICK
Got any persimmon sake?
THAT's expensive! HUSH.
CRIIICK

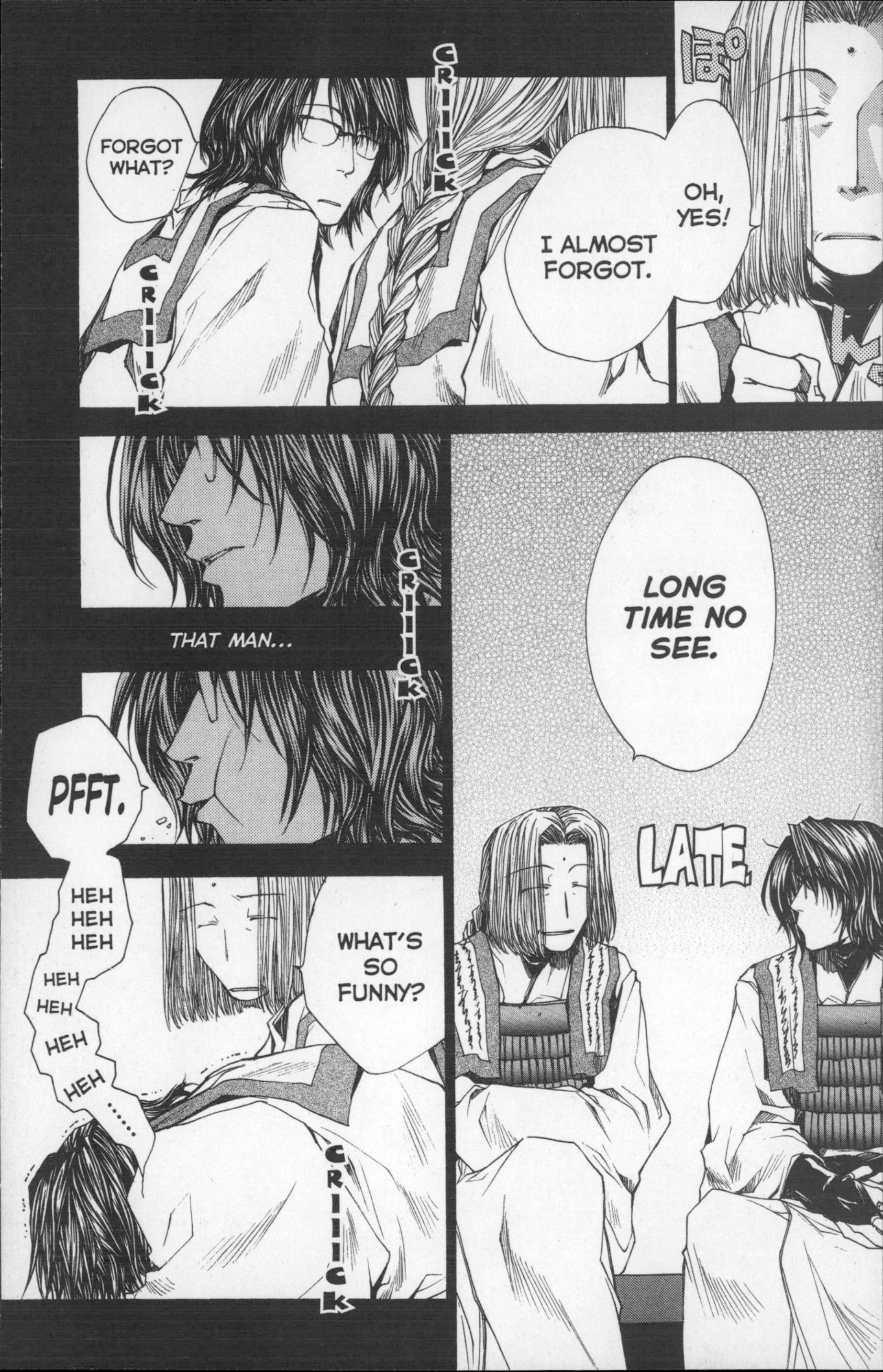
ぽ
OH, YES!
I ALMOST FORGOT.
CRIIICK
FORGOT WHAT?
CRIIICK
LONG TIME NO SEE.
LATE.
CRIIICK
THAT MAN...
PFFT.
WHAT'S SO FUNNY?
HEH HEH HEH
HEH HEH HEH HEH ......
CRIIICK

HEH HEH.
OH, WOW.
YOU REALLY DON'T CHANGE.
CRIIICK
YOU'RE THE SAME AS YOU EVER WERE, KOUMYOU.
CRIIICK
WELL, I SUPPOSE.
SHOULD I TAKE THAT AS A COMPLIMENT?
YOU KNOW WHAT?
THAT'S A SECRET.
CRIIICK
YOU HAD TO BE CAREFUL WITH THAT SORT OF SILENCE.
IT COULD EAT RIGHT INTO THE DARKNESS OF NIGHT.

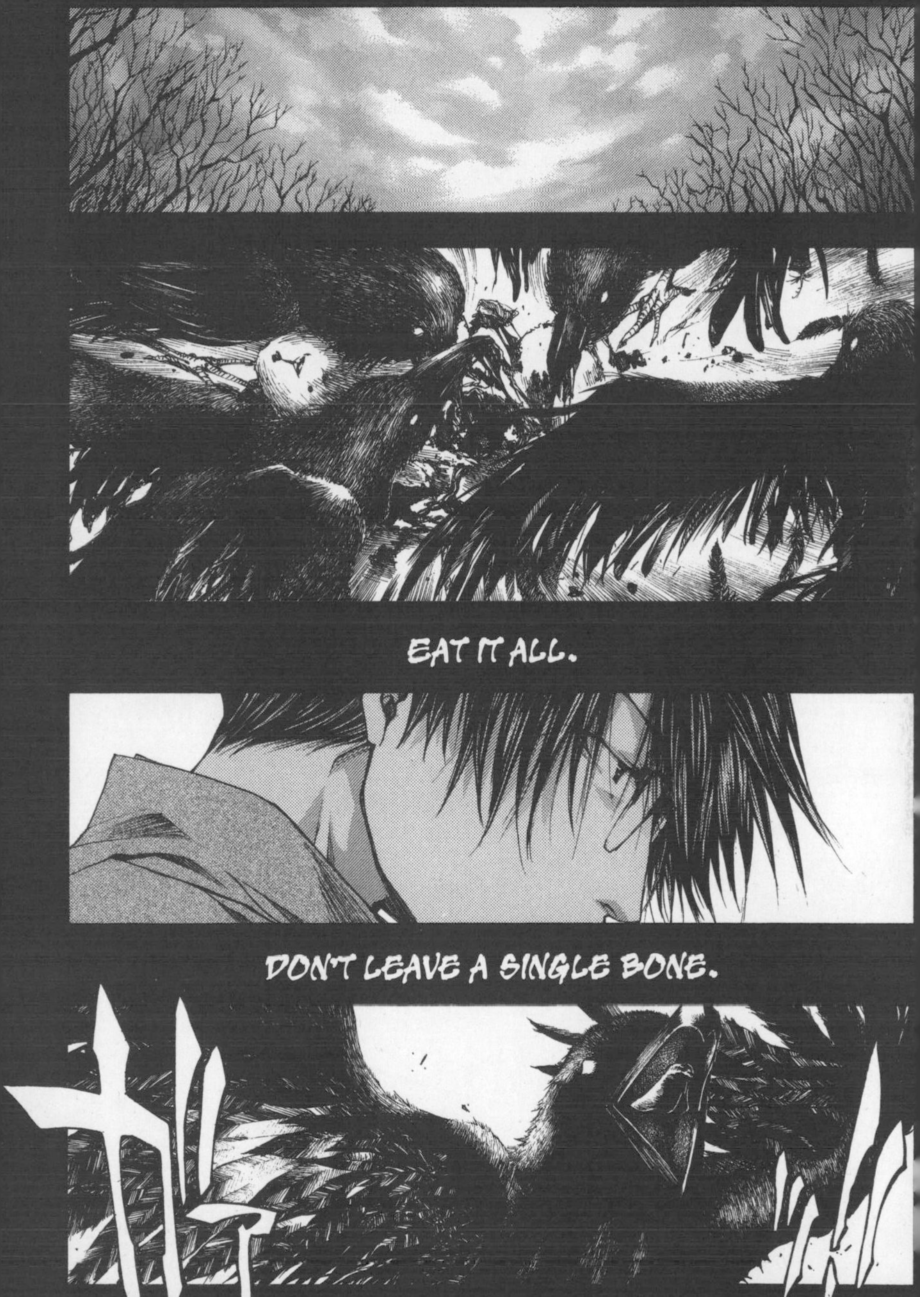
EAT IT ALL.
DON'T LEAVE A SINGLE BONE.

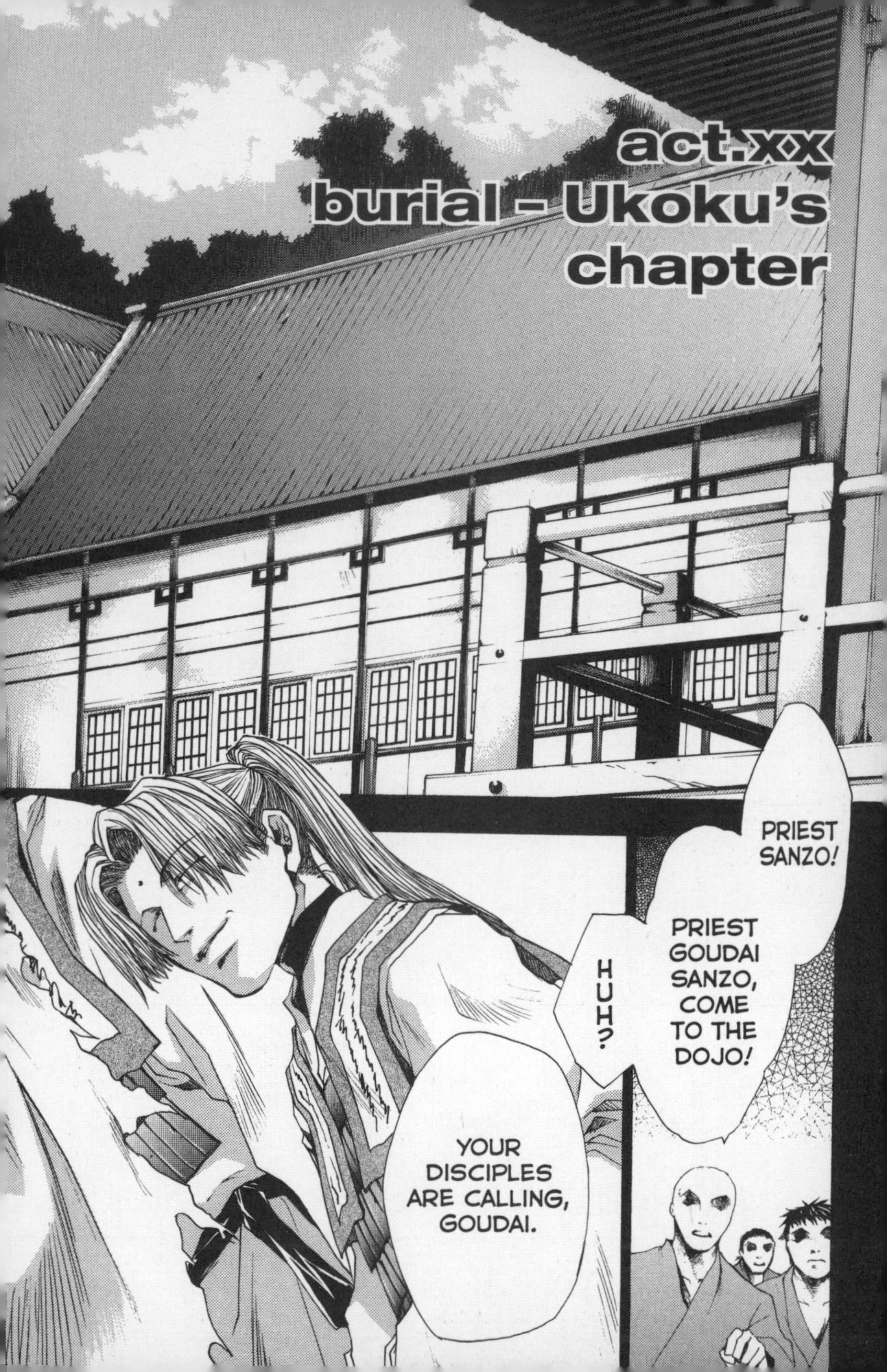
act.xx
burial - Ukoku's chapter
PRIEST SANZO!
PRIEST GOUDAI SANZO, COME TO THE DOJO!
HUH?
YOUR DISCIPLES ARE CALLING, GOUDAI.

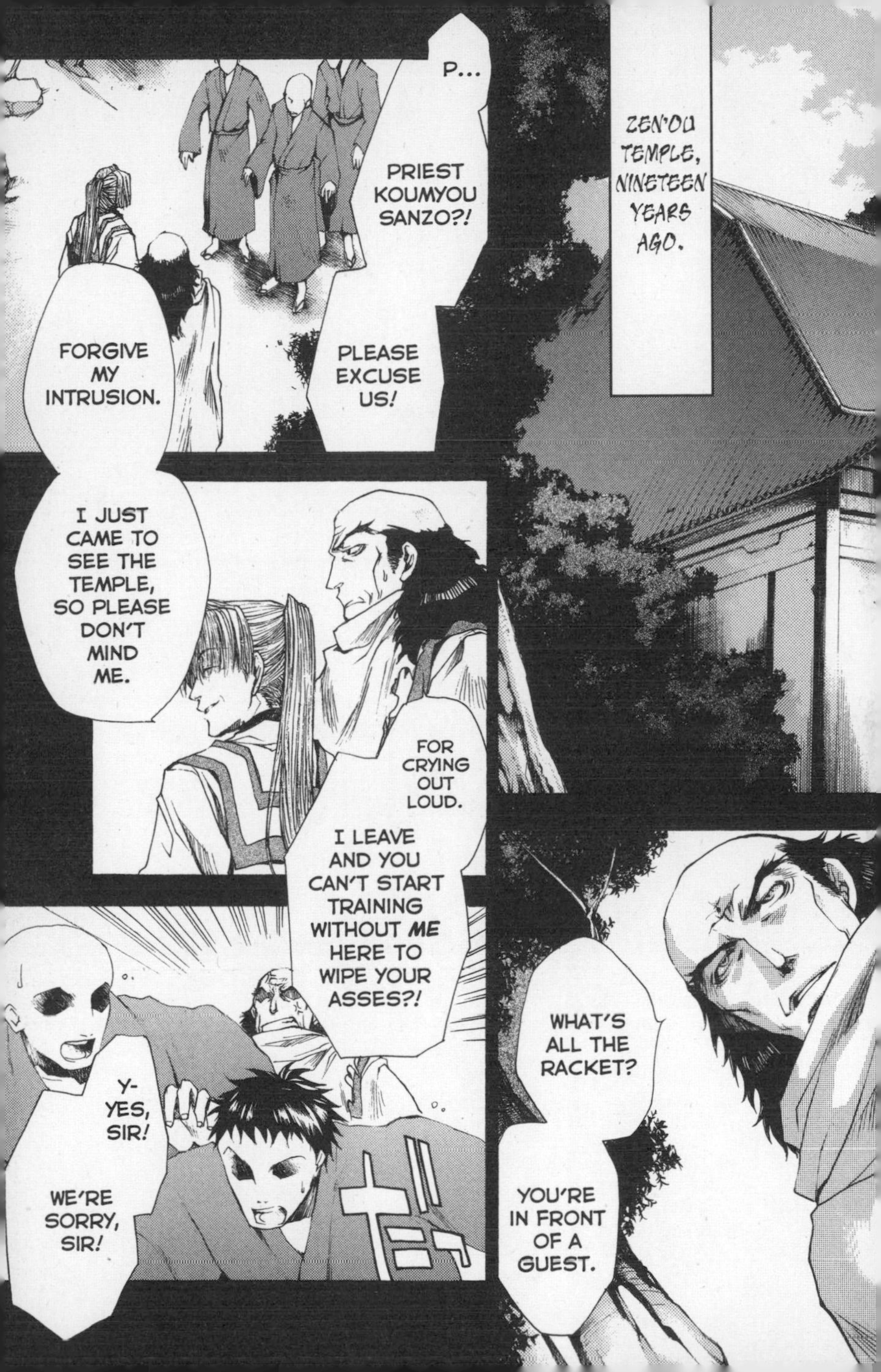
ZEN'OU TEMPLE, NINETEEN YEARS AGO.
P...
PRIEST KOUMYOU SANZO?!
PLEASE EXCUSE US!
FORGIVE MY INTRUSION.
I JUST CAME TO SEE THE TEMPLE, SO PLEASE DON'T MIND ME.
FOR CRYING OUT LOUD.
I LEAVE AND YOU CAN'T START TRAINING WITHOUT *ME* HERE TO WIPE YOUR ASSES?!
WHAT'S ALL THE RACKET?
YOU'RE IN FRONT OF A GUEST.
Y-YES, SIR!
WE'RE SORRY, SIR!

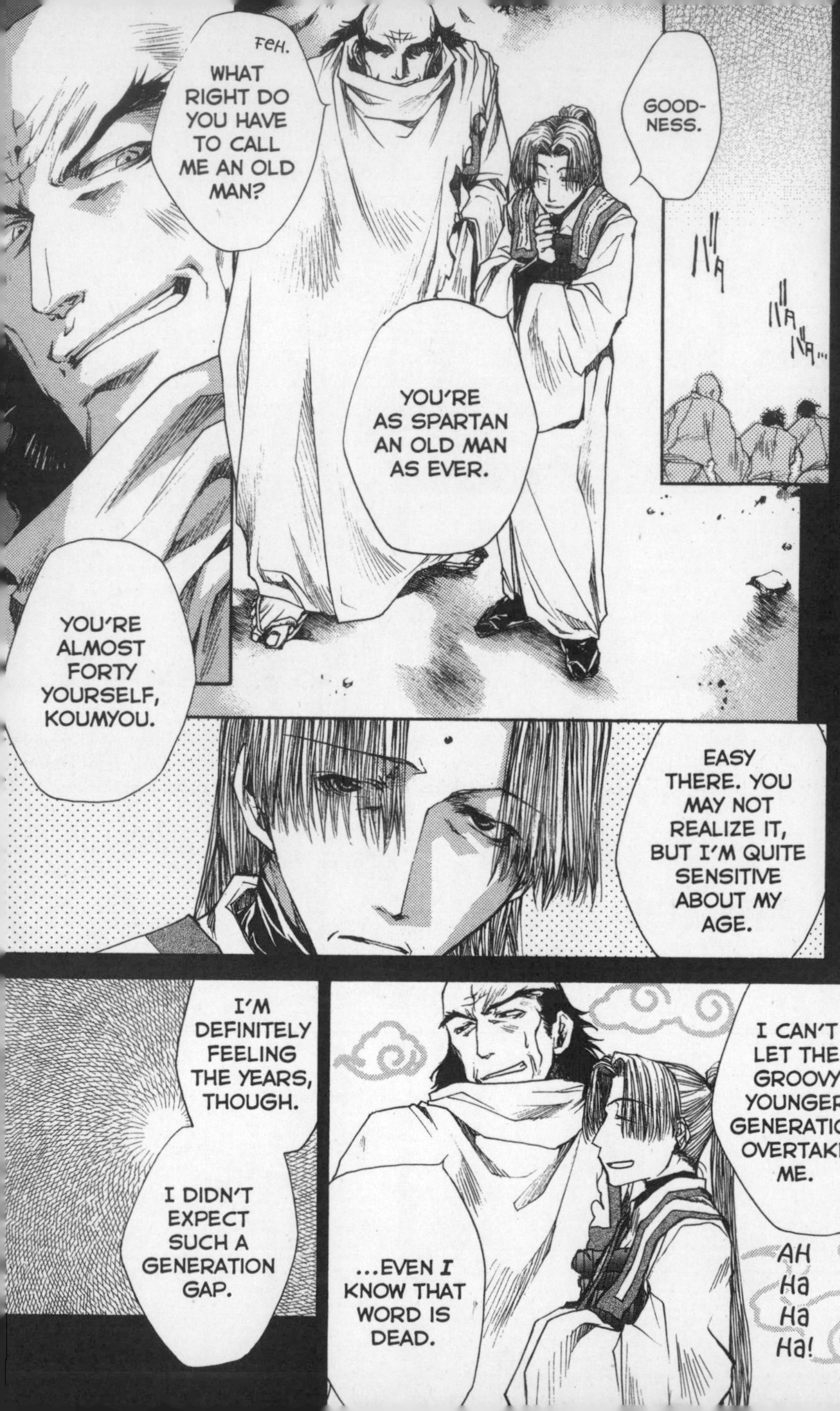
GOOD-NESS.
YOU'RE AS SPARTAN AN OLD MAN AS EVER.
FEH.
WHAT RIGHT DO YOU HAVE TO CALL ME AN OLD MAN?
YOU'RE ALMOST FORTY YOURSELF, KOUMYOU.
EASY THERE. YOU MAY NOT REALIZE IT, BUT I'M QUITE SENSITIVE ABOUT MY AGE.
I CAN'T LET THE GROOVY YOUNGER GENERATION OVERTAKE ME.
AH HA HA HA!
...EVEN *I* KNOW THAT WORD IS DEAD.
I'M DEFINITELY FEELING THE YEARS, THOUGH.
I DIDN'T EXPECT SUCH A GENERATION GAP.

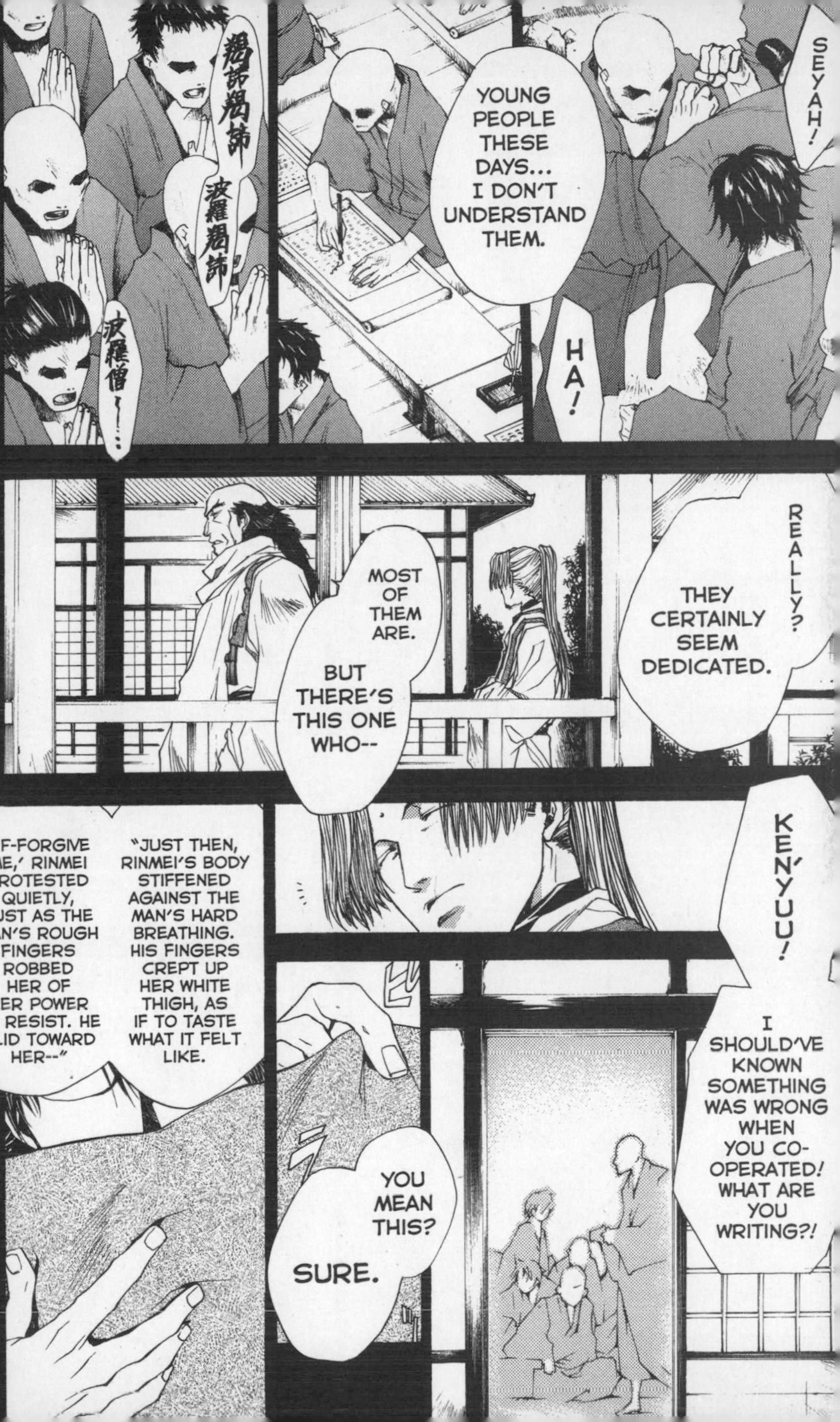
SEYAH!
HA!
YOUNG PEOPLE THESE DAYS... I DON'T UNDERSTAND THEM.
羯諦羯諦
波羅羯諦
波羅僧〜!…
REALLY?
THEY CERTAINLY SEEM DEDICATED.
MOST OF THEM ARE.
BUT THERE'S THIS ONE WHO--
KENYUU!
I SHOULD'VE KNOWN SOMETHING WAS WRONG WHEN YOU CO-OPERATED! WHAT ARE YOU WRITING?!
YOU MEAN THIS?
SURE.
"JUST THEN, RINMEI'S BODY STIFFENED AGAINST THE MAN'S HARD BREATHING. HIS FINGERS CREPT UP HER WHITE THIGH, AS IF TO TASTE WHAT IT FELT LIKE.
"'F-FORGIVE ME,' RINMEI PROTESTED QUIETLY, JUST AS THE MAN'S ROUGH FINGERS ROBBED HER OF HER POWER TO RESIST. HE SLID TOWARD HER--"

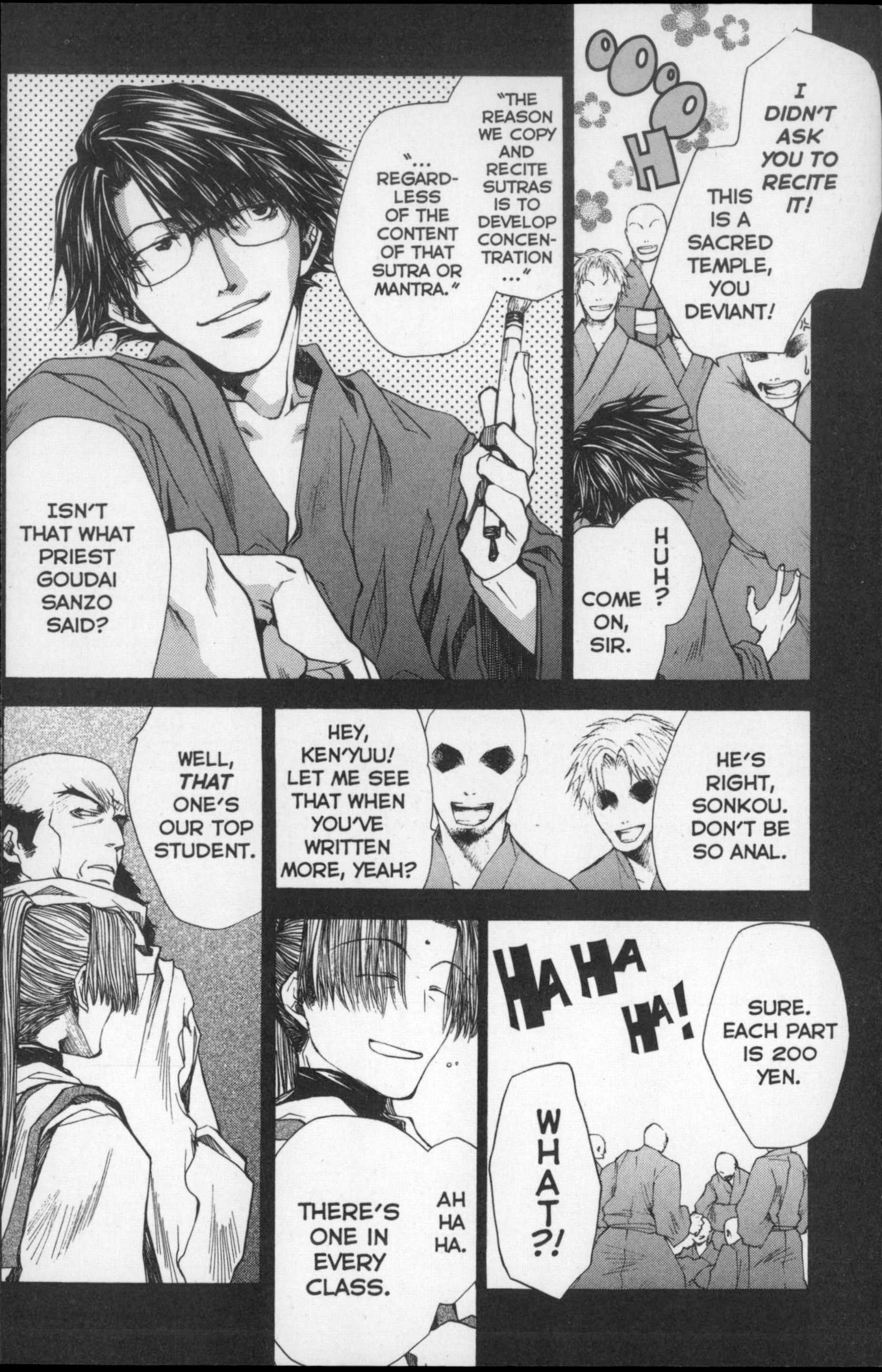
OOOOH
I DIDN'T ASK YOU TO RECITE IT!
THIS IS A SACRED TEMPLE, YOU DEVIANT!
HUH?
COME ON, SIR.
"THE REASON WE COPY AND RECITE SUTRAS IS TO DEVELOP CONCENTRATION..."
"...REGARDLESS OF THE CONTENT OF THAT SUTRA OR MANTRA."
ISN'T THAT WHAT PRIEST GOUDAI SANZO SAID?
HE'S RIGHT, SONKOU. DON'T BE SO ANAL.
HEY, KEN'YUU! LET ME SEE THAT WHEN YOU'VE WRITTEN MORE, YEAH?
HA HA HA!
SURE. EACH PART IS 200 YEN.
WHAT?!
AH HA HA.
THERE'S ONE IN EVERY CLASS.
WELL, *THAT* ONE'S OUR TOP STUDENT.

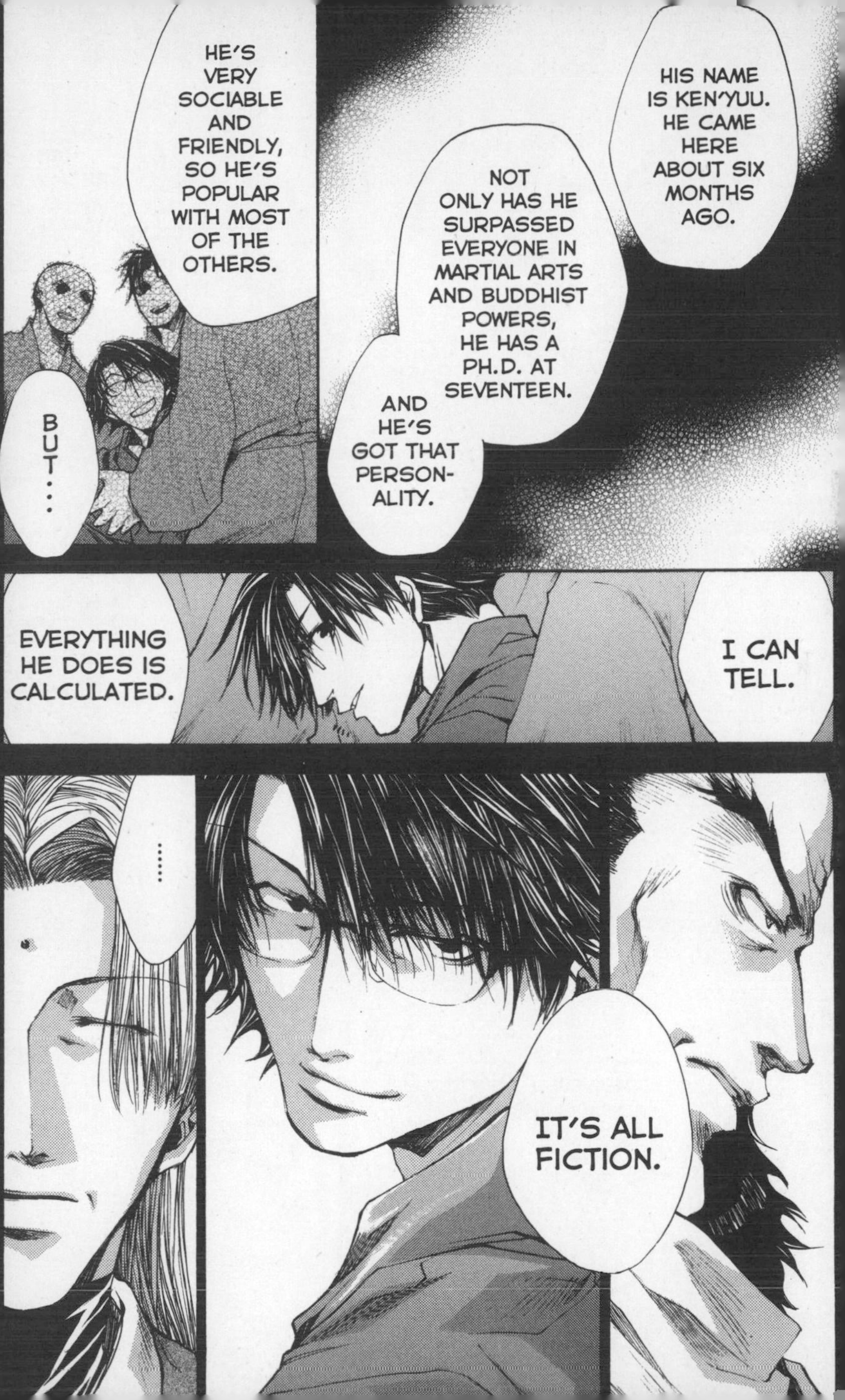
HIS NAME IS KEN'YUU. HE CAME HERE ABOUT SIX MONTHS AGO.
NOT ONLY HAS HE SURPASSED EVERYONE IN MARTIAL ARTS AND BUDDHIST POWERS, HE HAS A PH.D. AT SEVENTEEN.
AND HE'S GOT THAT PERSON-ALITY.
HE'S VERY SOCIABLE AND FRIENDLY, SO HE'S POPULAR WITH MOST OF THE OTHERS.
BUT...
I CAN TELL.
EVERYTHING HE DOES IS CALCULATED.
IT'S ALL FICTION.
......

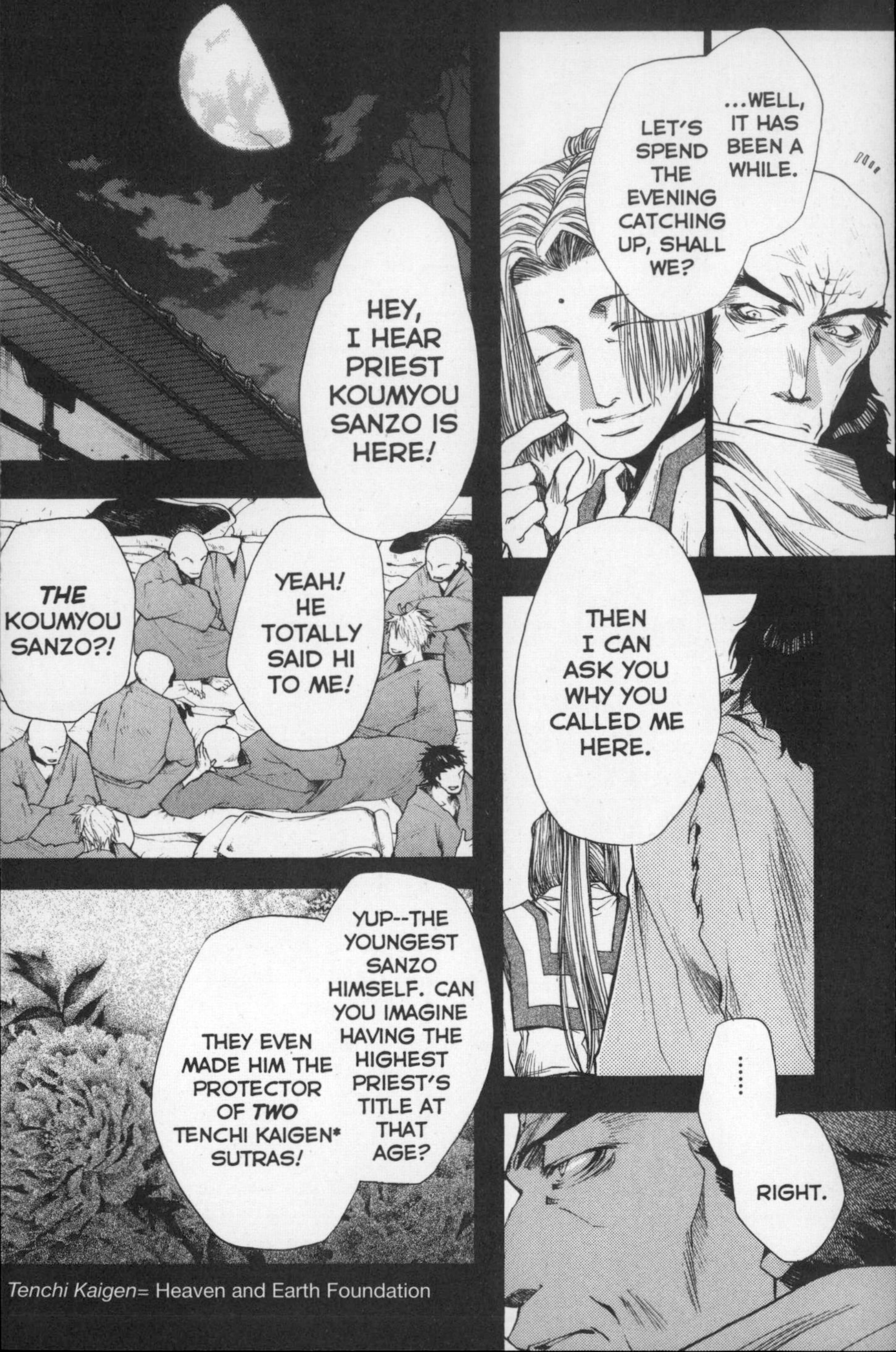
...WELL, IT HAS BEEN A WHILE.
LET'S SPEND THE EVENING CATCHING UP, SHALL WE?
HEY, I HEAR PRIEST KOUMYOU SANZO IS HERE!
THEN I CAN ASK YOU WHY YOU CALLED ME HERE.
YEAH! HE TOTALLY SAID HI TO ME!
THE KOUMYOU SANZO?!
......
YUP--THE YOUNGEST SANZO HIMSELF. CAN YOU IMAGINE HAVING THE HIGHEST PRIEST'S TITLE AT THAT AGE?
THEY EVEN MADE HIM THE PROTECTOR OF *TWO* TENCHI KAIGEN* SUTRAS!
RIGHT.

Tenchi Kaigen= Heaven and Earth Foundation

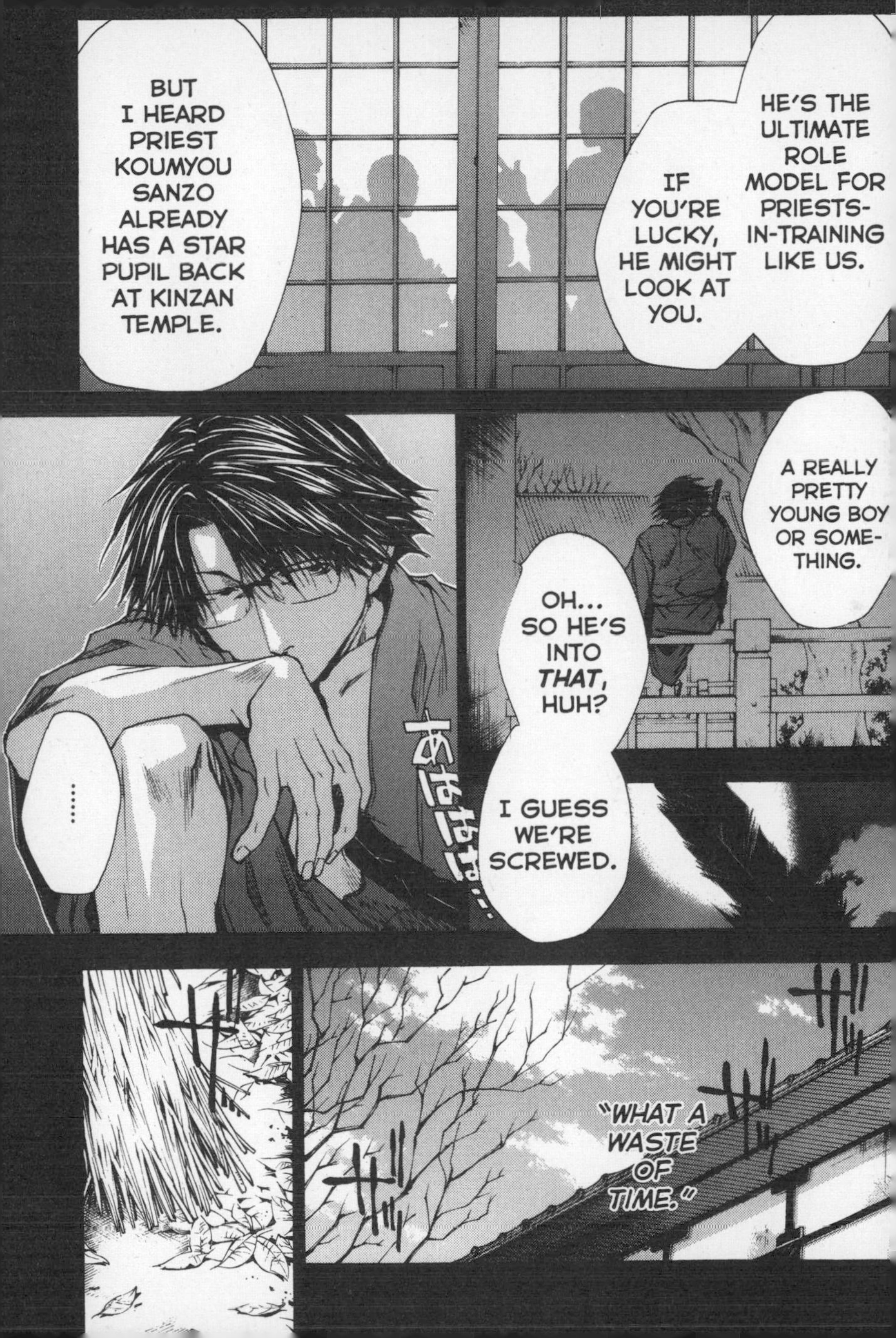
HE'S THE ULTIMATE ROLE MODEL FOR PRIESTS-IN-TRAINING LIKE US.
IF YOU'RE LUCKY, HE MIGHT LOOK AT YOU.
BUT I HEARD PRIEST KOUMYOU SANZO ALREADY HAS A STAR PUPIL BACK AT KINZAN TEMPLE.
A REALLY PRETTY YOUNG BOY OR SOME-THING.
OH... SO HE'S INTO *THAT*, HUH?
I GUESS WE'RE SCREWED.
あははは…
……
"WHAT A WASTE OF TIME."

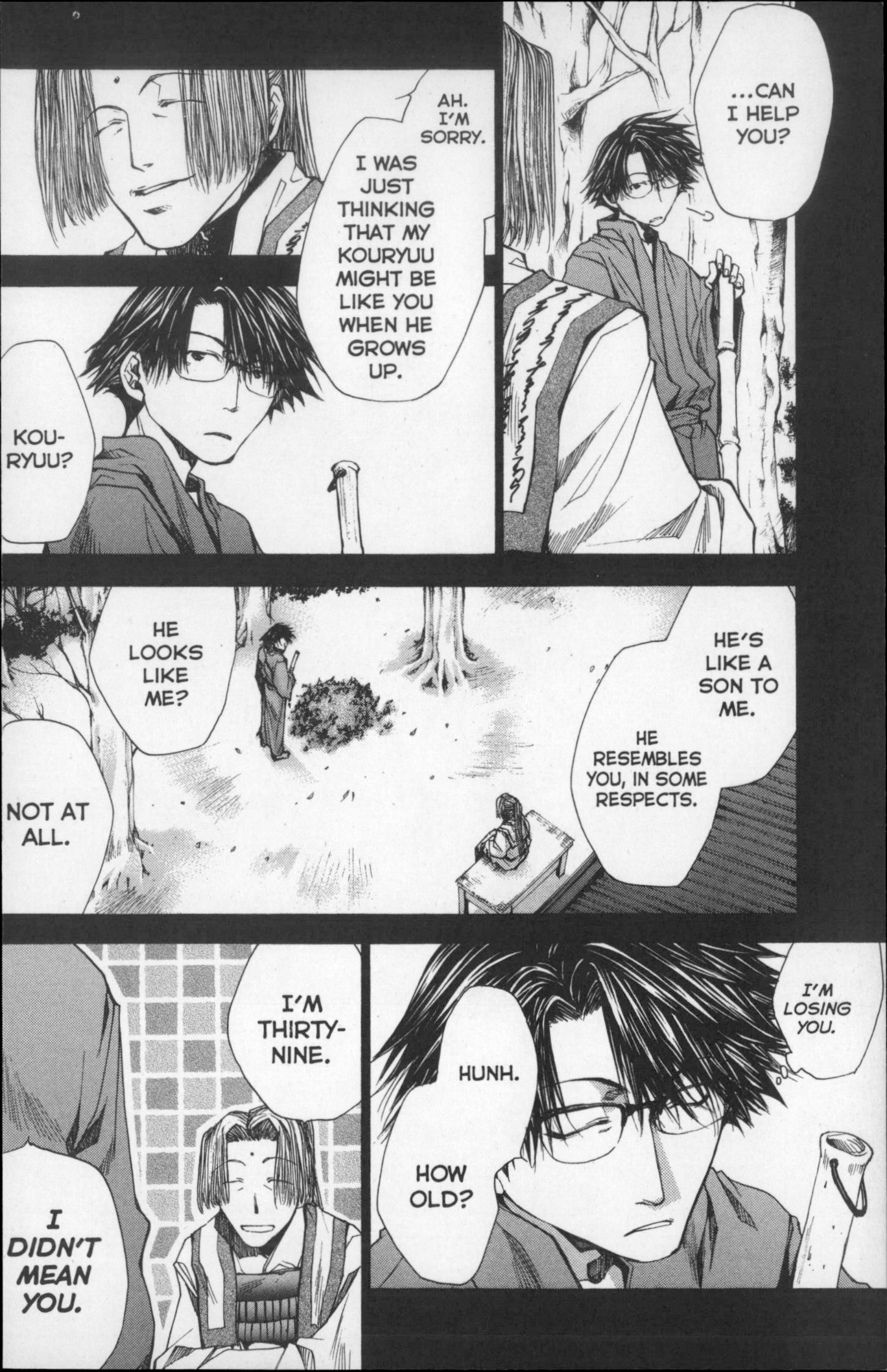
...CAN I HELP YOU?
AH. I'M SORRY.
I WAS JUST THINKING THAT MY KOURYUU MIGHT BE LIKE YOU WHEN HE GROWS UP.
KOU-RYUU?
HE'S LIKE A SON TO ME.
HE RESEMBLES YOU, IN SOME RESPECTS.
HE LOOKS LIKE ME?
NOT AT ALL.
I'M LOSING YOU.
HUNH.
HOW OLD?
I'M THIRTY-NINE.
I DIDN'T MEAN YOU.

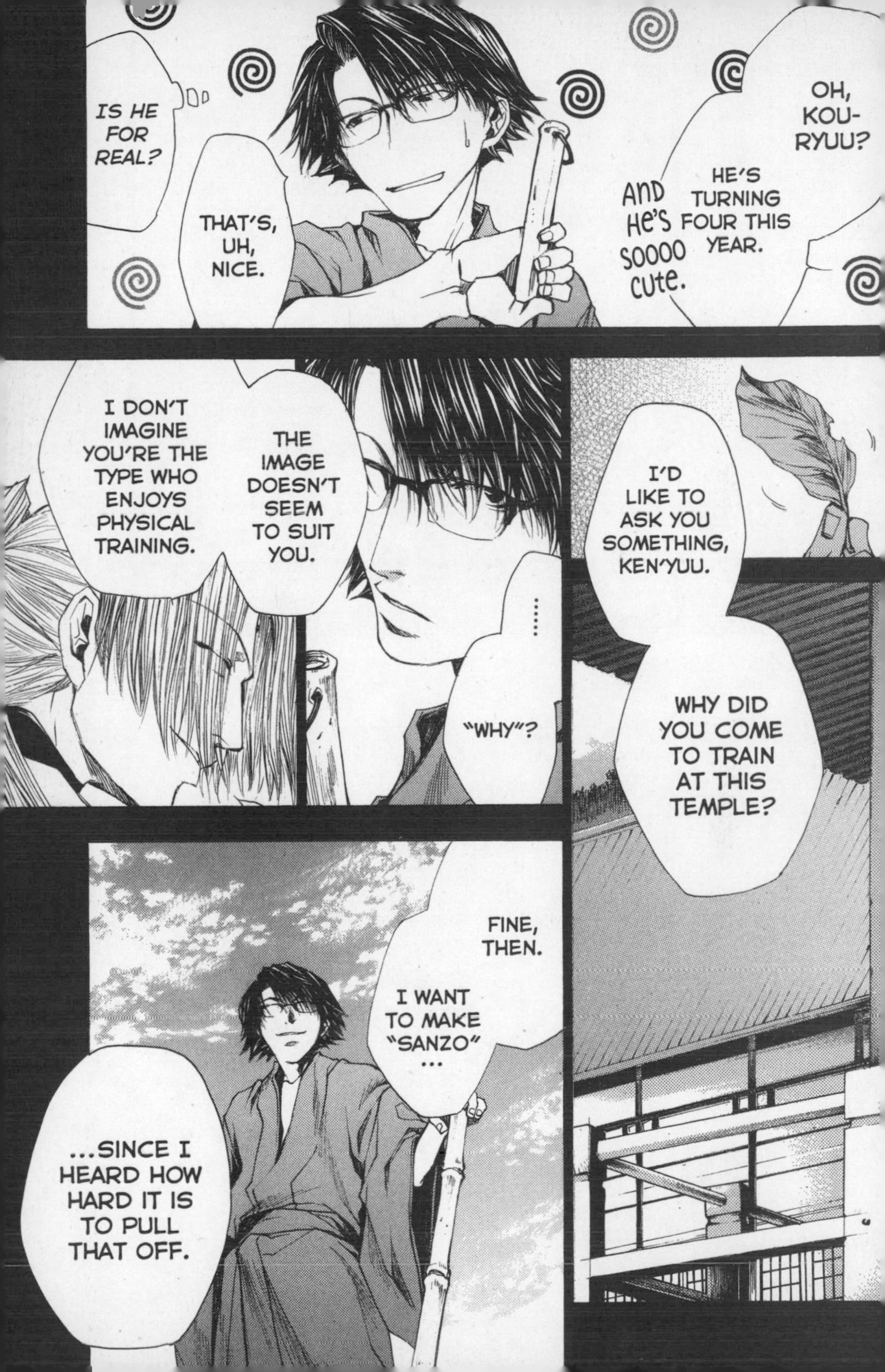
OH, KOU-RYUU?
HE'S TURNING FOUR THIS YEAR.
And He's soooo cute.
IS HE FOR REAL?
THAT'S, UH, NICE.
I'D LIKE TO ASK YOU SOMETHING, KEN'YUU.
WHY DID YOU COME TO TRAIN AT THIS TEMPLE?
......
"WHY"?
THE IMAGE DOESN'T SEEM TO SUIT YOU.
I DON'T IMAGINE YOU'RE THE TYPE WHO ENJOYS PHYSICAL TRAINING.
FINE, THEN.
I WANT TO MAKE "SANZO"...
...SINCE I HEARD HOW HARD IT IS TO PULL THAT OFF.

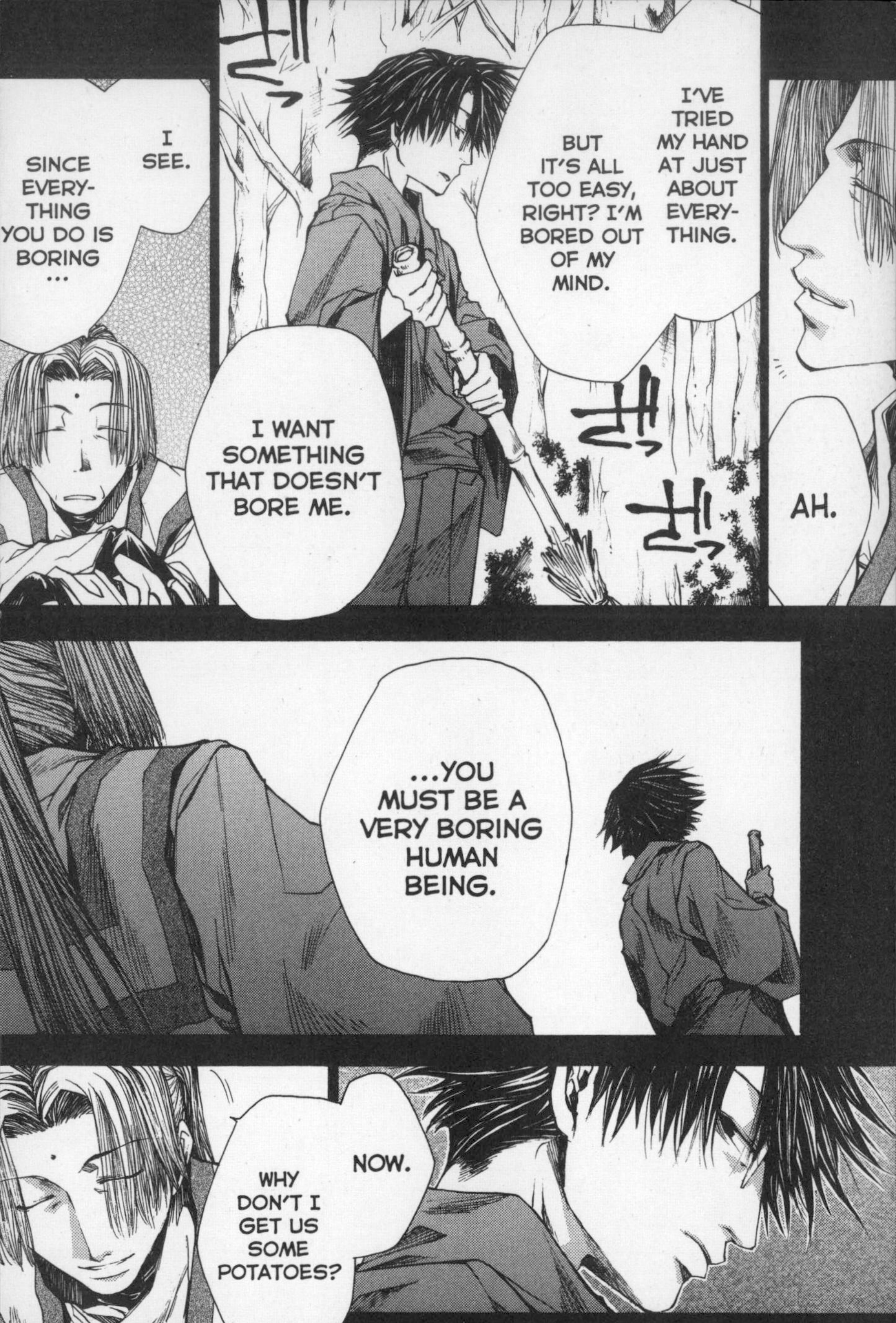
AH.
I'VE TRIED MY HAND AT JUST ABOUT EVERY-THING.
BUT IT'S ALL TOO EASY, RIGHT? I'M BORED OUT OF MY MIND.
I WANT SOMETHING THAT DOESN'T BORE ME.
I SEE.
SINCE EVERY-THING YOU DO IS BORING ...
...YOU MUST BE A VERY BORING HUMAN BEING.
NOW.
WHY DON'T I GET US SOME POTATOES?

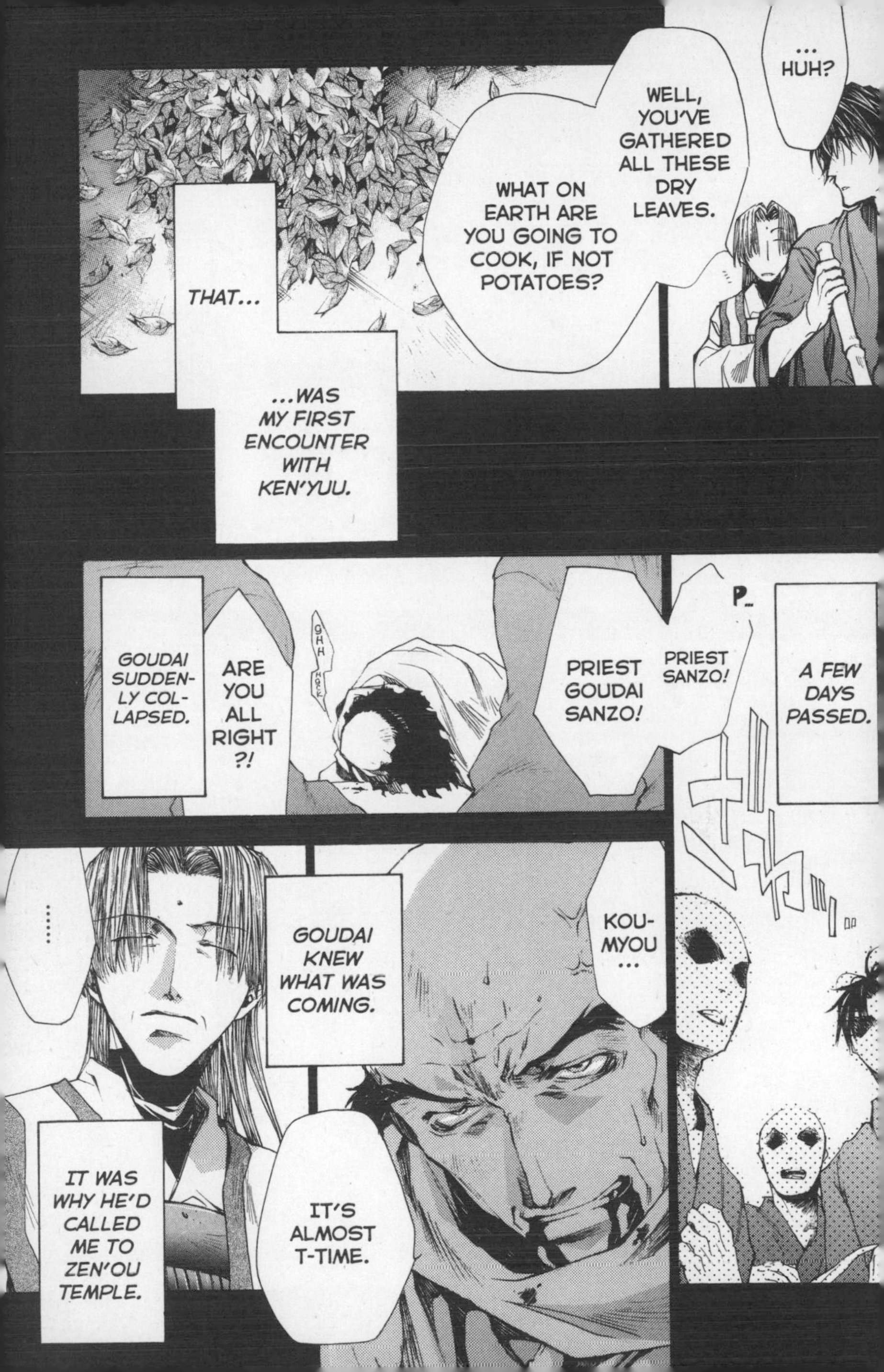
...HUH?
WELL, YOU'VE GATHERED ALL THESE DRY LEAVES.
WHAT ON EARTH ARE YOU GOING TO COOK, IF NOT POTATOES?
THAT...
...WAS MY FIRST ENCOUNTER WITH KEN'YUU.
A FEW DAYS PASSED.
P...
PRIEST SANZO!
PRIEST GOUDAI SANZO!
GHH HORK
ARE YOU ALL RIGHT?!
GOUDAI SUDDEN-LY COL-LAPSED.
KOU-MYOU...
GOUDAI KNEW WHAT WAS COMING.
IT'S ALMOST T-TIME.
......
IT WAS WHY HE'D CALLED ME TO ZEN'OU TEMPLE.

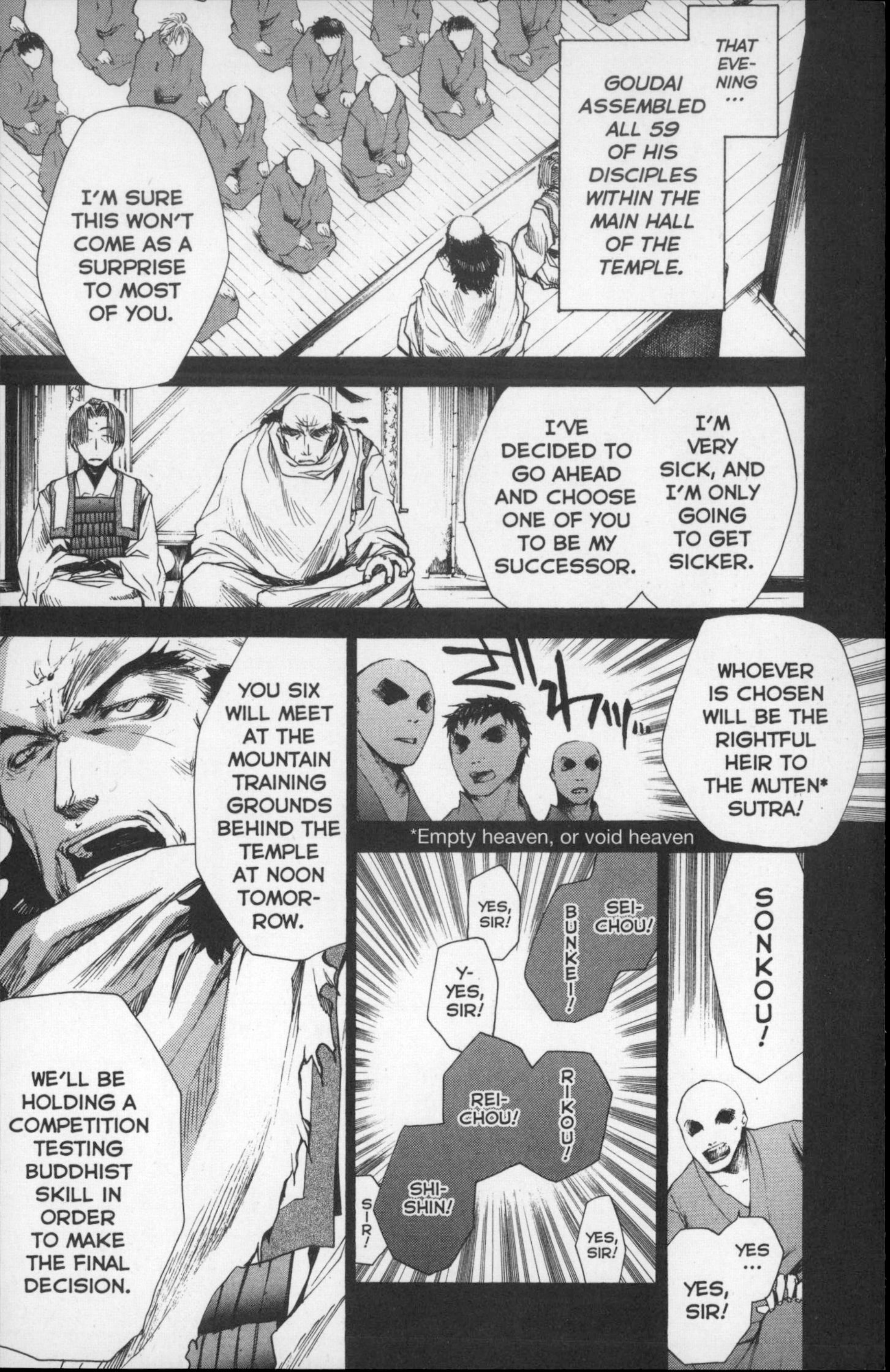
THAT EVENING...
GOUDAI ASSEMBLED ALL 59 OF HIS DISCIPLES WITHIN THE MAIN HALL OF THE TEMPLE.
I'M SURE THIS WON'T COME AS A SURPRISE TO MOST OF YOU.
I'M VERY SICK, AND I'M ONLY GOING TO GET SICKER.
I'VE DECIDED TO GO AHEAD AND CHOOSE ONE OF YOU TO BE MY SUCCESSOR.
WHOEVER IS CHOSEN WILL BE THE RIGHTFUL HEIR TO THE MUTEN* SUTRA!
SONKOU!
YES... YES, SIR!
SEI-CHOU!
BUNKEI!
YES, SIR!
Y-YES, SIR!
RIKOU!
REI-CHOU!
YES, SIR!
SHI-SHIN!
SIR!
YOU SIX WILL MEET AT THE MOUNTAIN TRAINING GROUNDS BEHIND THE TEMPLE AT NOON TOMORROW.
WE'LL BE HOLDING A COMPETITION TESTING BUDDHIST SKILL IN ORDER TO MAKE THE FINAL DECISION.
*Empty heaven, or void heaven

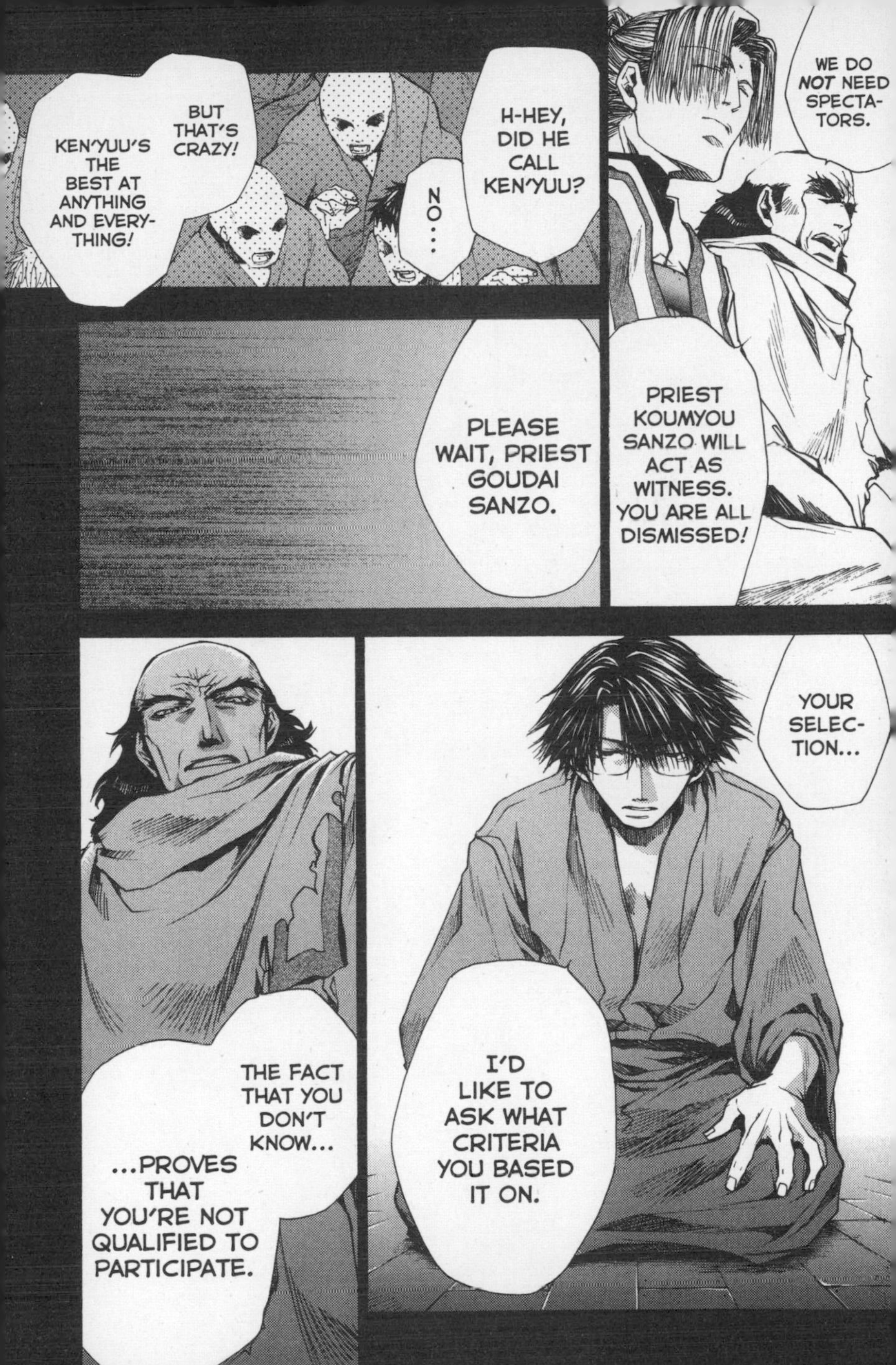
WE DO NOT NEED SPECTATORS.
PRIEST KOUMYOU SANZO WILL ACT AS WITNESS. YOU ARE ALL DISMISSED!
H-HEY, DID HE CALL KEN'YUU?
NO...
BUT THAT'S CRAZY!
KEN'YUU'S THE BEST AT ANYTHING AND EVERYTHING!
PLEASE WAIT, PRIEST GOUDAI SANZO.
YOUR SELECTION...
I'D LIKE TO ASK WHAT CRITERIA YOU BASED IT ON.
THE FACT THAT YOU DON'T KNOW...
...PROVES THAT YOU'RE NOT QUALIFIED TO PARTICIPATE.

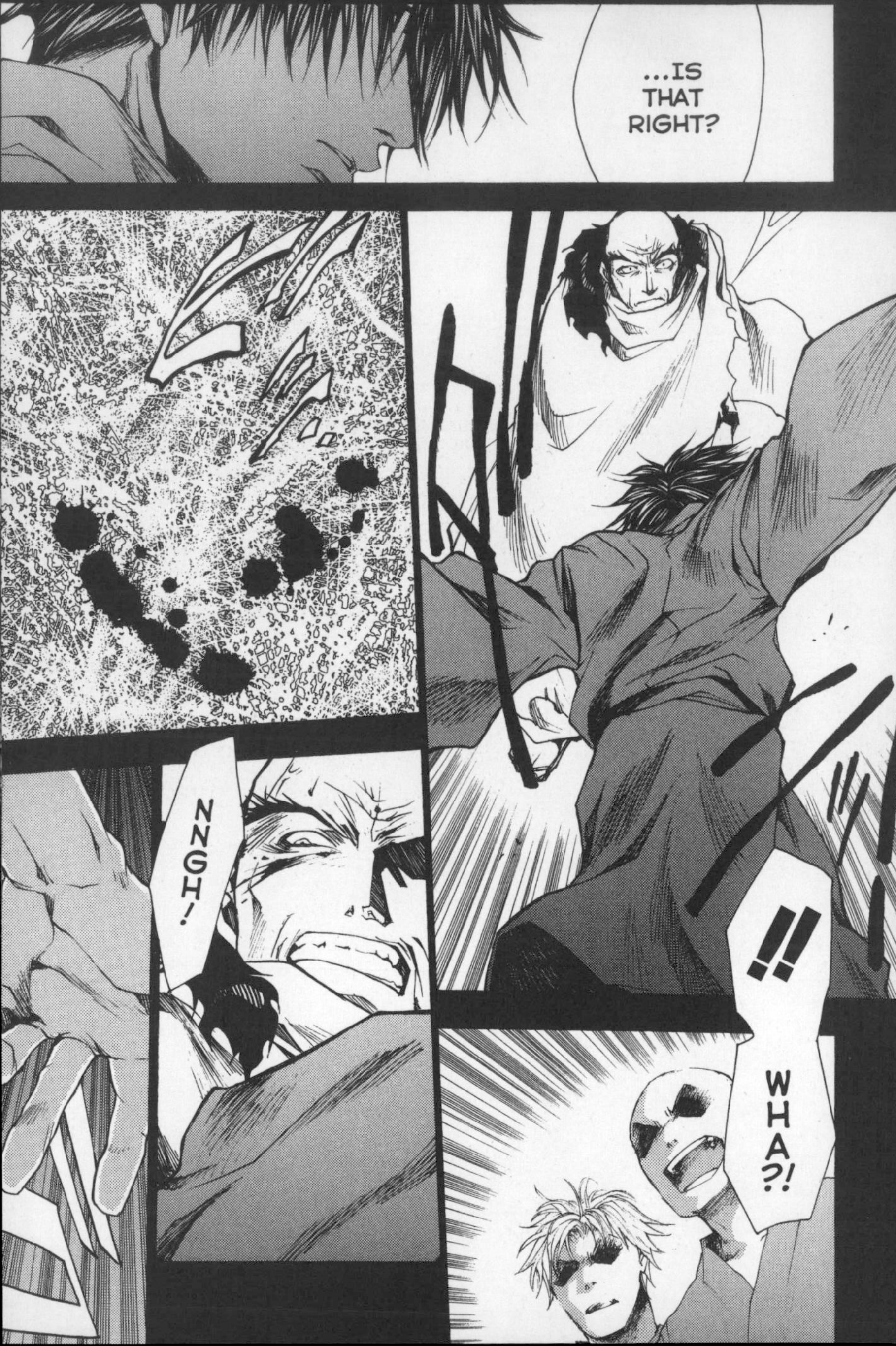
...IS THAT RIGHT?
!!
WHA?!
NNGH!

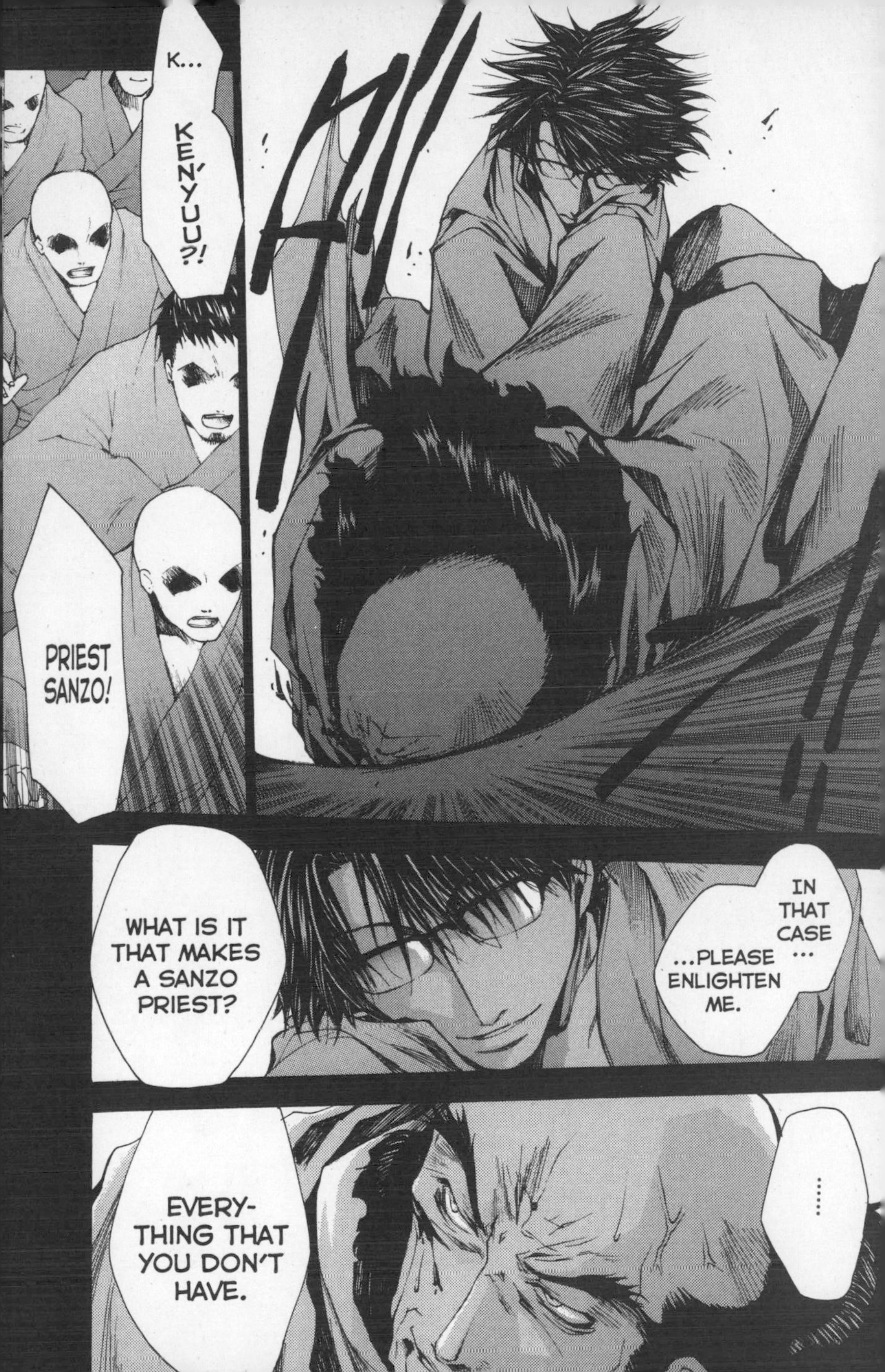
K...
KEN'YUU?!
PRIEST SANZO!
IN THAT CASE ...
...PLEASE ENLIGHTEN ME.
WHAT IS IT THAT MAKES A SANZO PRIEST?
......
EVERY-THING THAT YOU DON'T HAVE.

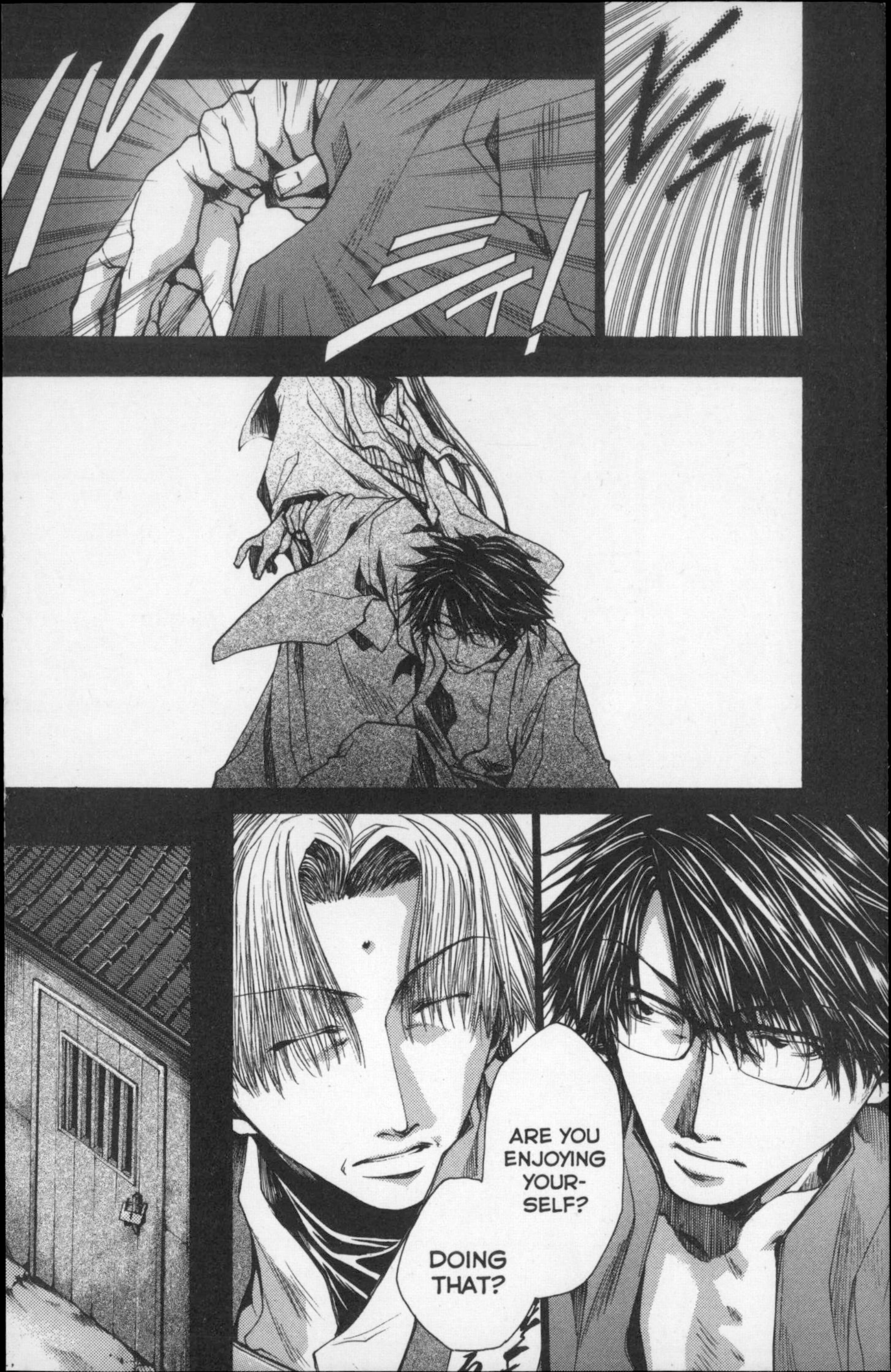
ARE YOU ENJOYING YOUR-SELF?
DOING THAT?

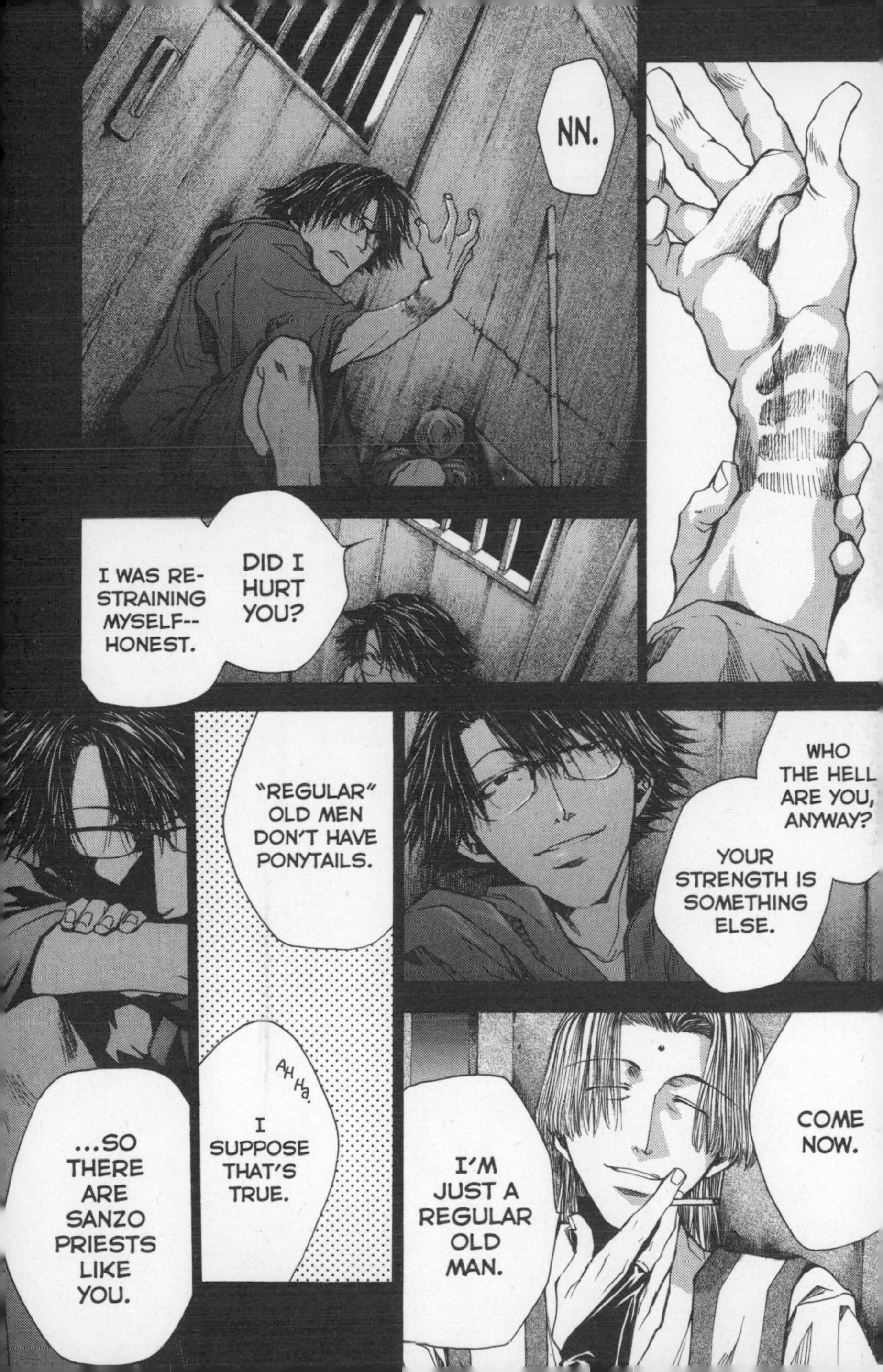
NN.
DID I HURT YOU?
I WAS RE-STRAINING MYSELF--HONEST.
WHO THE HELL ARE YOU, ANYWAY?
YOUR STRENGTH IS SOMETHING ELSE.
COME NOW.
I'M JUST A REGULAR OLD MAN.
"REGULAR" OLD MEN DON'T HAVE PONYTAILS.
AH HA.
I SUPPOSE THAT'S TRUE.
...SO THERE ARE SANZO PRIESTS LIKE YOU.

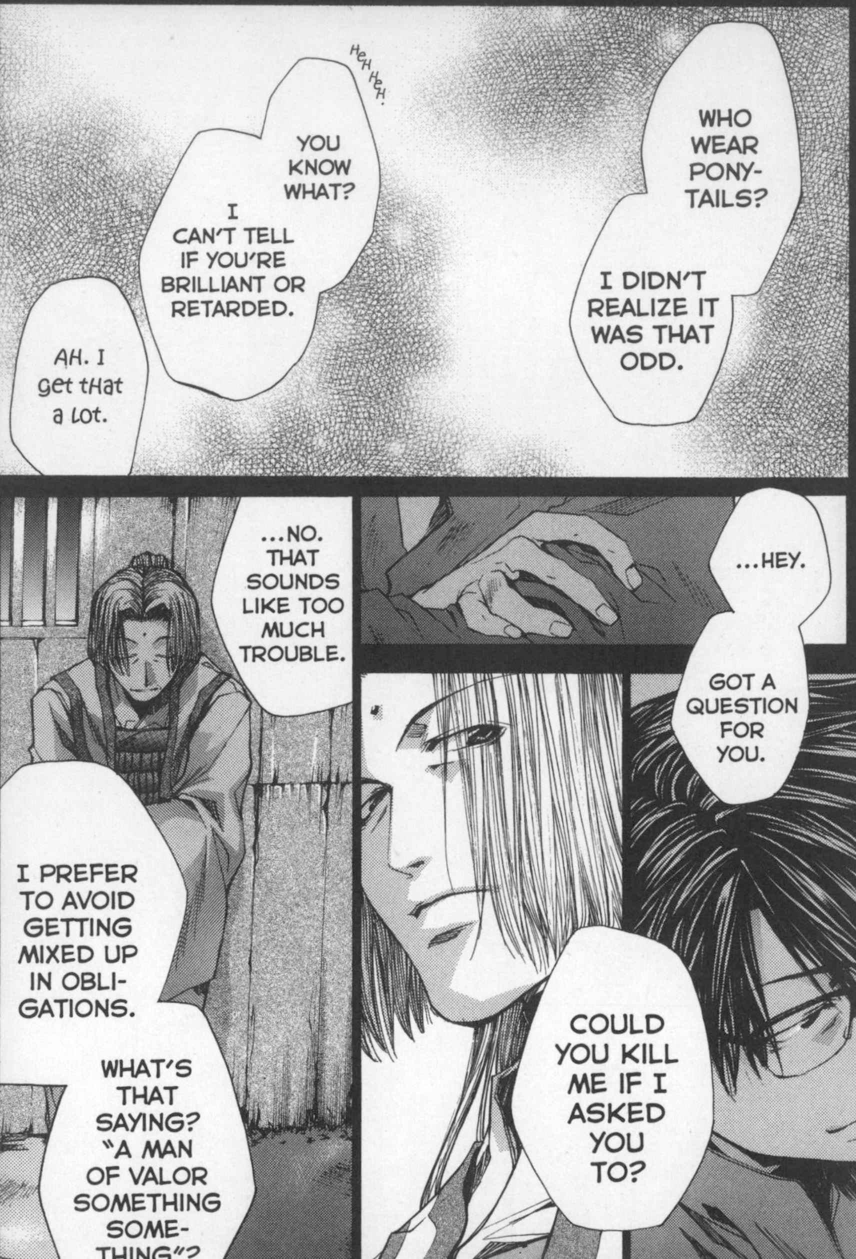
WHO WEAR PONY-TAILS?
I DIDN'T REALIZE IT WAS THAT ODD.
HEH HEH HEH.
YOU KNOW WHAT?
I CAN'T TELL IF YOU'RE BRILLIANT OR RETARDED.
AH. I get tHat a Lot.
...HEY.
GOT A QUESTION FOR YOU.
COULD YOU KILL ME IF I ASKED YOU TO?
...NO. THAT SOUNDS LIKE TOO MUCH TROUBLE.
I PREFER TO AVOID GETTING MIXED UP IN OBLI-GATIONS.
WHAT'S THAT SAYING? "A MAN OF VALOR SOMETHING SOME-THING"?

I CAN'T BE LIKE THAT.
IF I'M NOT IN AN EAT OR BE EATEN SITUATION...
...I DON'T FEEL ALIVE.
REALLY, THERE'S NOTHING I WANT.
EVERY-ONE LIVES BY DO OR DIE.
IT'S ALL ABOUT WINNING, AND MAKING FOOD OUT OF SOMEONE ELSE'S CORPSE.
YOU HAVE TO KEEP FEEDING OFF OF OTHER PEOPLE IN ORDER TO LIVE.
...SO YOU CAN EVENTUALLY BE EATEN YOURSELF?
THAT LIGHT.

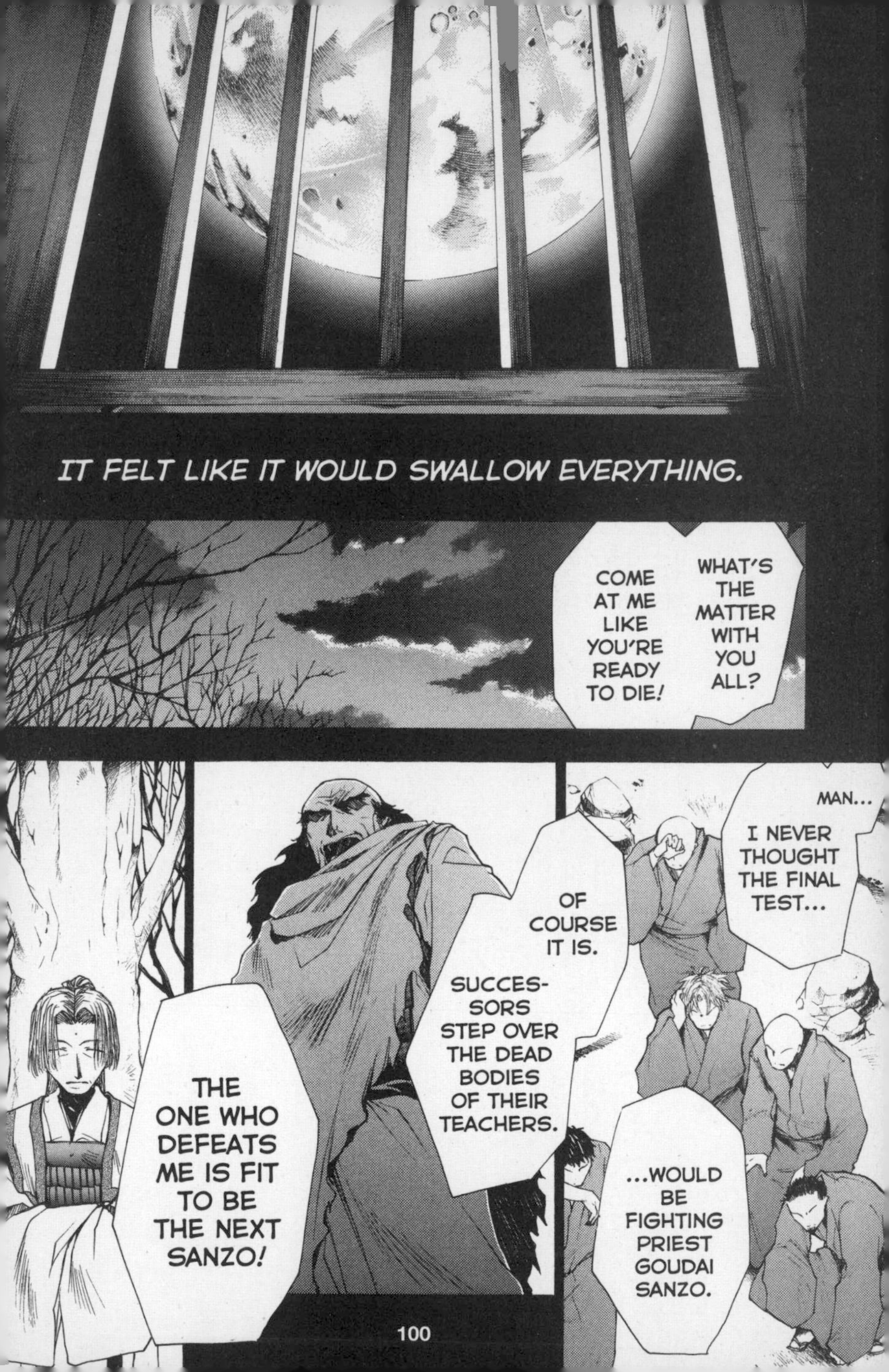
IT FELT LIKE IT WOULD SWALLOW EVERYTHING.
WHAT'S THE MATTER WITH YOU ALL?
COME AT ME LIKE YOU'RE READY TO DIE!
MAN...
I NEVER THOUGHT THE FINAL TEST...
...WOULD BE FIGHTING PRIEST GOUDAI SANZO.
OF COURSE IT IS.
SUCCES-SORS STEP OVER THE DEAD BODIES OF THEIR TEACHERS.
THE ONE WHO DEFEATS ME IS FIT TO BE THE NEXT SANZO!

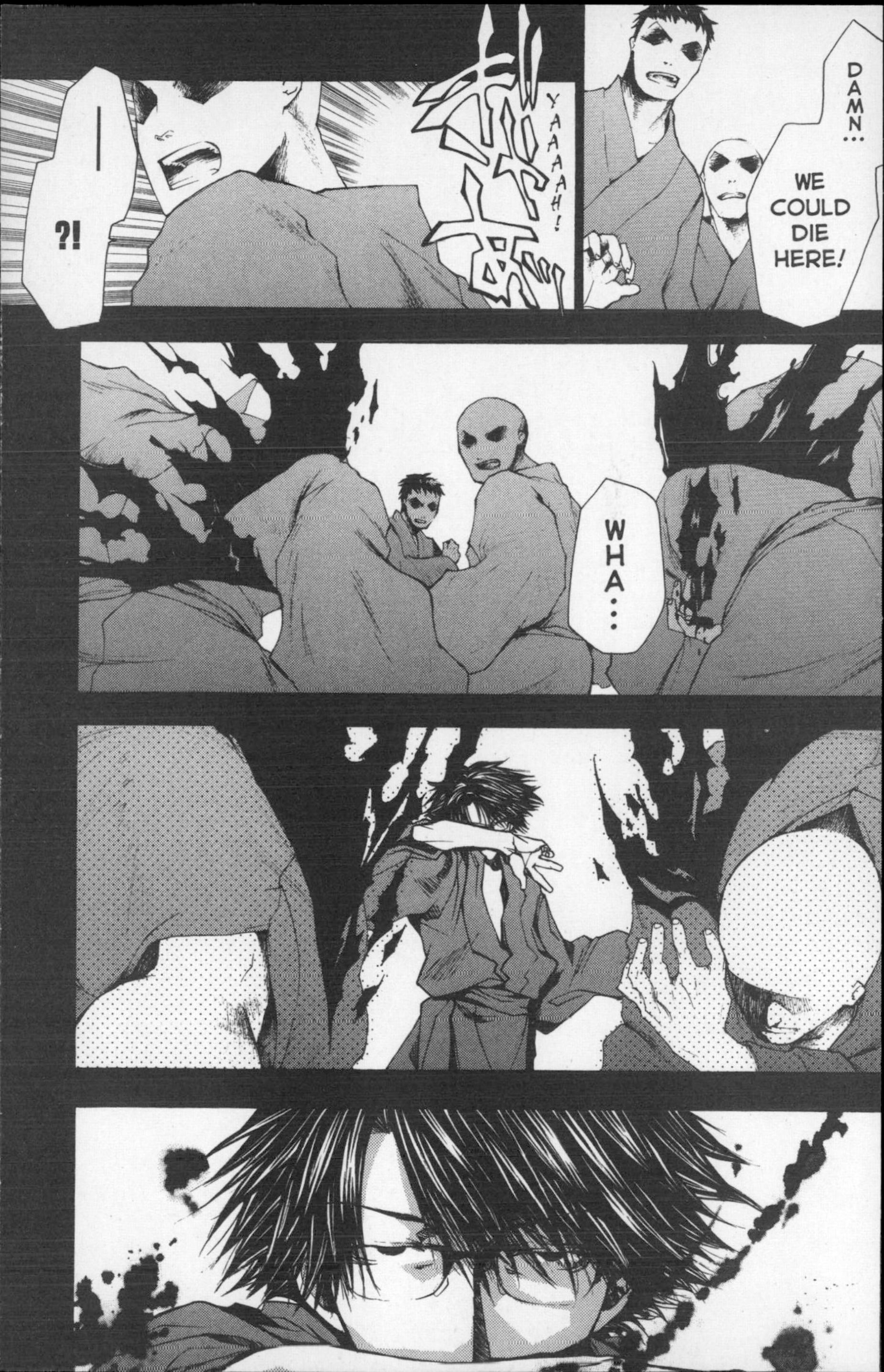
DAMN...
WE COULD DIE HERE!
YAAAAAH!
—
?!
WHA...

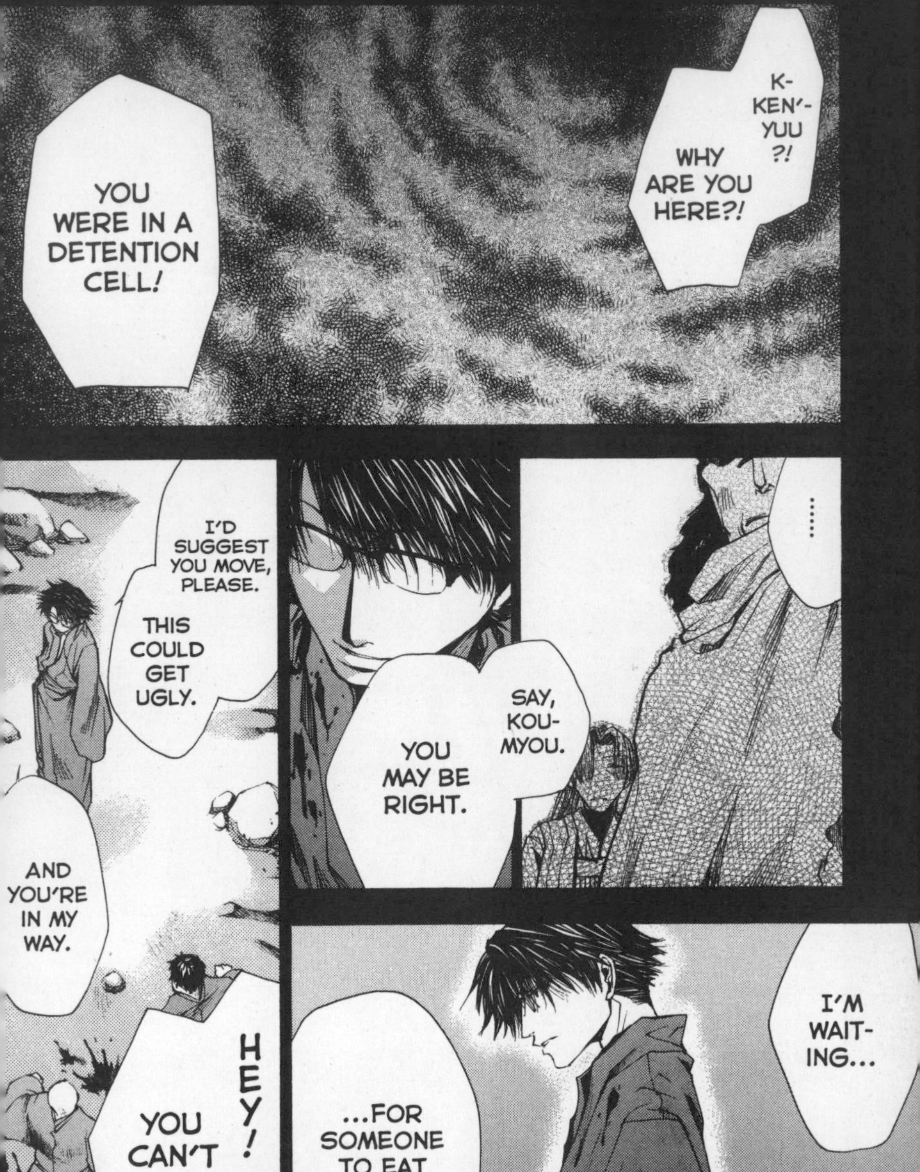
K-KEN'-YUU?!
WHY ARE YOU HERE?!
YOU WERE IN A DETENTION CELL!
......
SAY, KOU-MYOU.
YOU MAY BE RIGHT.
I'M WAITING...
...FOR SOMEONE TO EAT ME.
I'D SUGGEST YOU MOVE, PLEASE.
THIS COULD GET UGLY.
AND YOU'RE IN MY WAY.
HEY!
YOU CAN'T JUST--

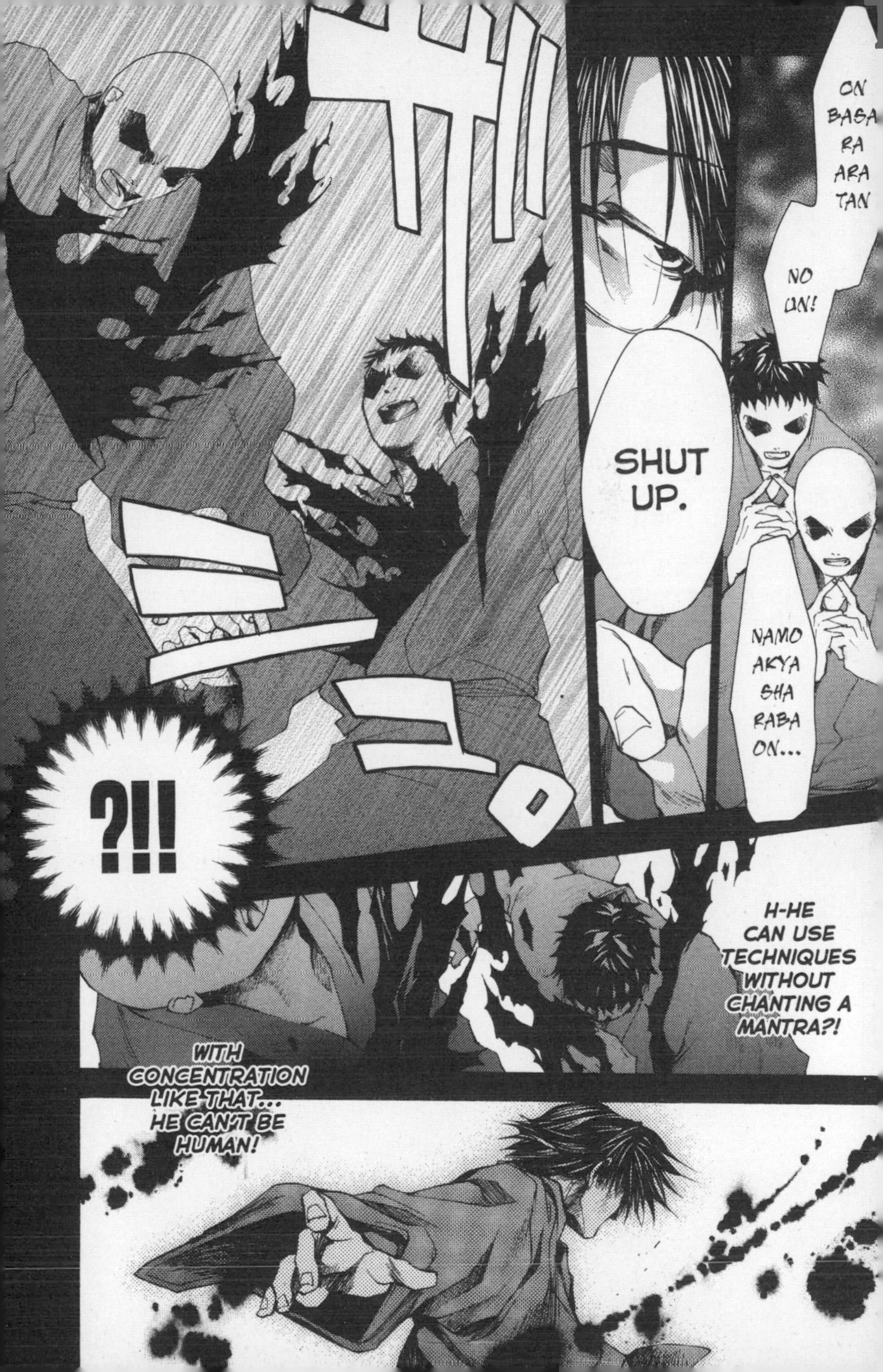
ON BASARA RA ARA TAN
NO UN!
NAMO AKYA SHA RABA ON...
SHUT UP.
?!!
H-HE CAN USE TECHNIQUES WITHOUT CHANTING A MANTRA?!
WITH CONCENTRATION LIKE THAT... HE CAN'T BE HUMAN!

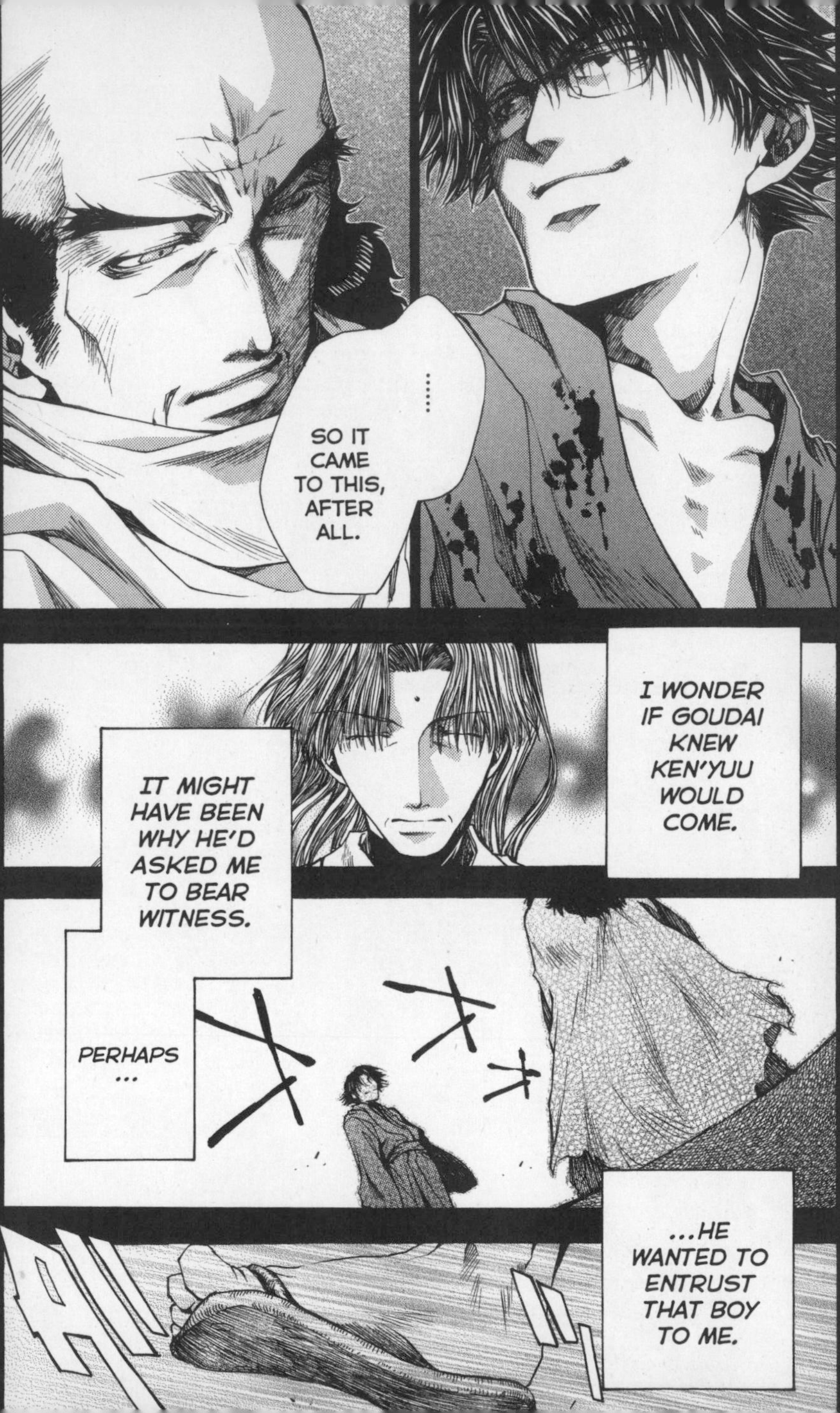
......
SO IT CAME TO THIS, AFTER ALL.
I WONDER IF GOUDAI KNEW KEN'YUU WOULD COME.
IT MIGHT HAVE BEEN WHY HE'D ASKED ME TO BEAR WITNESS.
PERHAPS ...
...HE WANTED TO ENTRUST THAT BOY TO ME.

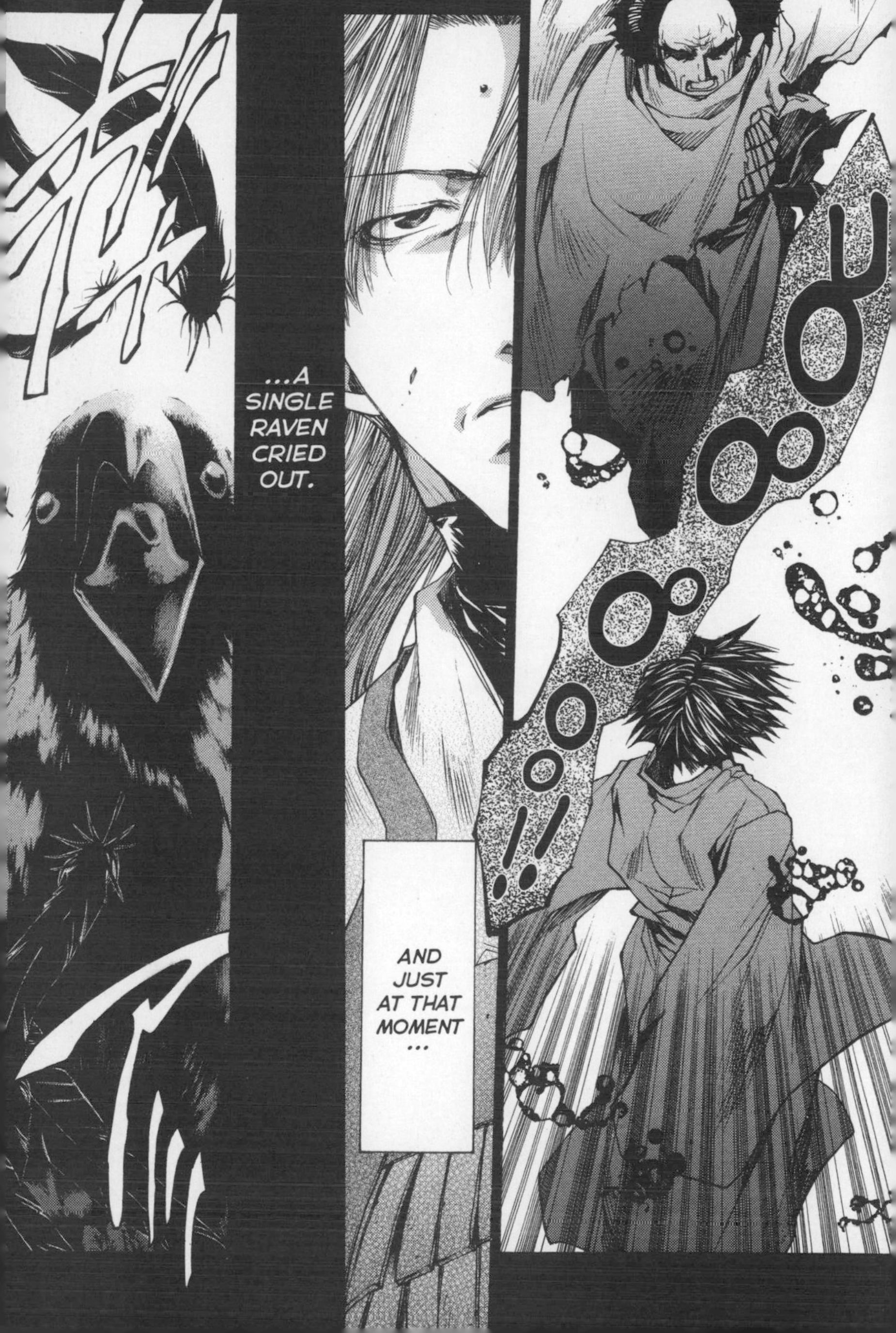
AND JUST AT THAT MOMENT ...
...A SINGLE RAVEN CRIED OUT.

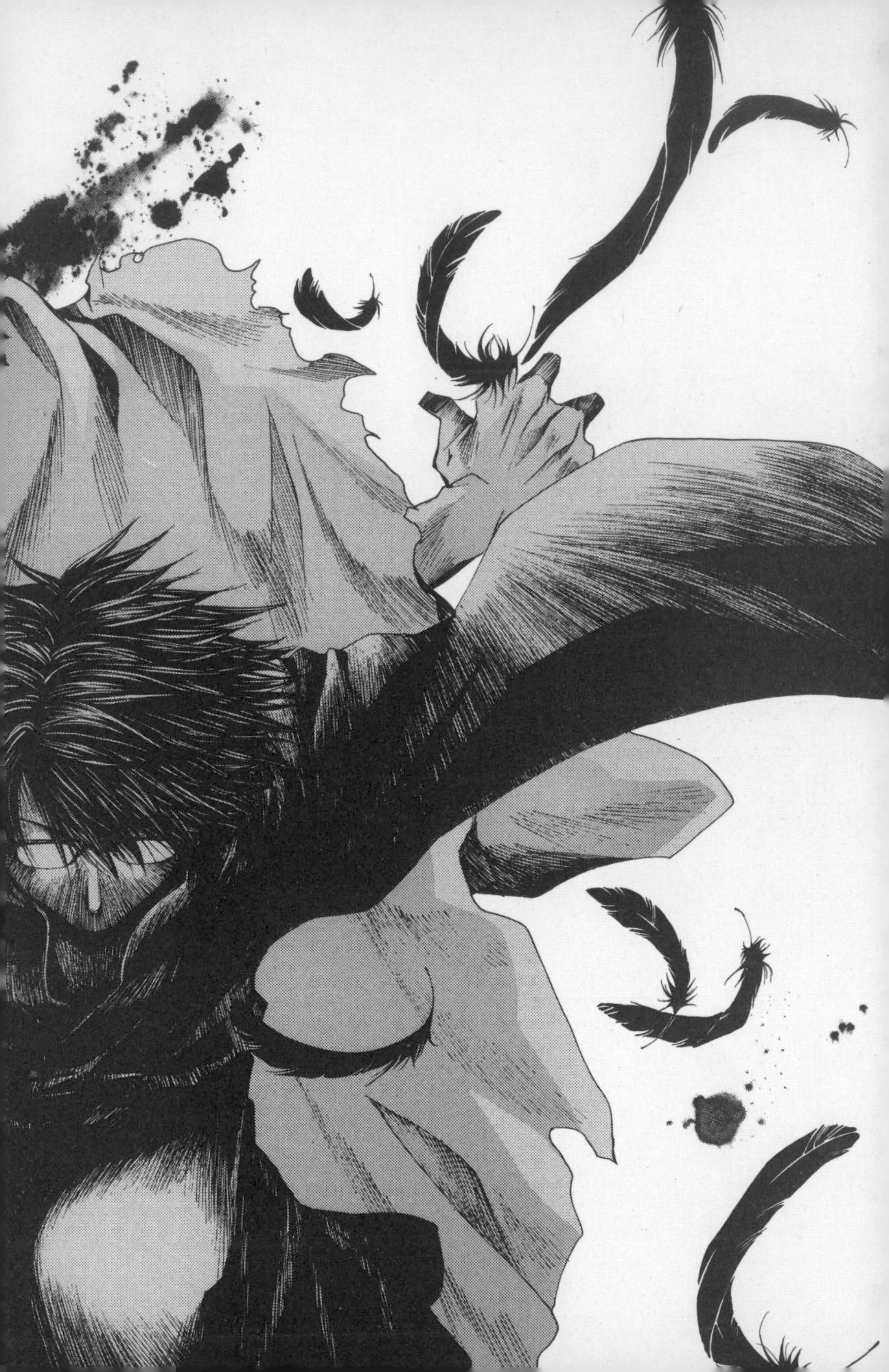

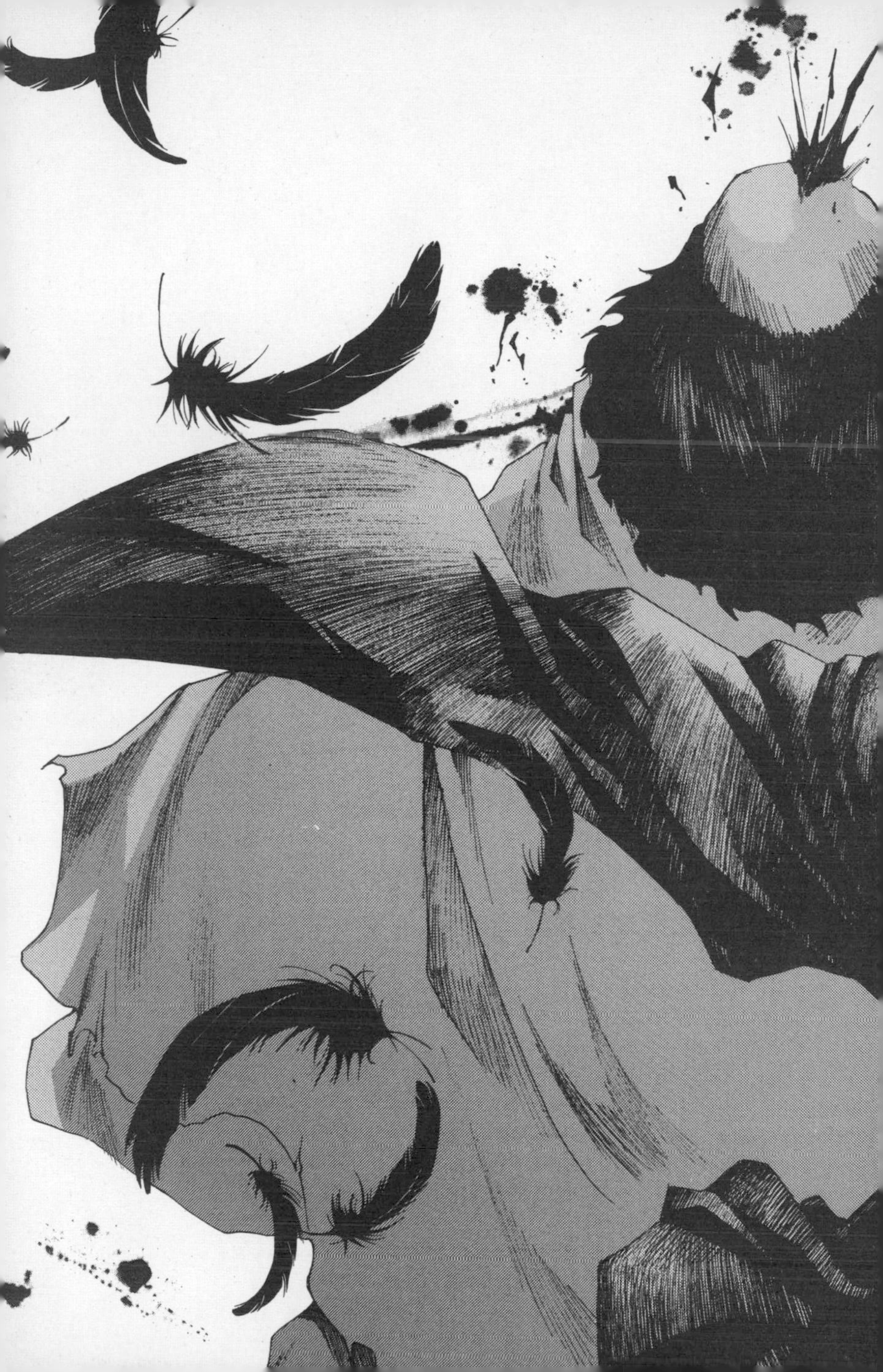

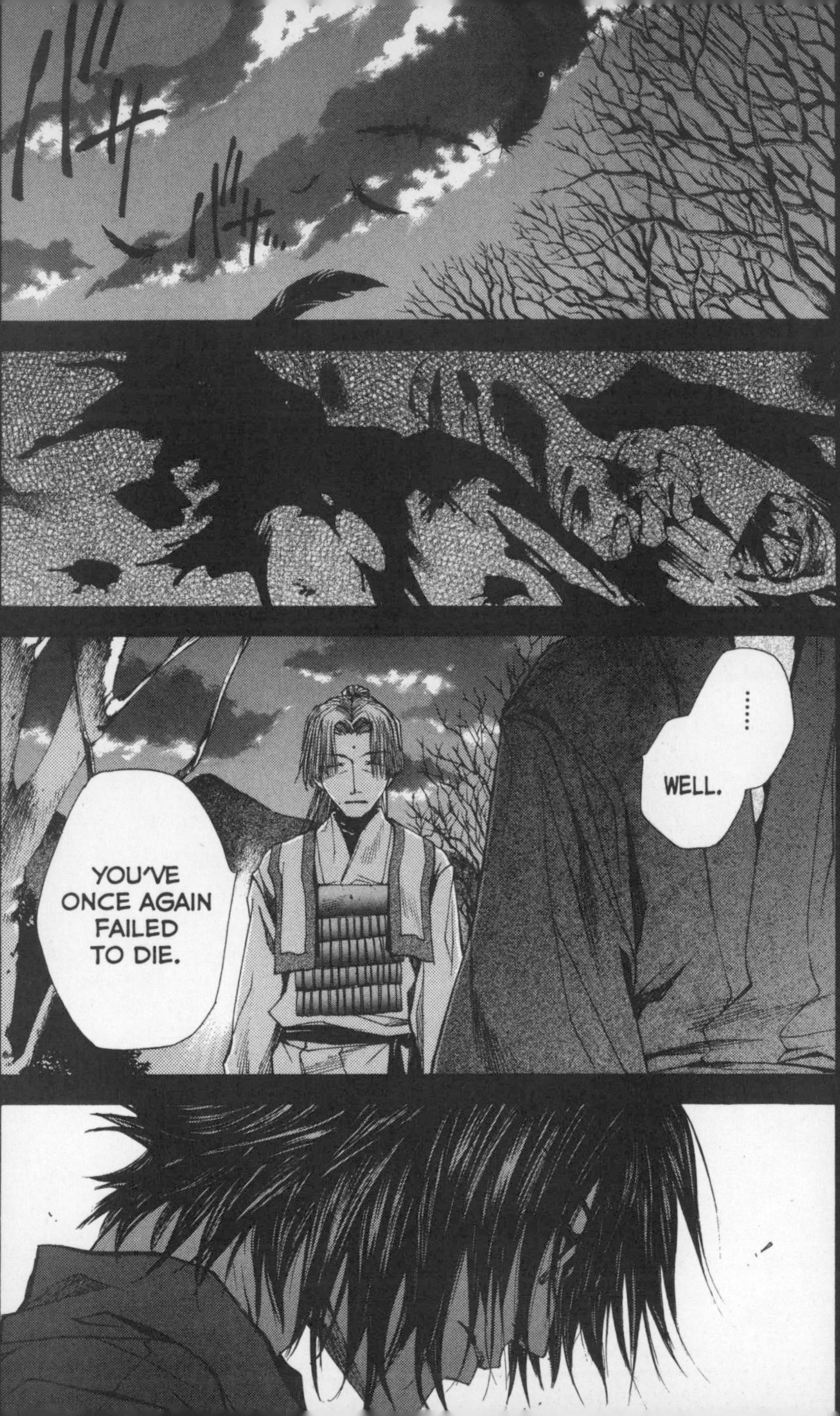
バサ
バサ…
……
WELL.
YOU'VE ONCE AGAIN FAILED TO DIE.

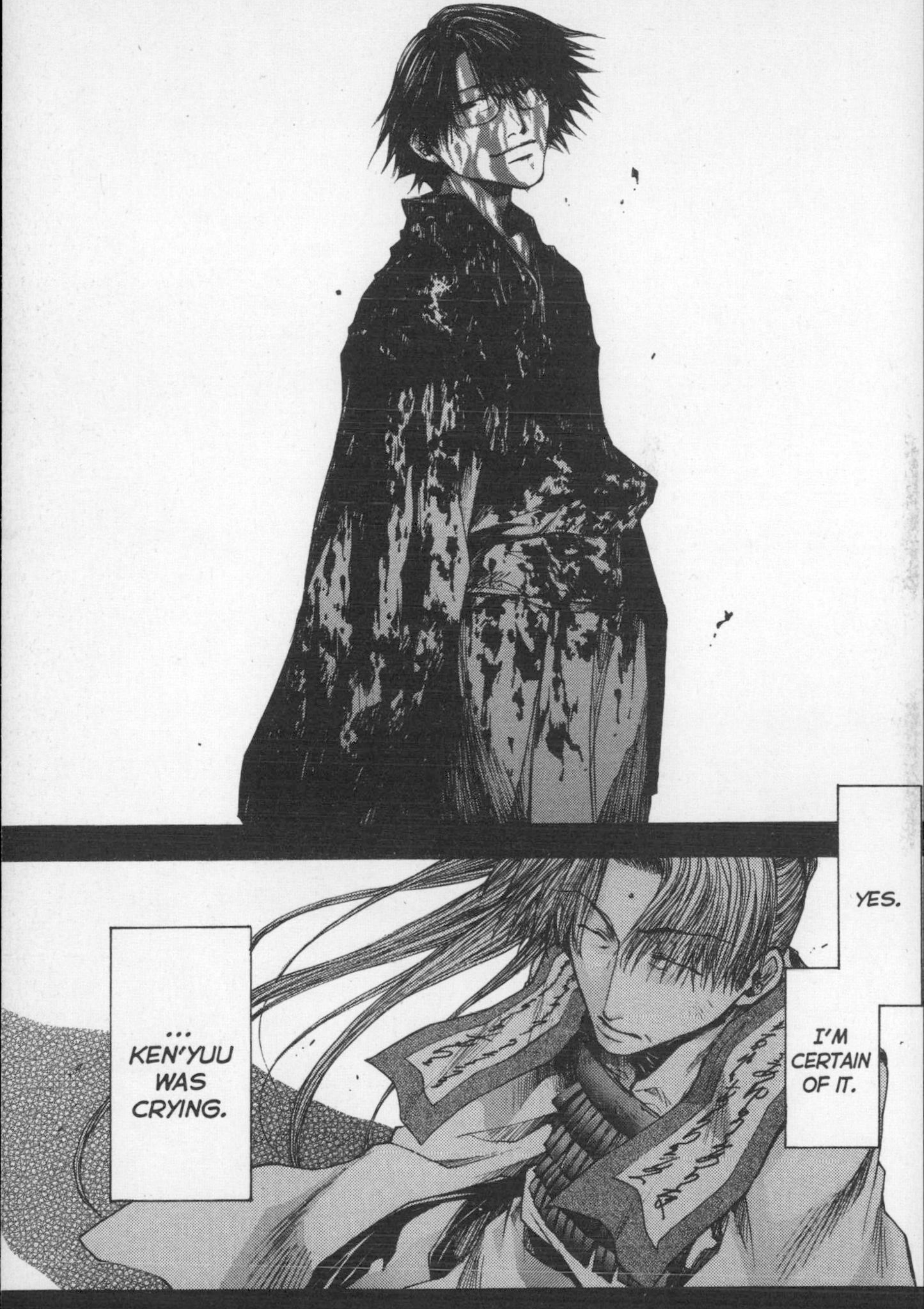
YES.
I'M CERTAIN OF IT.
... KEN'YUU WAS CRYING.

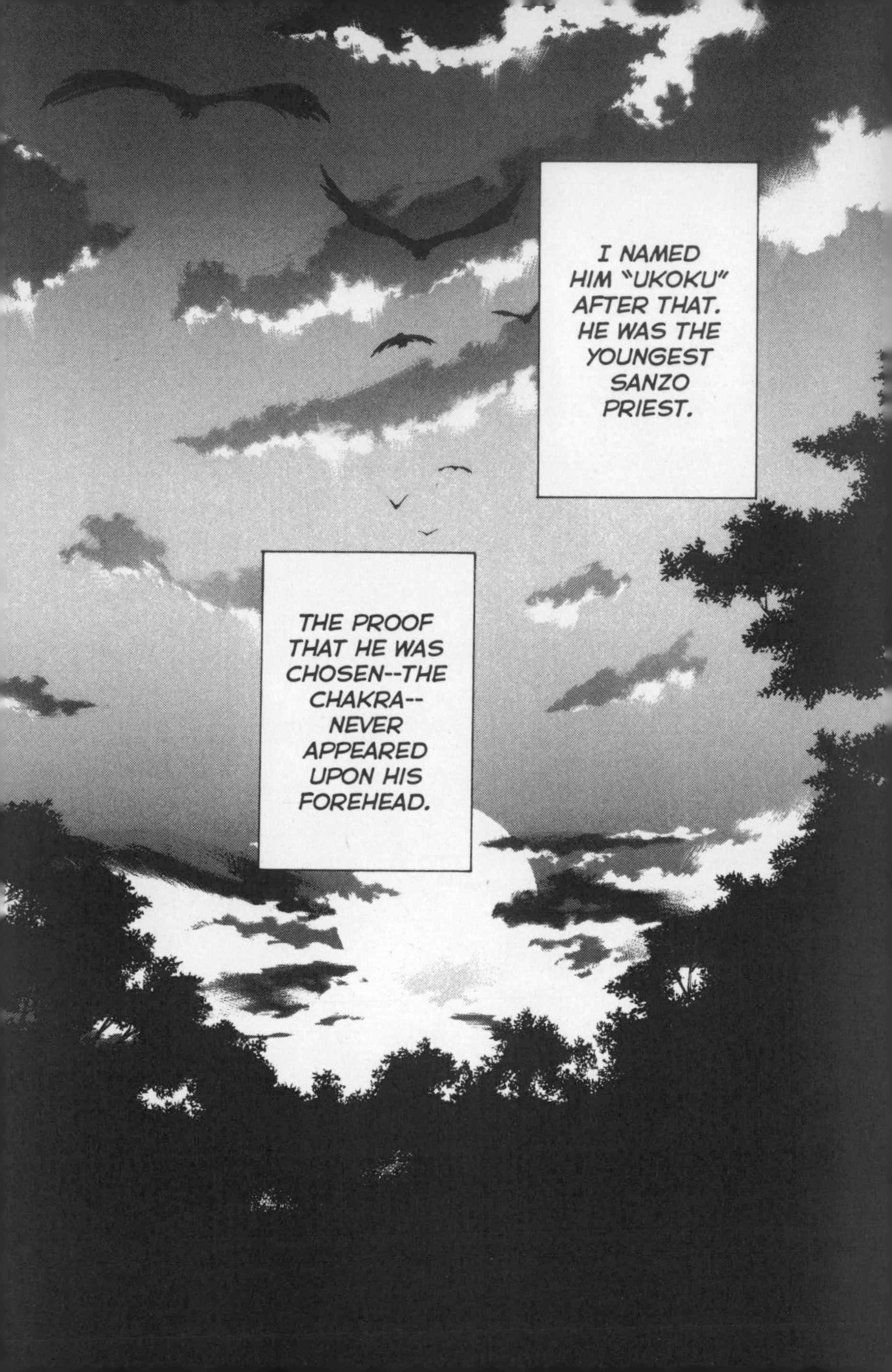
I NAMED HIM "UKOKU" AFTER THAT. HE WAS THE YOUNGEST SANZO PRIEST.
THE PROOF THAT HE WAS CHOSEN--THE CHAKRA--NEVER APPEARED UPON HIS FOREHEAD.

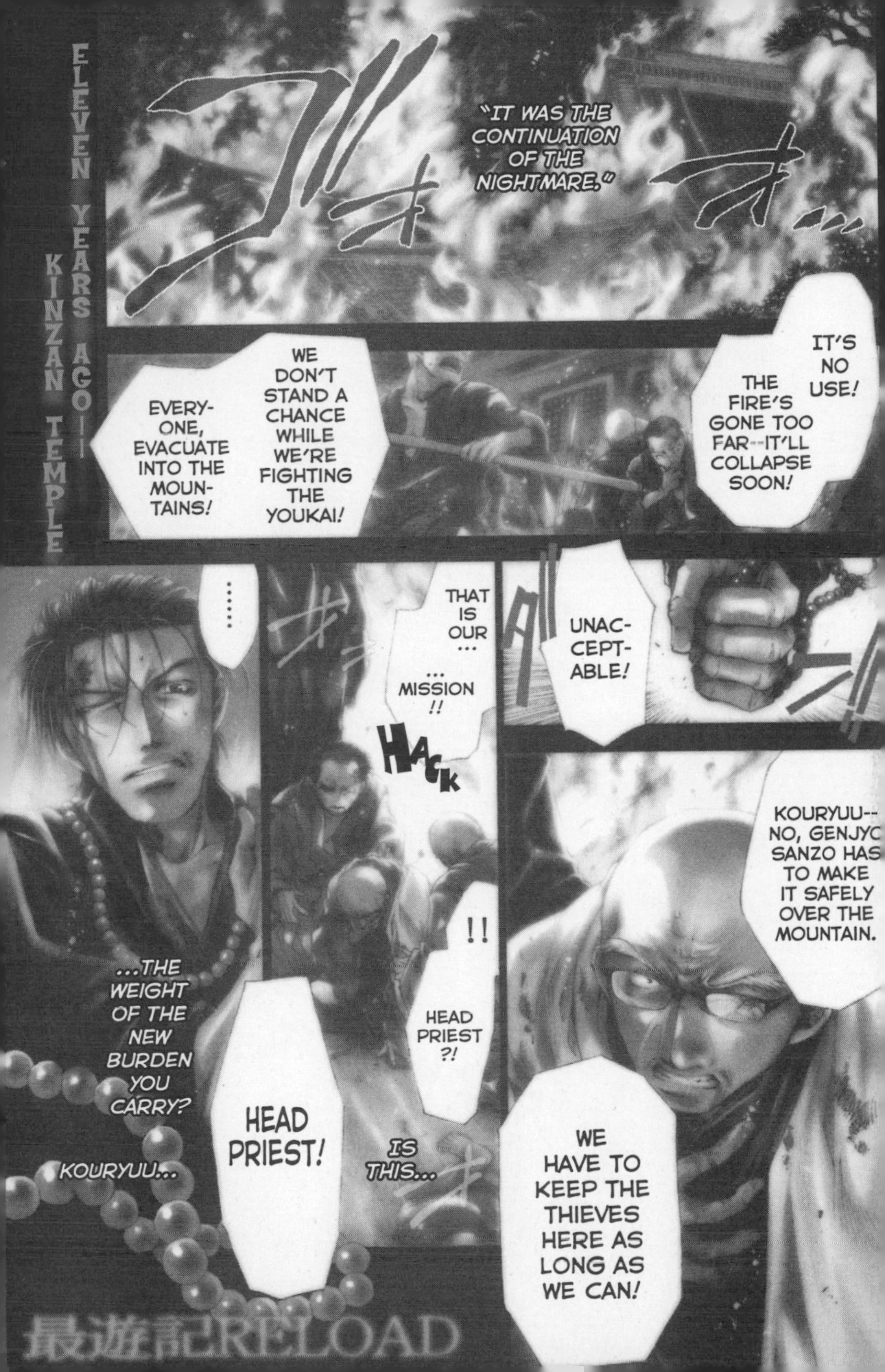
ゴォ
"IT WAS THE CONTINUATION OF THE NIGHTMARE."
オ...
IT'S NO USE! THE FIRE'S GONE TOO FAR--IT'LL COLLAPSE SOON!
WE DON'T STAND A CHANCE WHILE WE'RE FIGHTING THE YOUKAI!
EVERY-ONE, EVACUATE INTO THE MOUN-TAINS!
ELEVEN YEARS AGO -- KINZAN TEMPLE
UNAC-CEPT-ABLE!
KOURYUU--NO, GENJYO SANZO HAS TO MAKE IT SAFELY OVER THE MOUNTAIN.
WE HAVE TO KEEP THE THIEVES HERE AS LONG AS WE CAN!
THAT IS OUR...
...MISSION!!
HACK
!!
HEAD PRIEST?!
HEAD PRIEST!
IS THIS...
......
...THE WEIGHT OF THE NEW BURDEN YOU CARRY?
KOURYUU...
最遊記RELOAD

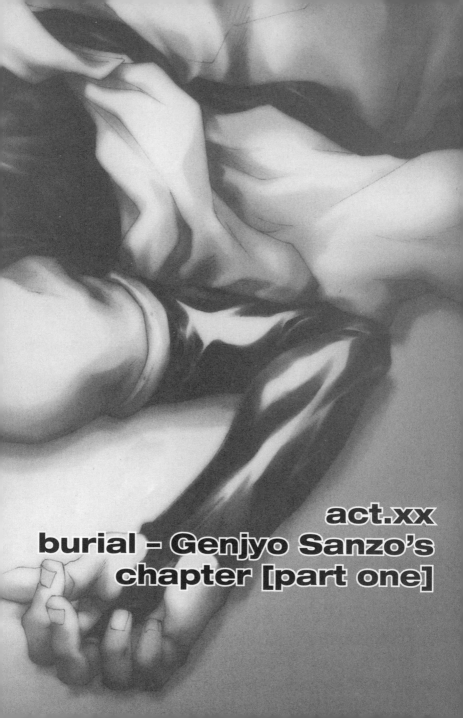

act.xx
burial – Genjyo Sanzo's
chapter [part one]

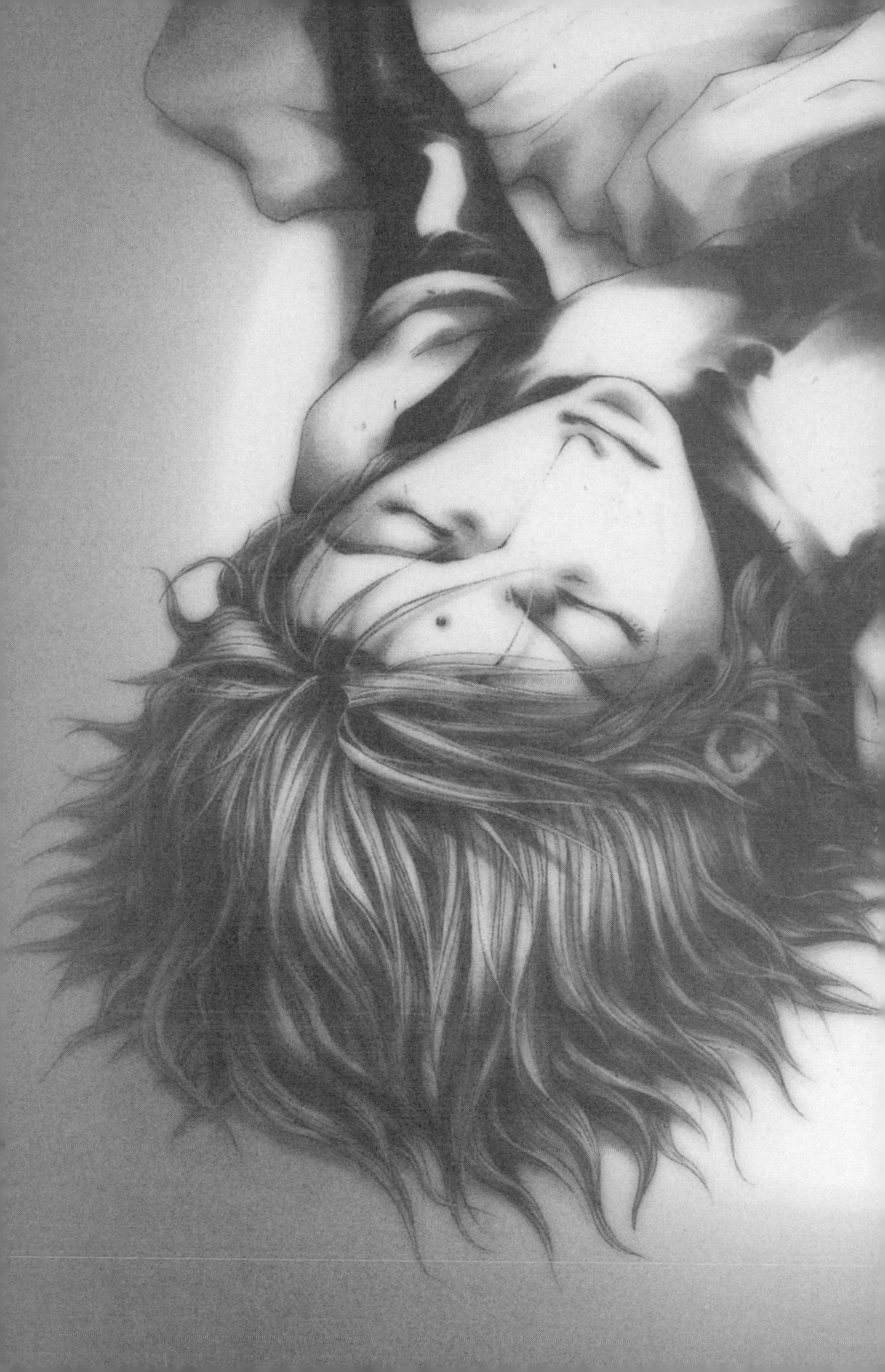

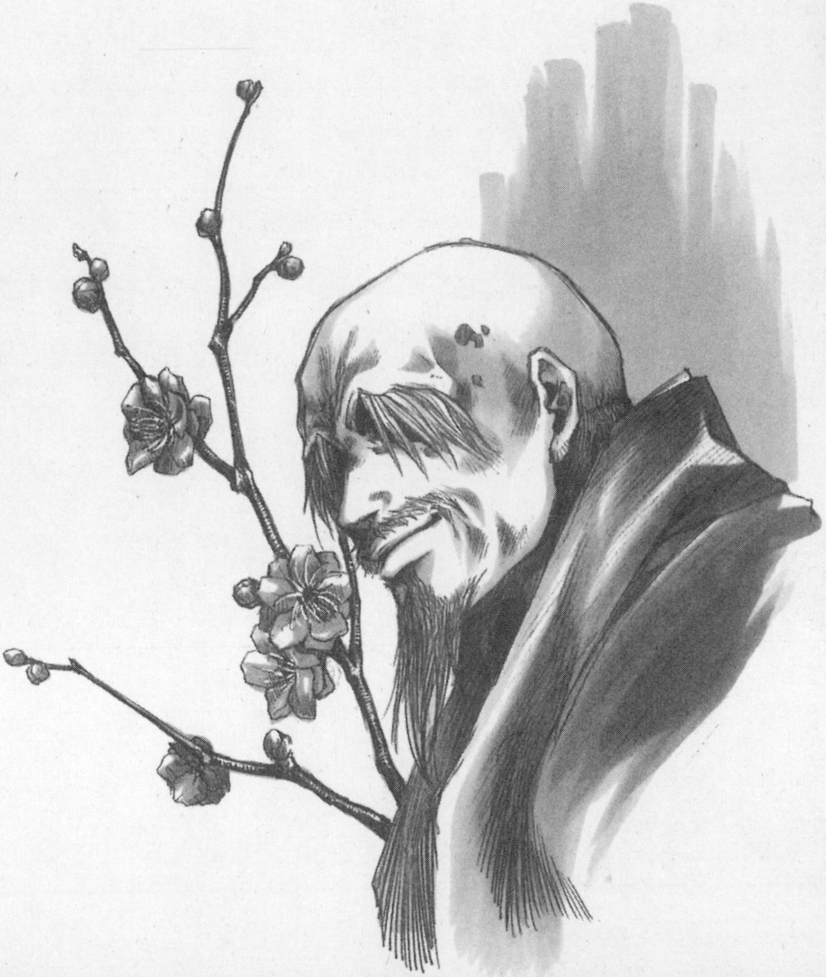

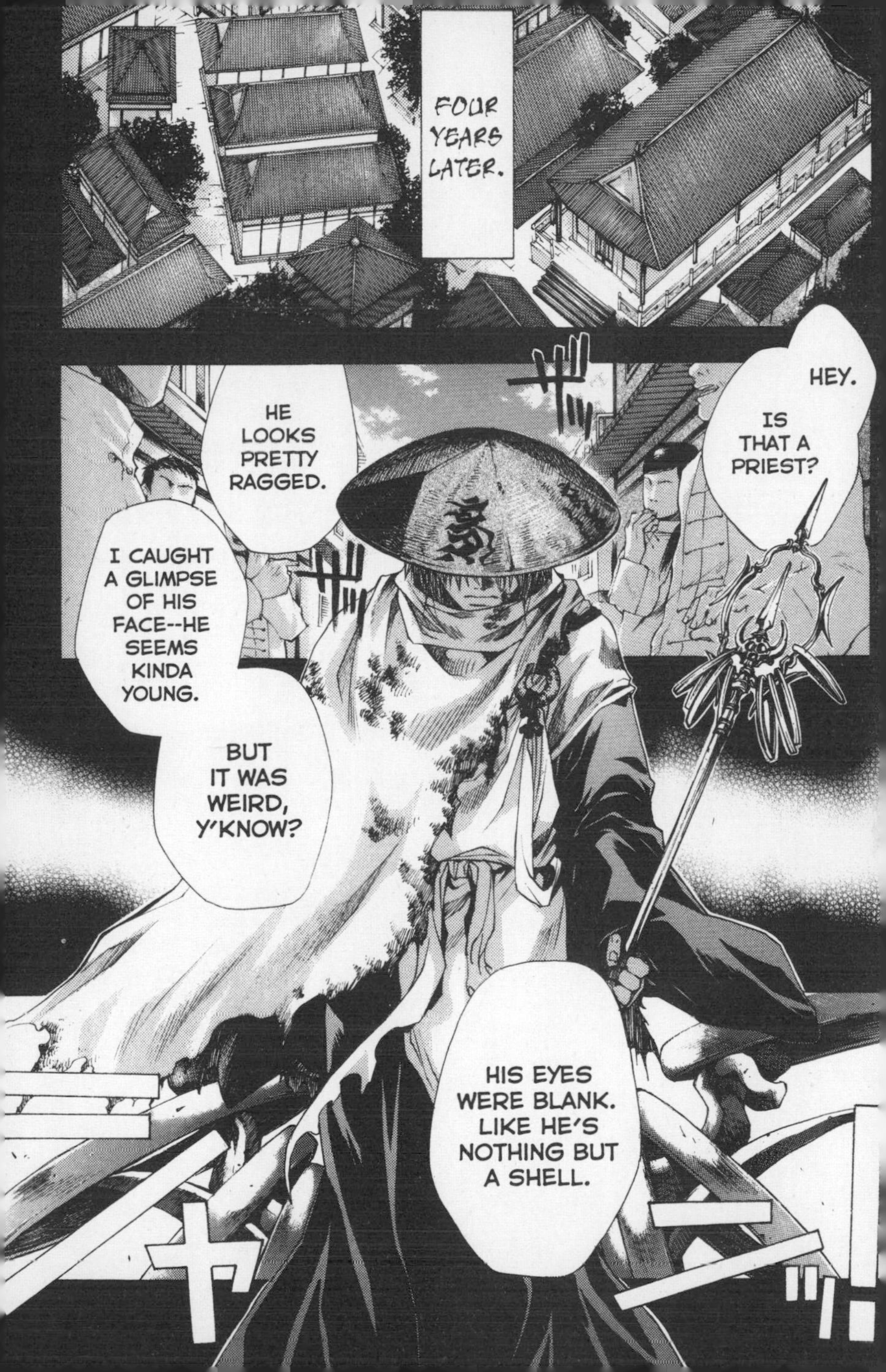
FOUR YEARS LATER.
HEY.
IS THAT A PRIEST?
HE LOOKS PRETTY RAGGED.
I CAUGHT A GLIMPSE OF HIS FACE--HE SEEMS KINDA YOUNG.
BUT IT WAS WEIRD, Y'KNOW?
HIS EYES WERE BLANK. LIKE HE'S NOTHING BUT A SHELL.

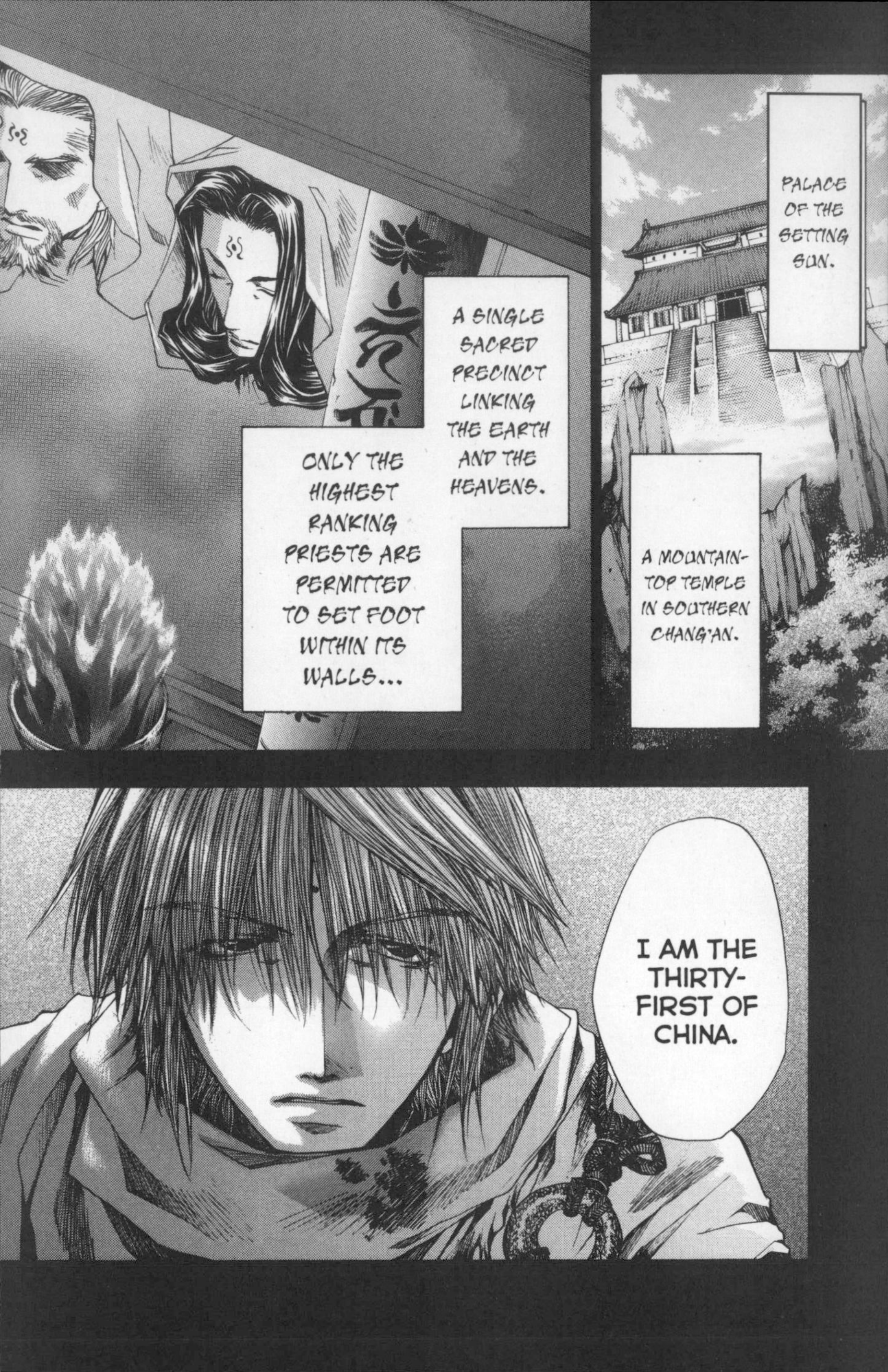
PALACE OF THE SETTING SUN.
A MOUNTAIN-TOP TEMPLE IN SOUTHERN CHANG'AN.
A SINGLE SACRED PRECINCT LINKING THE EARTH AND THE HEAVENS.
ONLY THE HIGHEST RANKING PRIESTS ARE PERMITTED TO SET FOOT WITHIN ITS WALLS...
I AM THE THIRTY-FIRST OF CHINA.

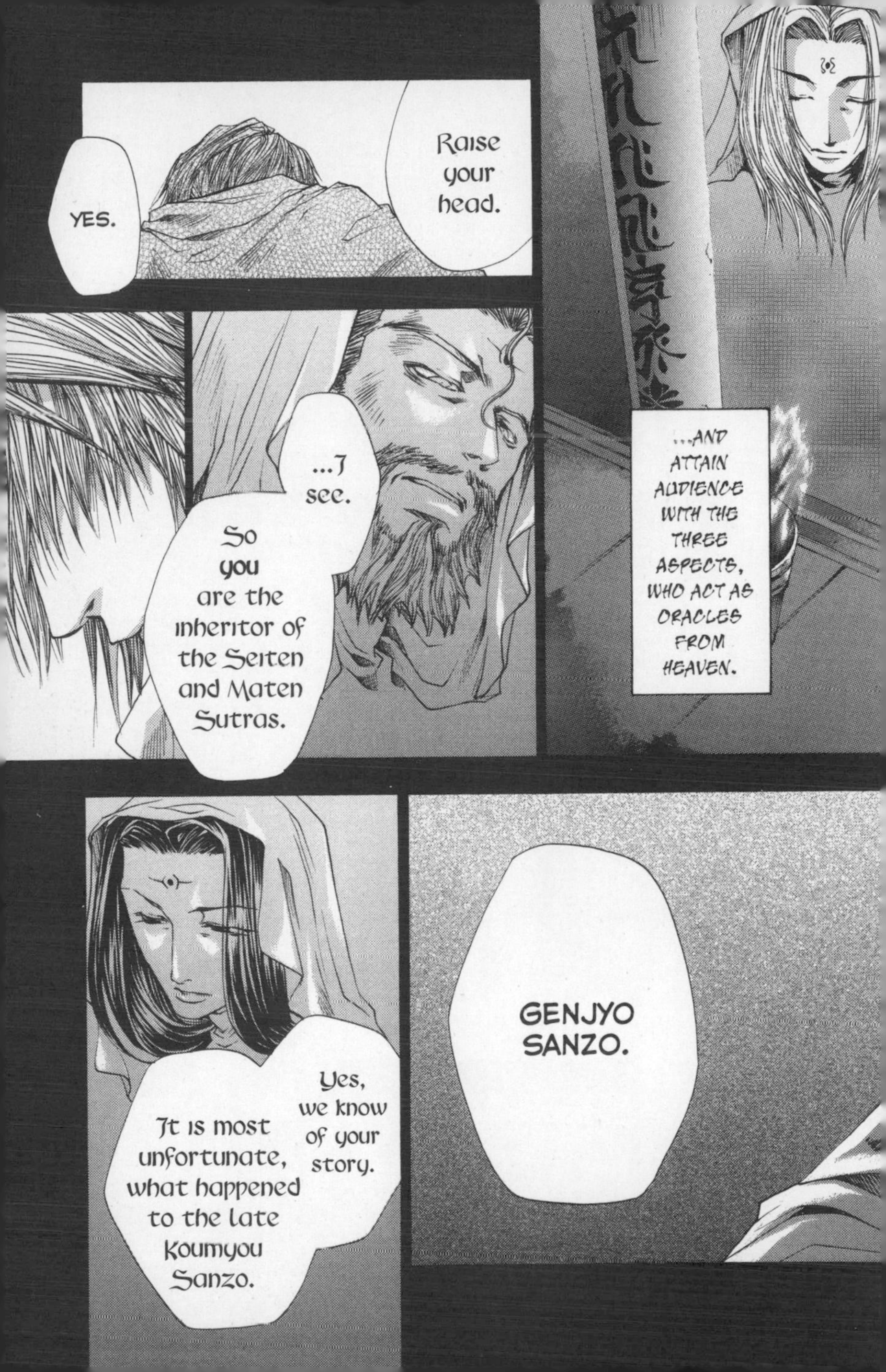
...AND ATTAIN AUDIENCE WITH THE THREE ASPECTS, WHO ACT AS ORACLES FROM HEAVEN.
Raise your head.
YES.
...I see.
So you are the inheritor of the Seiten and Maten Sutras.
GENJYO SANZO.
Yes, we know of your story.
It is most unfortunate, what happened to the late Koumyou Sanzo.

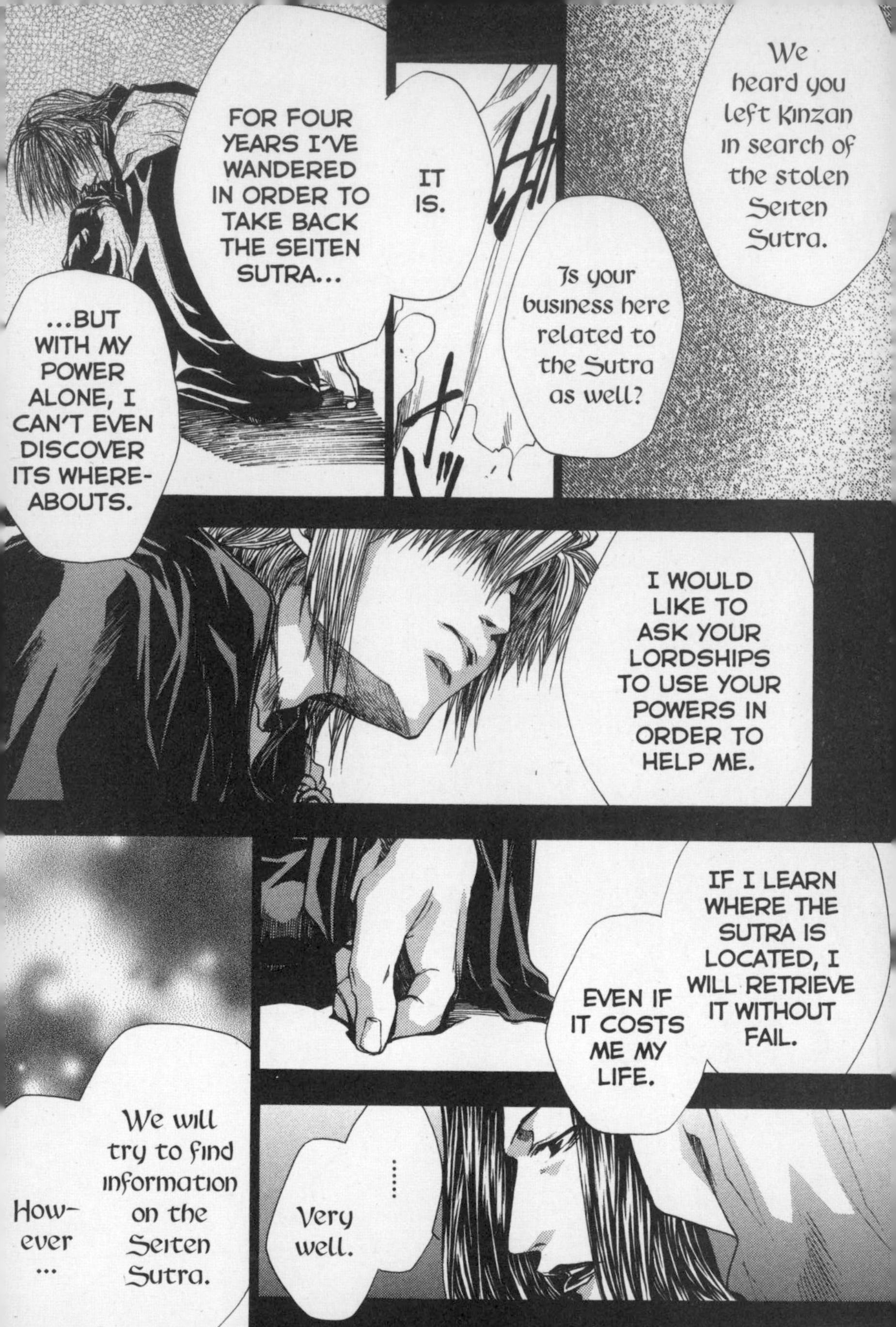
We heard you left Kinzan in search of the stolen Seiten Sutra.
Is your business here related to the Sutra as well?
IT IS.
FOR FOUR YEARS I'VE WANDERED IN ORDER TO TAKE BACK THE SEITEN SUTRA...
...BUT WITH MY POWER ALONE, I CAN'T EVEN DISCOVER ITS WHERE-ABOUTS.
I WOULD LIKE TO ASK YOUR LORDSHIPS TO USE YOUR POWERS IN ORDER TO HELP ME.
IF I LEARN WHERE THE SUTRA IS LOCATED, I WILL RETRIEVE IT WITHOUT FAIL.
EVEN IF IT COSTS ME MY LIFE.
......
Very well.
We will try to find information on the Seiten Sutra.
How-ever...

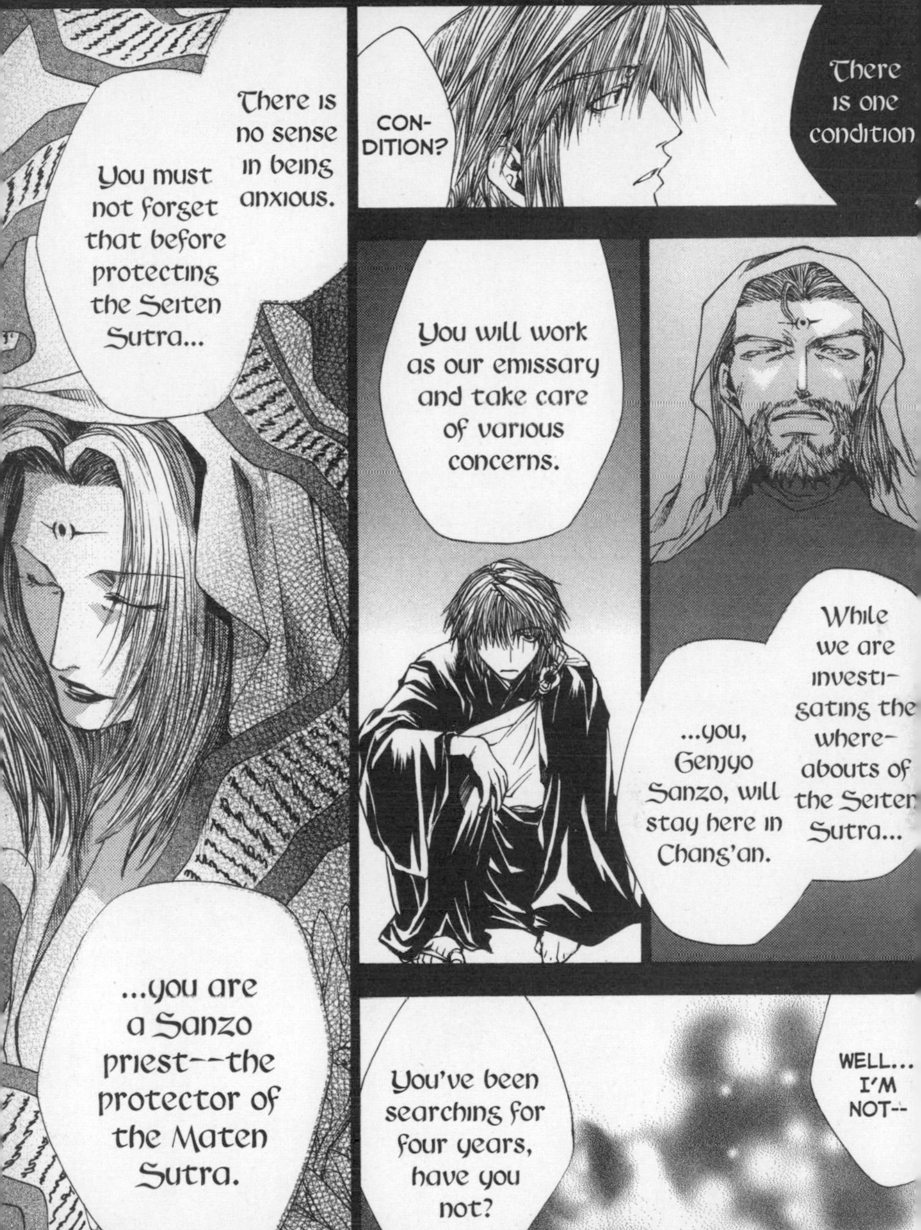
There is one condition
CON-DITION?
While we are investigating the whereabouts of the Seiten Sutra...
...you, Genjyo Sanzo, will stay here in Chang'an.
You will work as our emissary and take care of various concerns.
WELL... I'M NOT--
You've been searching for four years, have you not?
There is no sense in being anxious.
You must not forget that before protecting the Seiten Sutra...
...you are a Sanzo priest--the protector of the Maten Sutra.

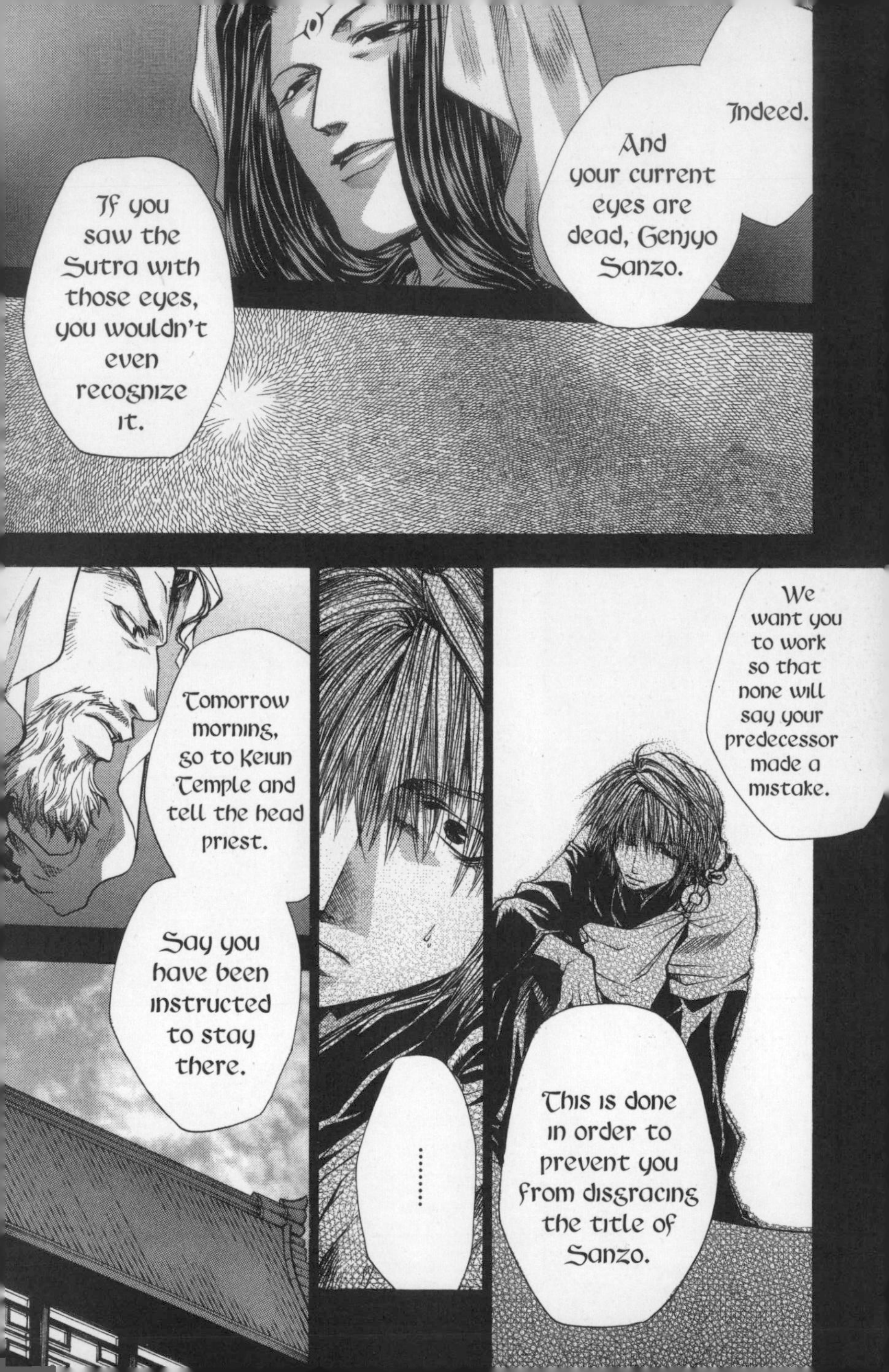
Indeed.
And your current eyes are dead, Genjyo Sanzo.
If you saw the Sutra with those eyes, you wouldn't even recognize it.
We want you to work so that none will say your predecessor made a mistake.
This is done in order to prevent you from disgracing the title of Sanzo.
……
Tomorrow morning, go to Keiun Temple and tell the head priest.
Say you have been instructed to stay there.

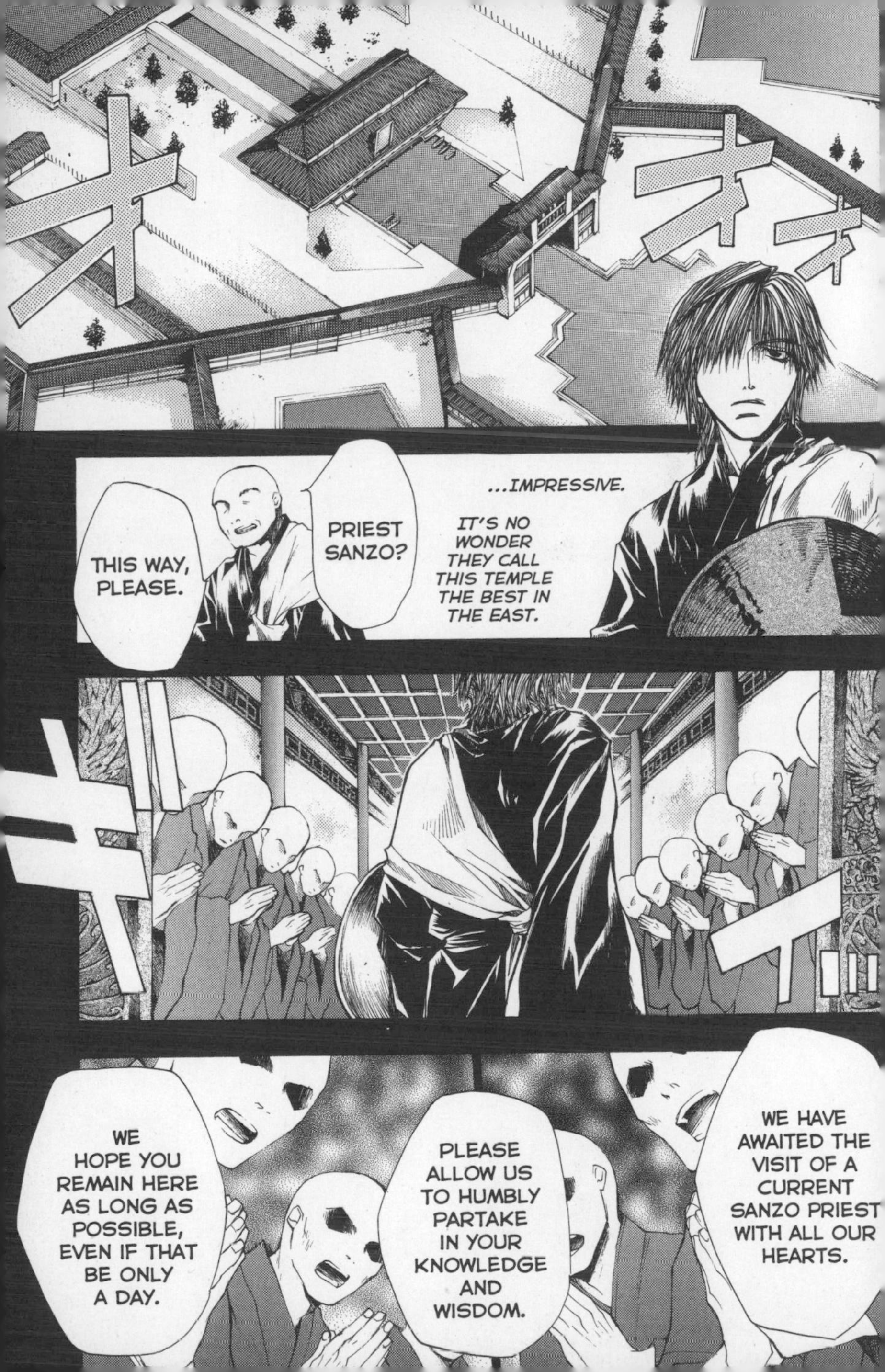
オォ
オ
...IMPRESSIVE.
IT'S NO WONDER THEY CALL THIS TEMPLE THE BEST IN THE EAST.
PRIEST SANZO?
THIS WAY, PLEASE.
WE HAVE AWAITED THE VISIT OF A CURRENT SANZO PRIEST WITH ALL OUR HEARTS.
PLEASE ALLOW US TO HUMBLY PARTAKE IN YOUR KNOWLEDGE AND WISDOM.
WE HOPE YOU REMAIN HERE AS LONG AS POSSIBLE, EVEN IF THAT BE ONLY A DAY.

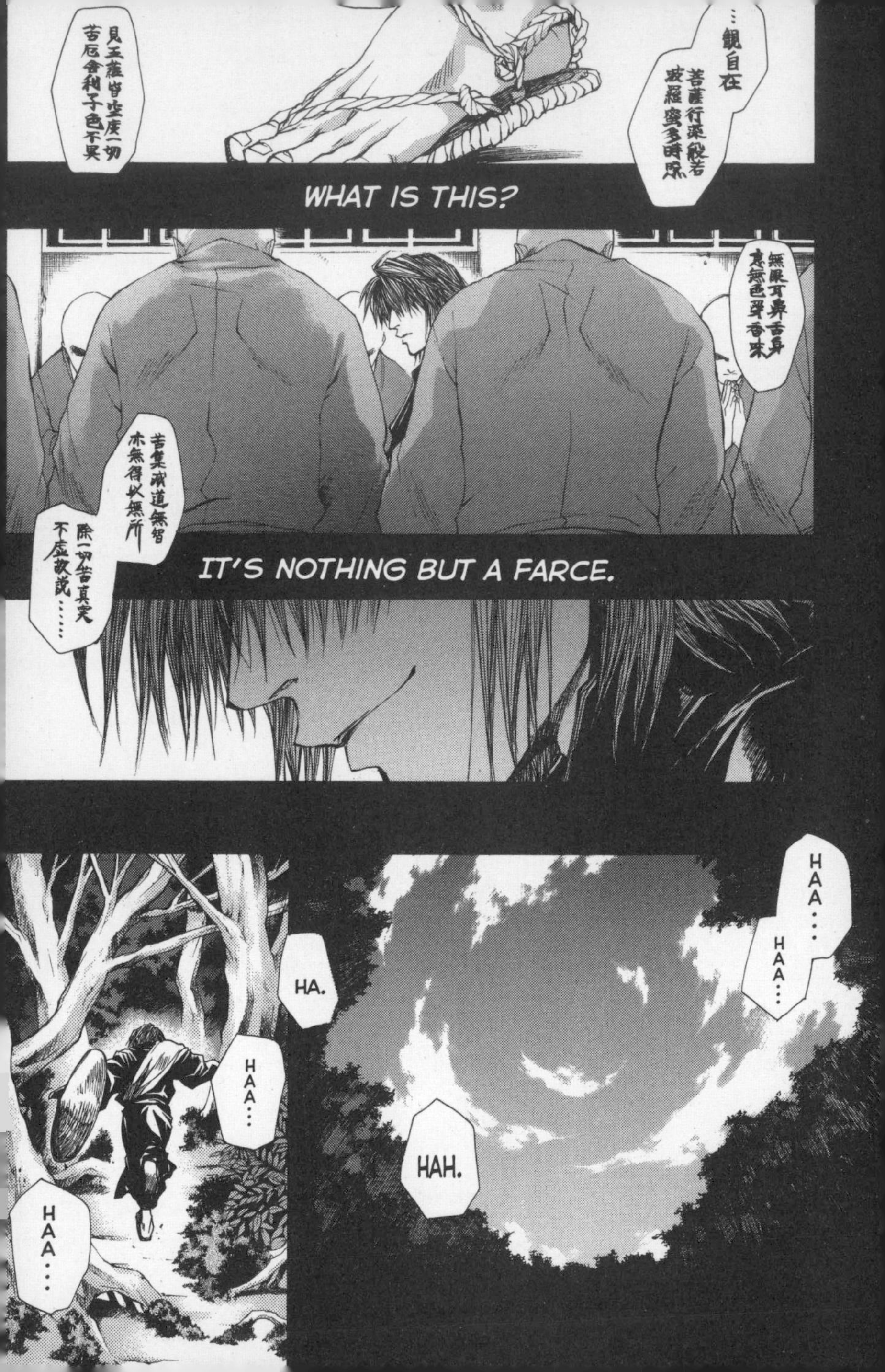
…觀自在菩薩行深般若波羅蜜多時照
見五蘊皆空度一切苦厄舍利子色不異
WHAT IS THIS?
無眼耳鼻舌身意無色聲香味
苦集滅道無智亦無得以無所
IT'S NOTHING BUT A FARCE.
除一切苦真實不虛故說……
HAA… HAA…
HAH.
HA.
HAA…
HAA…

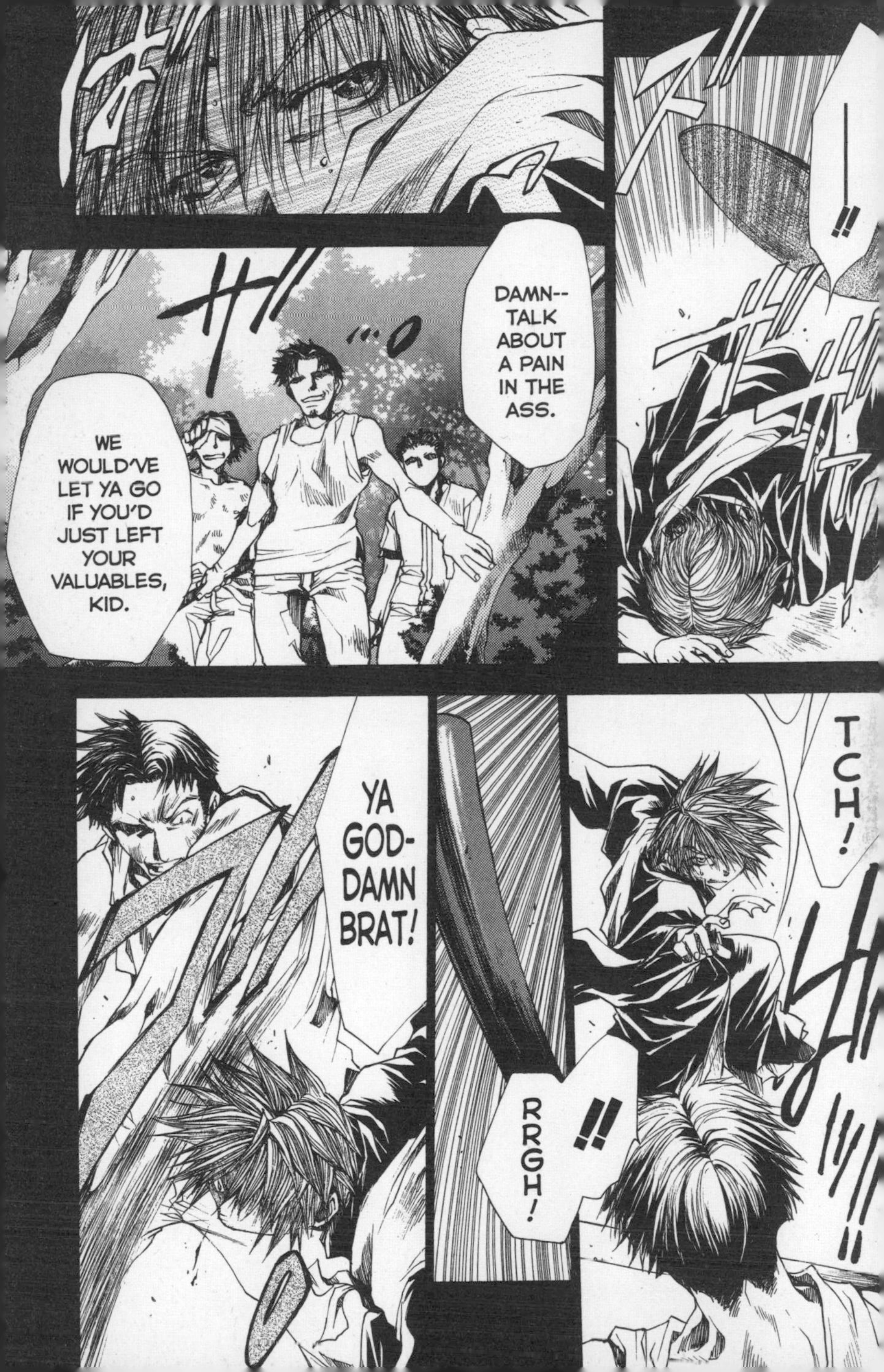
—!!
DAMN-- TALK ABOUT A PAIN IN THE ASS.
WE WOULD'VE LET YA GO IF YOU'D JUST LEFT YOUR VALUABLES, KID.
TCH!
!!
RRGH!
YA GOD-DAMN BRAT!

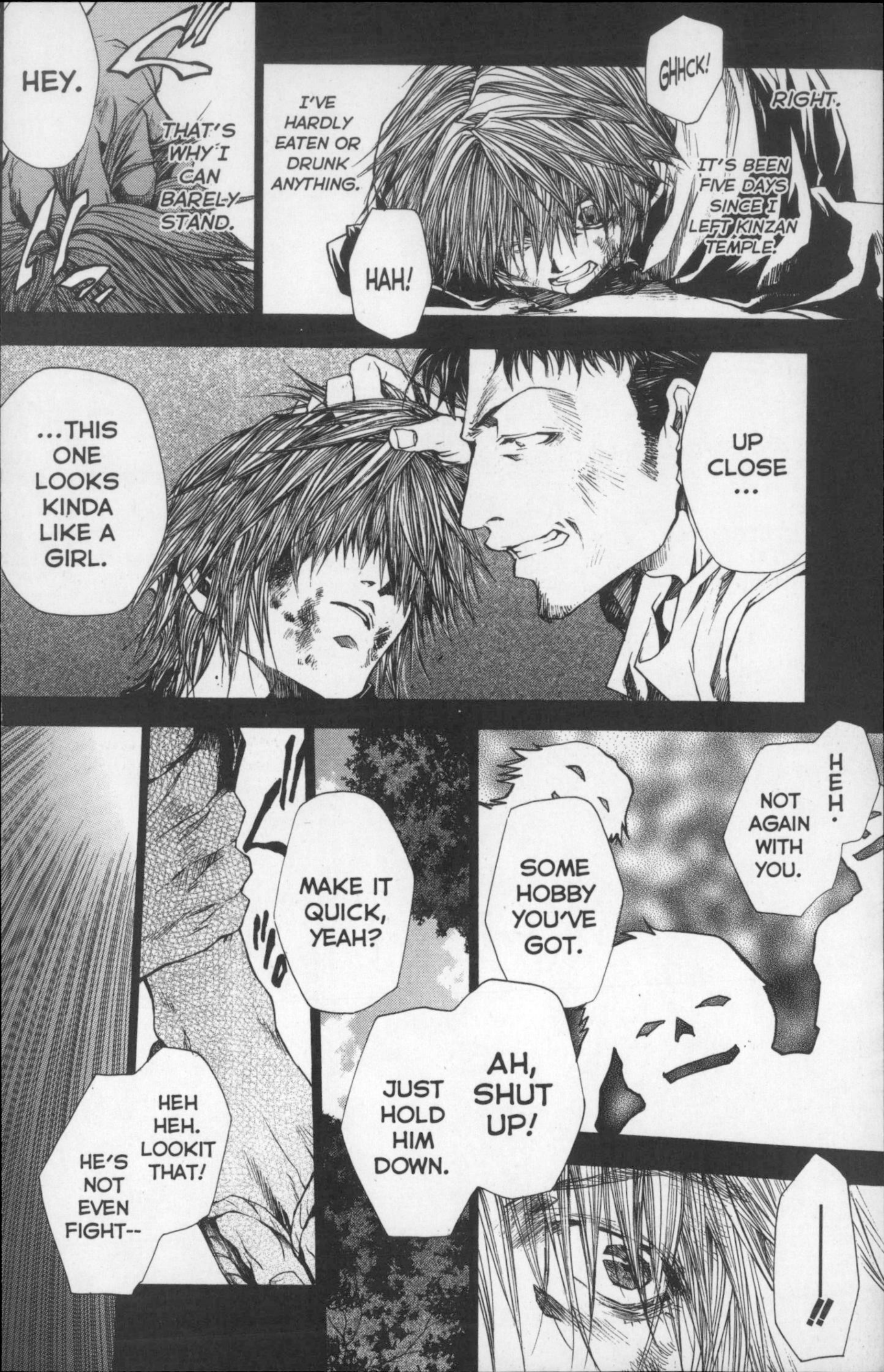
GHHCK!
RIGHT.
IT'S BEEN FIVE DAYS SINCE I LEFT KINZAN TEMPLE.
I'VE HARDLY EATEN OR DRUNK ANYTHING.
HAH!
HEY.
THAT'S WHY I CAN BARELY STAND.
UP CLOSE...
...THIS ONE LOOKS KINDA LIKE A GIRL.
HEH.
NOT AGAIN WITH YOU.
SOME HOBBY YOU'VE GOT.
AH, SHUT UP!
JUST HOLD HIM DOWN.
——!!
MAKE IT QUICK, YEAH?
HEH HEH. LOOKIT THAT!
HE'S NOT EVEN FIGHT--

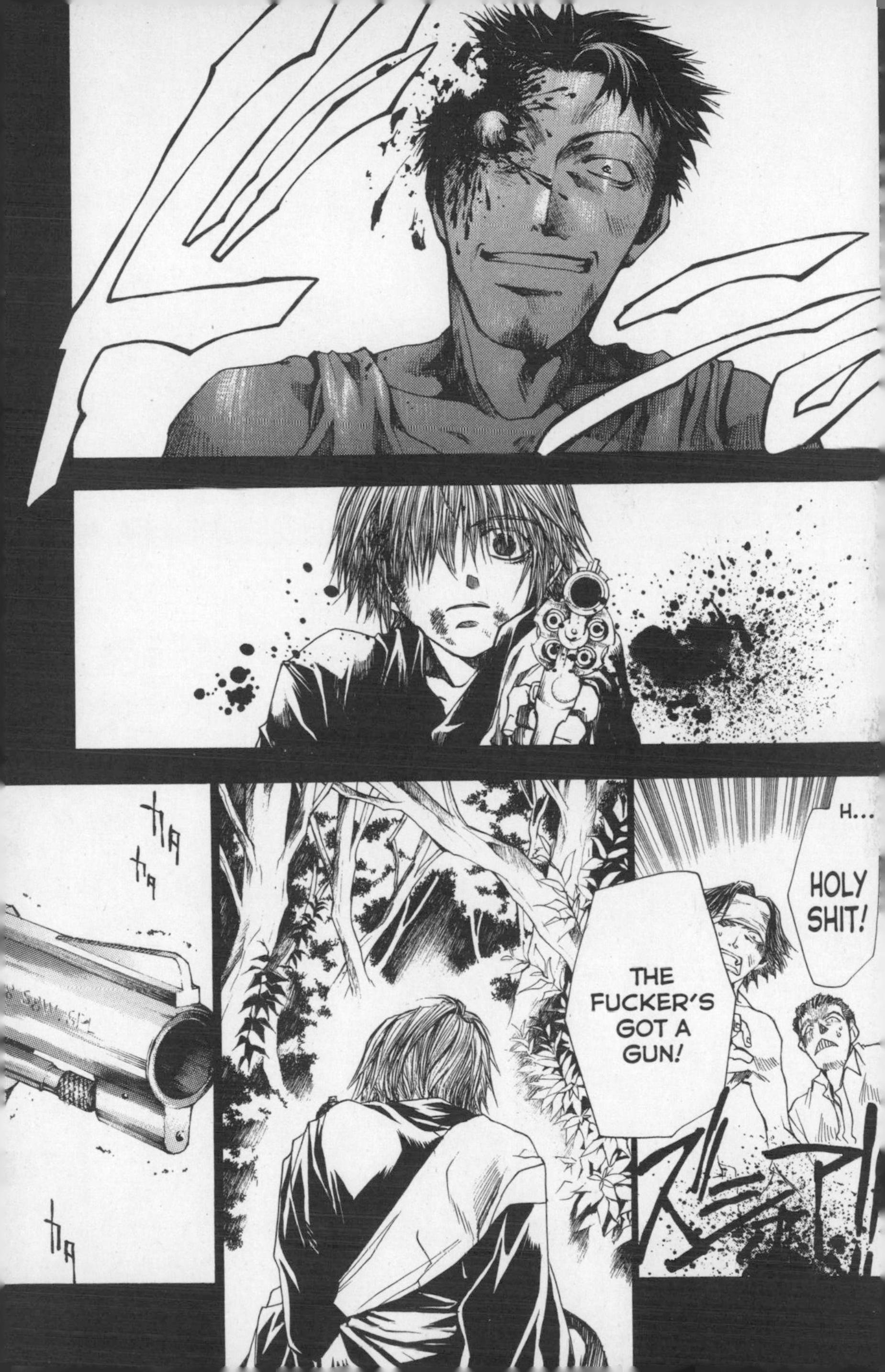
H...
HOLY SHIT!
THE FUCKER'S GOT A GUN!
HA
HA
HA

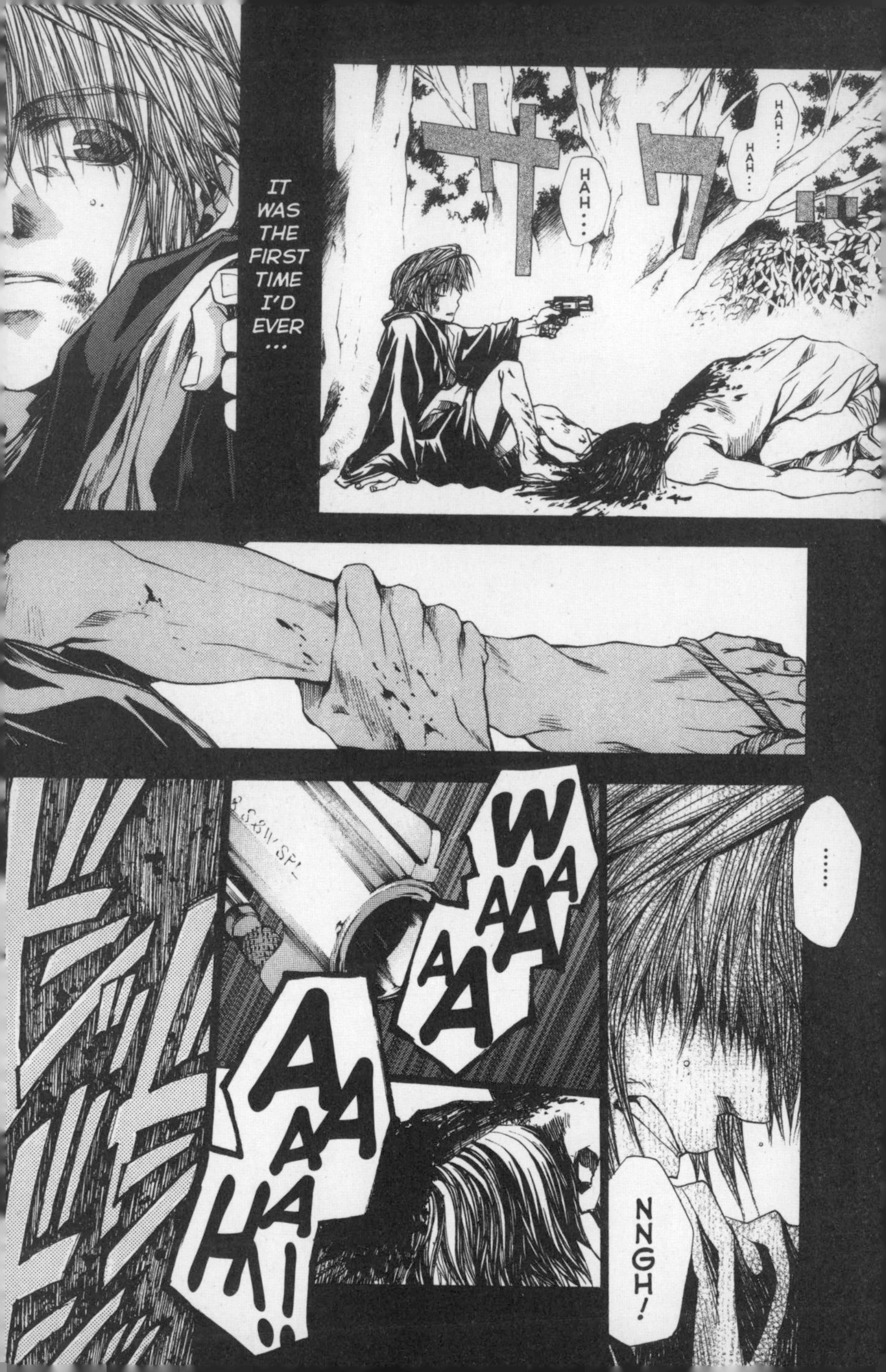
HAH...
HAH...
HAH...
IT WAS THE FIRST TIME I'D EVER...
......
NNGH!
WAAAAAA
AAAAHAH!!

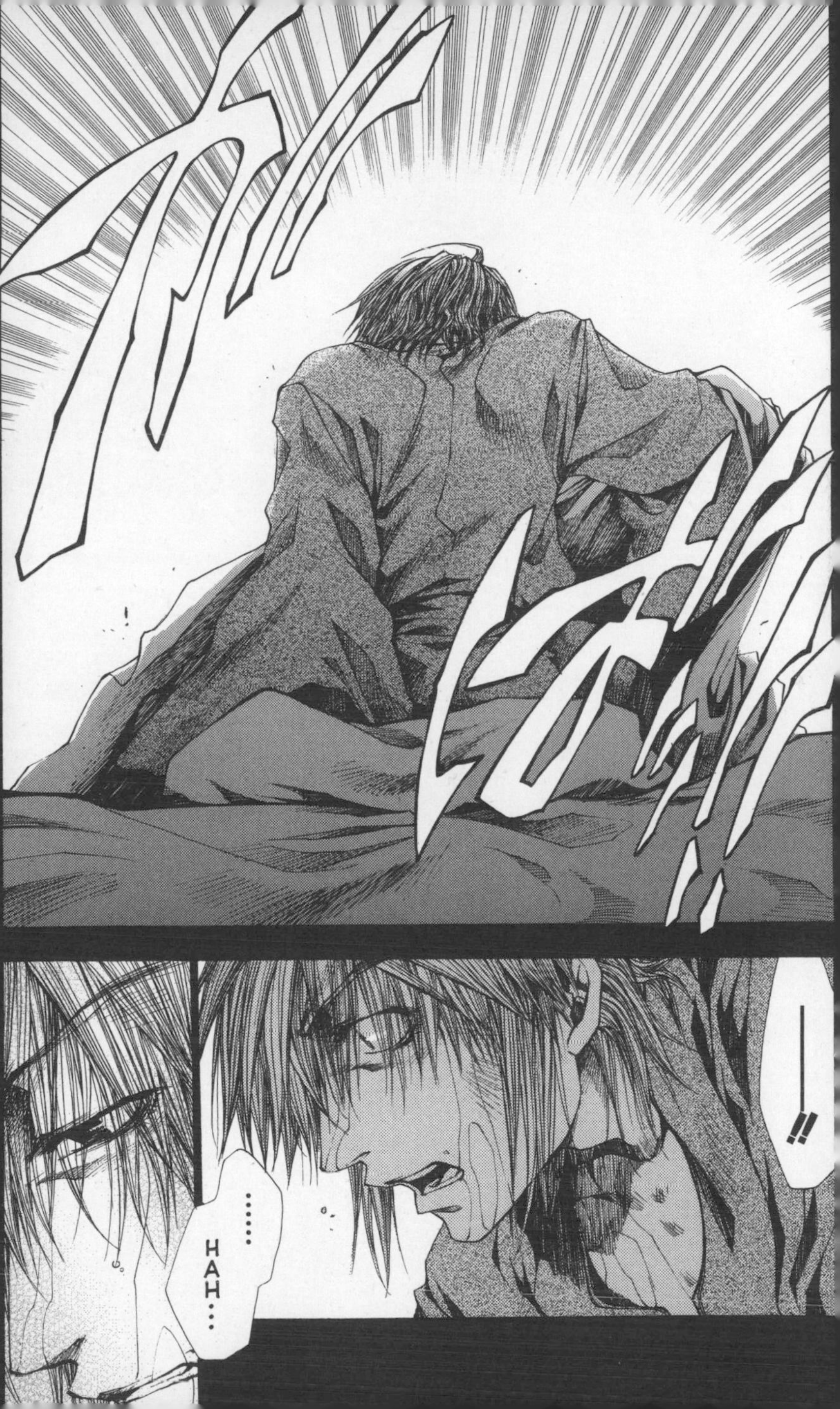
——!!
......
HAH...

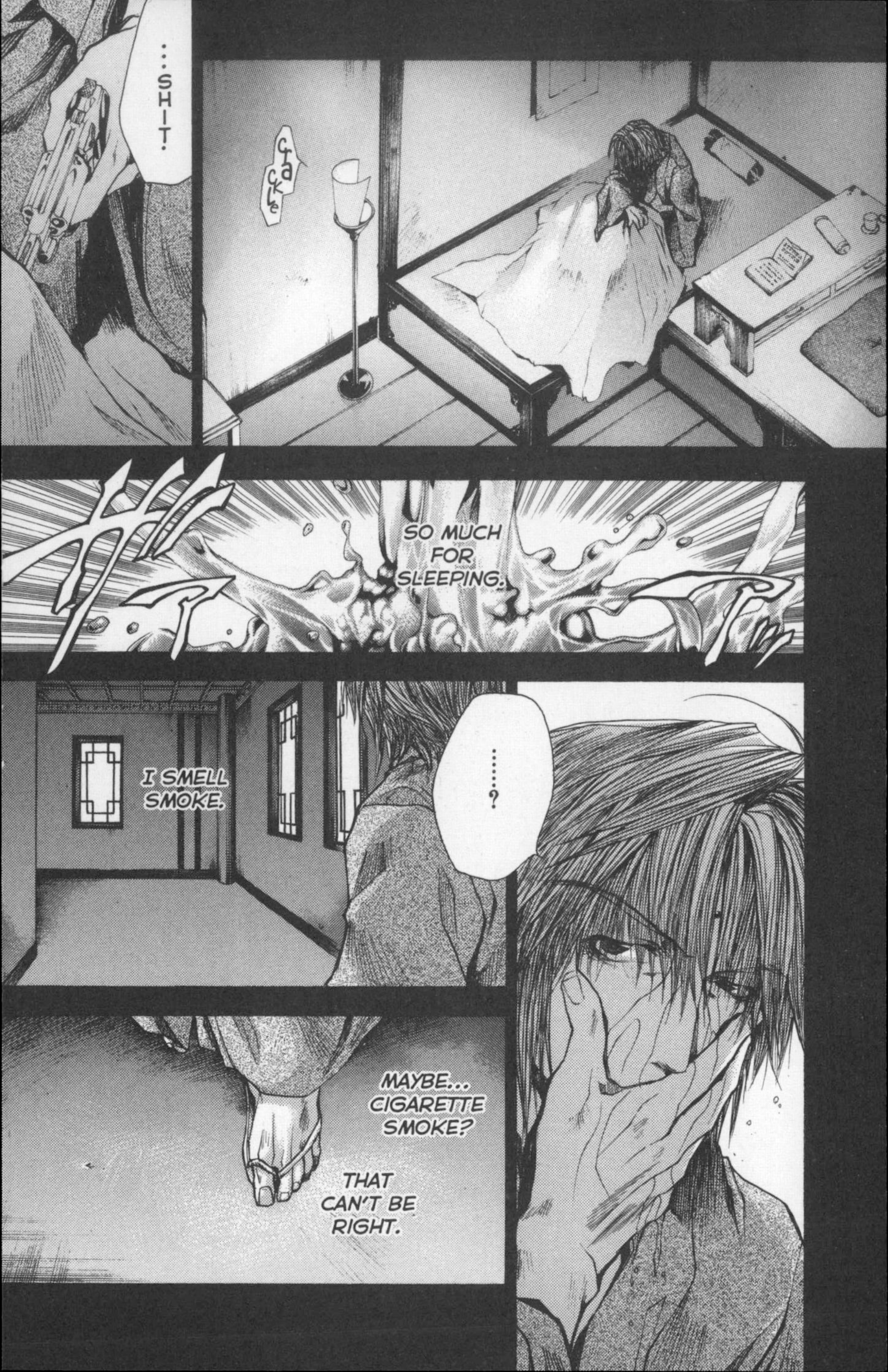

Crackle
...SHIT.
SO MUCH FOR SLEEPING.
......?
I SMELL SMOKE.
MAYBE... CIGARETTE SMOKE?
THAT CAN'T BE RIGHT.

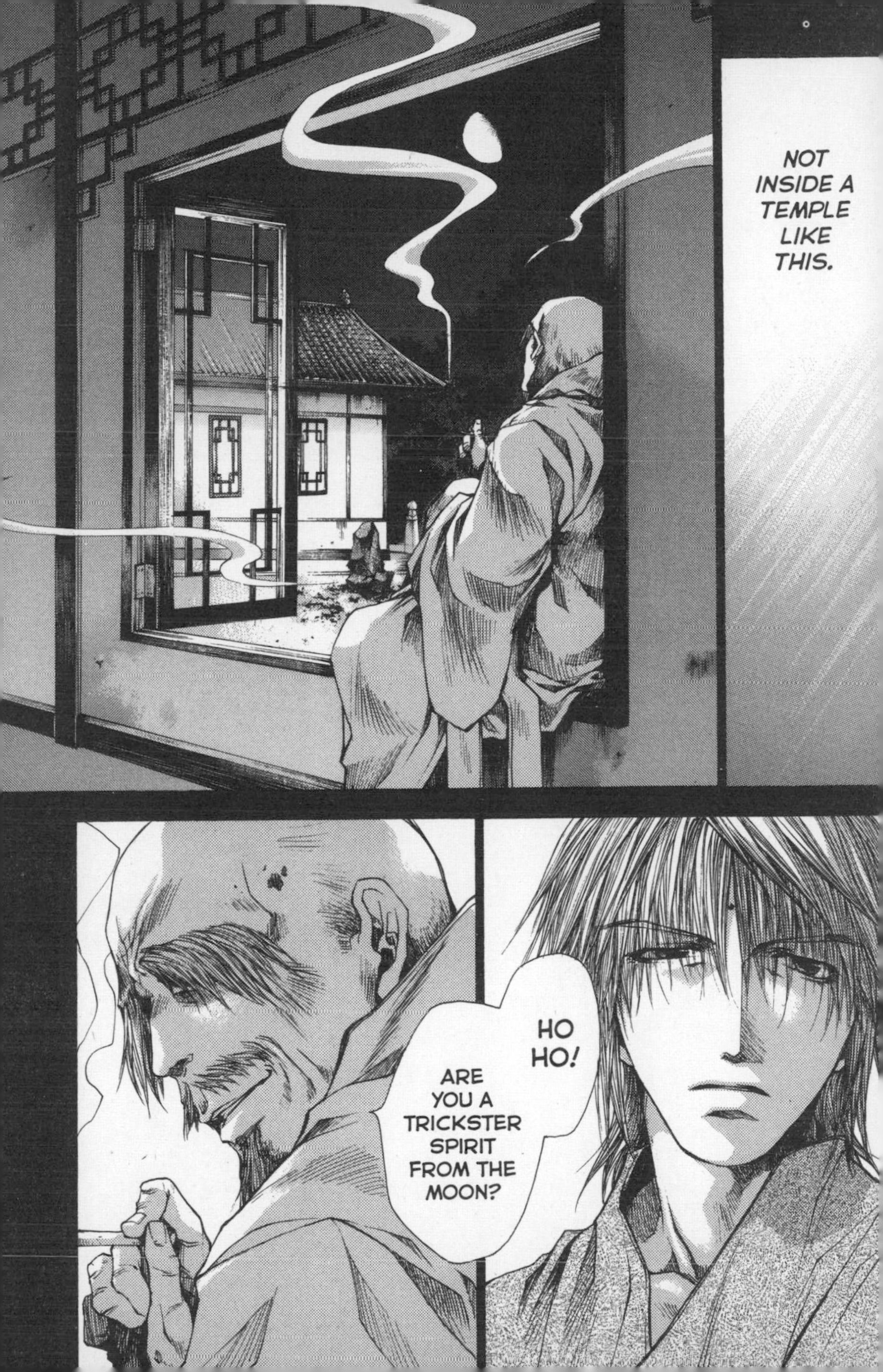
NOT INSIDE A TEMPLE LIKE THIS.
HO HO!
ARE YOU A TRICKSTER SPIRIT FROM THE MOON?

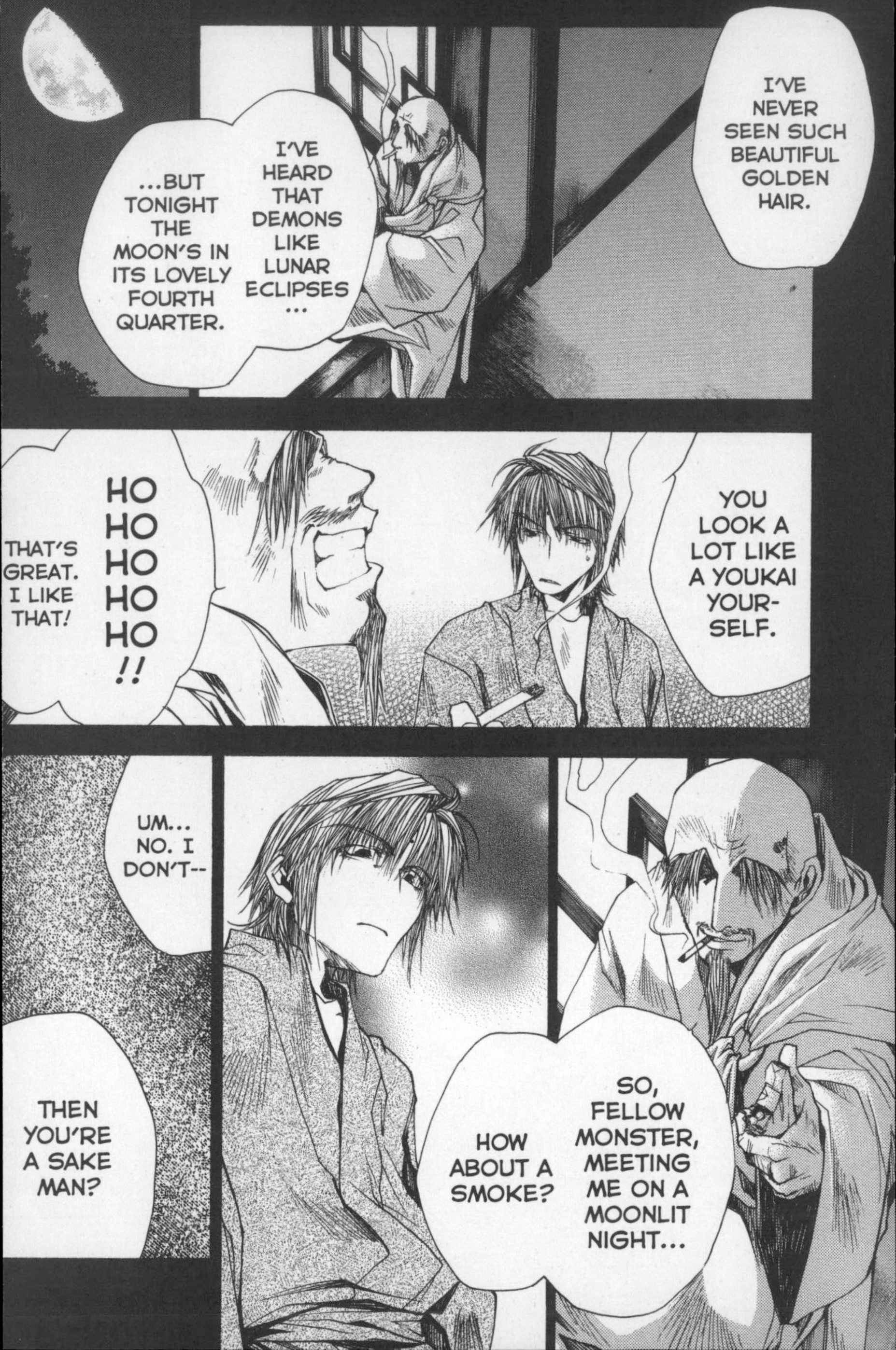
I'VE NEVER SEEN SUCH BEAUTIFUL GOLDEN HAIR.
I'VE HEARD THAT DEMONS LIKE LUNAR ECLIPSES...
...BUT TONIGHT THE MOON'S IN ITS LOVELY FOURTH QUARTER.
YOU LOOK A LOT LIKE A YOUKAI YOUR-SELF.
HO HO HO HO HO!!
THAT'S GREAT. I LIKE THAT!
SO, FELLOW MONSTER, MEETING ME ON A MOONLIT NIGHT...
HOW ABOUT A SMOKE?
UM... NO. I DON'T--
THEN YOU'RE A SAKE MAN?

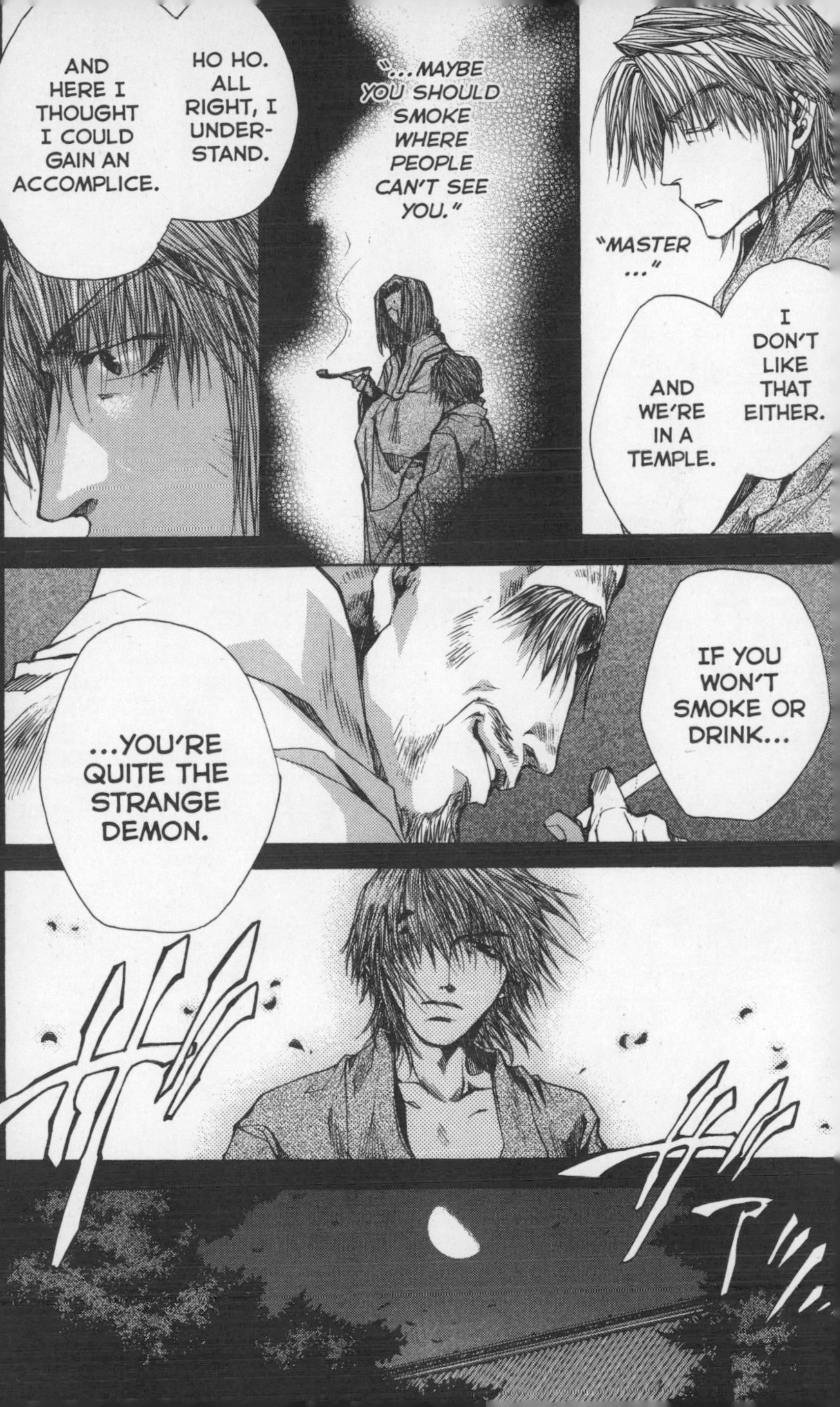
"MASTER ..."
I DON'T LIKE THAT EITHER.
AND WE'RE IN A TEMPLE.
"...MAYBE YOU SHOULD SMOKE WHERE PEOPLE CAN'T SEE YOU."
HO HO. ALL RIGHT, I UNDER-STAND.
AND HERE I THOUGHT I COULD GAIN AN ACCOMPLICE.
IF YOU WON'T SMOKE OR DRINK...
...YOU'RE QUITE THE STRANGE DEMON.

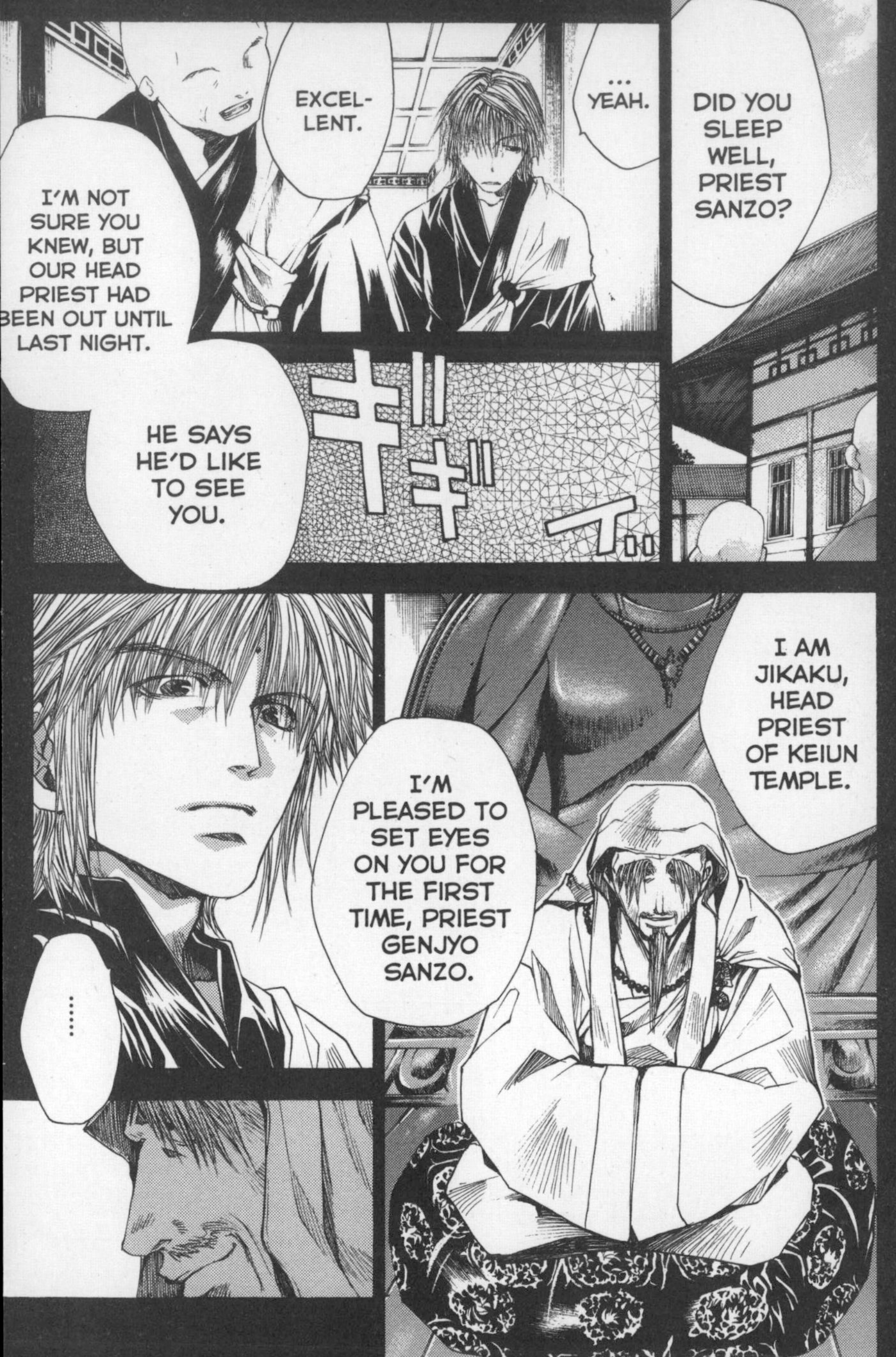
DID YOU SLEEP WELL, PRIEST SANZO?
... YEAH.
EXCEL-LENT.
I'M NOT SURE YOU KNEW, BUT OUR HEAD PRIEST HAD BEEN OUT UNTIL LAST NIGHT.
HE SAYS HE'D LIKE TO SEE YOU.
ギギイ..
I AM JIKAKU, HEAD PRIEST OF KEIUN TEMPLE.
I'M PLEASED TO SET EYES ON YOU FOR THE FIRST TIME, PRIEST GENJYO SANZO.
......

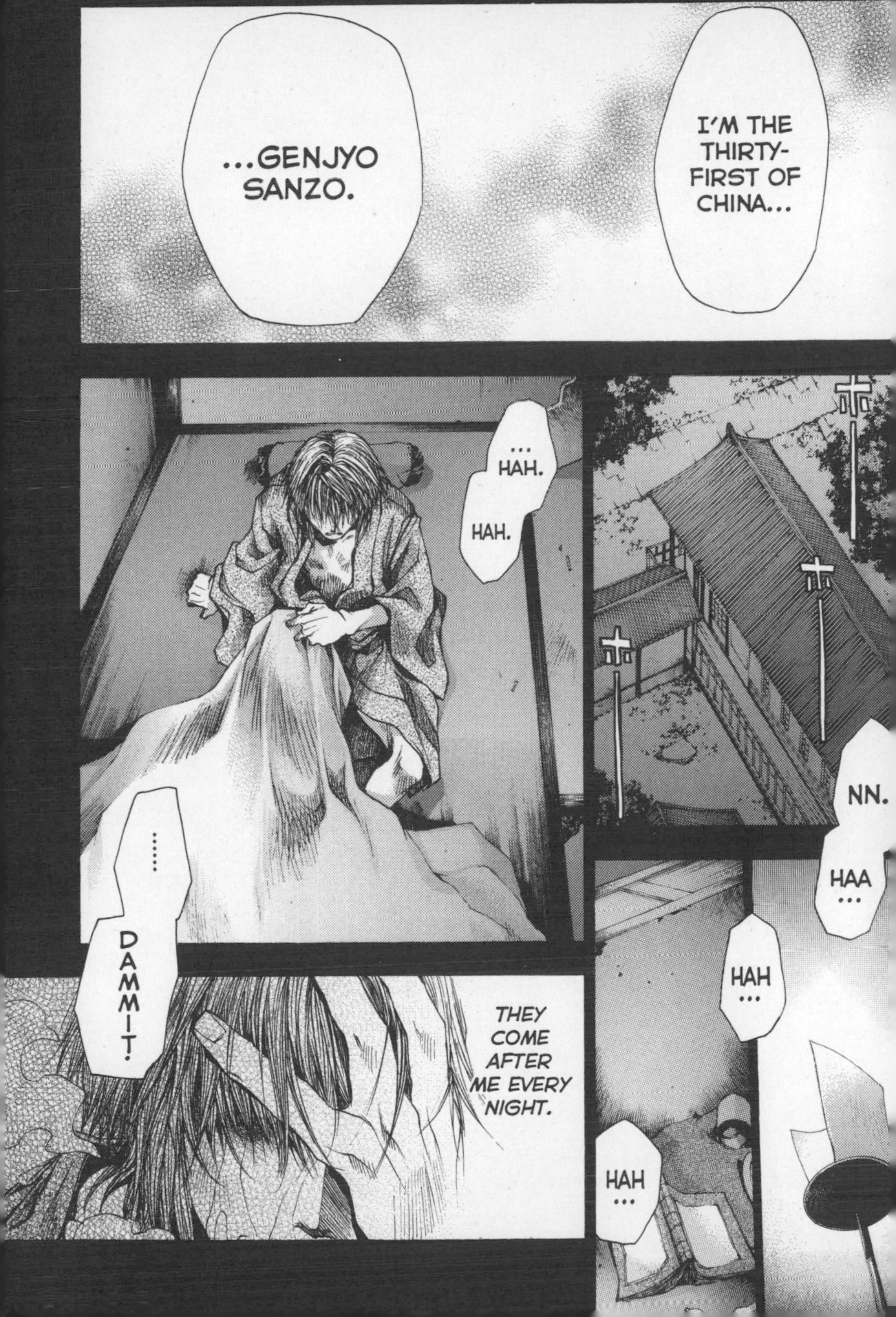
I'M THE THIRTY-FIRST OF CHINA...
...GENJYO SANZO.
NN.
HAA...
HAH...
HAH...
...HAH.
HAH.
......
DAMMIT!
THEY COME AFTER ME EVERY NIGHT.

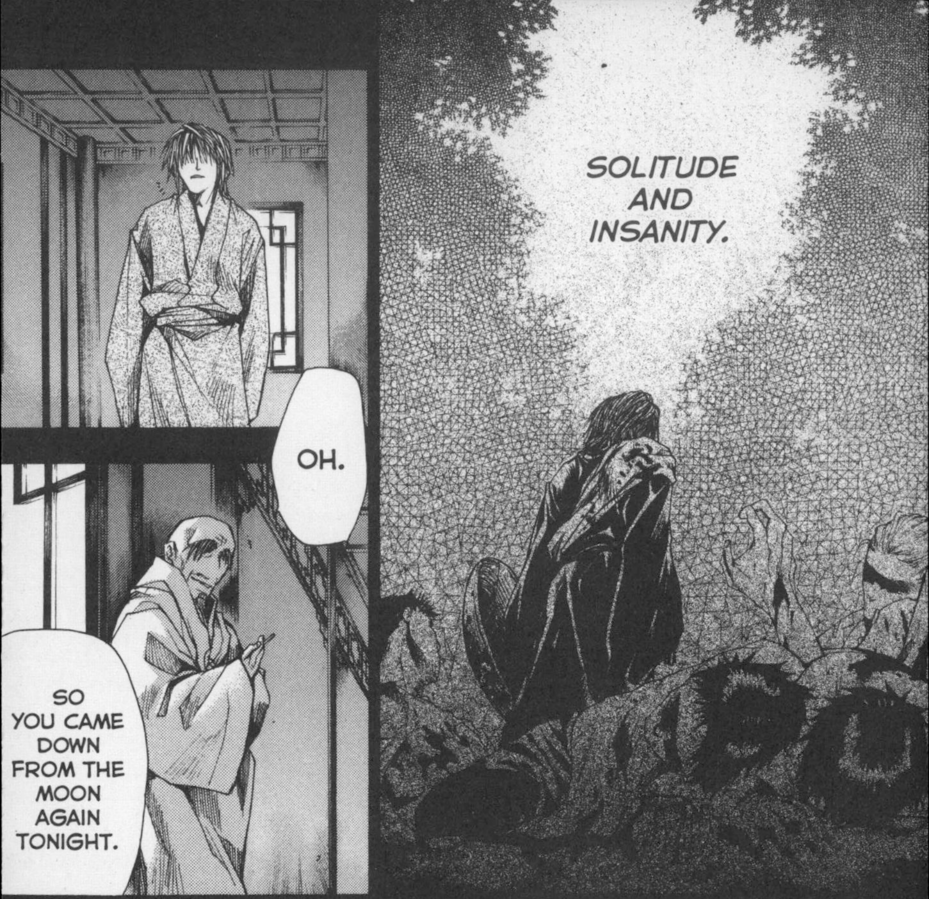
SOLITUDE AND INSANITY.
OH.
SO YOU CAME DOWN FROM THE MOON AGAIN TONIGHT.

*A mononoke is a vengeful spirit; a tanuki is a raccoon-like animal often thought to trick people.

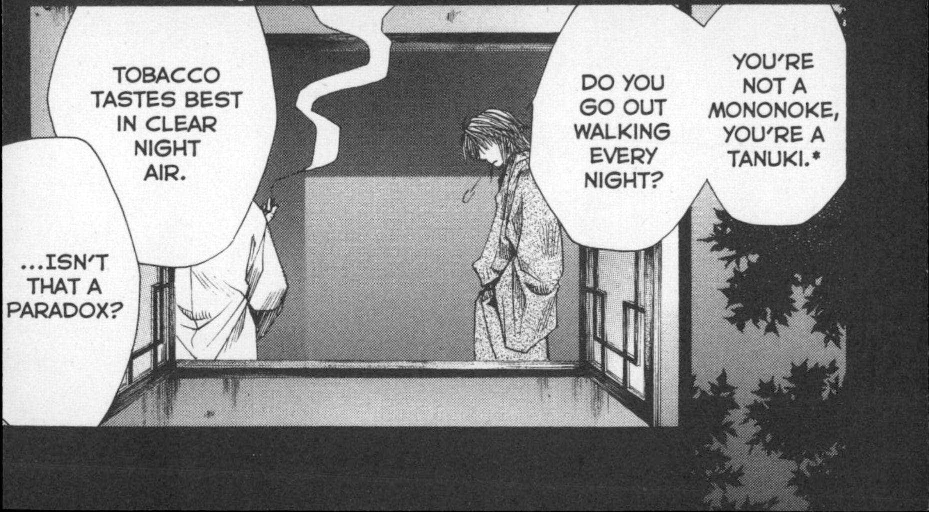
YOU'RE NOT A MONONOKE, YOU'RE A TANUKI.*
DO YOU GO OUT WALKING EVERY NIGHT?
TOBACCO TASTES BEST IN CLEAR NIGHT AIR.
...ISN'T THAT A PARADOX?

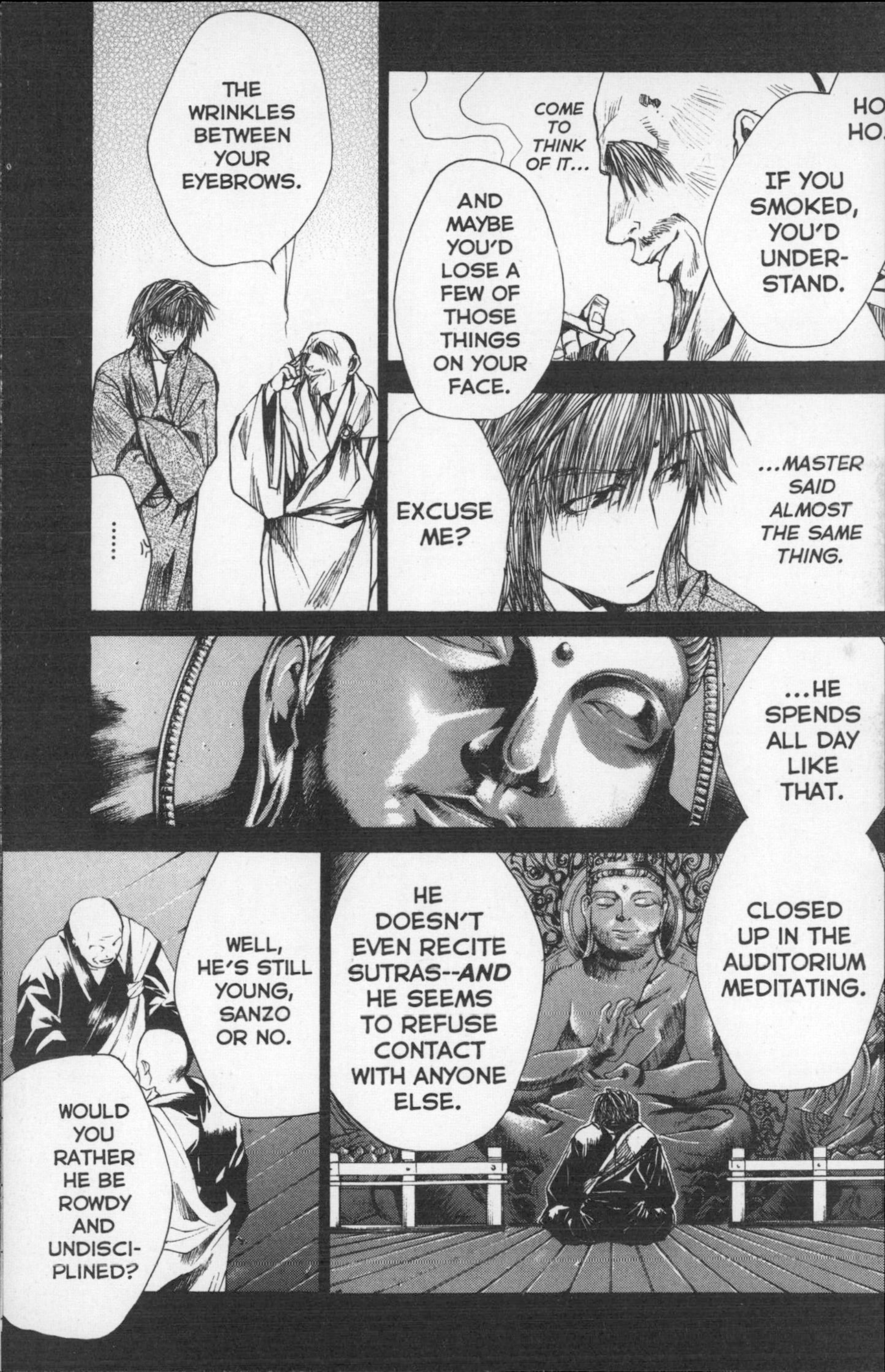
HO HO.
IF YOU SMOKED, YOU'D UNDERSTAND.
COME TO THINK OF IT...
AND MAYBE YOU'D LOSE A FEW OF THOSE THINGS ON YOUR FACE.
...MASTER SAID ALMOST THE SAME THING.
EXCUSE ME?
THE WRINKLES BETWEEN YOUR EYEBROWS.
......
...HE SPENDS ALL DAY LIKE THAT.
CLOSED UP IN THE AUDITORIUM MEDITATING.
HE DOESN'T EVEN RECITE SUTRAS--*AND* HE SEEMS TO REFUSE CONTACT WITH ANYONE ELSE.
WELL, HE'S STILL YOUNG, SANZO OR NO.
WOULD YOU RATHER HE BE ROWDY AND UNDISCIPLINED?

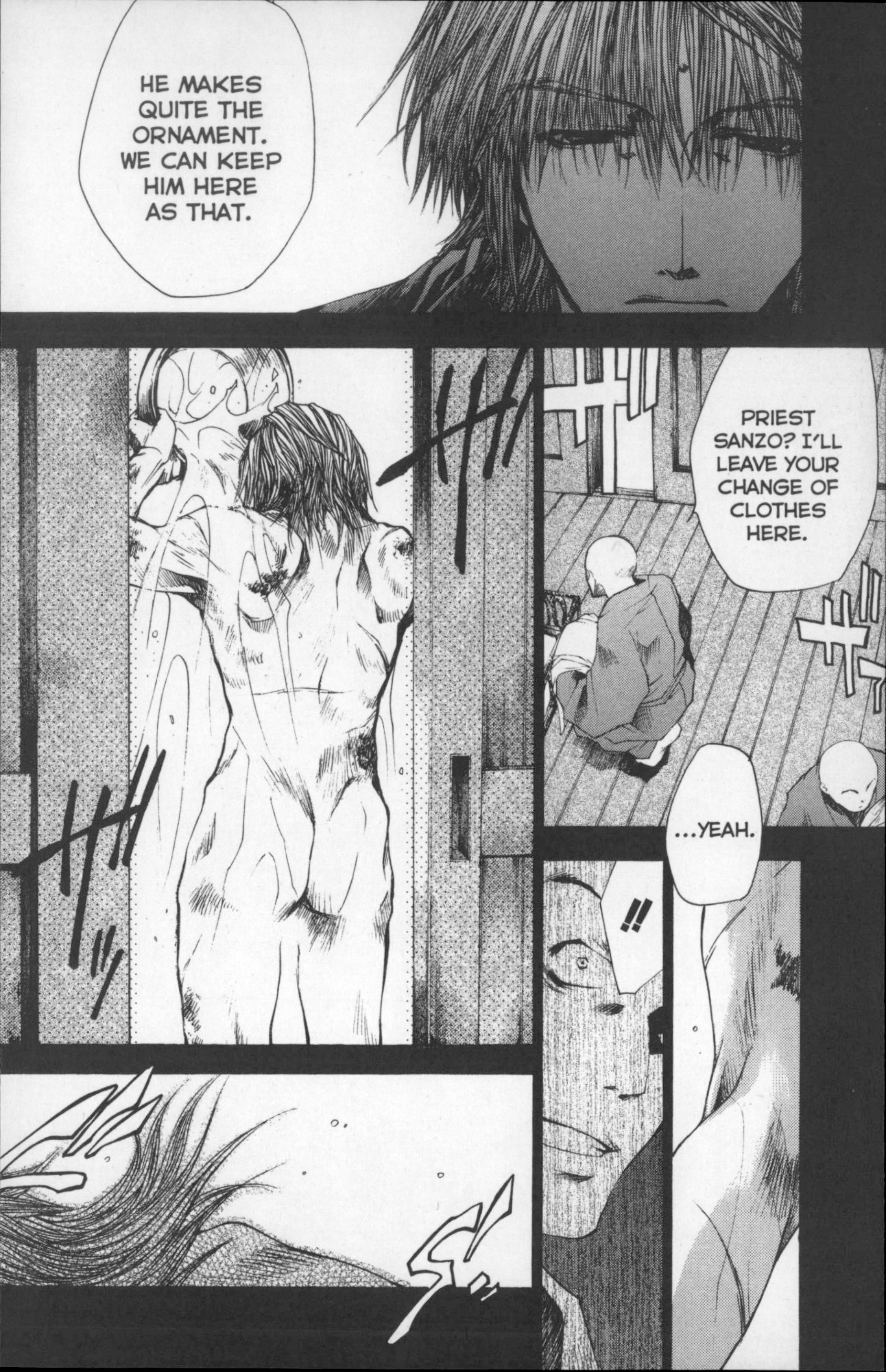
HE MAKES QUITE THE ORNAMENT. WE CAN KEEP HIM HERE AS THAT.
PRIEST SANZO? I'LL LEAVE YOUR CHANGE OF CLOTHES HERE.
...YEAH.
!!

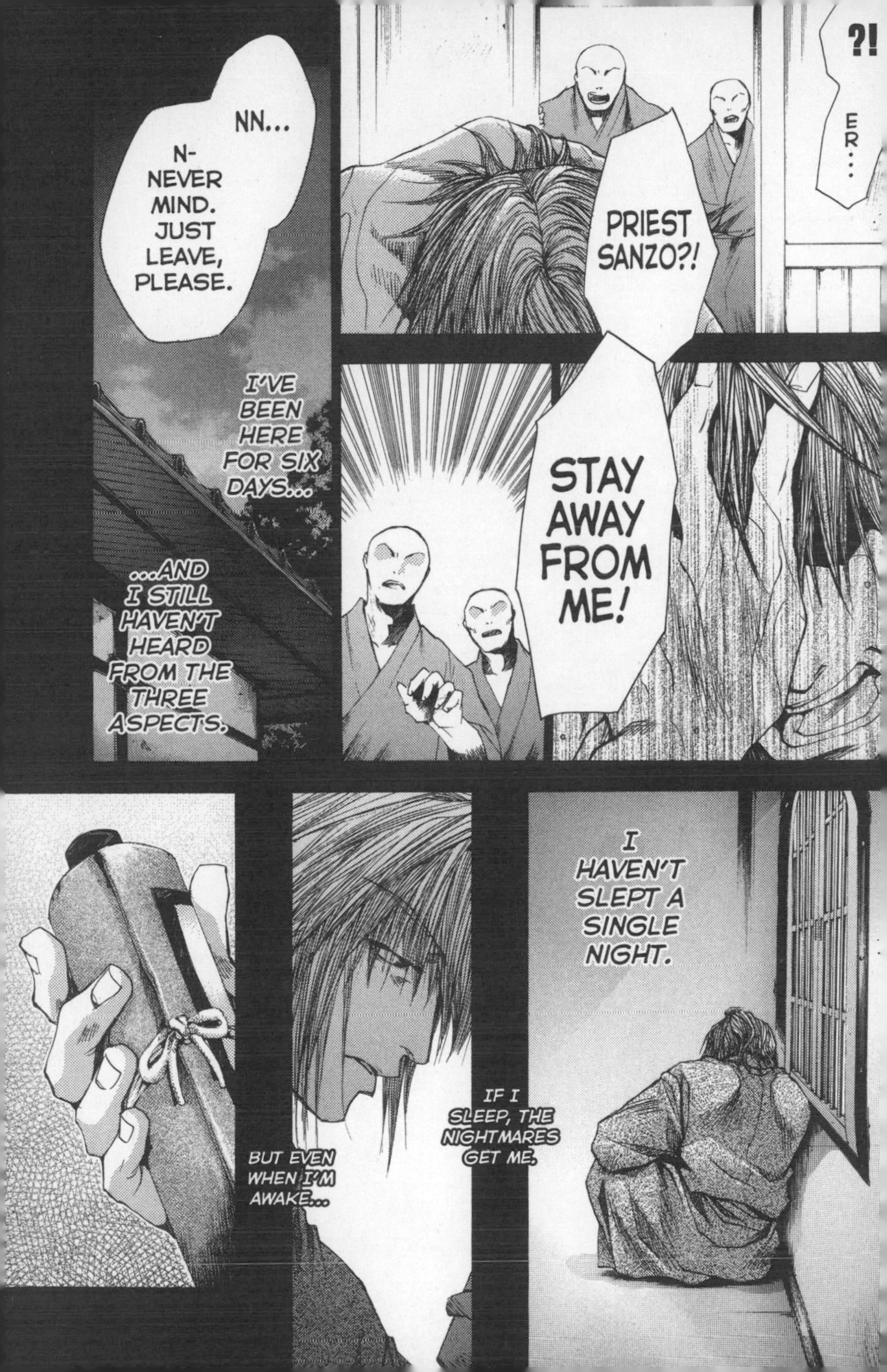
?!
ER...
PRIEST SANZO?!
STAY AWAY FROM ME!
NN...
N-NEVER MIND. JUST LEAVE, PLEASE.
I'VE BEEN HERE FOR SIX DAYS...
...AND I STILL HAVEN'T HEARD FROM THE THREE ASPECTS.
I HAVEN'T SLEPT A SINGLE NIGHT.
IF I SLEEP, THE NIGHTMARES GET ME.
BUT EVEN WHEN I'M AWAKE...

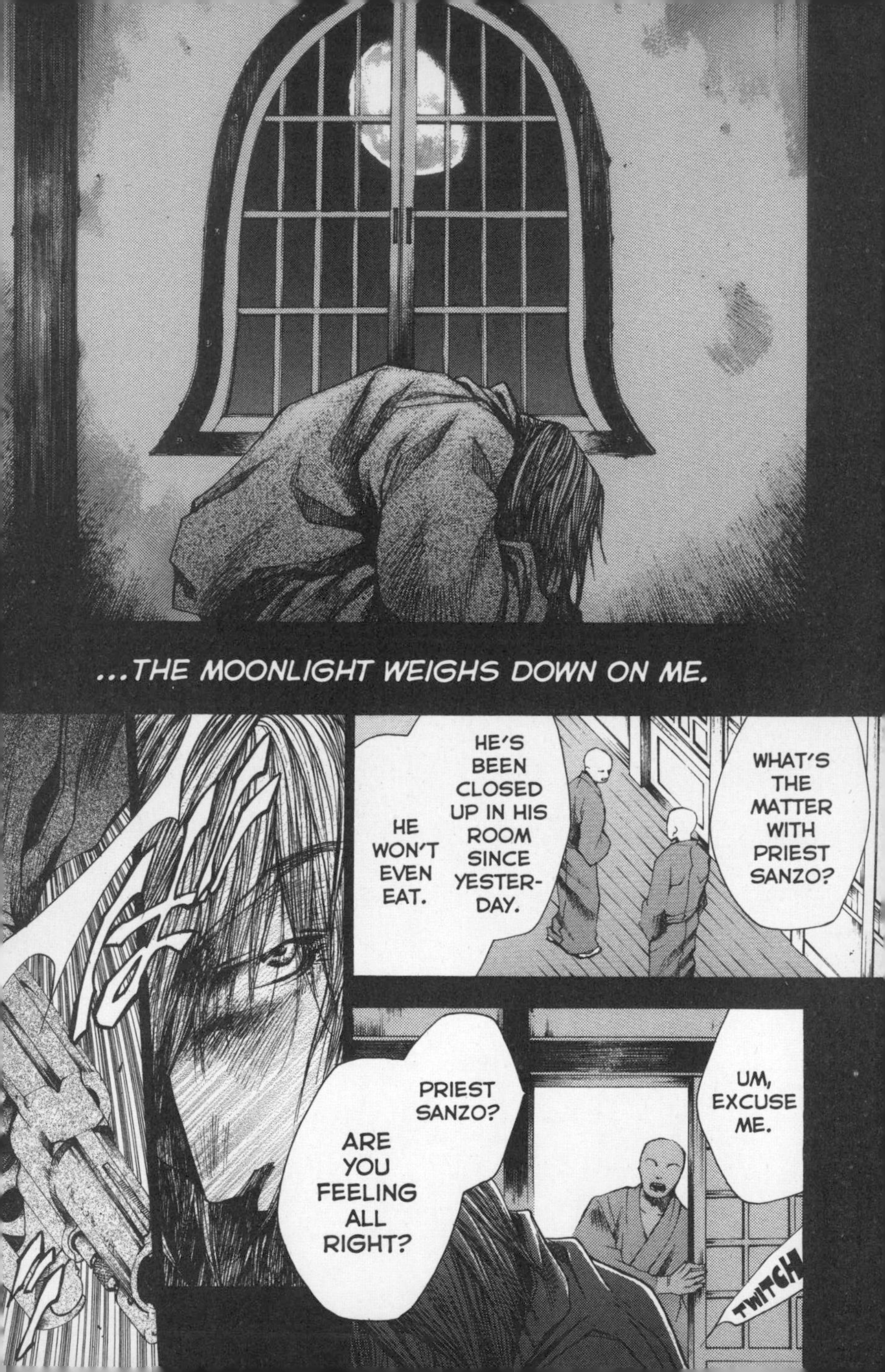
...THE MOONLIGHT WEIGHS DOWN ON ME.
WHAT'S THE MATTER WITH PRIEST SANZO?
HE'S BEEN CLOSED UP IN HIS ROOM SINCE YESTER-DAY.
HE WON'T EVEN EAT.
UM, EXCUSE ME.
PRIEST SANZO?
ARE YOU FEELING ALL RIGHT?
TWITCH

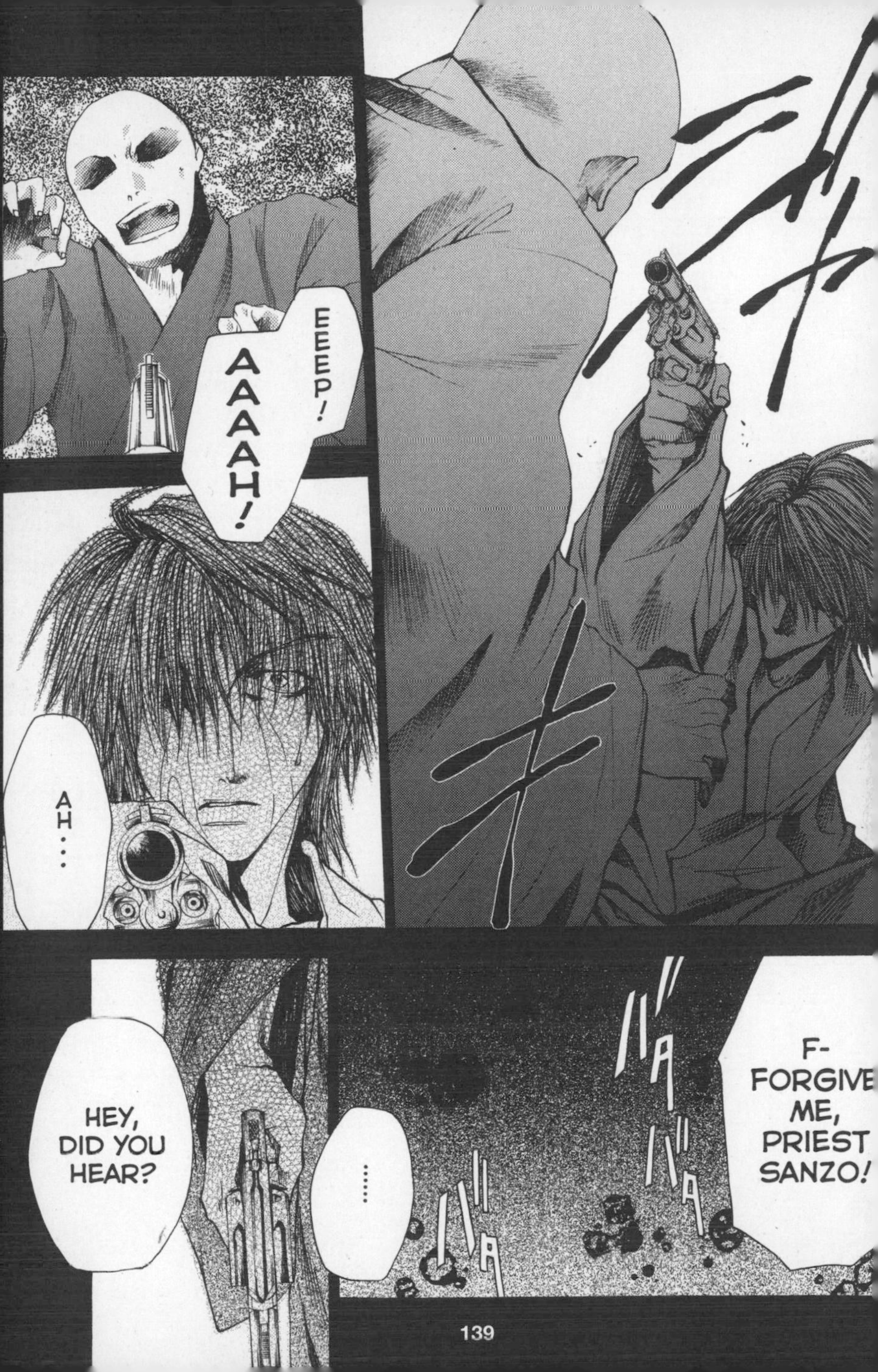
EEEP! AAAAH!
AH...
F-FORGIVE ME, PRIEST SANZO!
......
HEY, DID YOU HEAR?

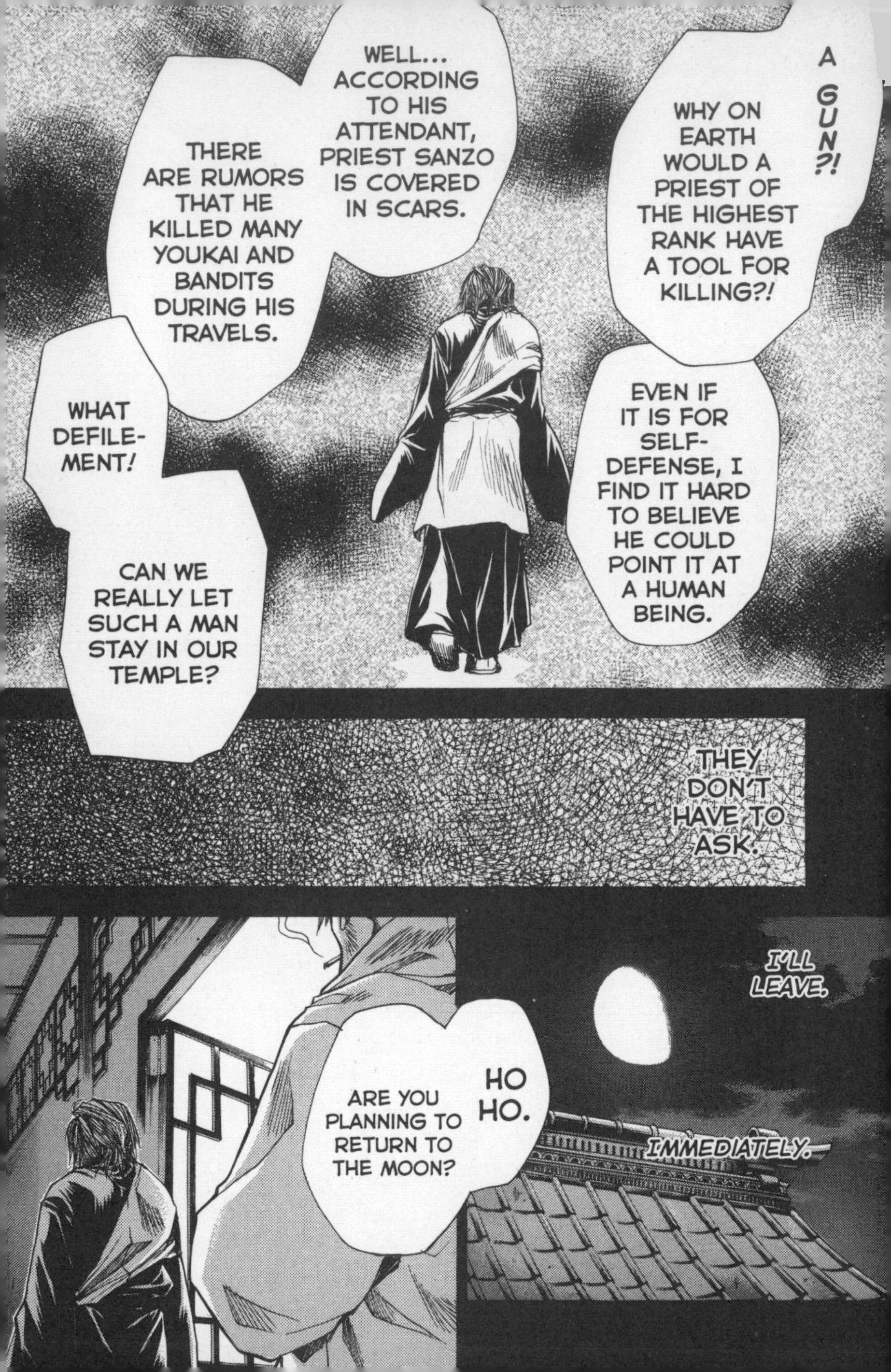
A GUN?!
WHY ON EARTH WOULD A PRIEST OF THE HIGHEST RANK HAVE A TOOL FOR KILLING?!
WELL... ACCORDING TO HIS ATTENDANT, PRIEST SANZO IS COVERED IN SCARS.
THERE ARE RUMORS THAT HE KILLED MANY YOUKAI AND BANDITS DURING HIS TRAVELS.
EVEN IF IT IS FOR SELF-DEFENSE, I FIND IT HARD TO BELIEVE HE COULD POINT IT AT A HUMAN BEING.
WHAT DEFILEMENT!
CAN WE REALLY LET SUCH A MAN STAY IN OUR TEMPLE?
THEY DON'T HAVE TO ASK.
I'LL LEAVE.
IMMEDIATELY.
HO HO.
ARE YOU PLANNING TO RETURN TO THE MOON?

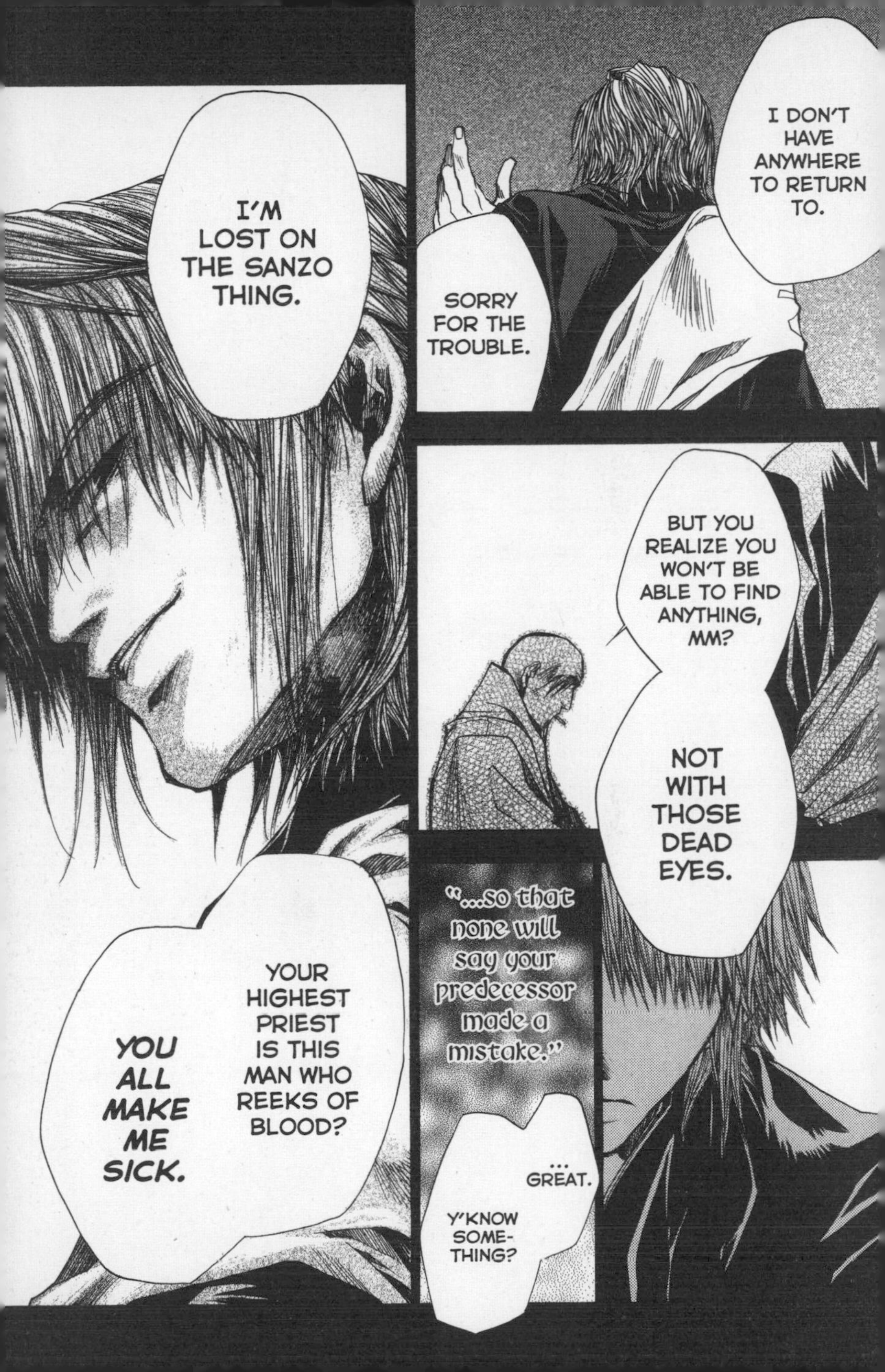
I DON'T HAVE ANYWHERE TO RETURN TO.
SORRY FOR THE TROUBLE.
BUT YOU REALIZE YOU WON'T BE ABLE TO FIND ANYTHING, MM?
NOT WITH THOSE DEAD EYES.
"...so that none will say your predecessor made a mistake."
...GREAT.
Y'KNOW SOME-THING?
I'M LOST ON THE SANZO THING.
YOUR HIGHEST PRIEST IS THIS MAN WHO REEKS OF BLOOD?
YOU ALL MAKE ME SICK.

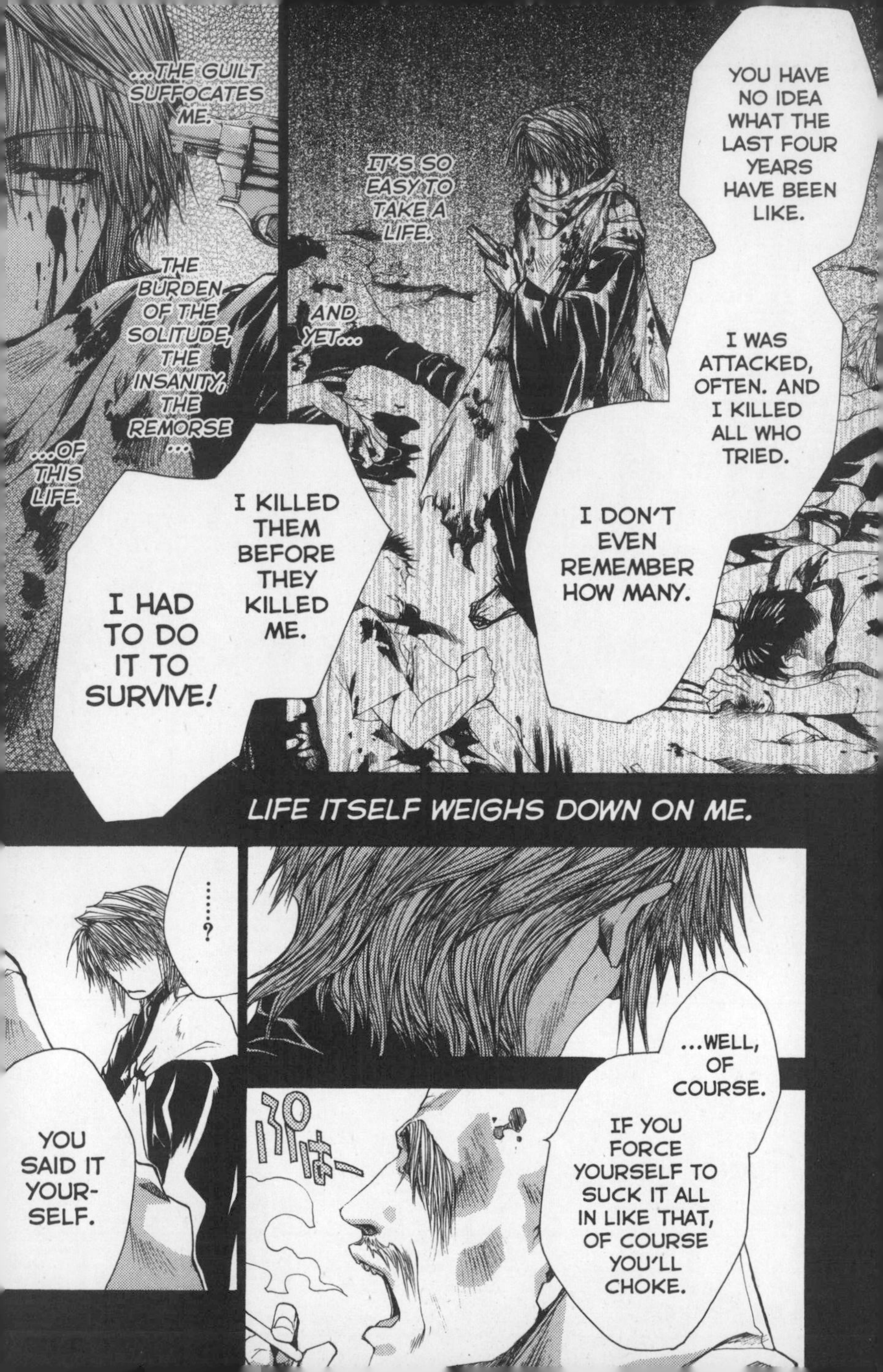

YOU HAVE NO IDEA WHAT THE LAST FOUR YEARS HAVE BEEN LIKE.
IT'S SO EASY TO TAKE A LIFE.
AND YET...
I WAS ATTACKED, OFTEN. AND I KILLED ALL WHO TRIED.
I DON'T EVEN REMEMBER HOW MANY.
I KILLED THEM BEFORE THEY KILLED ME.
I HAD TO DO IT TO SURVIVE!
...THE GUILT SUFFOCATES ME.
THE BURDEN OF THE SOLITUDE, THE INSANITY, THE REMORSE...
...OF THIS LIFE.
LIFE ITSELF WEIGHS DOWN ON ME.
...WELL, OF COURSE.
ぷはー
IF YOU FORCE YOURSELF TO SUCK IT ALL IN LIKE THAT, OF COURSE YOU'LL CHOKE.
......?
YOU SAID IT YOURSELF.

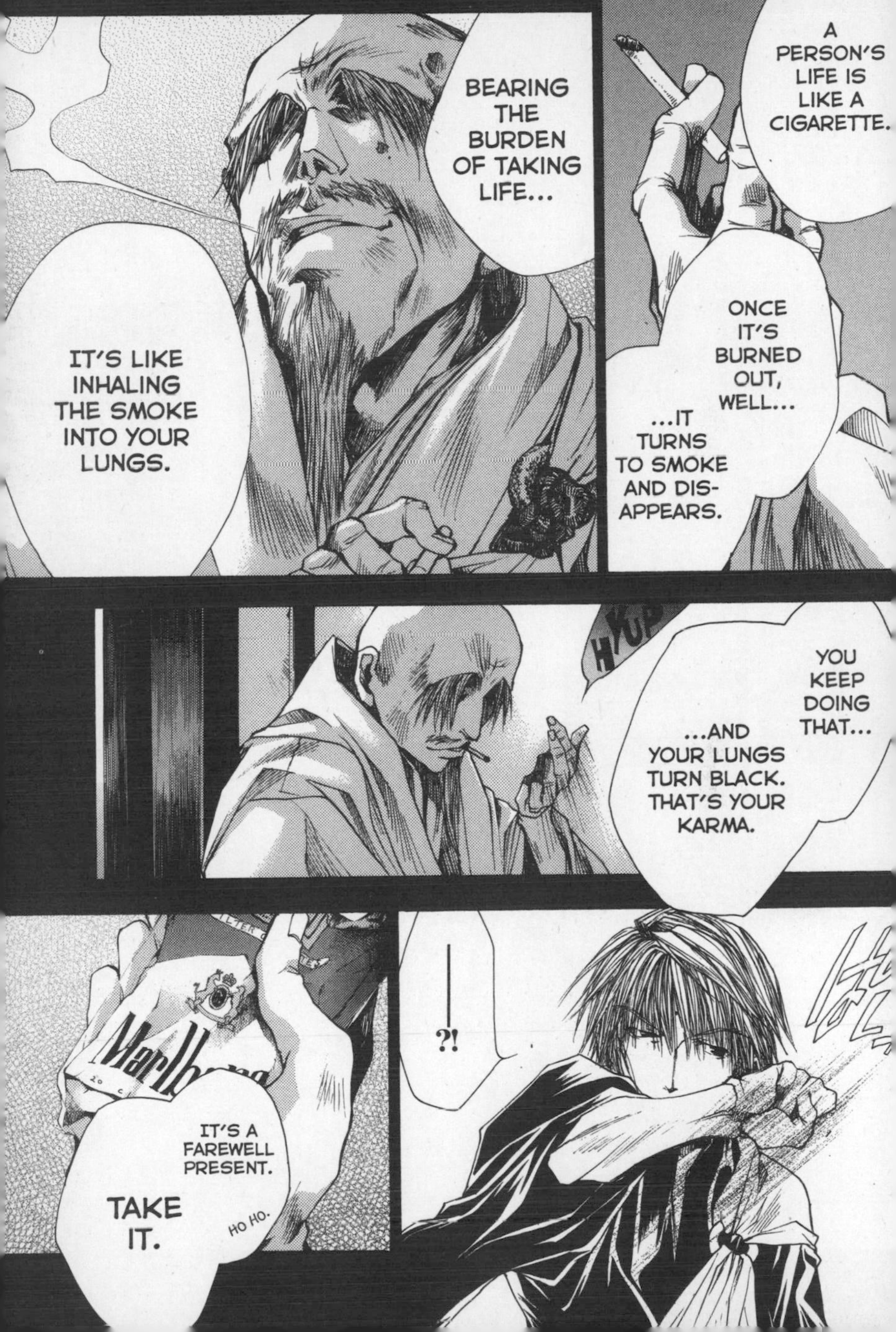
A PERSON'S LIFE IS LIKE A CIGARETTE.
ONCE IT'S BURNED OUT, WELL...
...IT TURNS TO SMOKE AND DIS-APPEARS.
BEARING THE BURDEN OF TAKING LIFE...
IT'S LIKE INHALING THE SMOKE INTO YOUR LUNGS.
HYUP
YOU KEEP DOING THAT...
...AND YOUR LUNGS TURN BLACK. THAT'S YOUR KARMA.
—?!
Marlboro
IT'S A FAREWELL PRESENT.
TAKE IT.
HO HO.

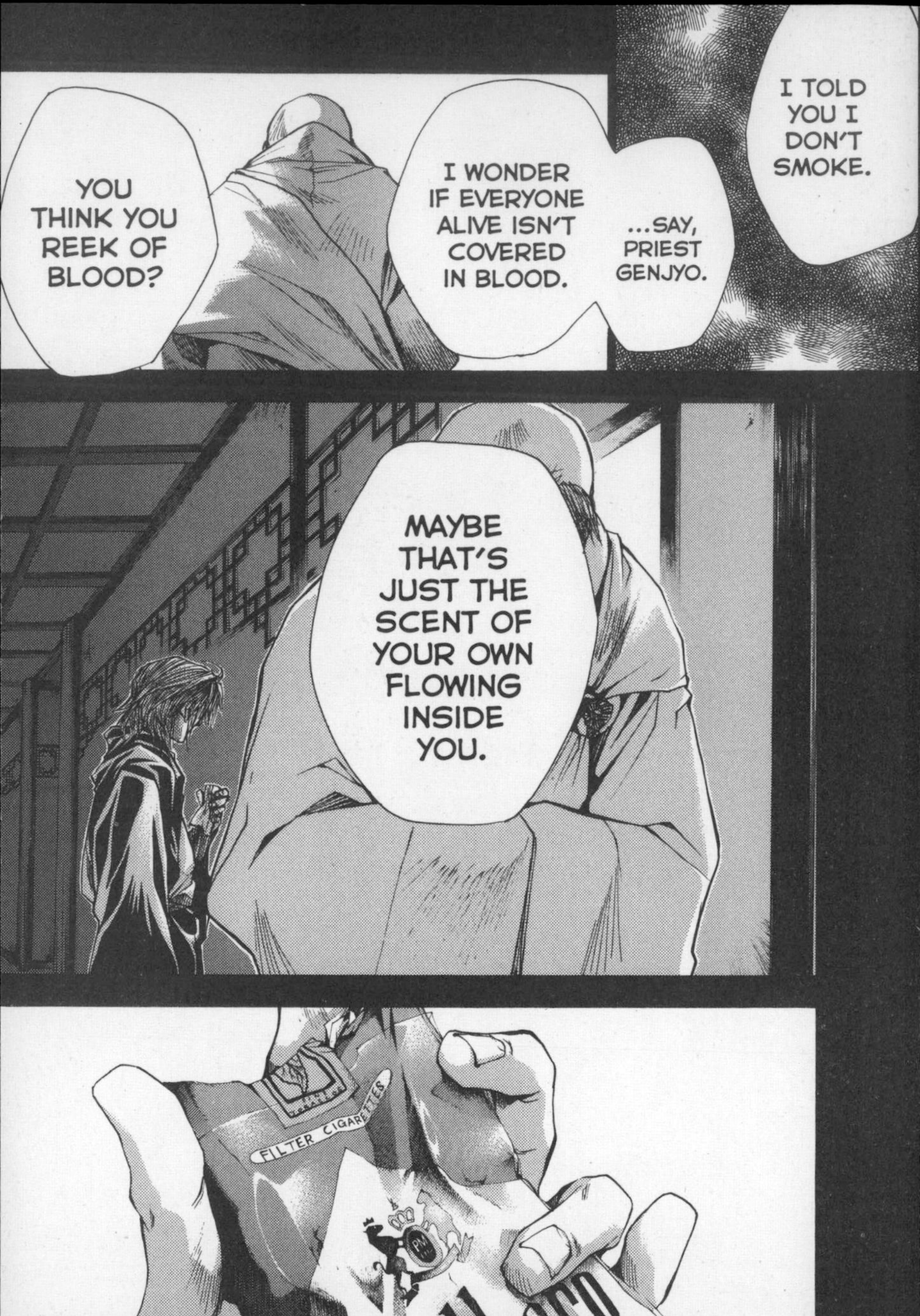
I TOLD YOU I DON'T SMOKE.
...SAY, PRIEST GENJYO.
I WONDER IF EVERYONE ALIVE ISN'T COVERED IN BLOOD.
YOU THINK YOU REEK OF BLOOD?
MAYBE THAT'S JUST THE SCENT OF YOUR OWN FLOWING INSIDE YOU.
FILTER CIGARETTES

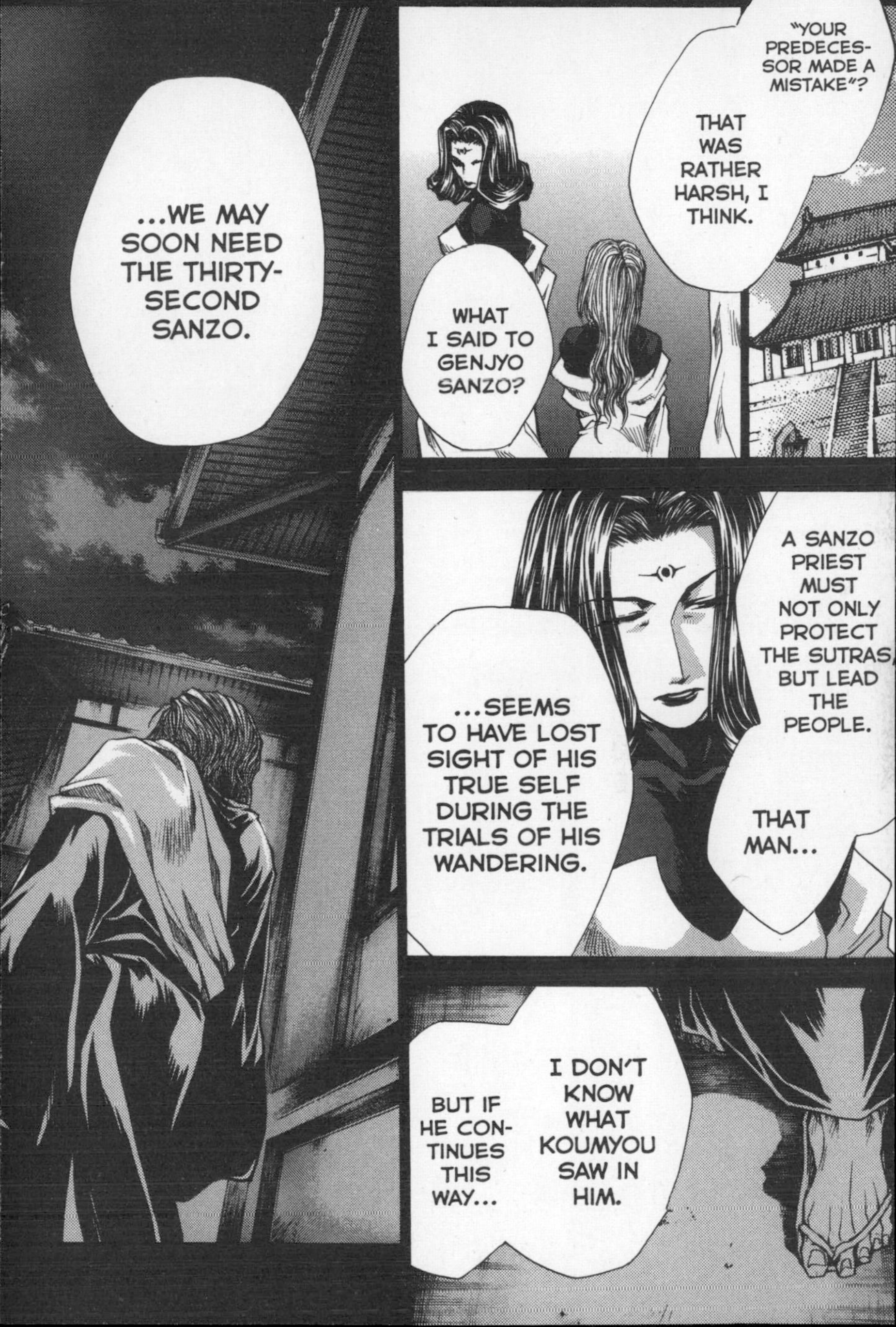
"YOUR PREDECES-SOR MADE A MISTAKE"?
THAT WAS RATHER HARSH, I THINK.
WHAT I SAID TO GENJYO SANZO?
A SANZO PRIEST MUST NOT ONLY PROTECT THE SUTRAS, BUT LEAD THE PEOPLE.
THAT MAN...
...SEEMS TO HAVE LOST SIGHT OF HIS TRUE SELF DURING THE TRIALS OF HIS WANDERING.
I DON'T KNOW WHAT KOUMYOU SAW IN HIM.
BUT IF HE CON-TINUES THIS WAY...
...WE MAY SOON NEED THE THIRTY-SECOND SANZO.

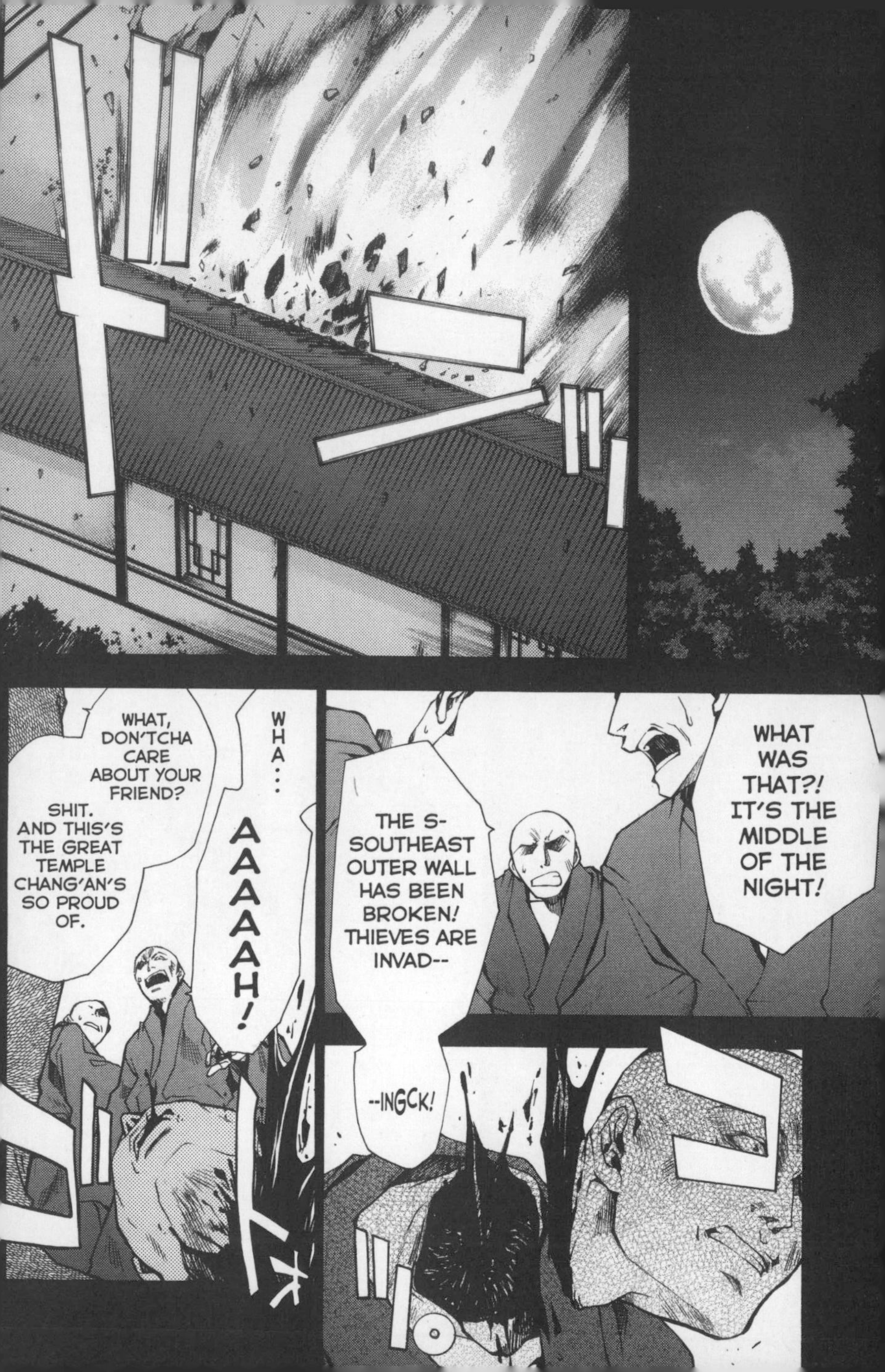

WHAT WAS THAT?! IT'S THE MIDDLE OF THE NIGHT!
THE S-SOUTHEAST OUTER WALL HAS BEEN BROKEN! THIEVES ARE INVAD--
--INGCK!
WHA... AAAAAH!
WHAT, DON'TCHA CARE ABOUT YOUR FRIEND?
SHIT. AND THIS'S THE GREAT TEMPLE CHANG'AN'S SO PROUD OF.

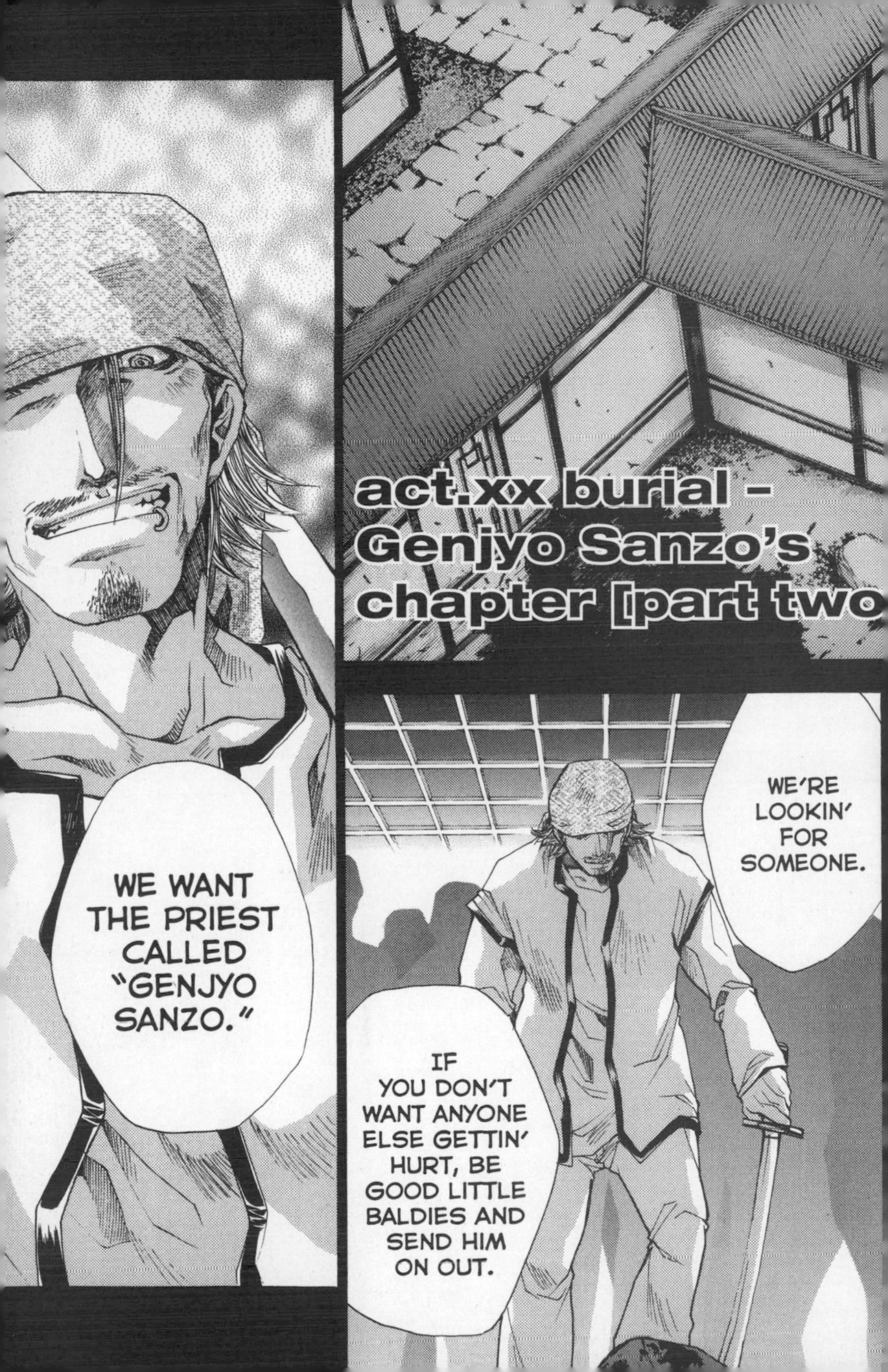
act.xx burial - Genjyo Sanzo's chapter [part two
WE'RE LOOKIN' FOR SOMEONE.
IF YOU DON'T WANT ANYONE ELSE GETTIN' HURT, BE GOOD LITTLE BALDIES AND SEND HIM ON OUT.
WE WANT THE PRIEST CALLED "GENJYO SANZO."

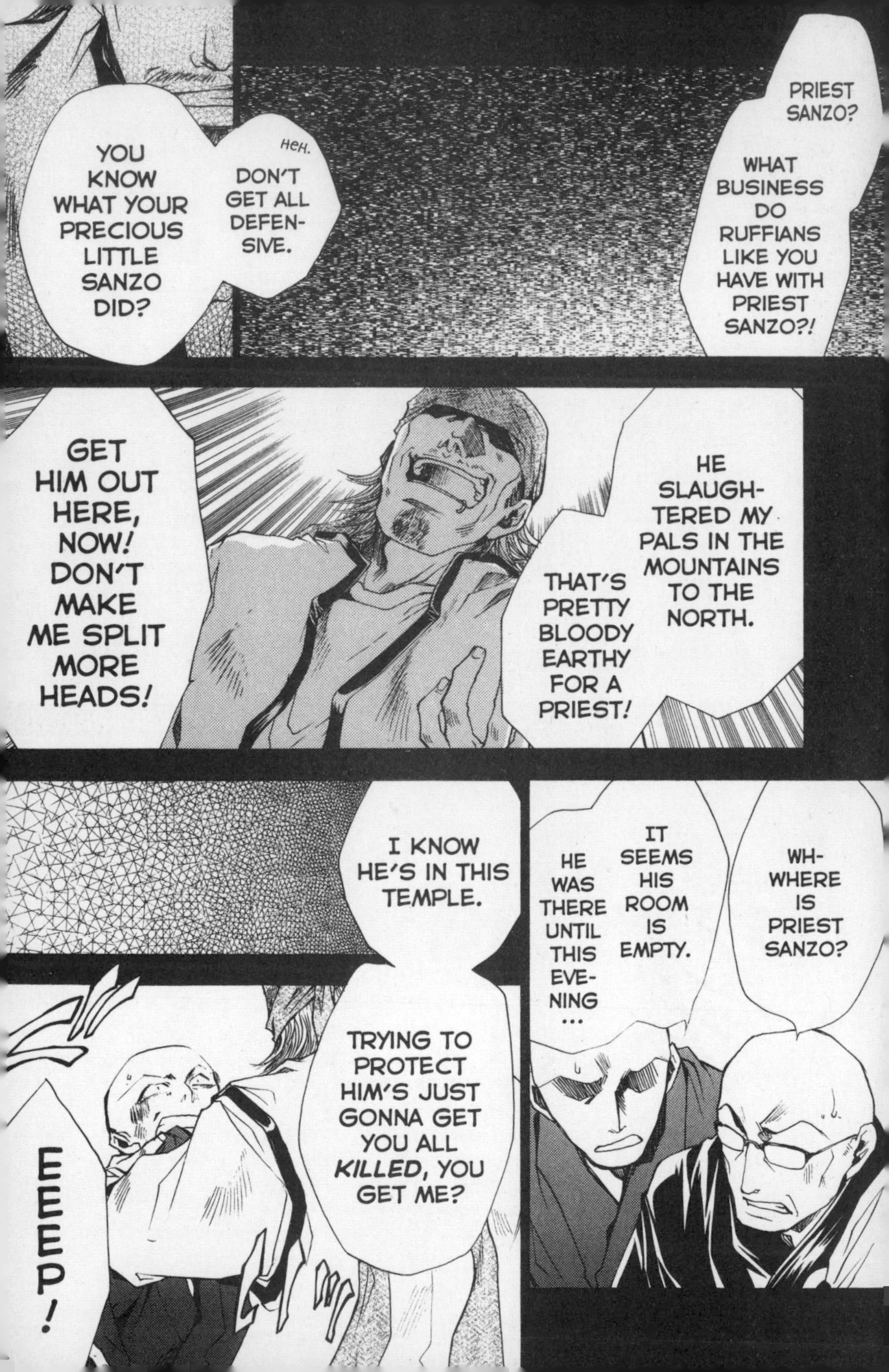
PRIEST SANZO?
WHAT BUSINESS DO RUFFIANS LIKE YOU HAVE WITH PRIEST SANZO?!
HEH.
DON'T GET ALL DEFENSIVE.
YOU KNOW WHAT YOUR PRECIOUS LITTLE SANZO DID?
HE SLAUGHTERED MY PALS IN THE MOUNTAINS TO THE NORTH.
THAT'S PRETTY BLOODY EARTHY FOR A PRIEST!
GET HIM OUT HERE, NOW! DON'T MAKE ME SPLIT MORE HEADS!
WH-WHERE IS PRIEST SANZO?
IT SEEMS HIS ROOM IS EMPTY.
HE WAS THERE UNTIL THIS EVENING...
I KNOW HE'S IN THIS TEMPLE.
TRYING TO PROTECT HIM'S JUST GONNA GET YOU ALL *KILLED*, YOU GET ME?
EEEP!

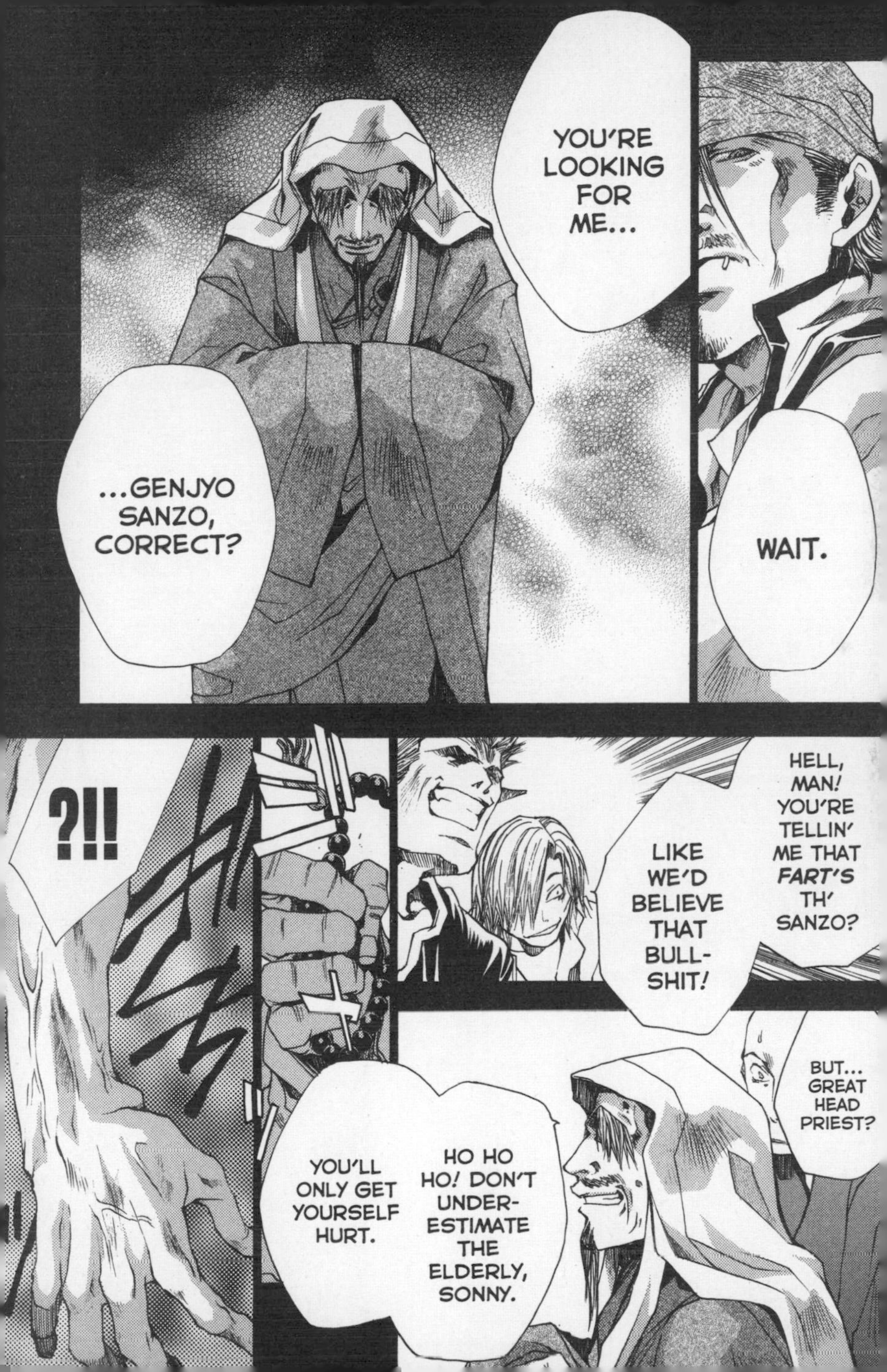
WAIT.
YOU'RE LOOKING FOR ME...
...GENJYO SANZO, CORRECT?
HELL, MAN! YOU'RE TELLIN' ME THAT *FART'S* TH' SANZO?
LIKE WE'D BELIEVE THAT BULL-SHIT!
BUT... GREAT HEAD PRIEST?
HO HO HO! DON'T UNDER-ESTIMATE THE ELDERLY, SONNY.
YOU'LL ONLY GET YOURSELF HURT.
?!!

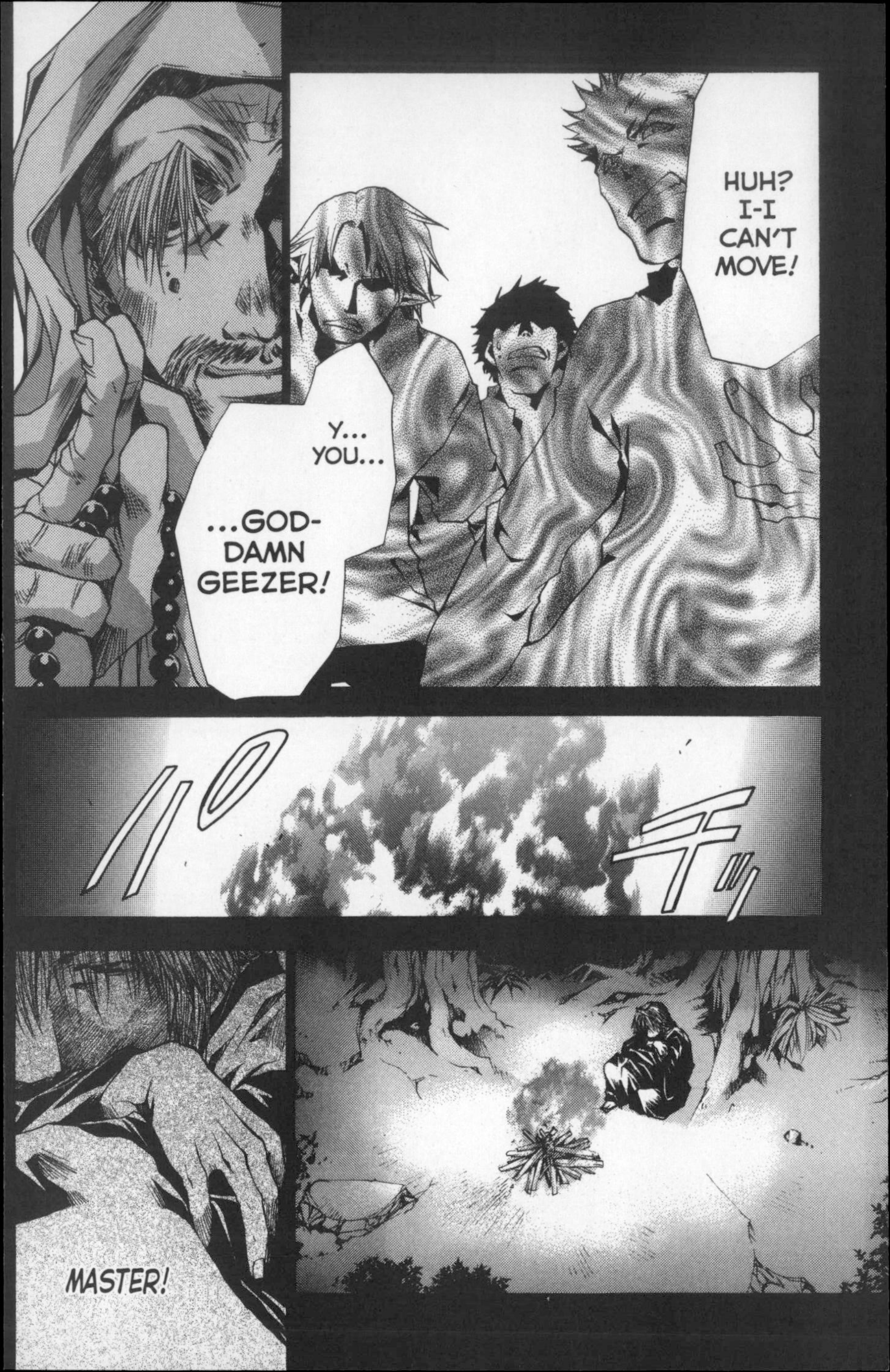
HUH? I-I CAN'T MOVE!
Y... YOU...
...GOD-DAMN GEEZER!
パチッ
MASTER!

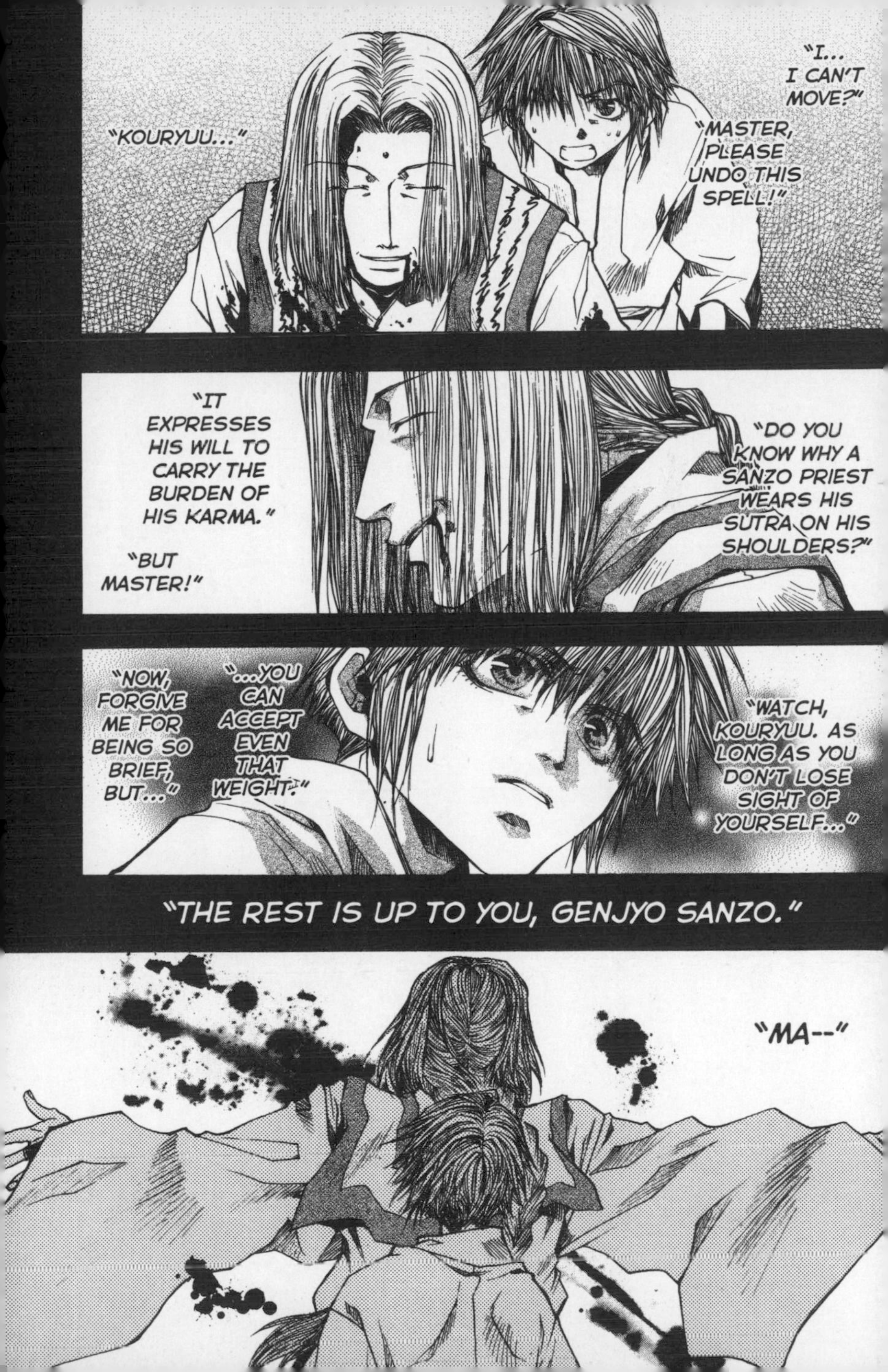
"I... I CAN'T MOVE?"
"MASTER, PLEASE UNDO THIS SPELL!"
"KOURYUU..."
"DO YOU KNOW WHY A SANZO PRIEST WEARS HIS SUTRA ON HIS SHOULDERS?"
"IT EXPRESSES HIS WILL TO CARRY THE BURDEN OF HIS KARMA."
"BUT MASTER!"
"WATCH, KOURYUU. AS LONG AS YOU DON'T LOSE SIGHT OF YOURSELF..."
"...YOU CAN ACCEPT EVEN THAT WEIGHT."
"NOW, FORGIVE ME FOR BEING SO BRIEF, BUT..."
"THE REST IS UP TO YOU, GENJYO SANZO."
"MA--"

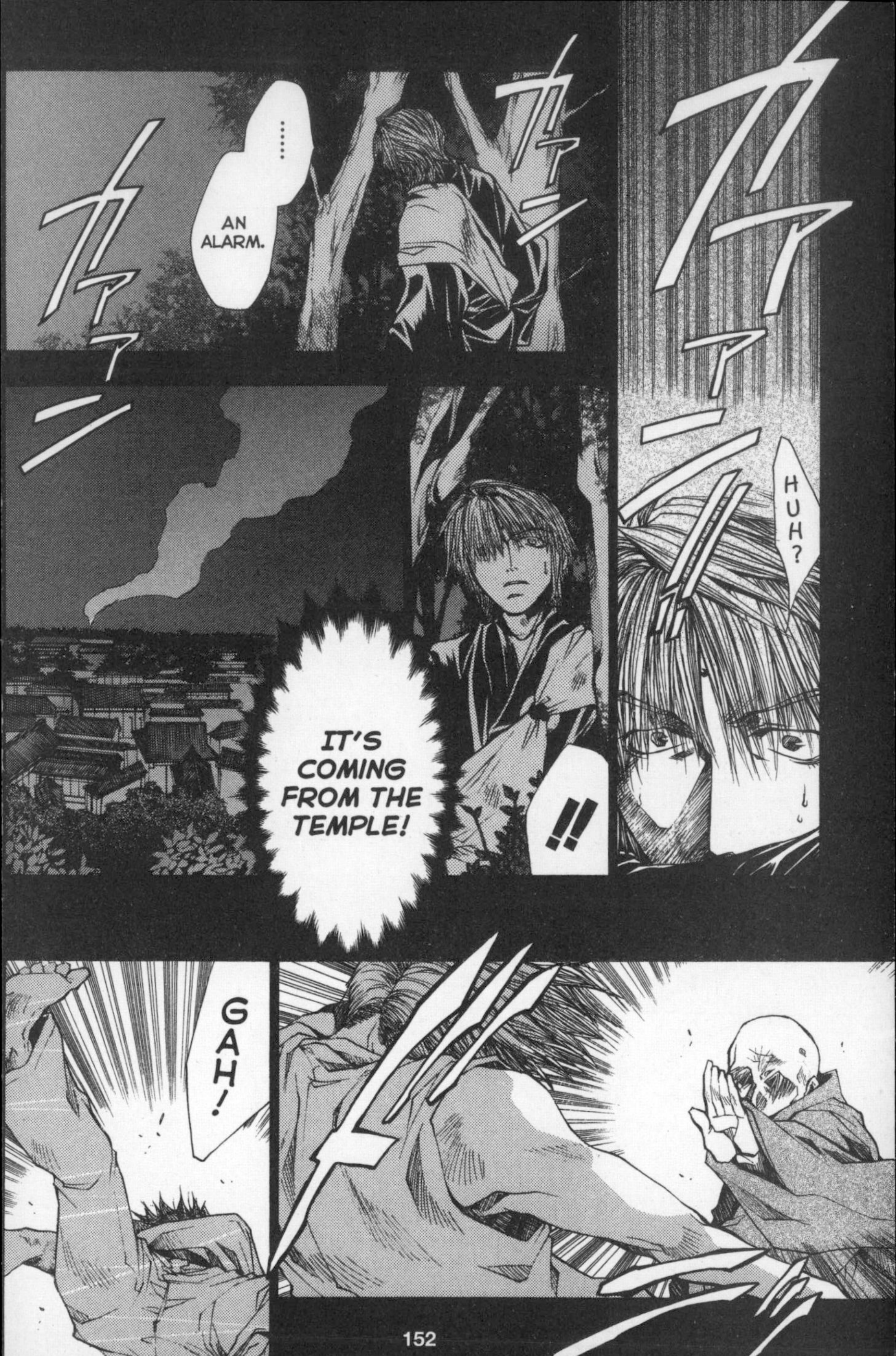
HUH?
......
AN ALARM.
!!
IT'S COMING FROM THE TEMPLE!
GAH!

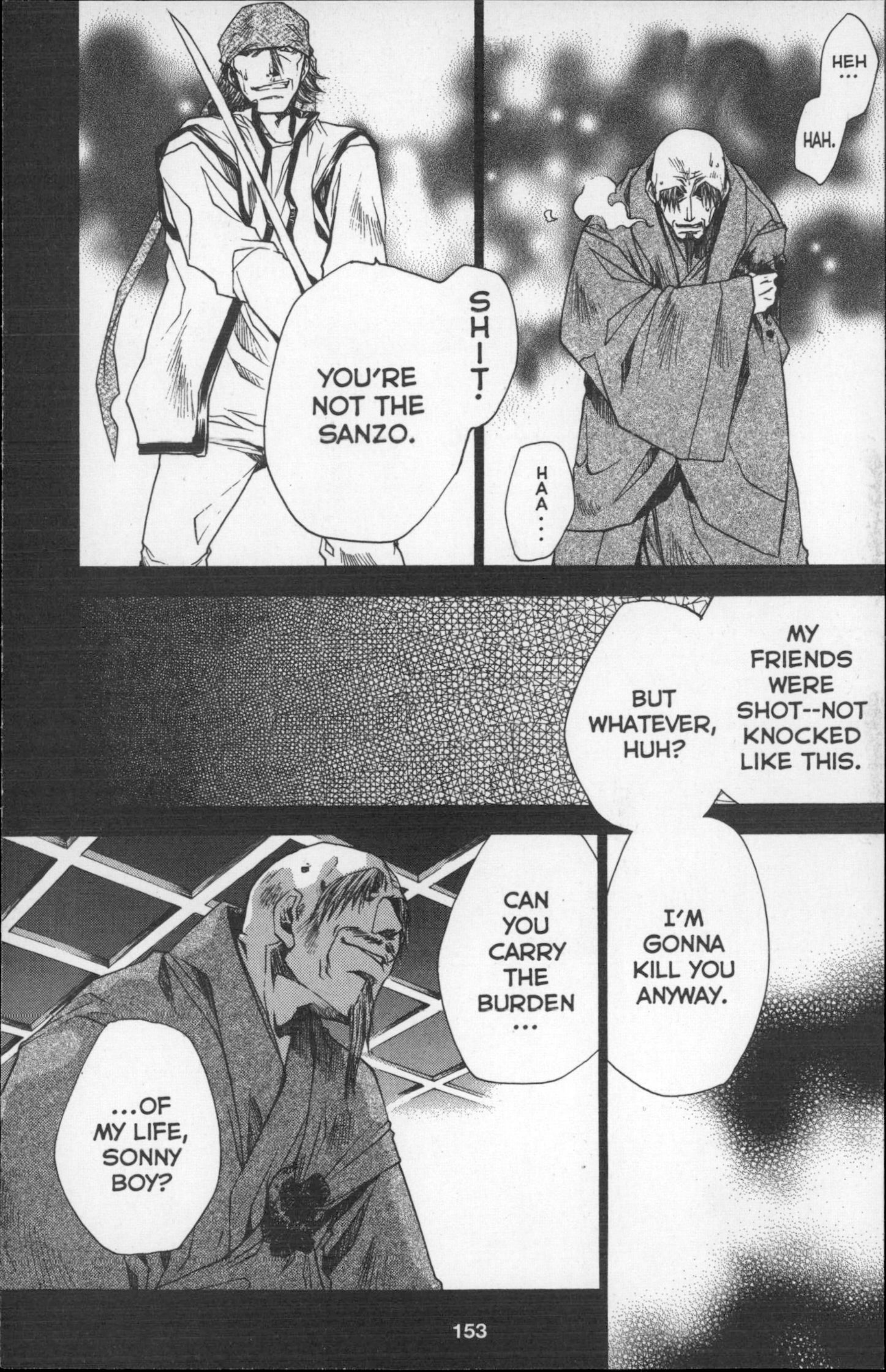
HEH... HAH.
HAA...
SHIT!
YOU'RE NOT THE SANZO.
MY FRIENDS WERE SHOT--NOT KNOCKED LIKE THIS.
BUT WHATEVER, HUH?
I'M GONNA KILL YOU ANYWAY.
CAN YOU CARRY THE BURDEN...
...OF MY LIFE, SONNY BOY?

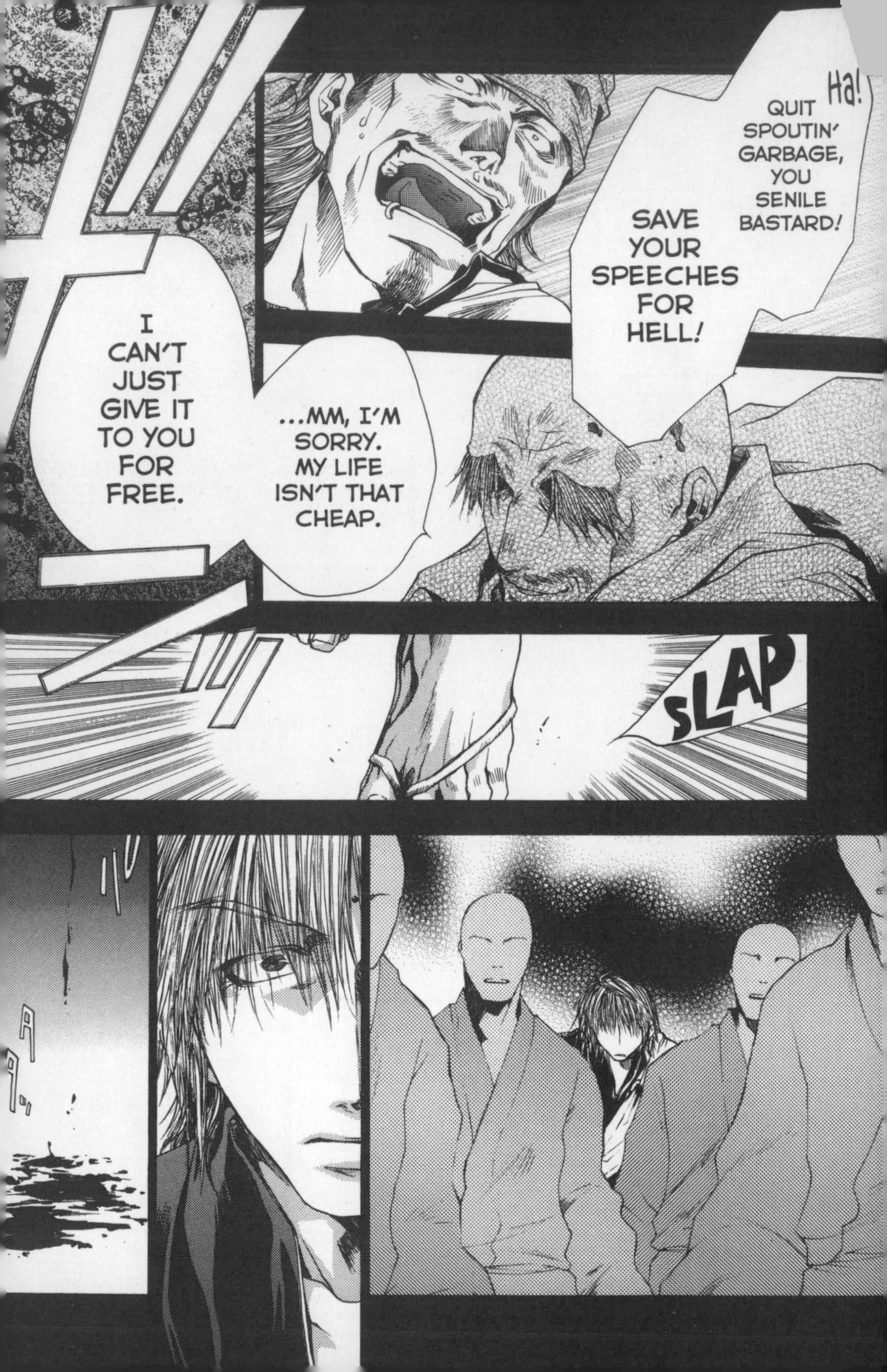
Ha!
QUIT SPOUTIN' GARBAGE, YOU SENILE BASTARD!
SAVE YOUR SPEECHES FOR HELL!
...MM, I'M SORRY. MY LIFE ISN'T THAT CHEAP.
I CAN'T JUST GIVE IT TO YOU FOR FREE.
SLAP

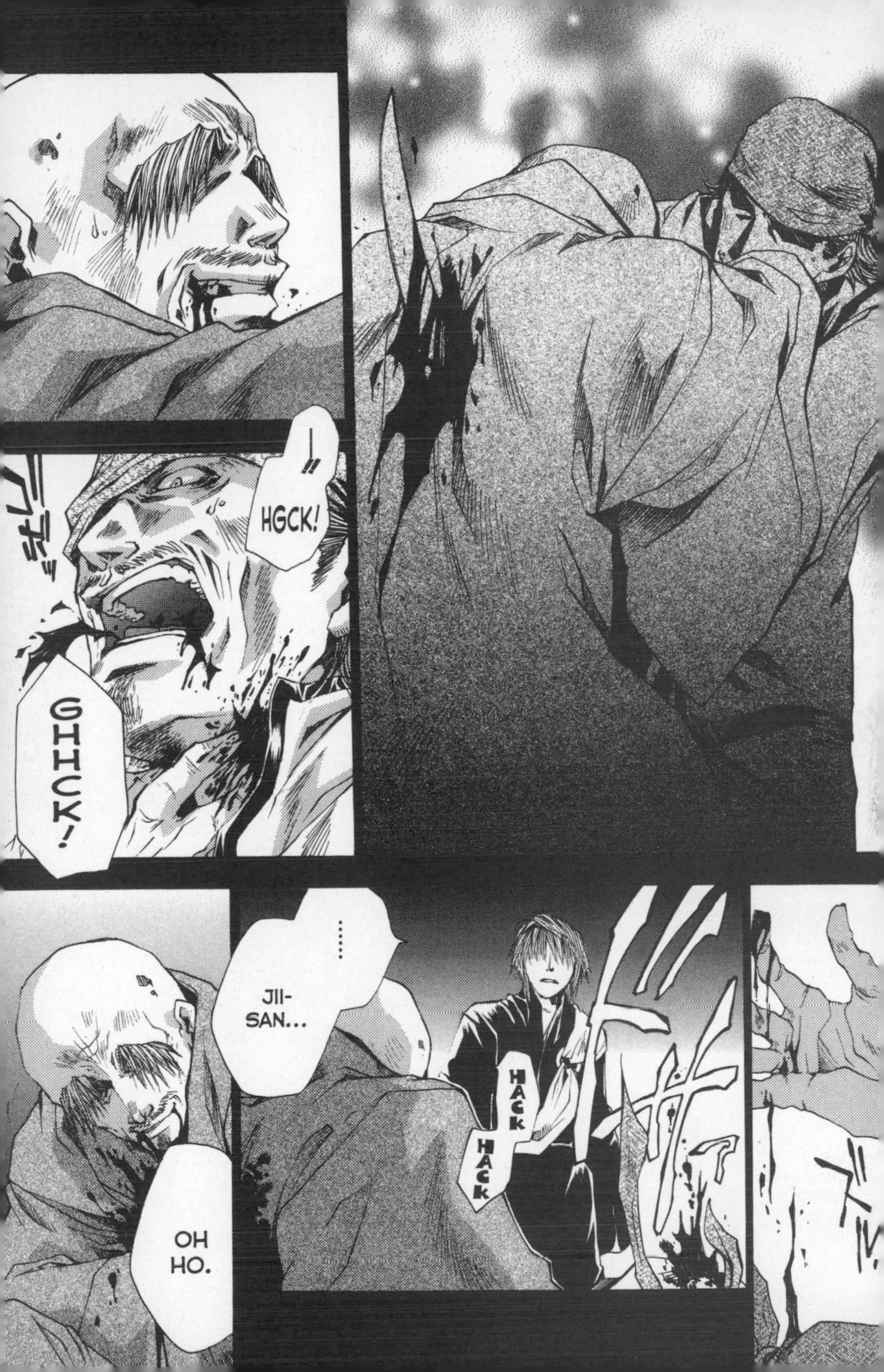
HGCK!
GHHCK!
HACK
HACK
......
JII-SAN...
OH HO.

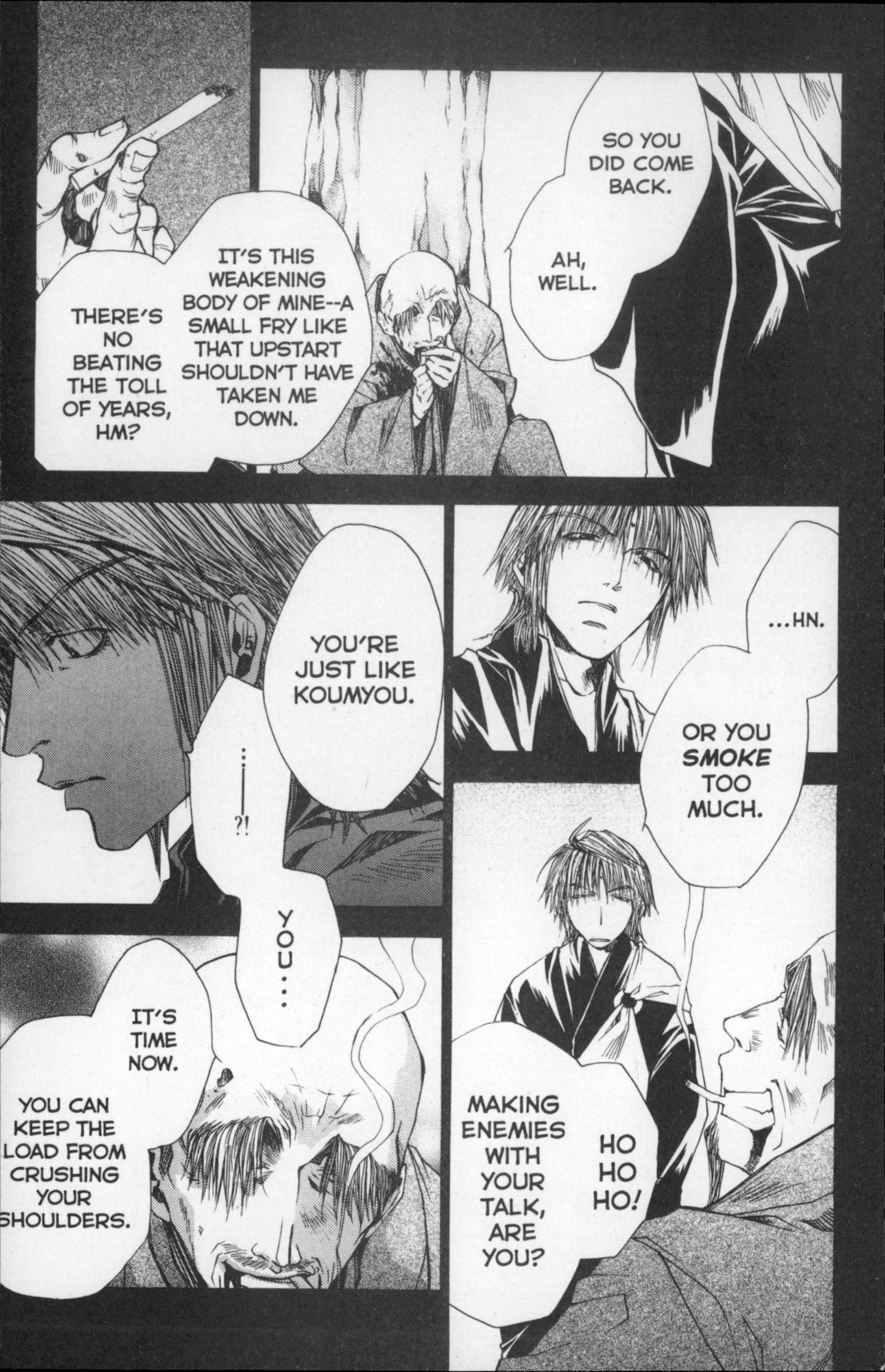
SO YOU DID COME BACK.
AH, WELL.
IT'S THIS WEAKENING BODY OF MINE--A SMALL FRY LIKE THAT UPSTART SHOULDN'T HAVE TAKEN ME DOWN.
THERE'S NO BEATING THE TOLL OF YEARS, HM?
...HN.
OR YOU **SMOKE** TOO MUCH.
MAKING ENEMIES WITH YOUR TALK, ARE YOU?
HO HO HO!
YOU'RE JUST LIKE KOUMYOU.
——?!
YOU...
IT'S TIME NOW.
YOU CAN KEEP THE LOAD FROM CRUSHING YOUR SHOULDERS.

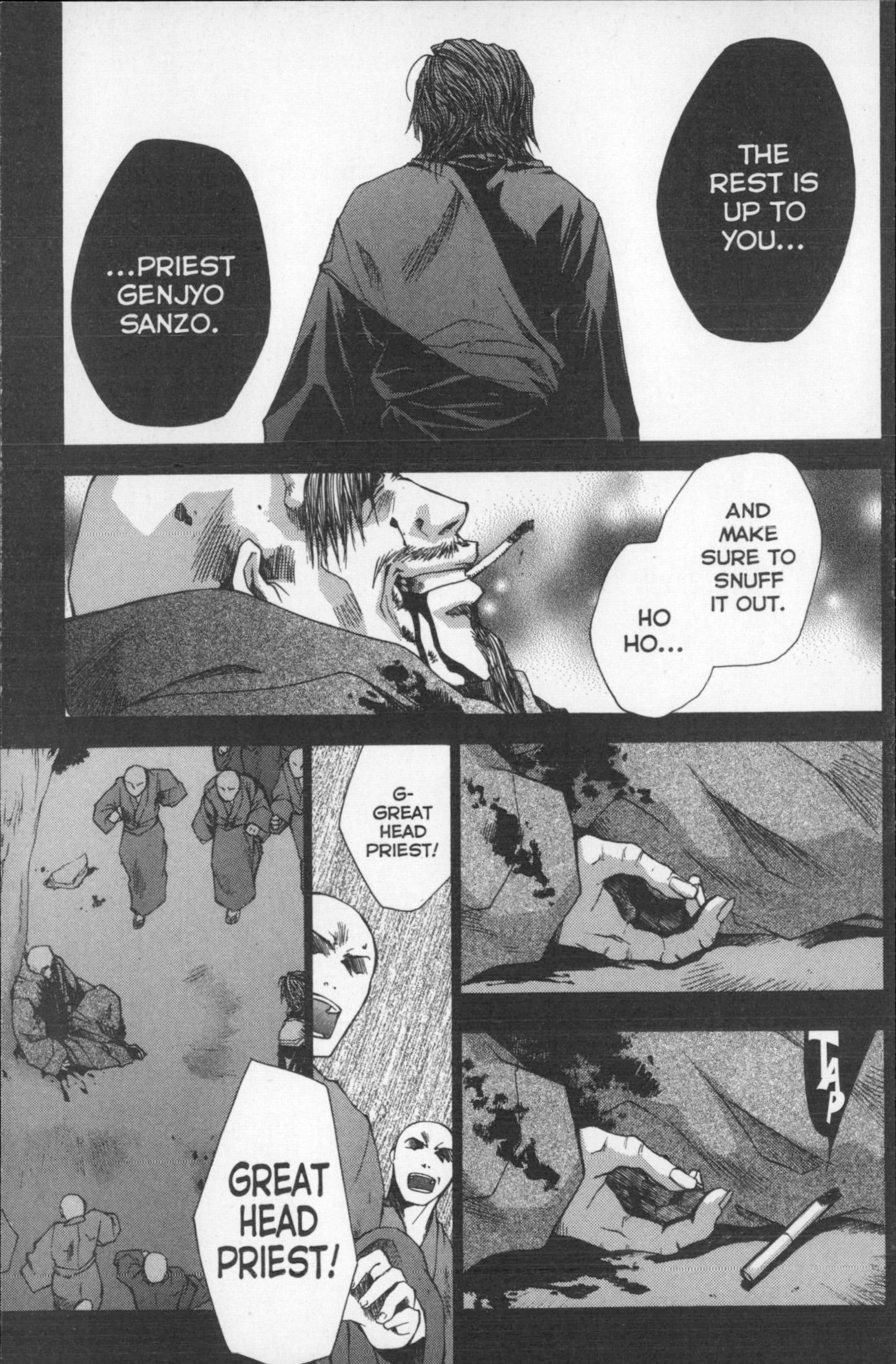
THE REST IS UP TO YOU...
...PRIEST GENJYO SANZO.
AND MAKE SURE TO SNUFF IT OUT.
HO HO...
TAP
G- GREAT HEAD PRIEST!
GREAT HEAD PRIEST!

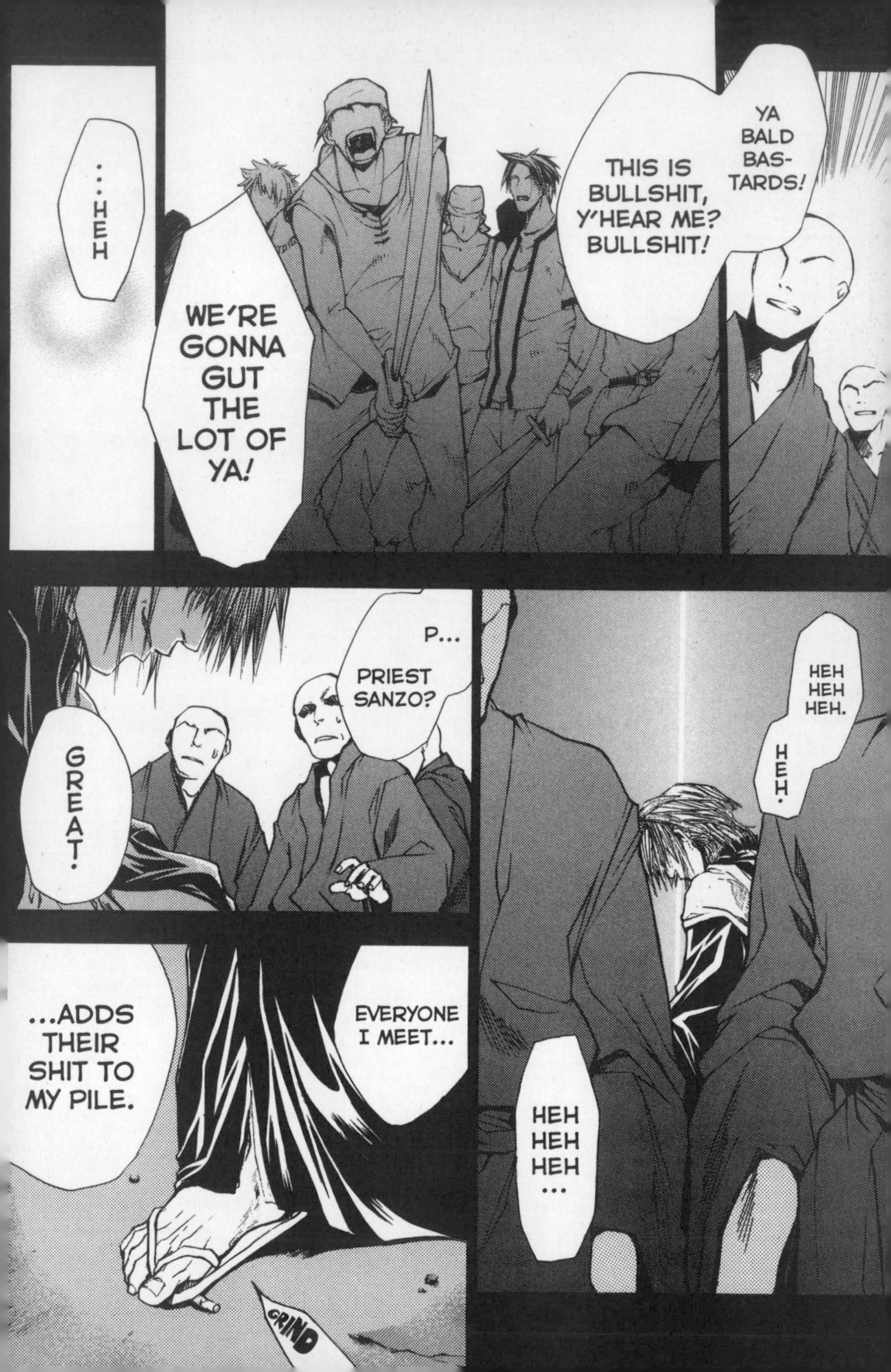
THIS IS BULLSHIT, Y'HEAR ME? BULLSHIT!
YA BALD BAS-TARDS!
WE'RE GONNA GUT THE LOT OF YA!
...HEH
HEH HEH HEH.
HEH.
HEH HEH HEH...
P... PRIEST SANZO?
GREAT.
EVERYONE I MEET...
...ADDS THEIR SHIT TO MY PILE.
GRIND

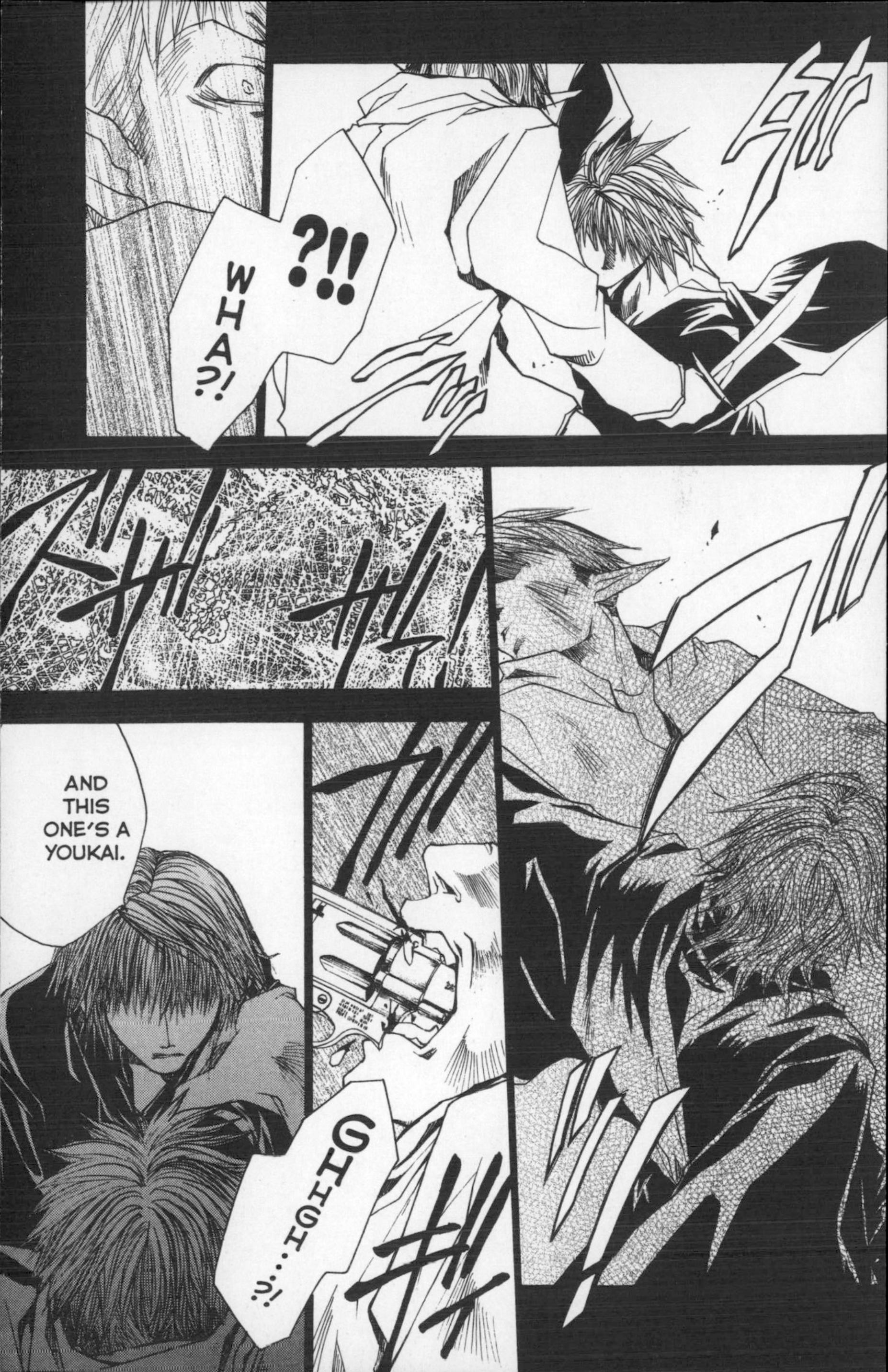

?!!
WHA?!
GHHGH...?!
AND THIS ONE'S A YOUKAI.

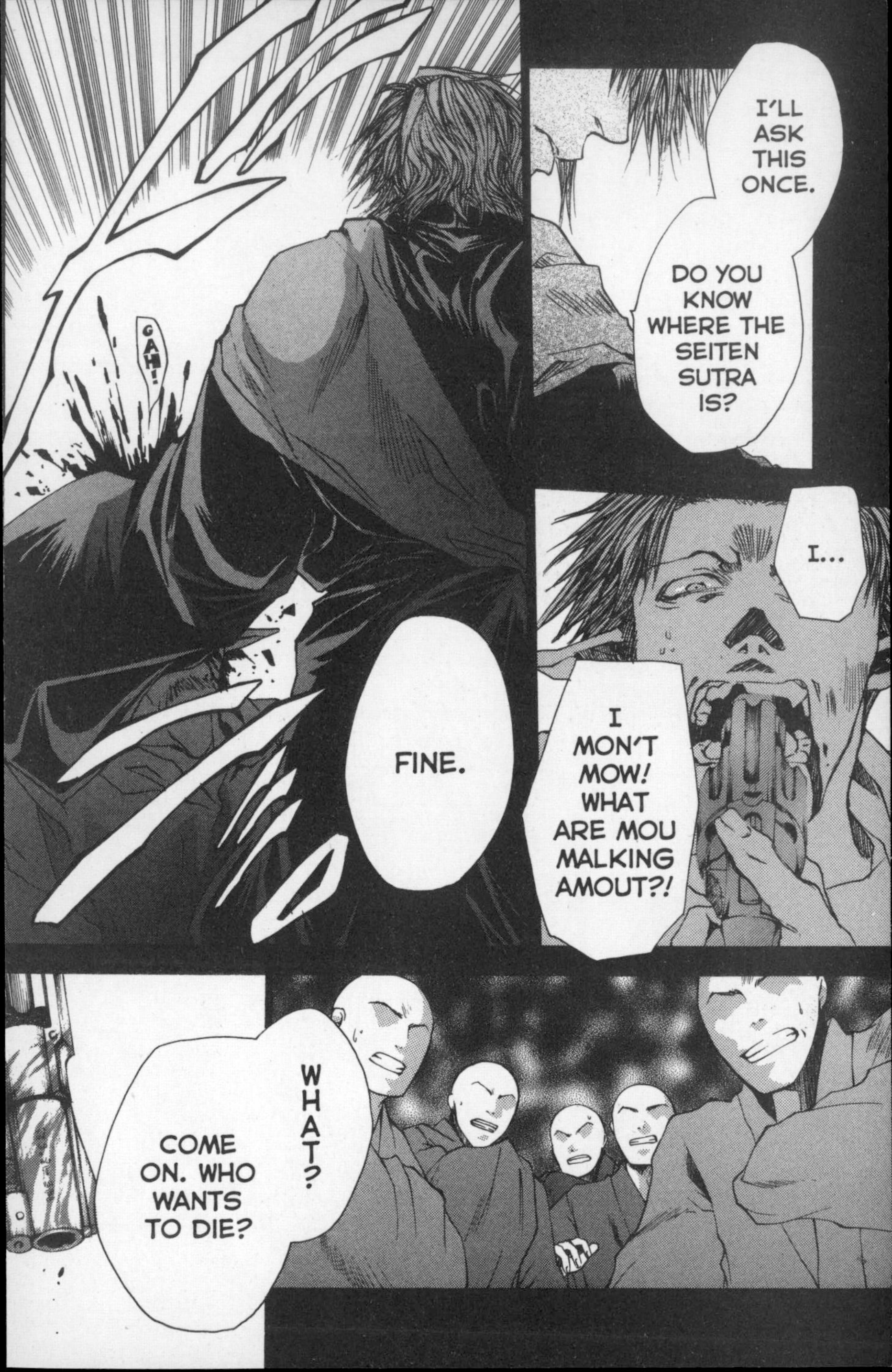
I'LL ASK THIS ONCE.
DO YOU KNOW WHERE THE SEITEN SUTRA IS?
I...
I MON'T MOW! WHAT ARE MOU MALKING AMOUT?!
FINE.
GAH!
WHAT?
COME ON. WHO WANTS TO DIE?

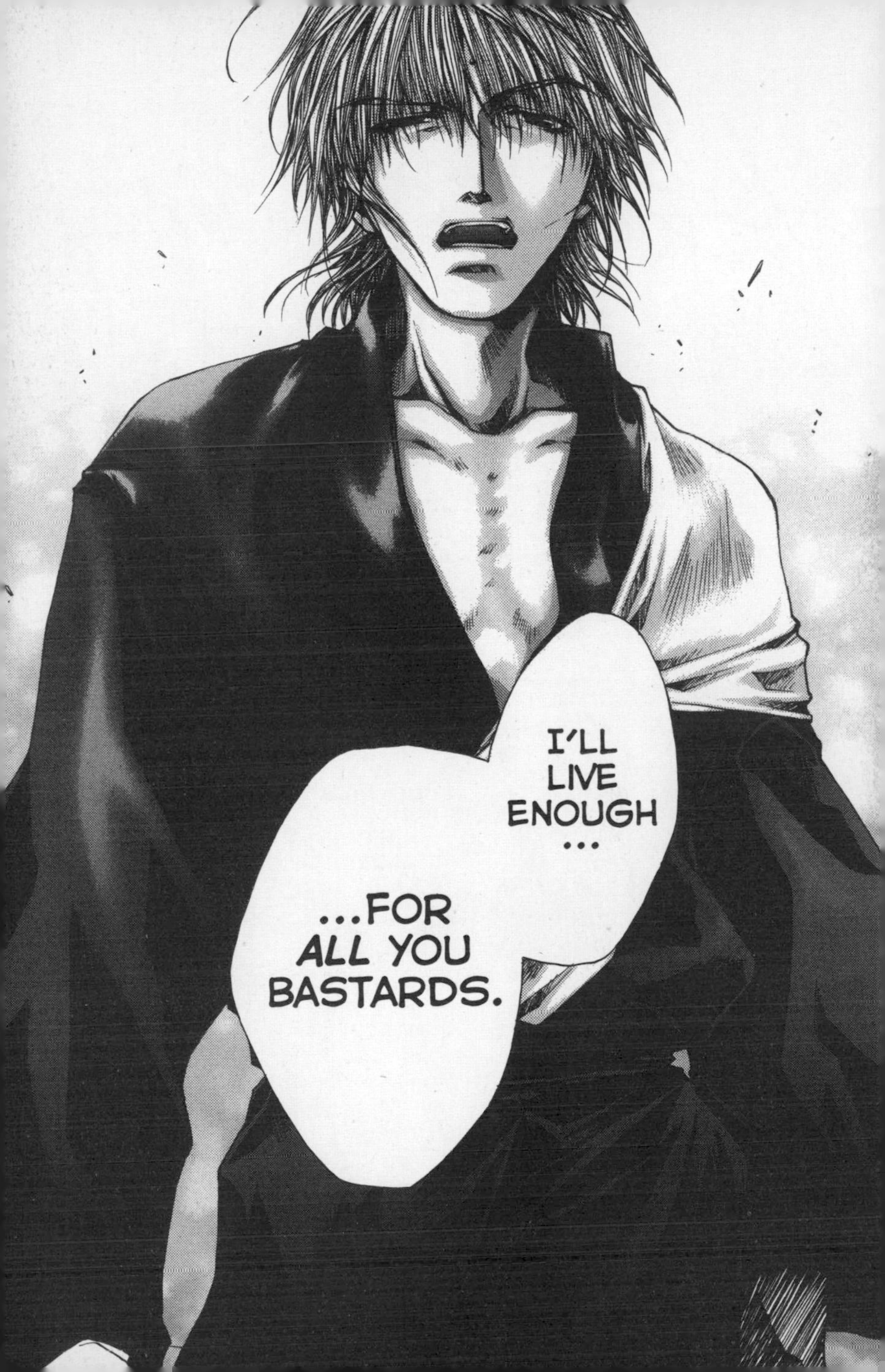
I'LL LIVE ENOUGH...
...FOR ALL YOU BASTARDS.

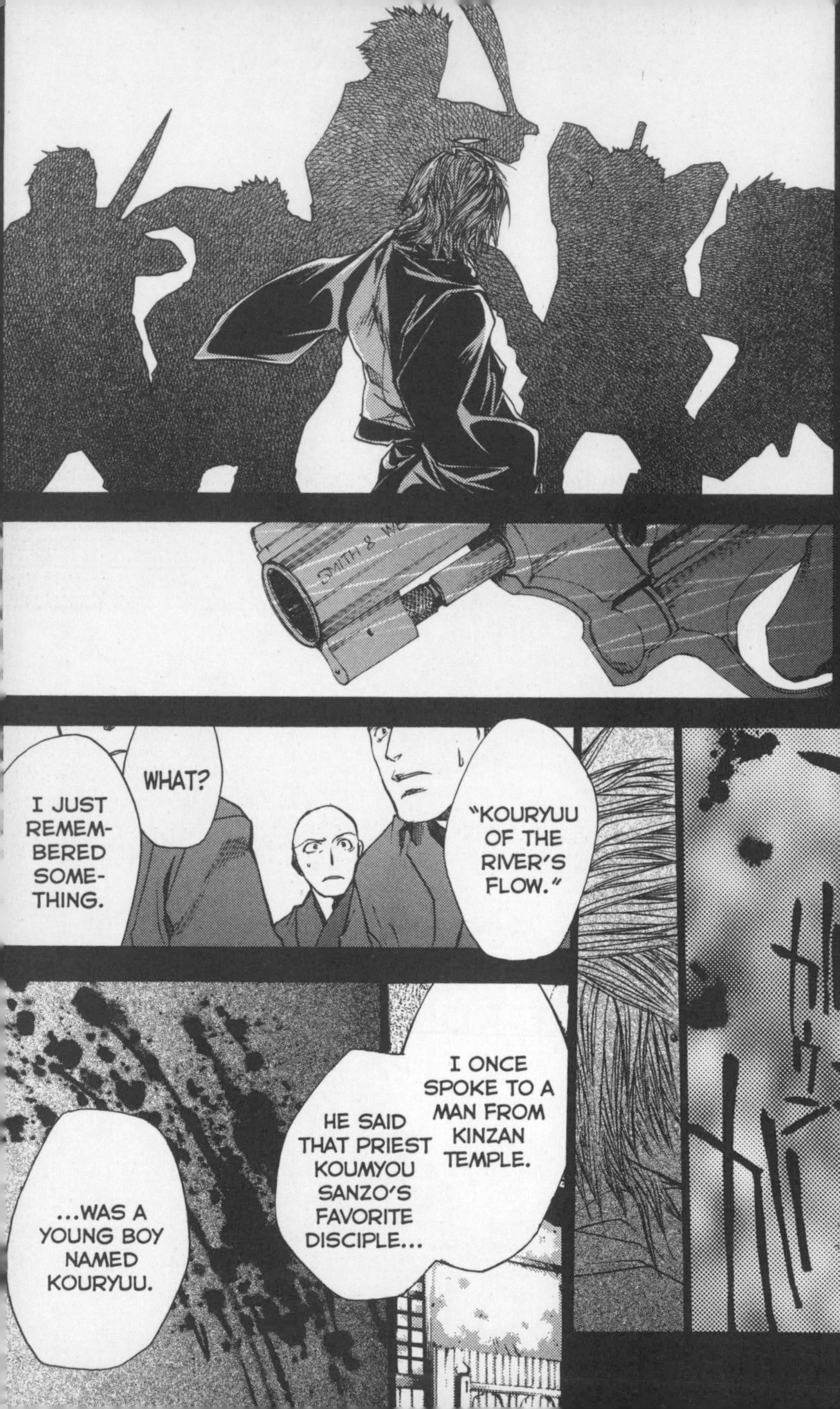
"KOURYUU OF THE RIVER'S FLOW."
WHAT?
I JUST REMEMBERED SOMETHING.
I ONCE SPOKE TO A MAN FROM KINZAN TEMPLE.
HE SAID THAT PRIEST KOUMYOU SANZO'S FAVORITE DISCIPLE...
...WAS A YOUNG BOY NAMED KOURYUU.

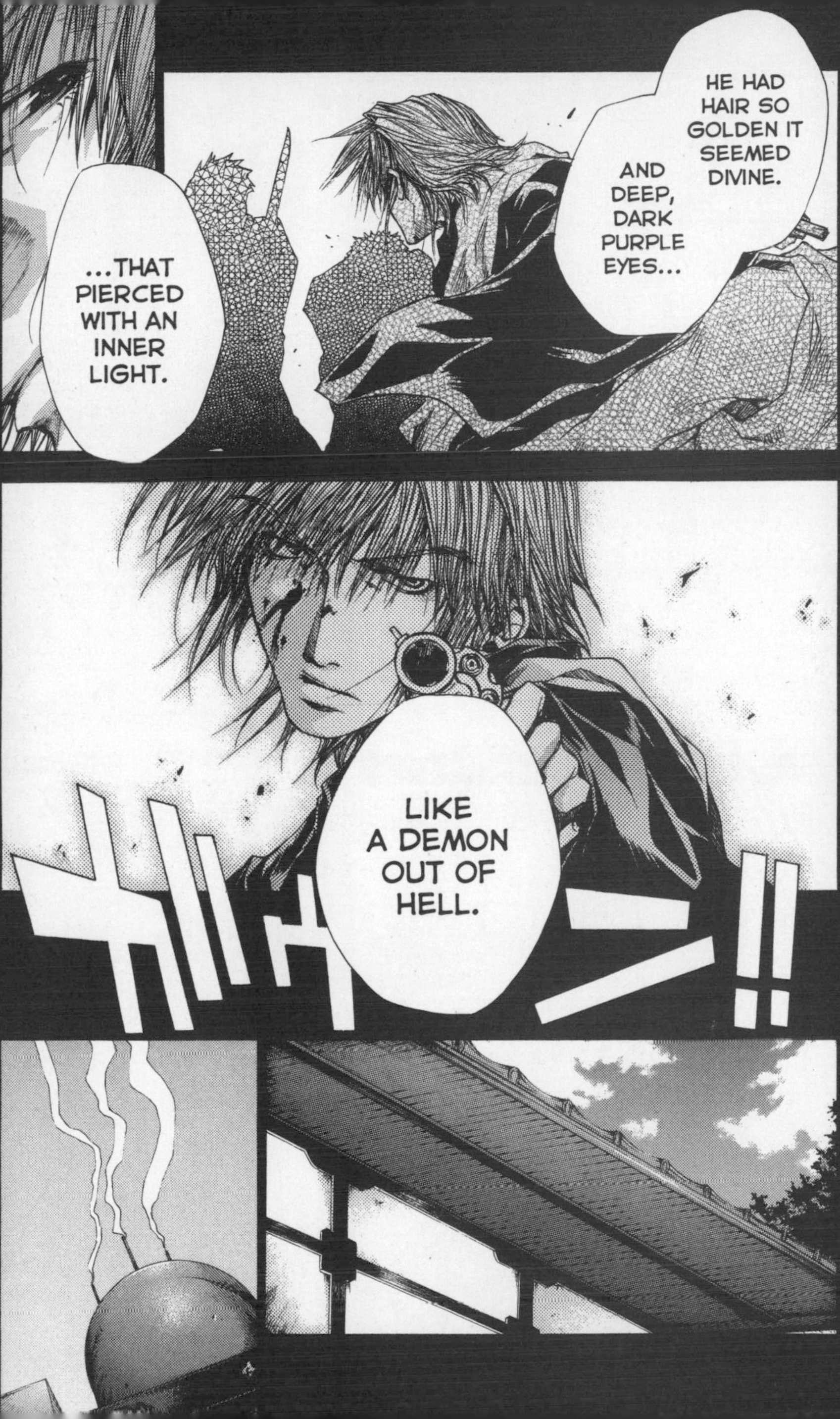
HE HAD HAIR SO GOLDEN IT SEEMED DIVINE.
AND DEEP, DARK PURPLE EYES...
...THAT PIERCED WITH AN INNER LIGHT.
LIKE A DEMON OUT OF HELL.

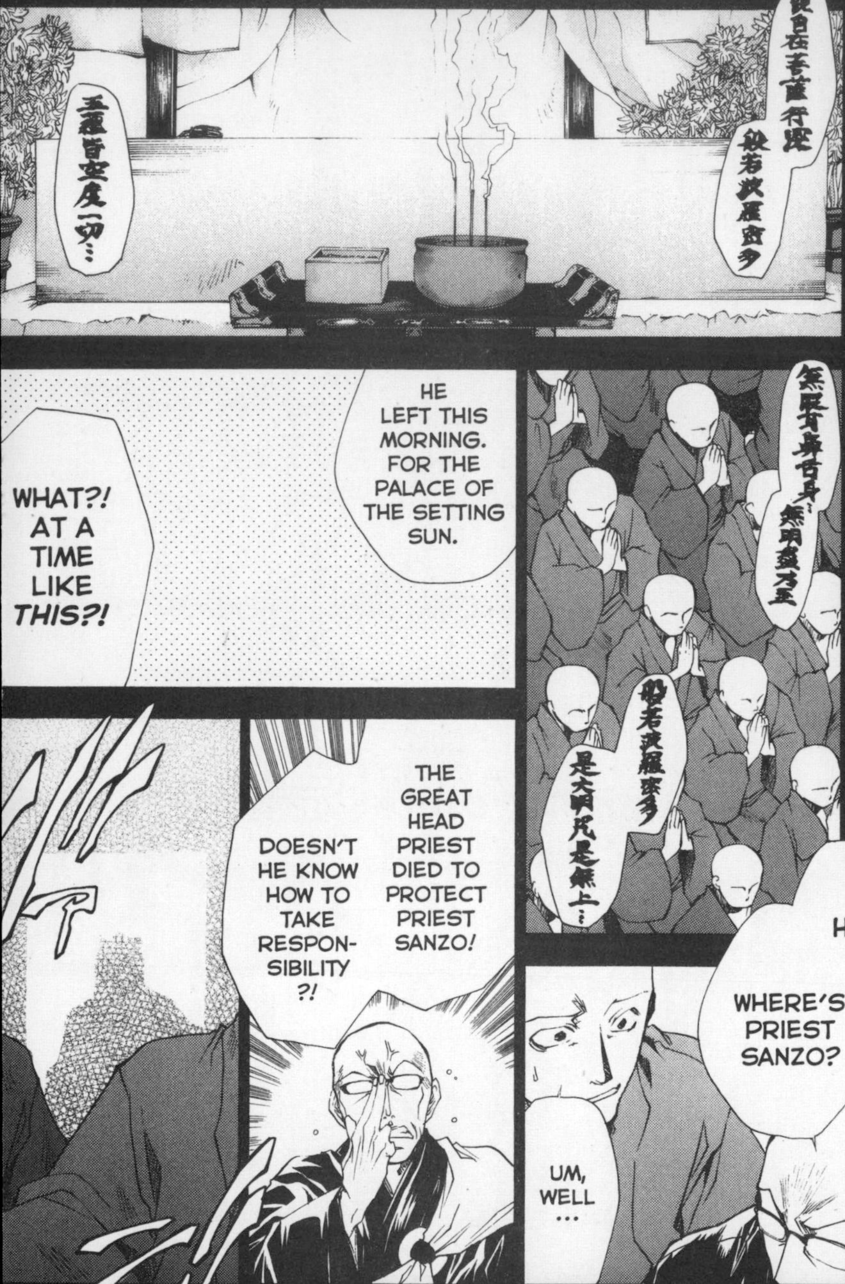

観自在菩薩行深
般若波羅蜜多
五蘊皆空度一切…
無眼耳鼻舌身
無明盡乃至
HE LEFT THIS MORNING. FOR THE PALACE OF THE SETTING SUN.
WHAT?! AT A TIME LIKE *THIS?!*
般若波羅蜜多
是大明咒是無上…
HEY.
WHERE'S PRIEST SANZO?
UM, WELL...
THE GREAT HEAD PRIEST DIED TO PROTECT PRIEST SANZO!
DOESN'T HE KNOW HOW TO TAKE RESPON-SIBILITY ?!

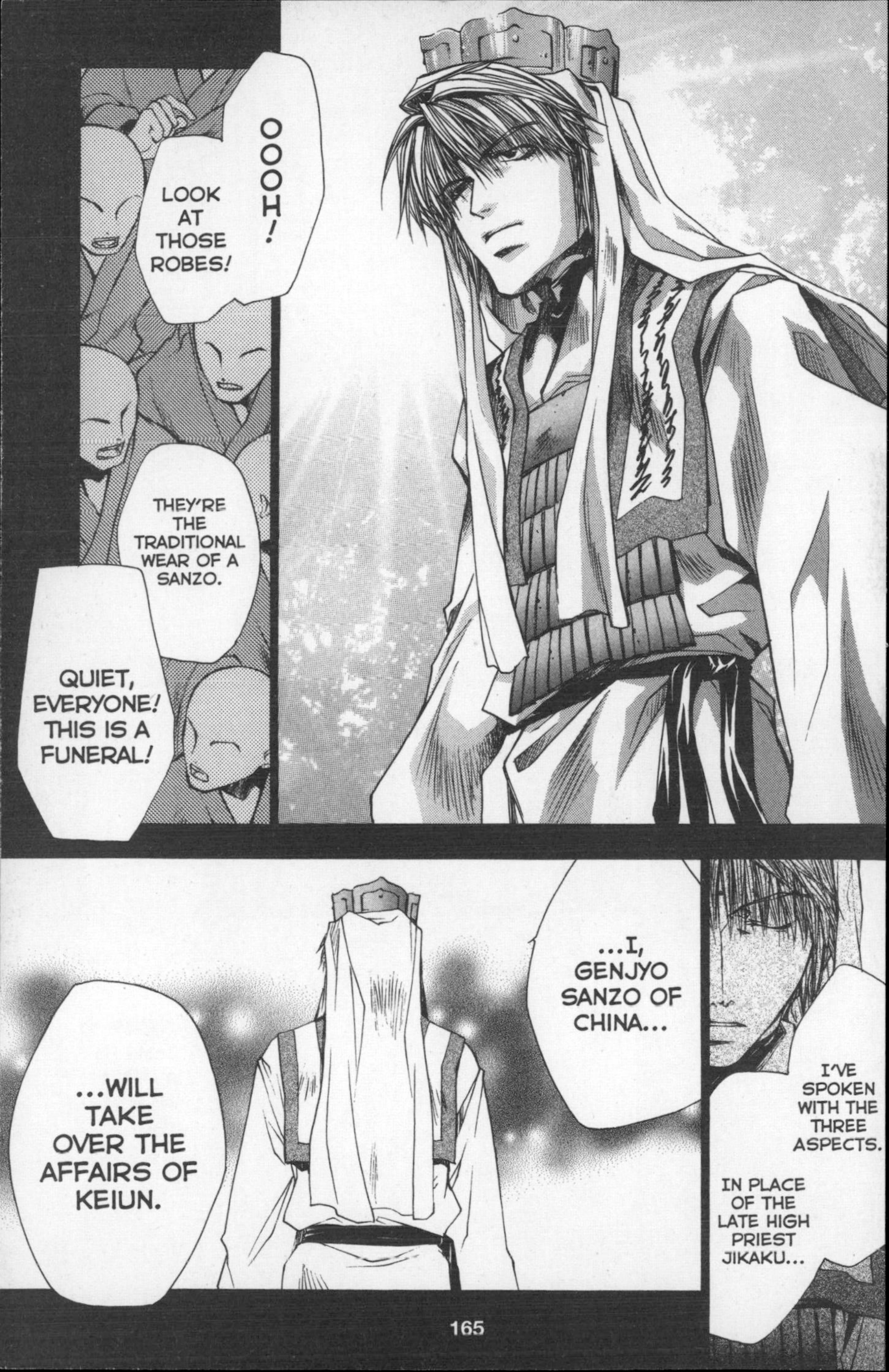
OOOH!
LOOK AT THOSE ROBES!
THEY'RE THE TRADITIONAL WEAR OF A SANZO.
QUIET, EVERYONE! THIS IS A FUNERAL!
I'VE SPOKEN WITH THE THREE ASPECTS.
IN PLACE OF THE LATE HIGH PRIEST JIKAKU...
...I, GENJYO SANZO OF CHINA...
...WILL TAKE OVER THE AFFAIRS OF KEIUN.

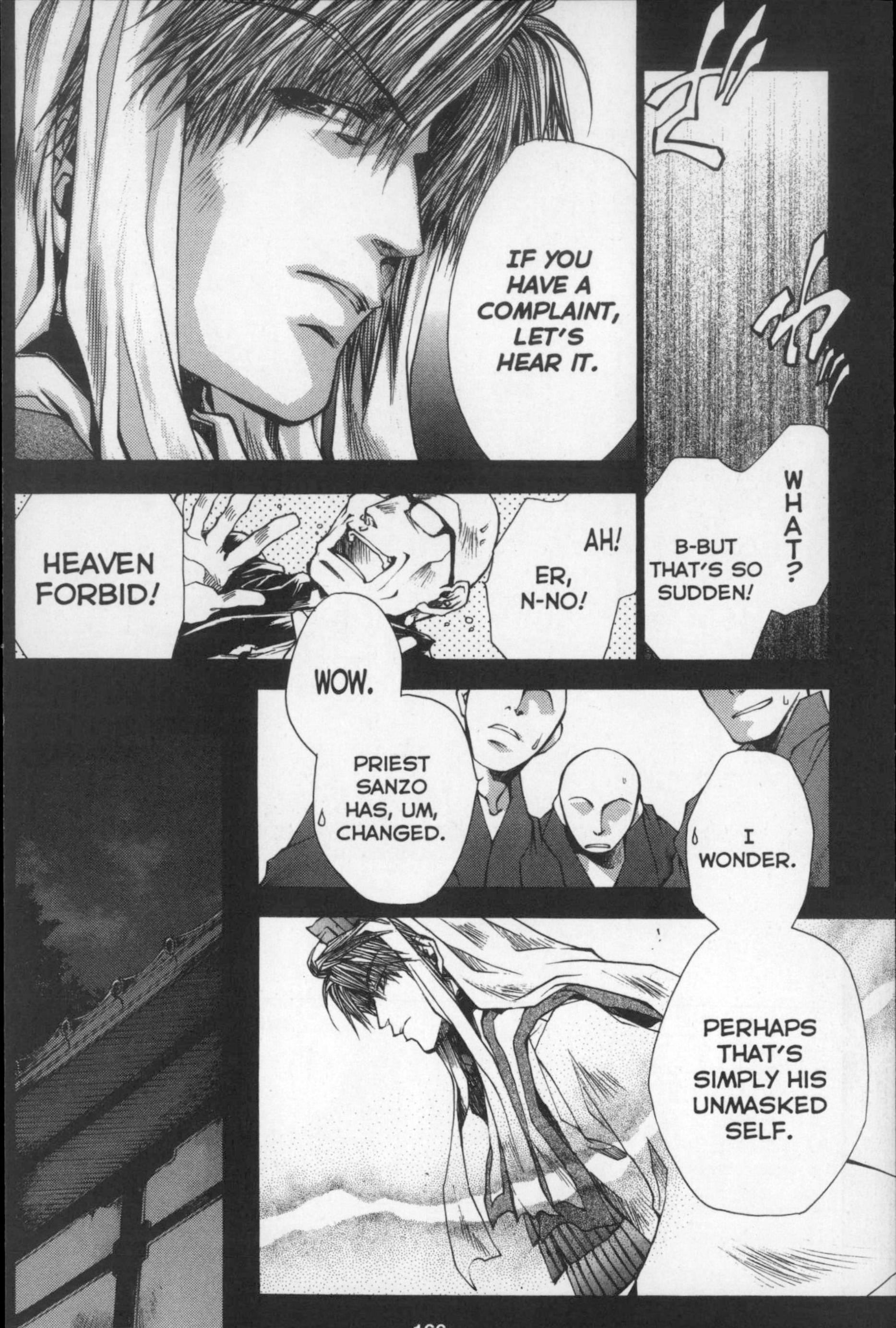
IF YOU HAVE A COMPLAINT, LET'S HEAR IT.
WHAT?
B-BUT THAT'S SO SUDDEN!
AH!
ER, N-NO!
HEAVEN FORBID!
WOW.
PRIEST SANZO HAS, UM, CHANGED.
I WONDER.
PERHAPS THAT'S SIMPLY HIS UNMASKED SELF.

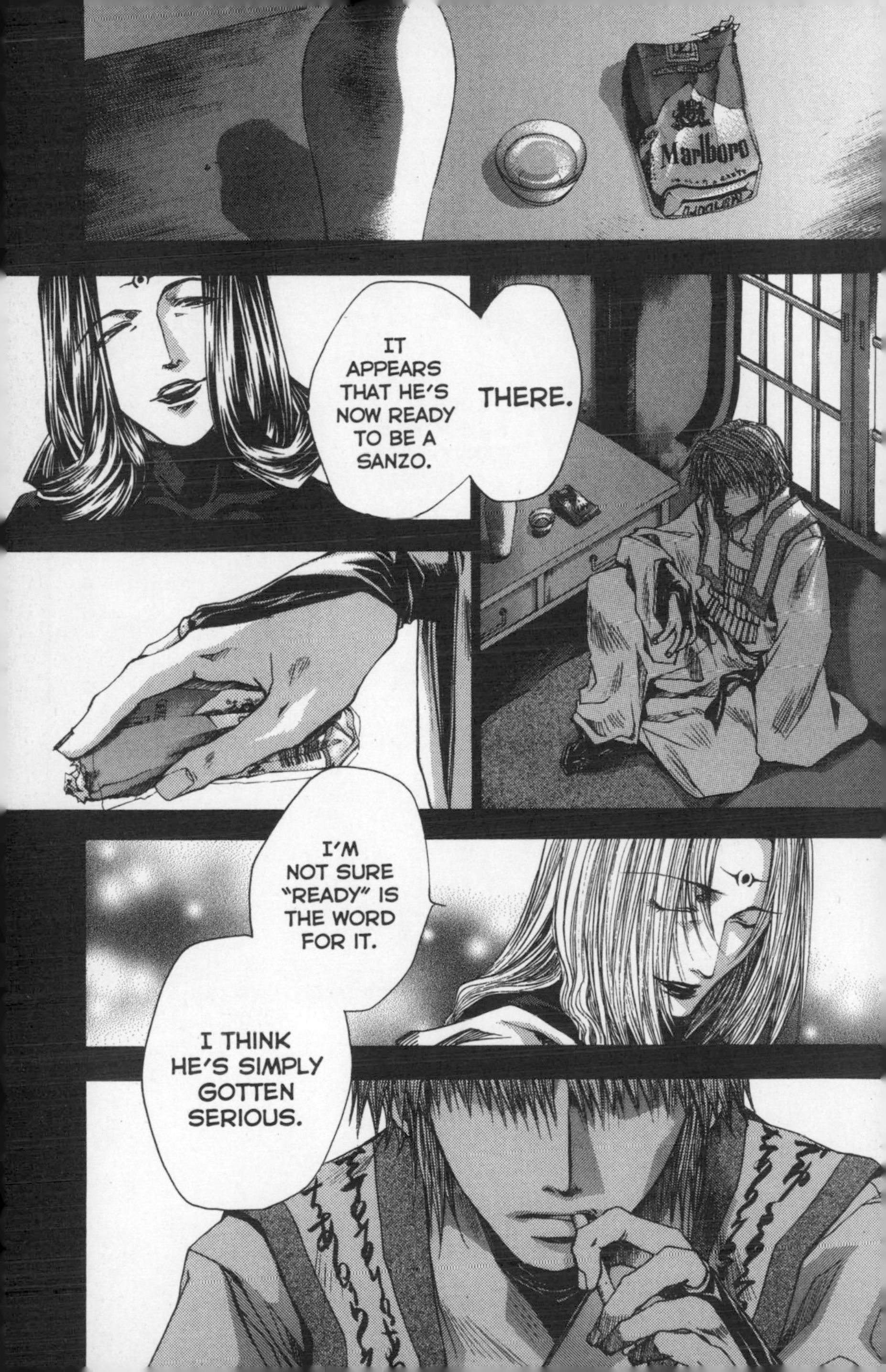
Marlboro
THERE.
IT APPEARS THAT HE'S NOW READY TO BE A SANZO.
I'M NOT SURE "READY" IS THE WORD FOR IT.
I THINK HE'S SIMPLY GOTTEN SERIOUS.

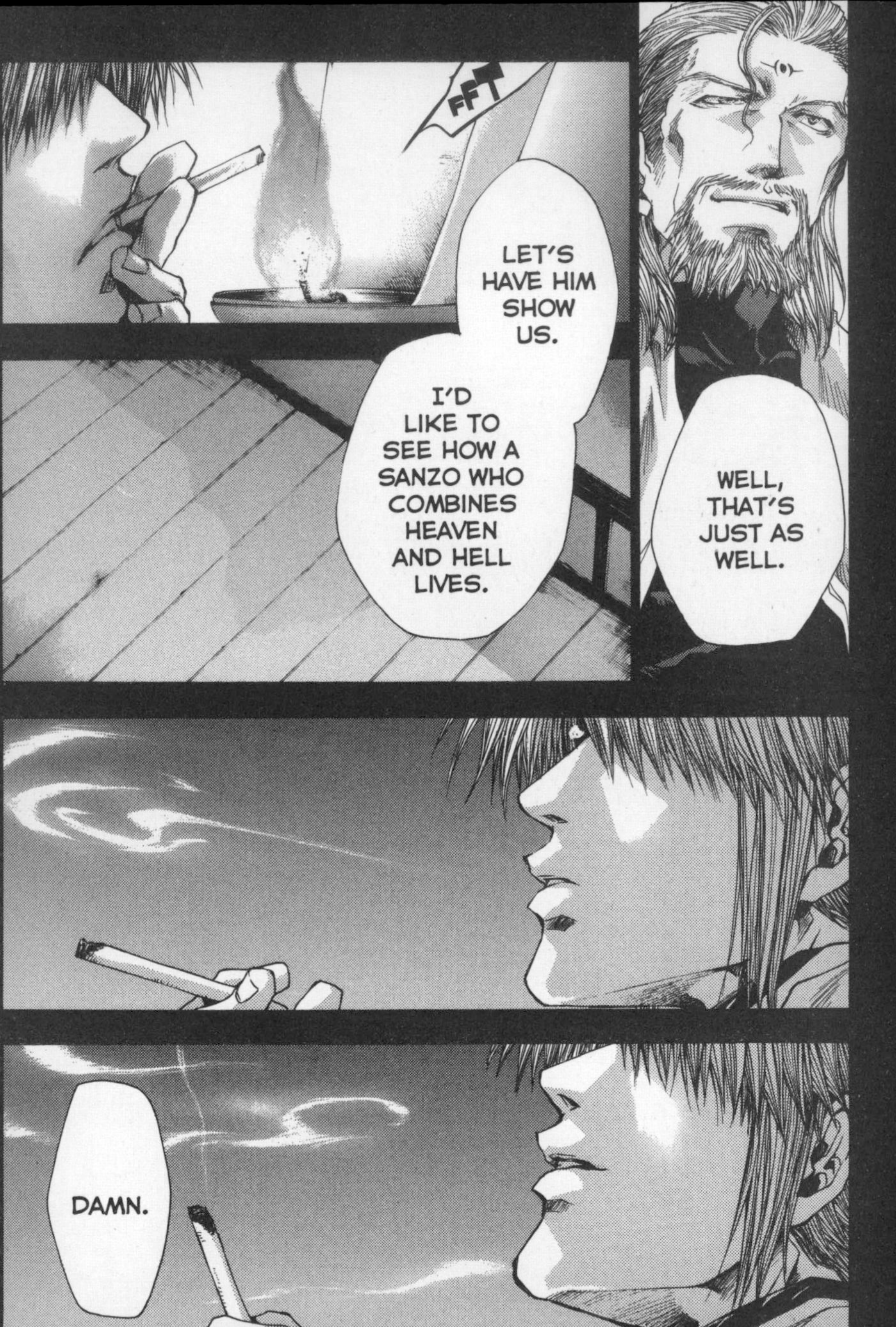
WELL, THAT'S JUST AS WELL.
FFT
LET'S HAVE HIM SHOW US.
I'D LIKE TO SEE HOW A SANZO WHO COMBINES HEAVEN AND HELL LIVES.
DAMN.

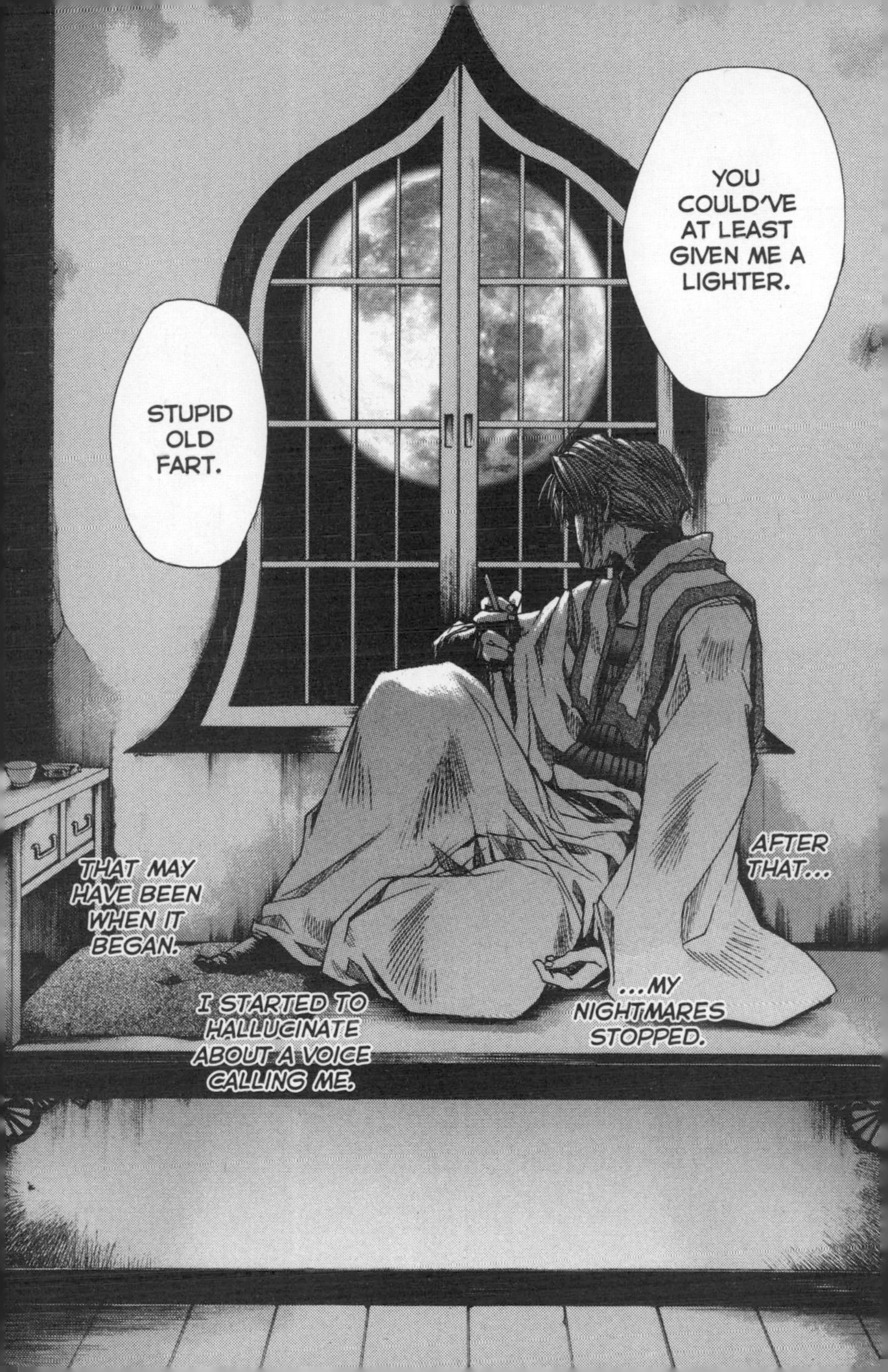
YOU COULD'VE AT LEAST GIVEN ME A LIGHTER.
STUPID OLD FART.
AFTER THAT...
...MY NIGHTMARES STOPPED.
THAT MAY HAVE BEEN WHEN IT BEGAN.
I STARTED TO HALLUCINATE ABOUT A VOICE CALLING ME.

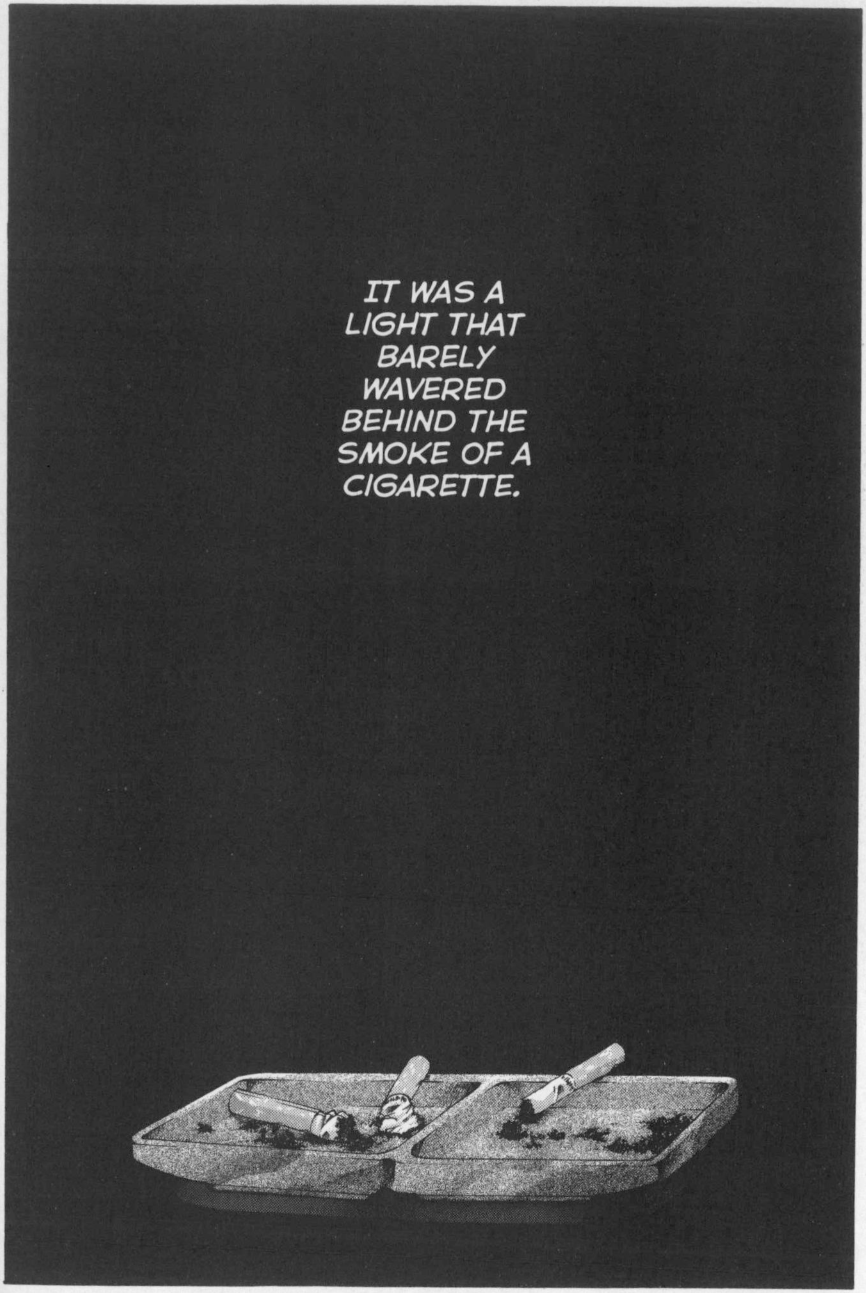
IT WAS A LIGHT THAT BARELY WAVERED BEHIND THE SMOKE OF A CIGARETTE.

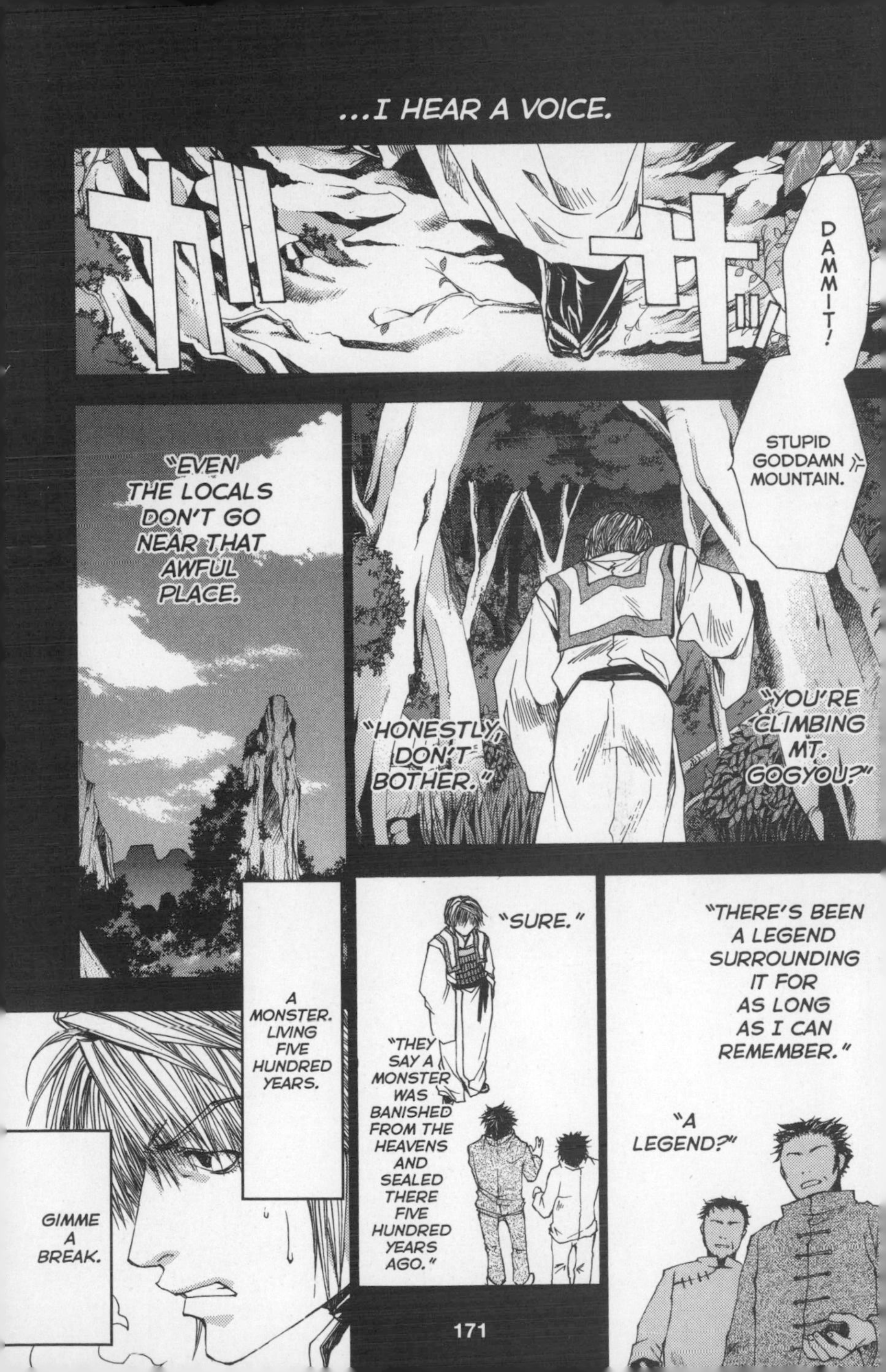
...I HEAR A VOICE.
DAMMIT!
STUPID GODDAMN MOUNTAIN.
"YOU'RE CLIMBING MT. GOGYOU?"
"HONESTLY, DON'T BOTHER."
"EVEN THE LOCALS DON'T GO NEAR THAT AWFUL PLACE.
"THERE'S BEEN A LEGEND SURROUNDING IT FOR AS LONG AS I CAN REMEMBER."
"A LEGEND?"
"SURE."
"THEY SAY A MONSTER WAS BANISHED FROM THE HEAVENS AND SEALED THERE FIVE HUNDRED YEARS AGO."
A MONSTER. LIVING FIVE HUNDRED YEARS.
GIMME A BREAK.

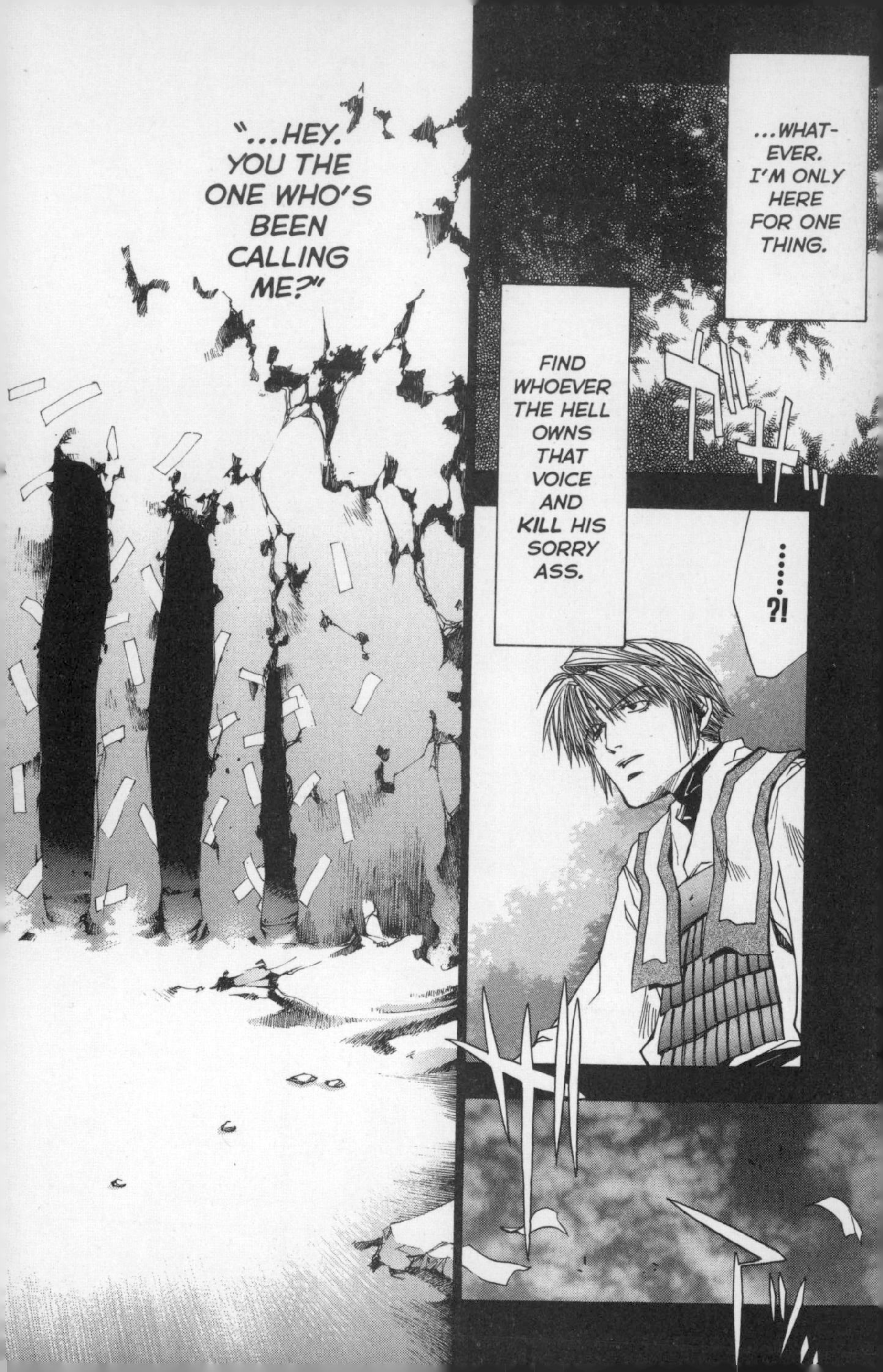
...WHAT-EVER. I'M ONLY HERE FOR ONE THING.
FIND WHOEVER THE HELL OWNS THAT VOICE AND KILL HIS SORRY ASS.
......?!
"...HEY. YOU THE ONE WHO'S BEEN CALLING ME?"

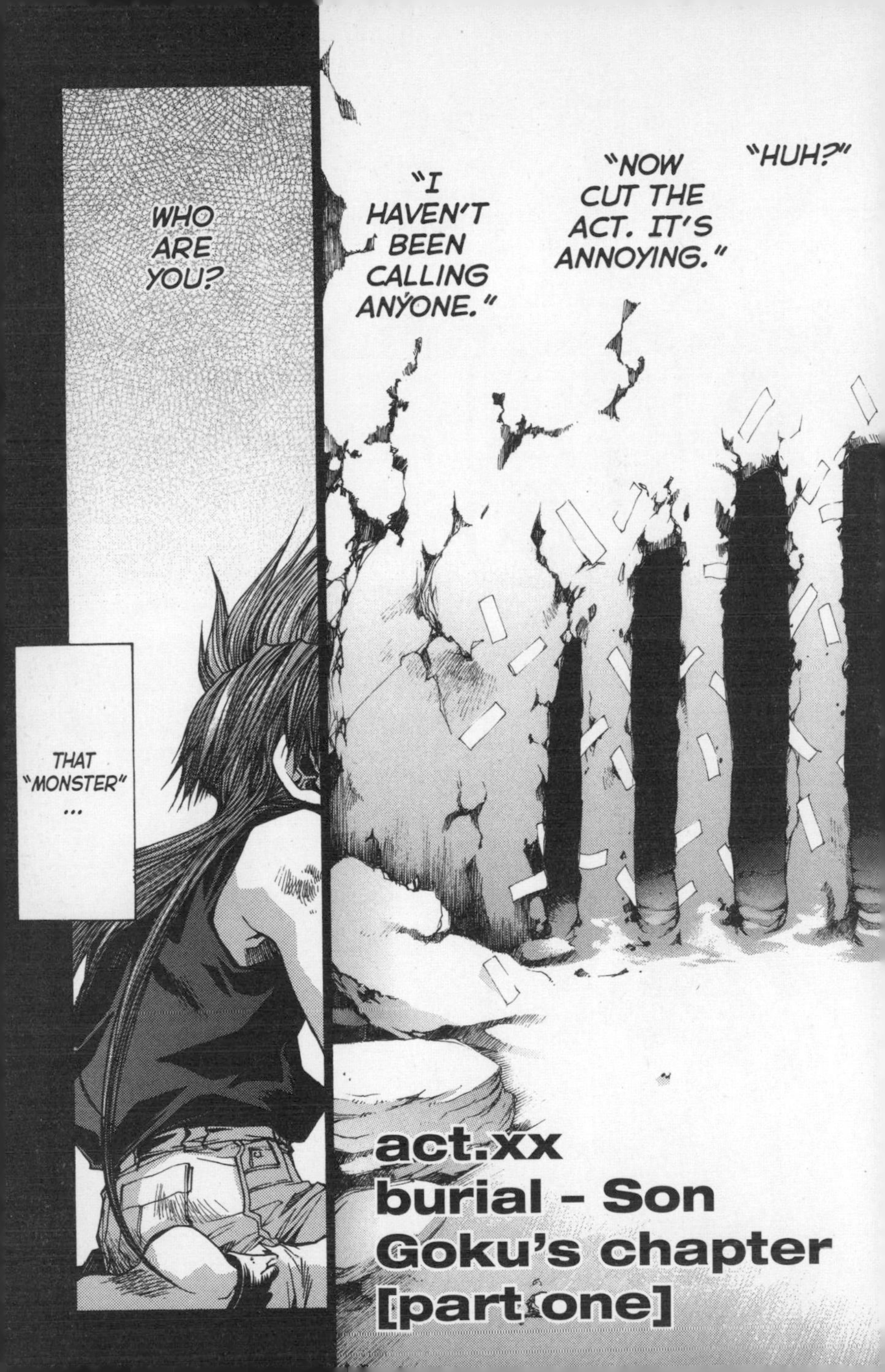
"HUH?"
"NOW CUT THE ACT. IT'S ANNOYING."
"I HAVEN'T BEEN CALLING ANYONE."
act.xx burial - Son Goku's chapter [part one]
WHO ARE YOU?
THAT "MONSTER" ...

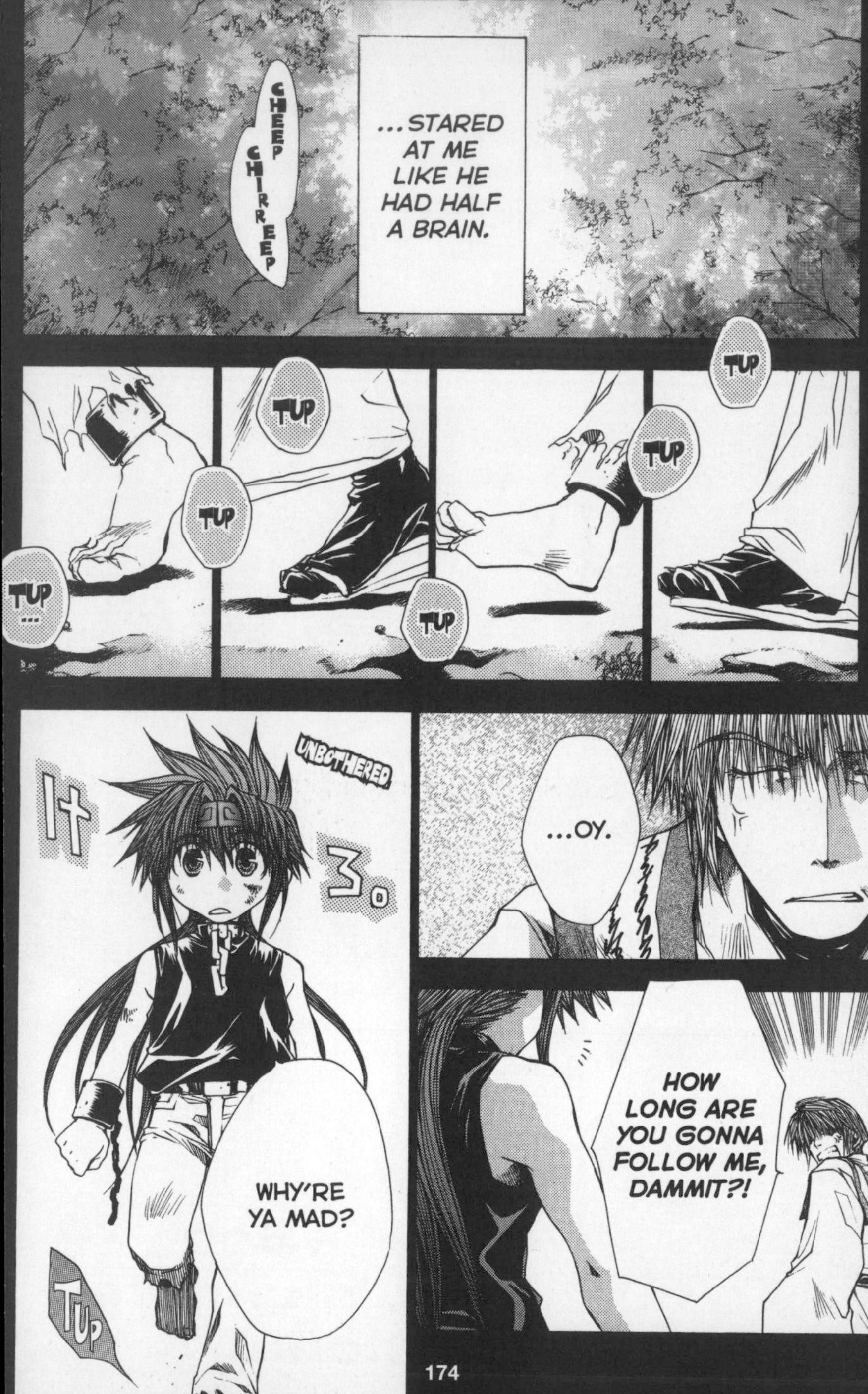
...STARED AT ME LIKE HE HAD HALF A BRAIN.
CHEEP CHIRREEP
TUP
TUP
TUP
TUP
TUP
TUP ...
...OY.
HOW LONG ARE YOU GONNA FOLLOW ME, DAMMIT?!
UNBOTHERED.
WHY'RE YA MAD?
TUP

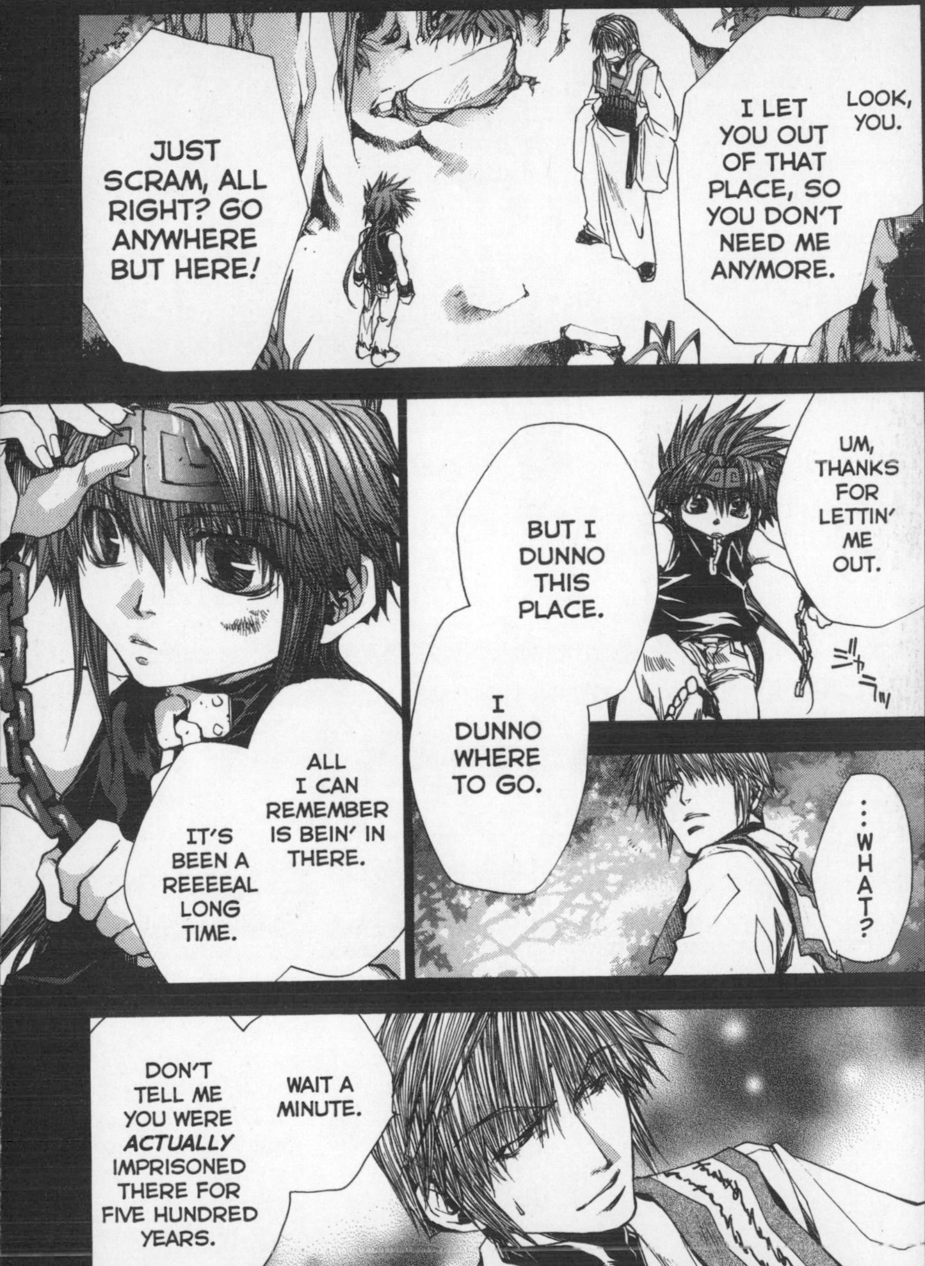
LOOK, YOU.
I LET YOU OUT OF THAT PLACE, SO YOU DON'T NEED ME ANYMORE.
JUST SCRAM, ALL RIGHT? GO ANYWHERE BUT HERE!
UM, THANKS FOR LETTIN' ME OUT.
BUT I DUNNO THIS PLACE.
I DUNNO WHERE TO GO.
...WHAT?
ALL I CAN REMEMBER IS BEIN' IN THERE.
IT'S BEEN A REEEEAL LONG TIME.
WAIT A MINUTE.
DON'T TELL ME YOU WERE *ACTUALLY* IMPRISONED THERE FOR FIVE HUNDRED YEARS.

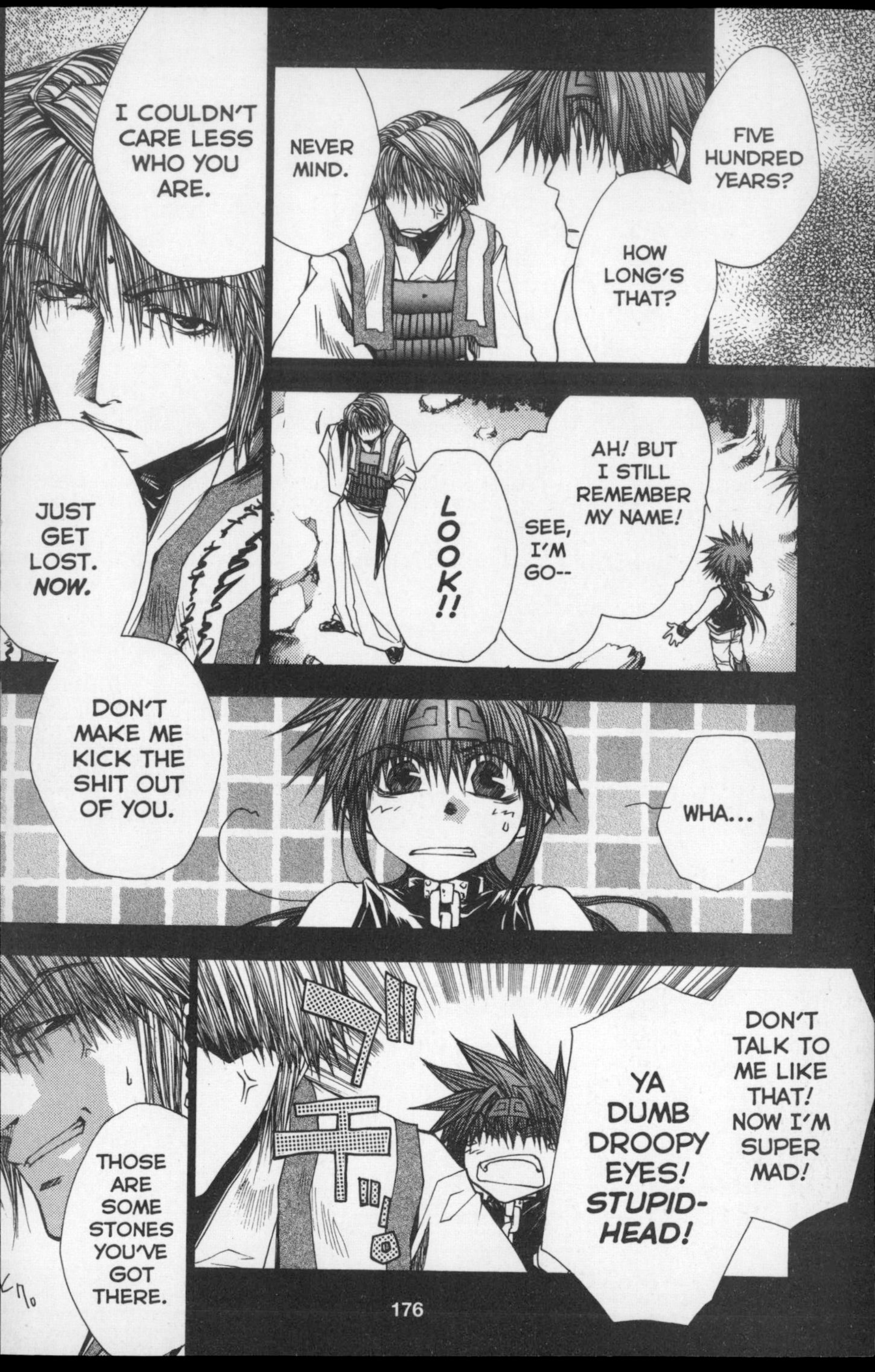
FIVE HUNDRED YEARS?
HOW LONG'S THAT?
NEVER MIND.
AH! BUT I STILL REMEMBER MY NAME!
SEE, I'M GO--
LOOK!!
I COULDN'T CARE LESS WHO YOU ARE.
JUST GET LOST. *NOW.*
WHA...
DON'T MAKE ME KICK THE SHIT OUT OF YOU.
DON'T TALK TO ME LIKE THAT! NOW I'M SUPER MAD!
YA DUMB DROOPY EYES! *STUPID-HEAD!*
THOSE ARE SOME STONES YOU'VE GOT THERE.

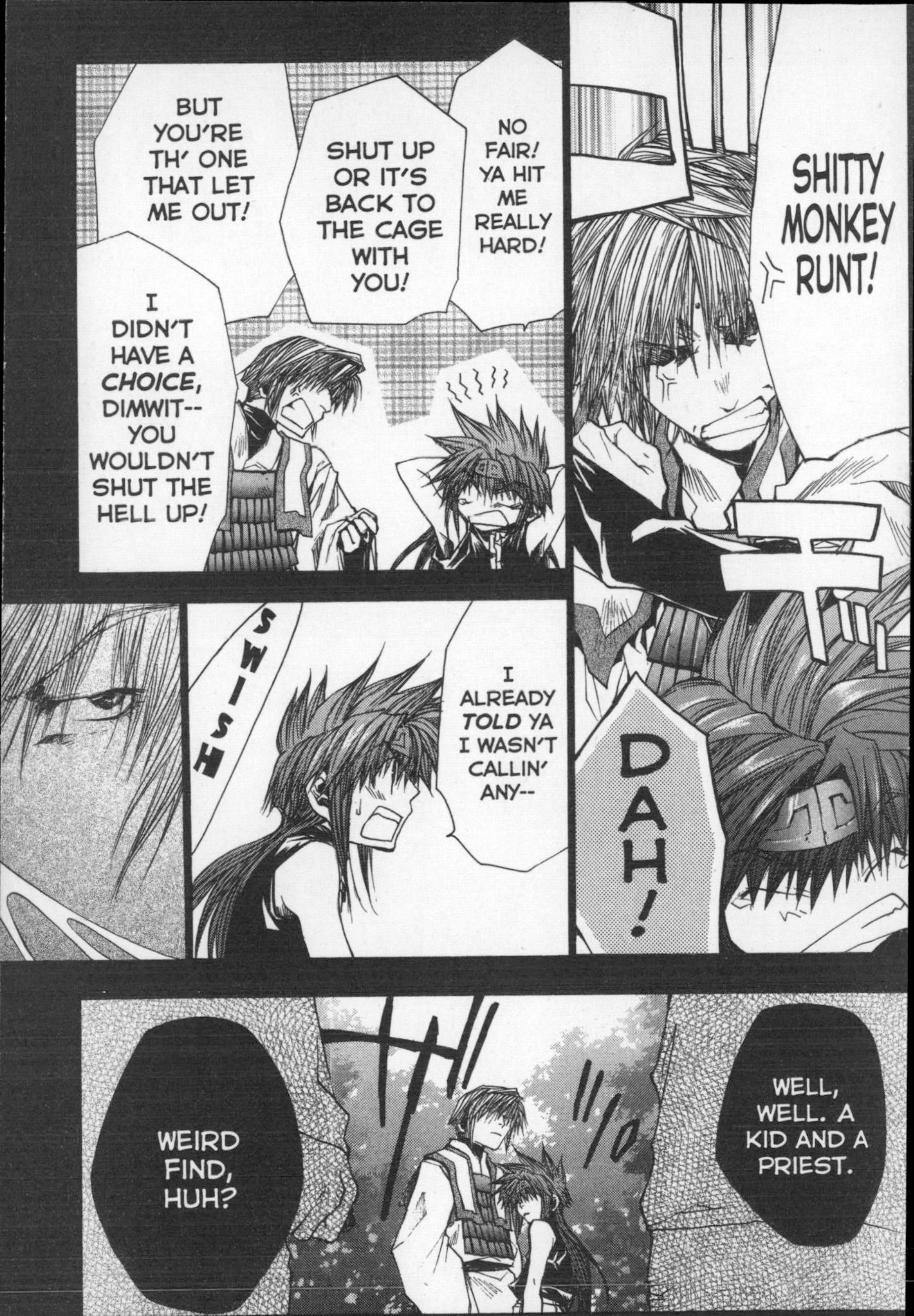
SHITTY MONKEY RUNT!
DAH!
NO FAIR! YA HIT ME REALLY HARD!
SHUT UP OR IT'S BACK TO THE CAGE WITH YOU!
BUT YOU'RE TH' ONE THAT LET ME OUT!
I DIDN'T HAVE A *CHOICE*, DIMWIT-- YOU WOULDN'T SHUT THE HELL UP!
I ALREADY *TOLD* YA I WASN'T CALLIN' ANY--
SWISH
WELL, WELL. A KID AND A PRIEST.
WEIRD FIND, HUH?

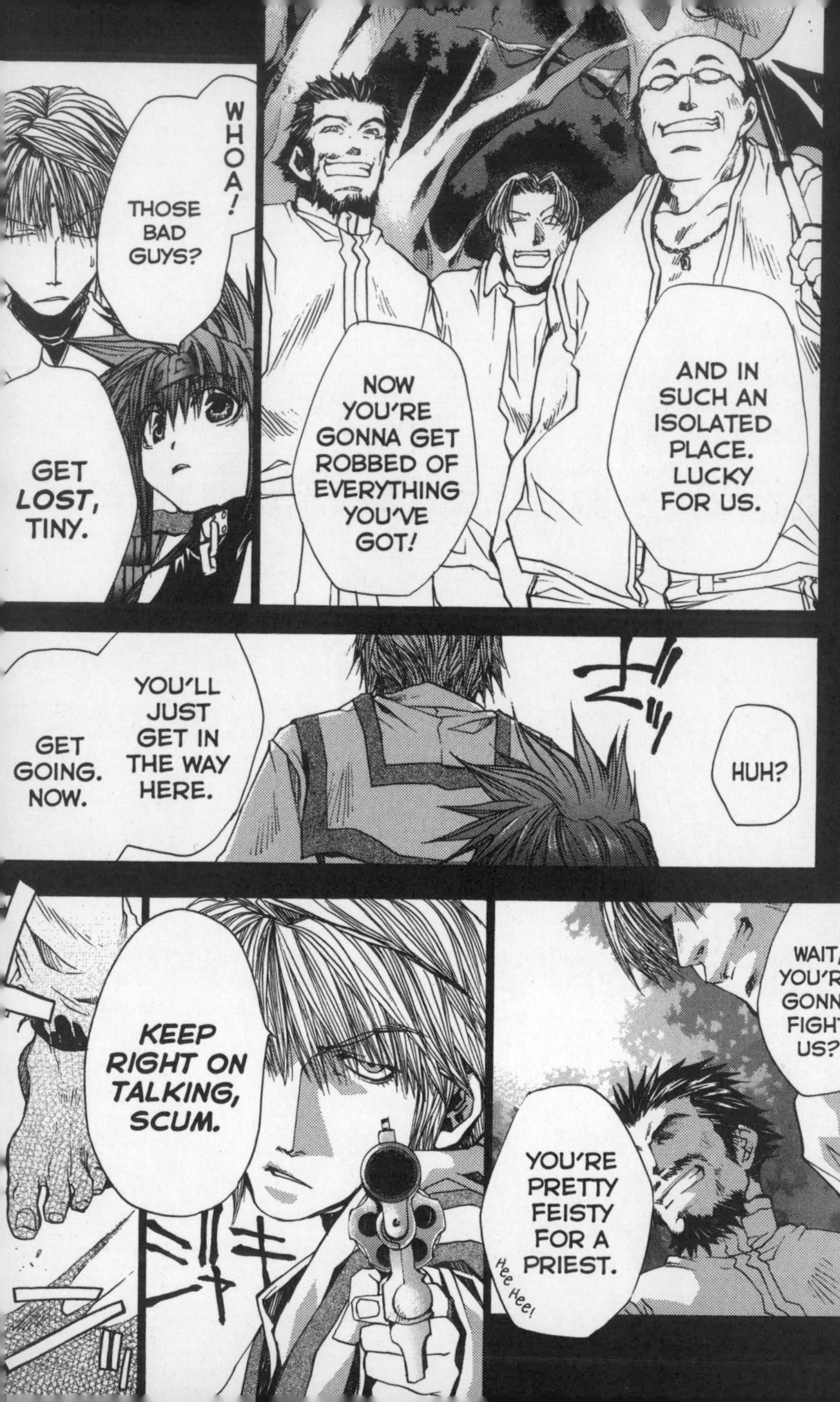
AND IN SUCH AN ISOLATED PLACE. LUCKY FOR US.
NOW YOU'RE GONNA GET ROBBED OF EVERYTHING YOU'VE GOT!
WHOA!
THOSE BAD GUYS?
GET *LOST*, TINY.
HUH?
YOU'LL JUST GET IN THE WAY HERE.
GET GOING. NOW.
WAIT, YOU'RE GONNA FIGHT US?
YOU'RE PRETTY FEISTY FOR A PRIEST.
Hee Hee!
KEEP RIGHT ON TALKING, SCUM.

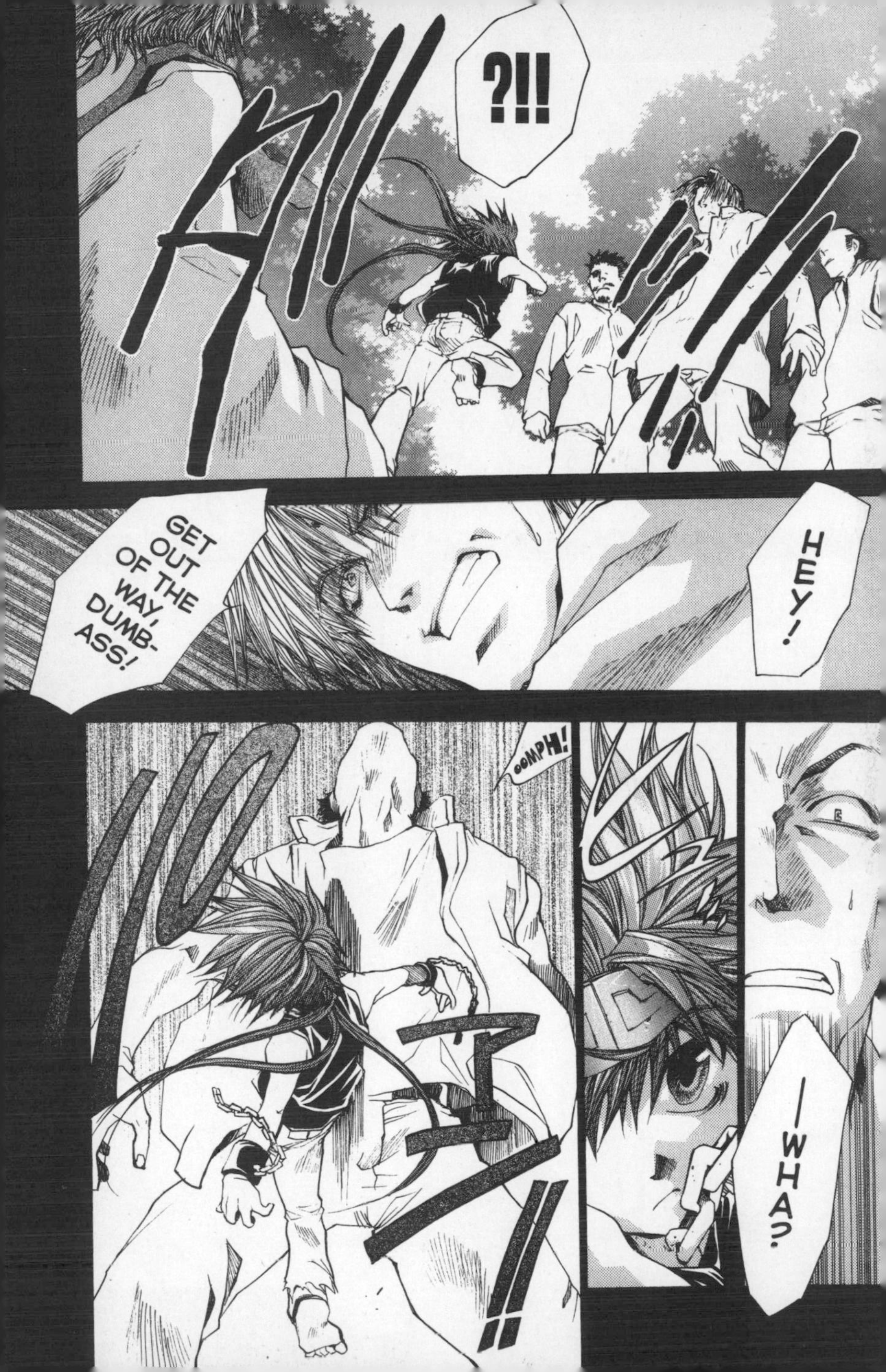
?!!
HEY!
GET OUT OF THE WAY, DUMB-ASS!
WHA?
OOMPH!

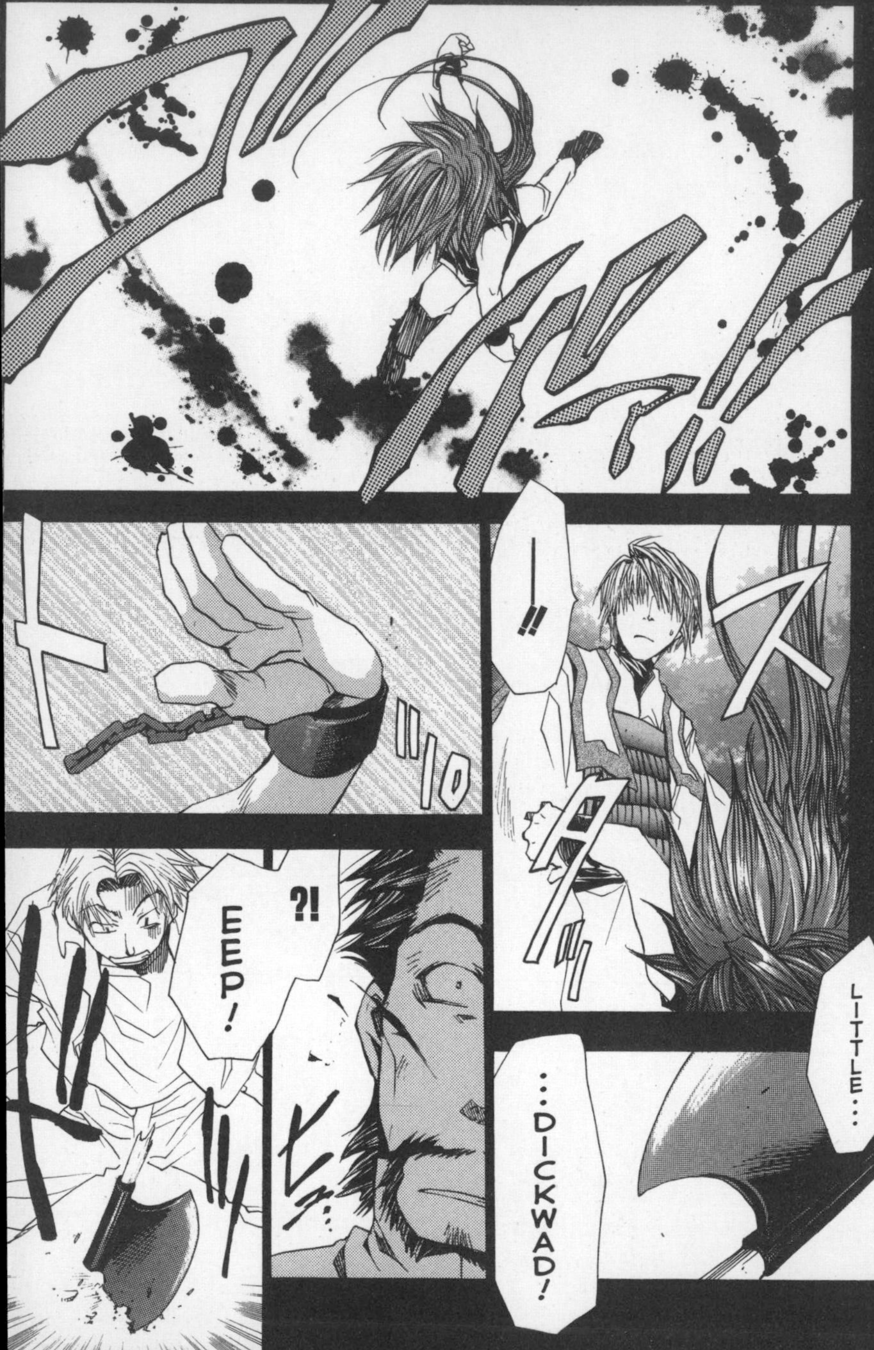
!!
LITTLE...
...DICKWAD!
?!
EEP!

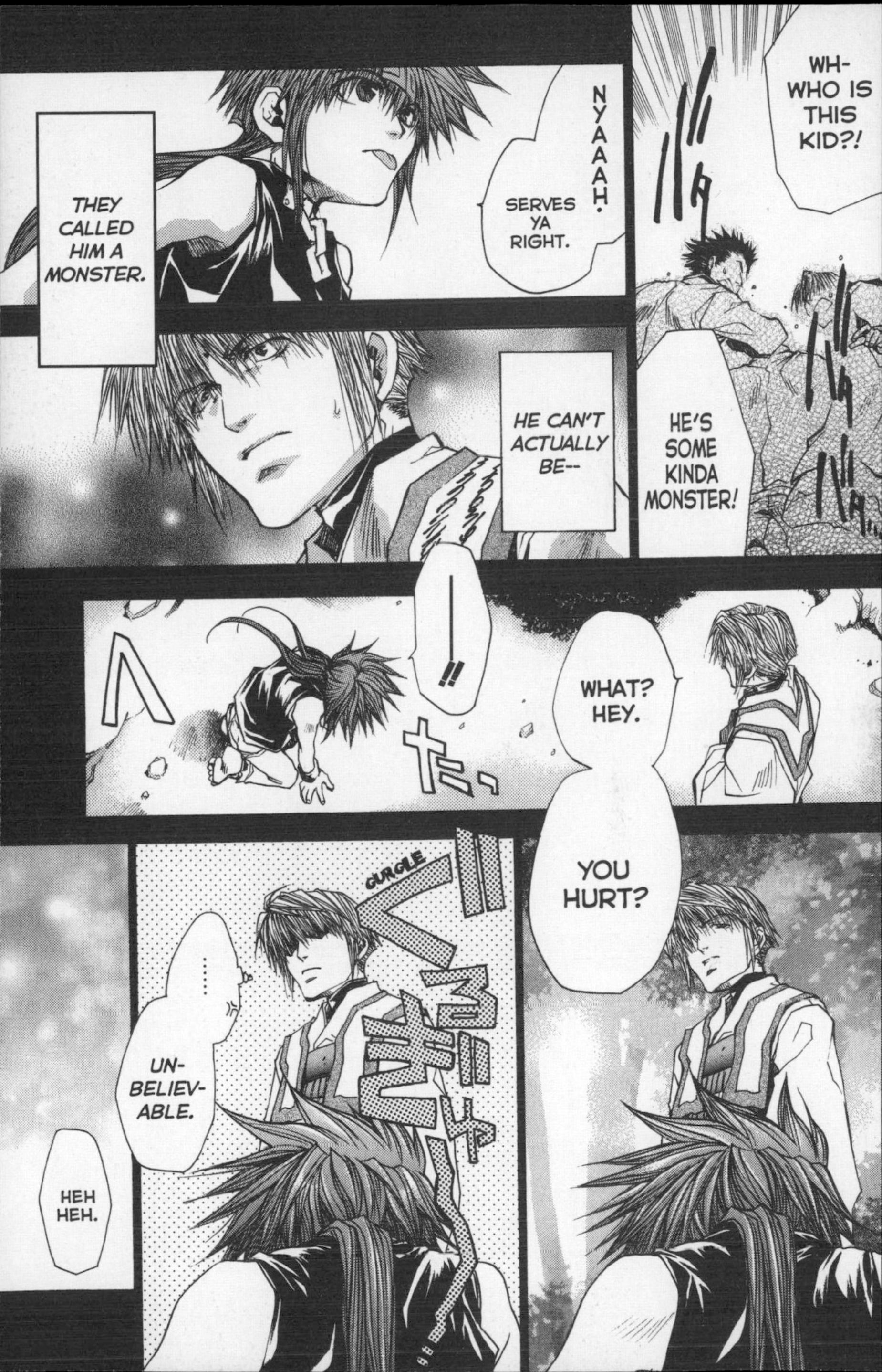

WH- WHO IS THIS KID?!
HE'S SOME KINDA MONSTER!
NYAAAAH.
SERVES YA RIGHT.
THEY CALLED HIM A MONSTER.
HE CAN'T ACTUALLY BE--
WHAT? HEY.
—!!
YOU HURT?
GURGLE
......
UN-BELIEV-ABLE.
HEH HEH.

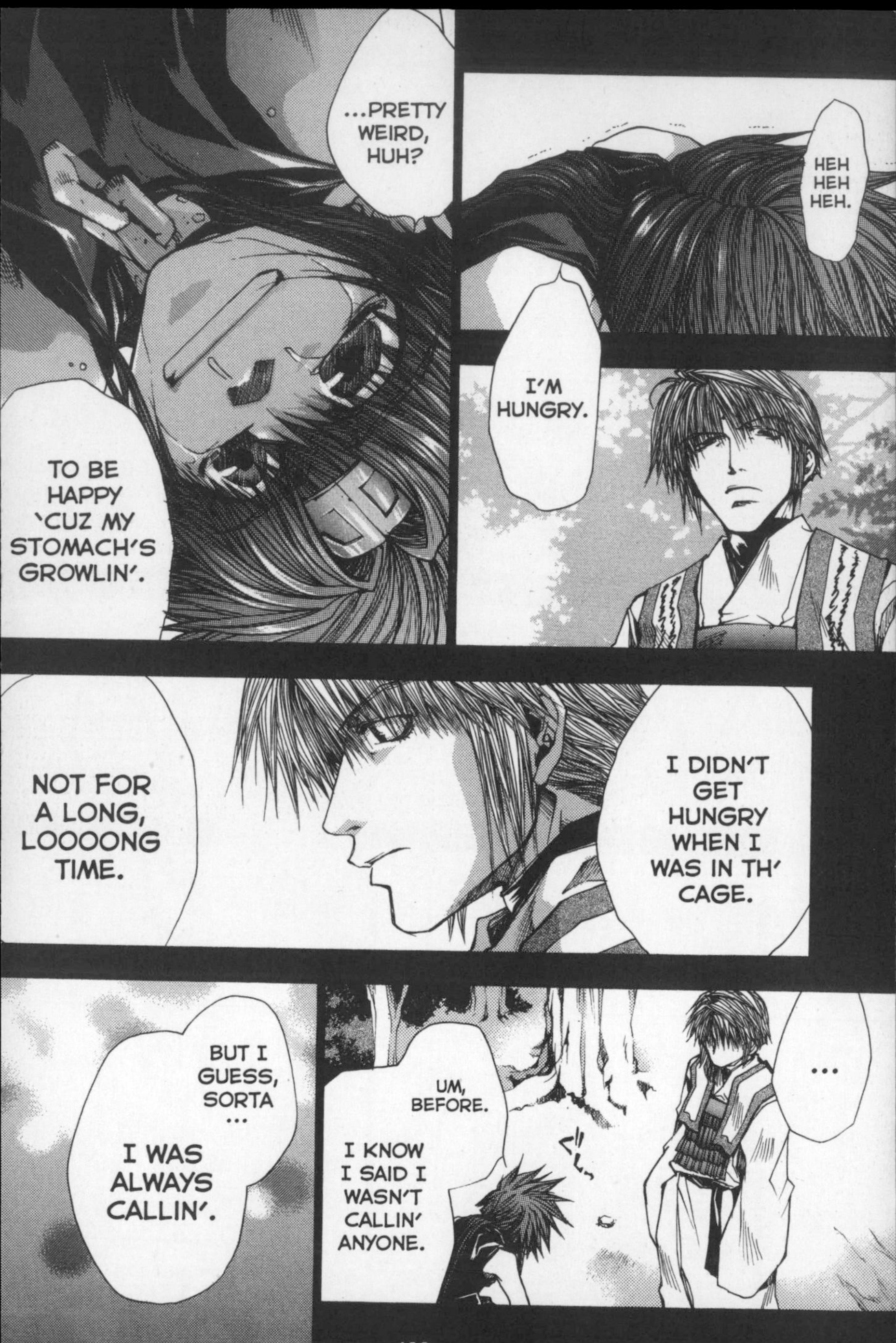
HEH HEH HEH.
I'M HUNGRY.
...PRETTY WEIRD, HUH?
TO BE HAPPY 'CUZ MY STOMACH'S GROWLIN'.
I DIDN'T GET HUNGRY WHEN I WAS IN TH' CAGE.
NOT FOR A LONG, LOOOONG TIME.
...
UM, BEFORE.
I KNOW I SAID I WASN'T CALLIN' ANYONE.
BUT I GUESS, SORTA ...
I WAS ALWAYS CALLIN'.

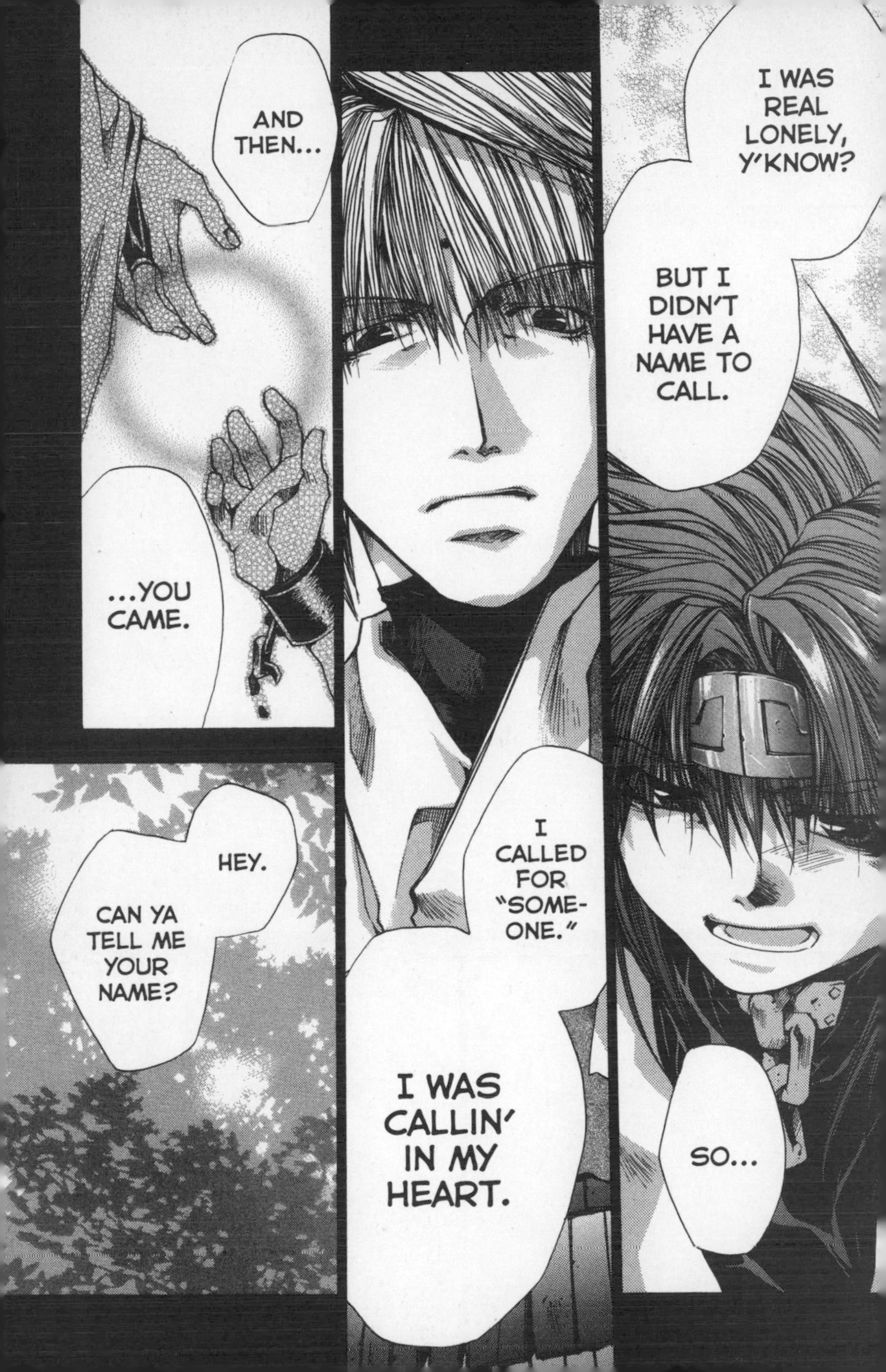
I WAS REAL LONELY, Y'KNOW?
BUT I DIDN'T HAVE A NAME TO CALL.
SO...
I CALLED FOR "SOME-ONE."
I WAS CALLIN' IN MY HEART.
AND THEN...
...YOU CAME.
HEY.
CAN YA TELL ME YOUR NAME?

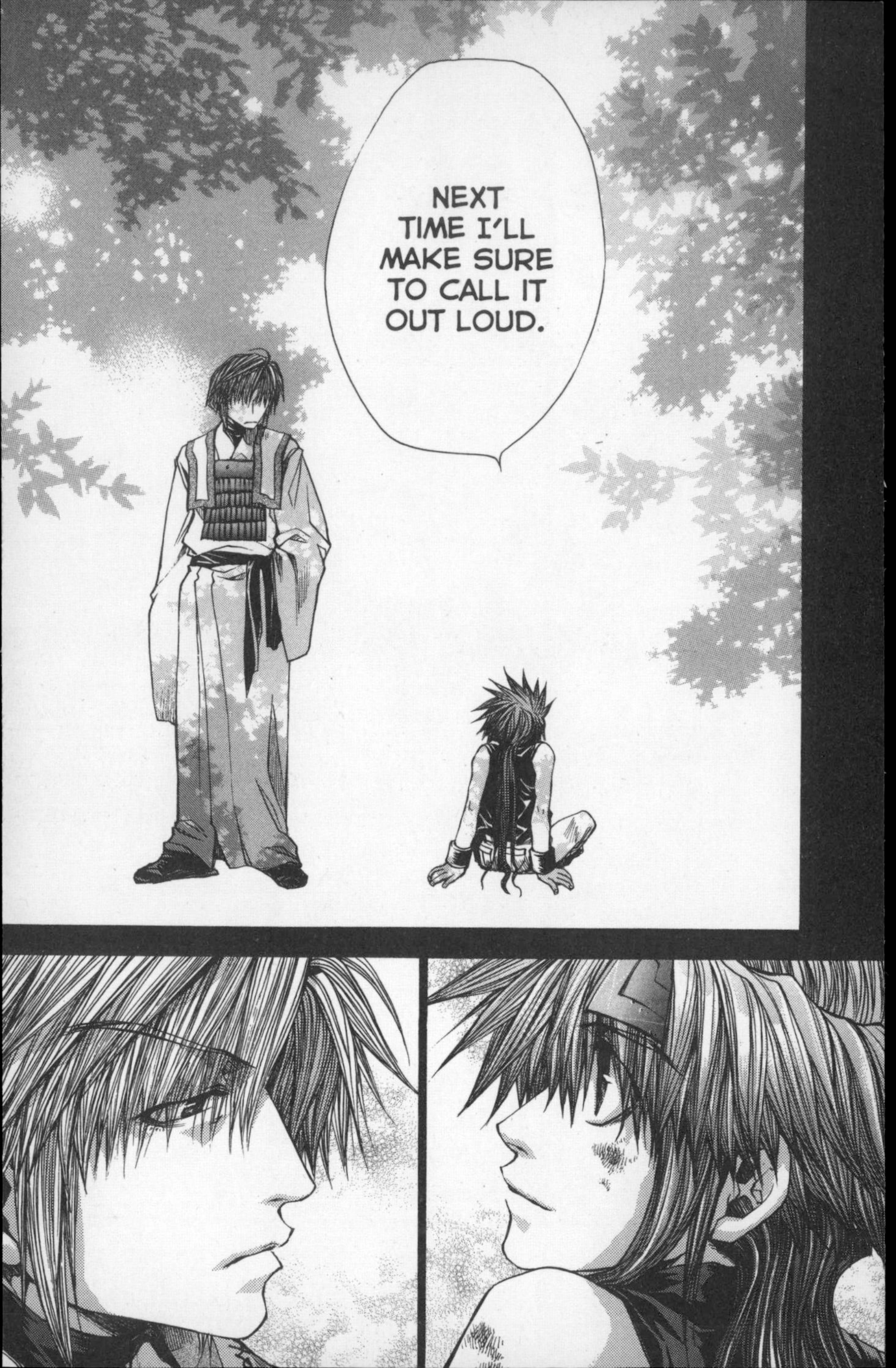
NEXT TIME I'LL MAKE SURE TO CALL IT OUT LOUD.

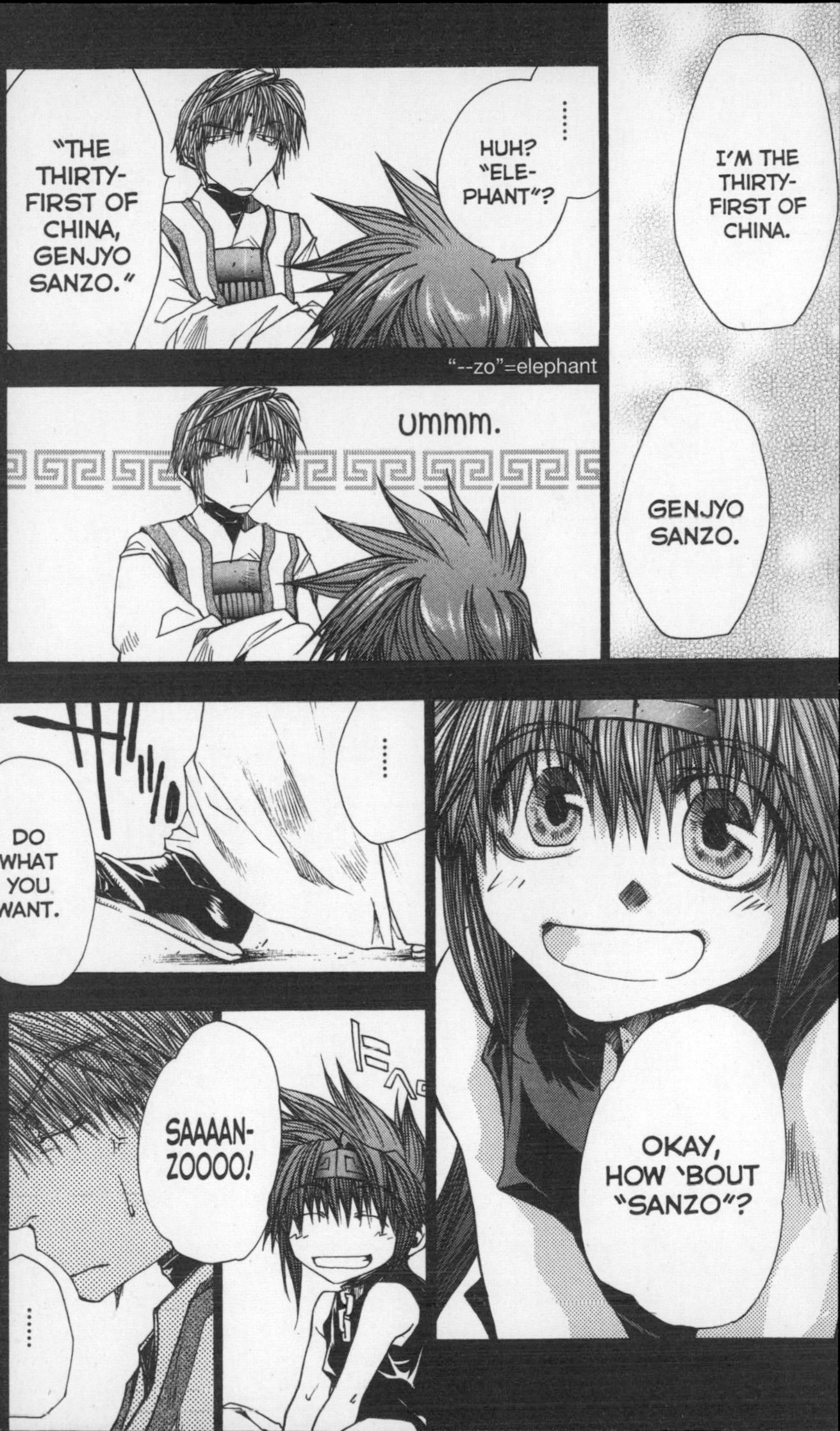
I'M THE THIRTY-FIRST OF CHINA.
GENJYO SANZO.
......
HUH? "ELE-PHANT"?
"THE THIRTY-FIRST OF CHINA, GENJYO SANZO."
"--zo"=elephant
UMMM.
OKAY, HOW 'BOUT "SANZO"?
......
DO WHAT YOU WANT.
SAAAAN-ZOOOO!
......

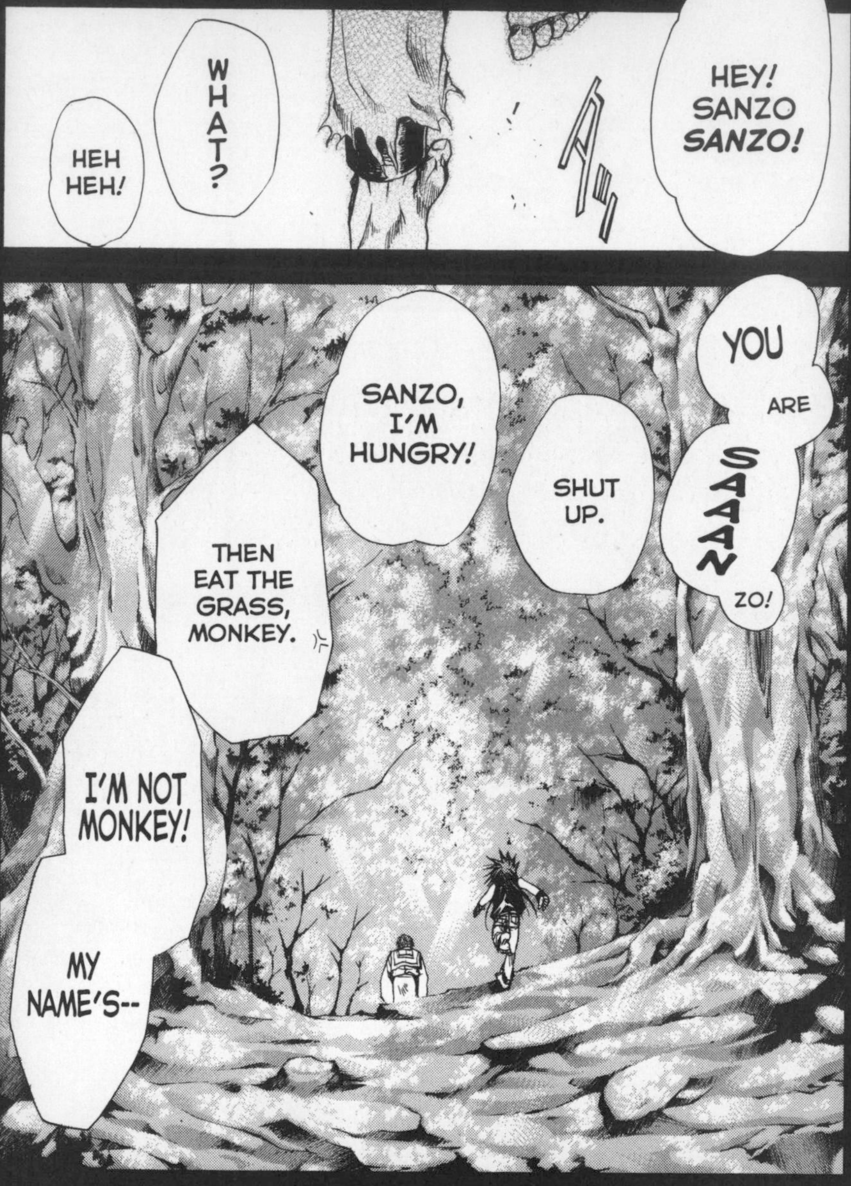
HEY! SANZO SANZO!
WHAT?
HEH HEH!
YOU ARE SAAAANZO!
SANZO, I'M HUNGRY!
SHUT UP.
THEN EAT THE GRASS, MONKEY.
I'M NOT MONKEY!
MY NAME'S--

YOU'RE GOING TO BE STAYING WITH ME FOR A WHILE...
IT'S NOT AS IF I HAVE ANY CHOICE.

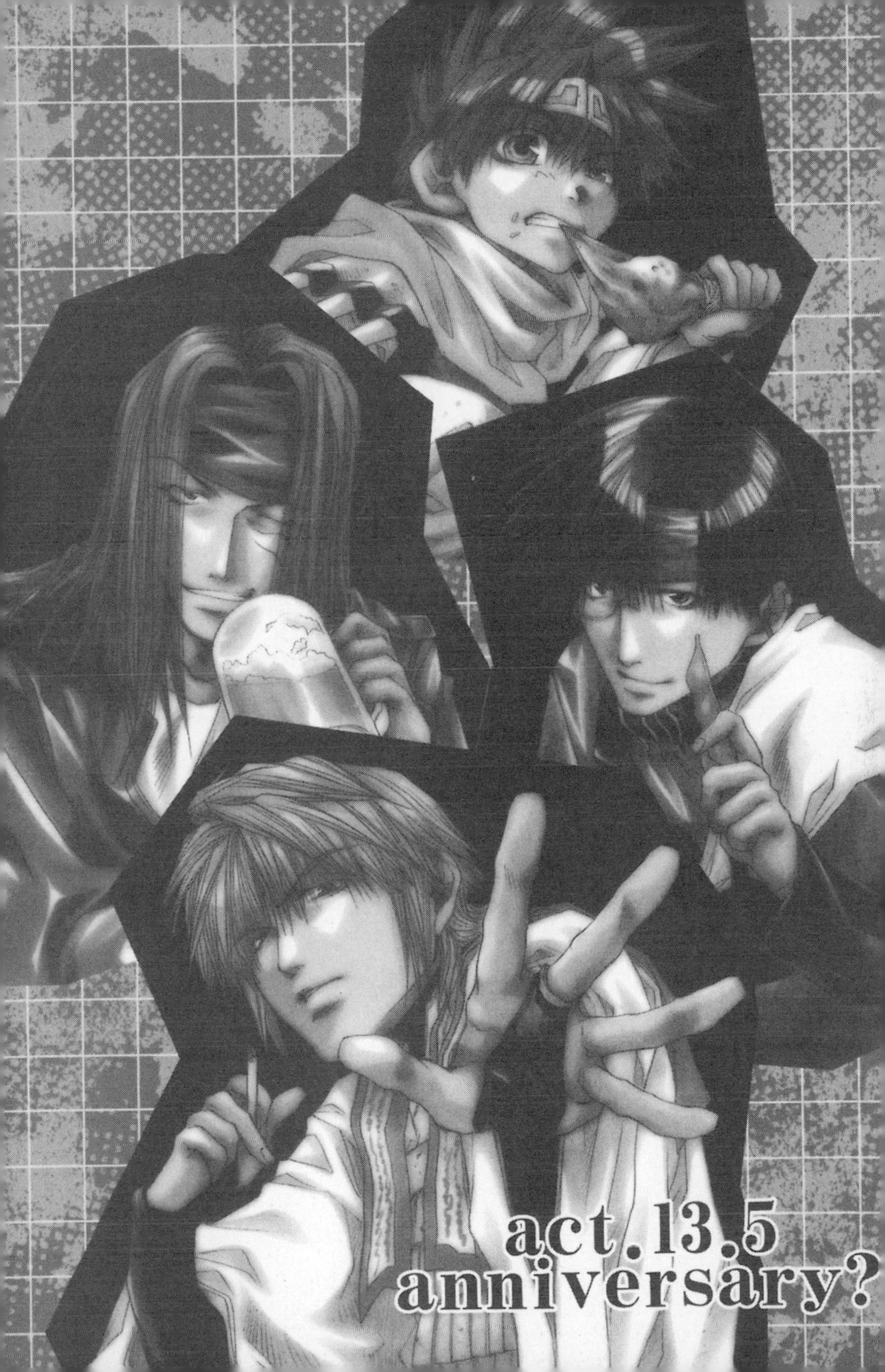
act.13.5
anniversary?

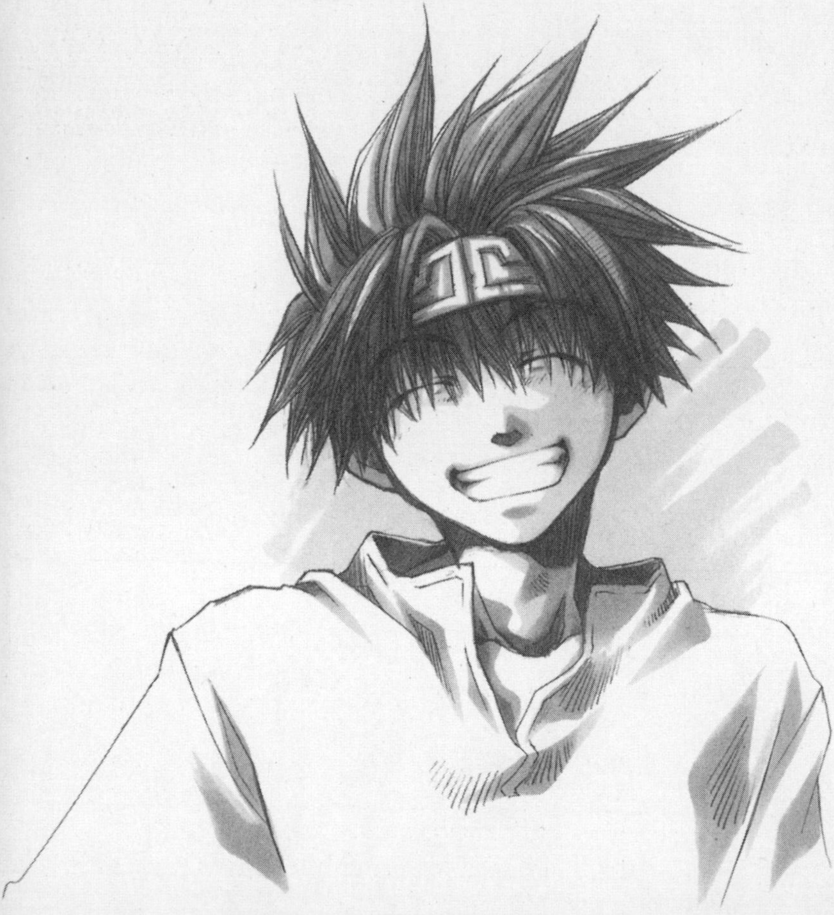

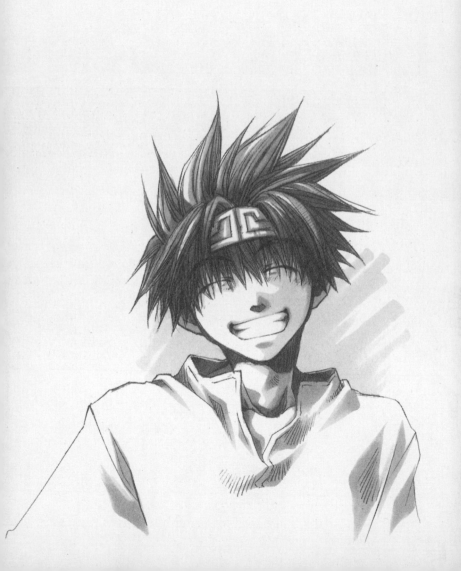

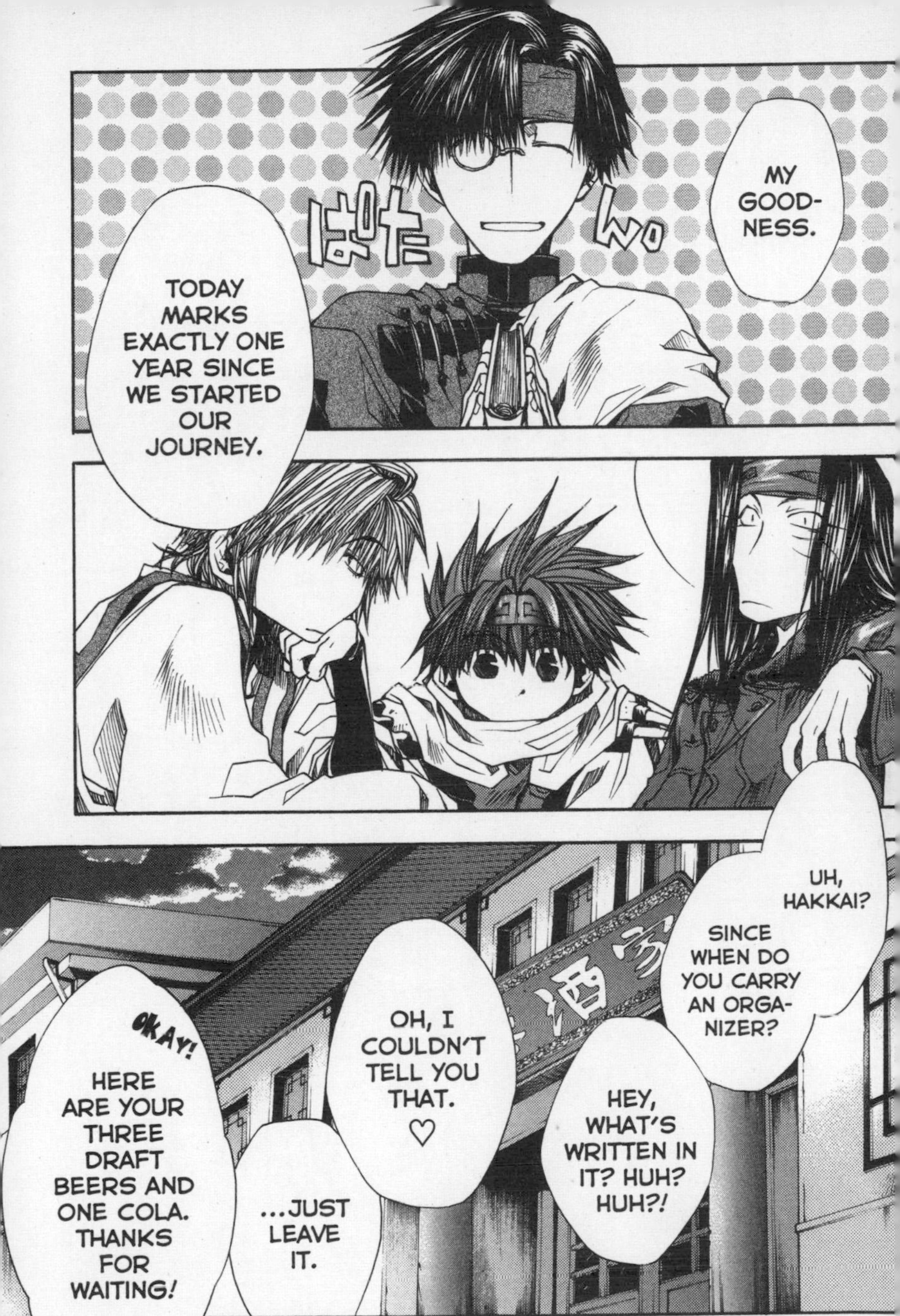
MY GOODNESS.
ぱたん
TODAY MARKS EXACTLY ONE YEAR SINCE WE STARTED OUR JOURNEY.
UH, HAKKAI?
SINCE WHEN DO YOU CARRY AN ORGANIZER?
OH, I COULDN'T TELL YOU THAT. ♡
HEY, WHAT'S WRITTEN IN IT? HUH? HUH?!
...JUST LEAVE IT.
OKAY!
HERE ARE YOUR THREE DRAFT BEERS AND ONE COLA. THANKS FOR WAITING!

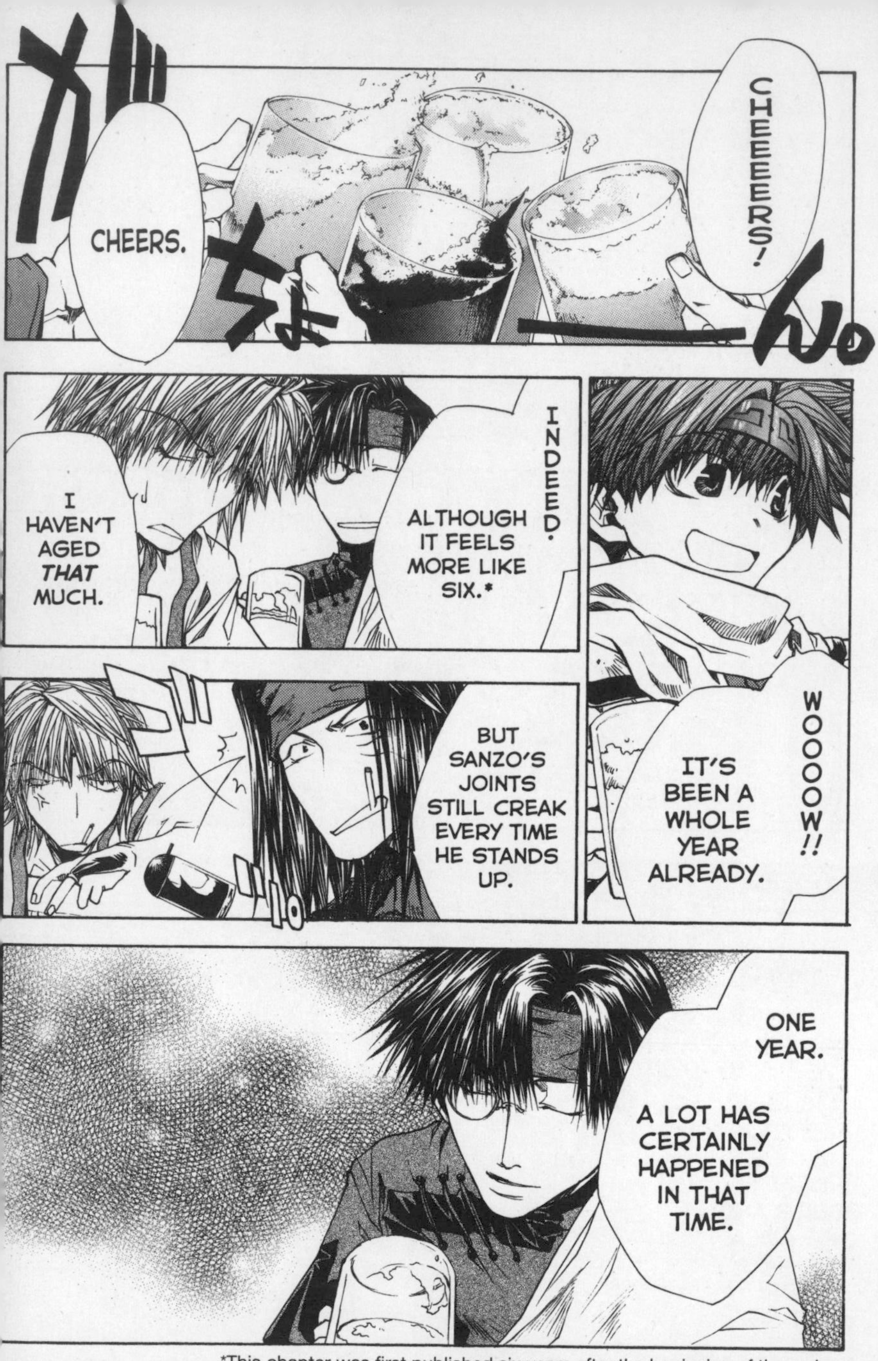
CHEEEERS!
CHEERS.
WOOOOOW!!
IT'S BEEN A WHOLE YEAR ALREADY.
INDEED.
ALTHOUGH IT FEELS MORE LIKE SIX.*
I HAVEN'T AGED *THAT* MUCH.
BUT SANZO'S JOINTS STILL CREAK EVERY TIME HE STANDS UP.
ONE YEAR.
A LOT HAS CERTAINLY HAPPENED IN THAT TIME.

*This chapter was first published six years after the beginning of the series.

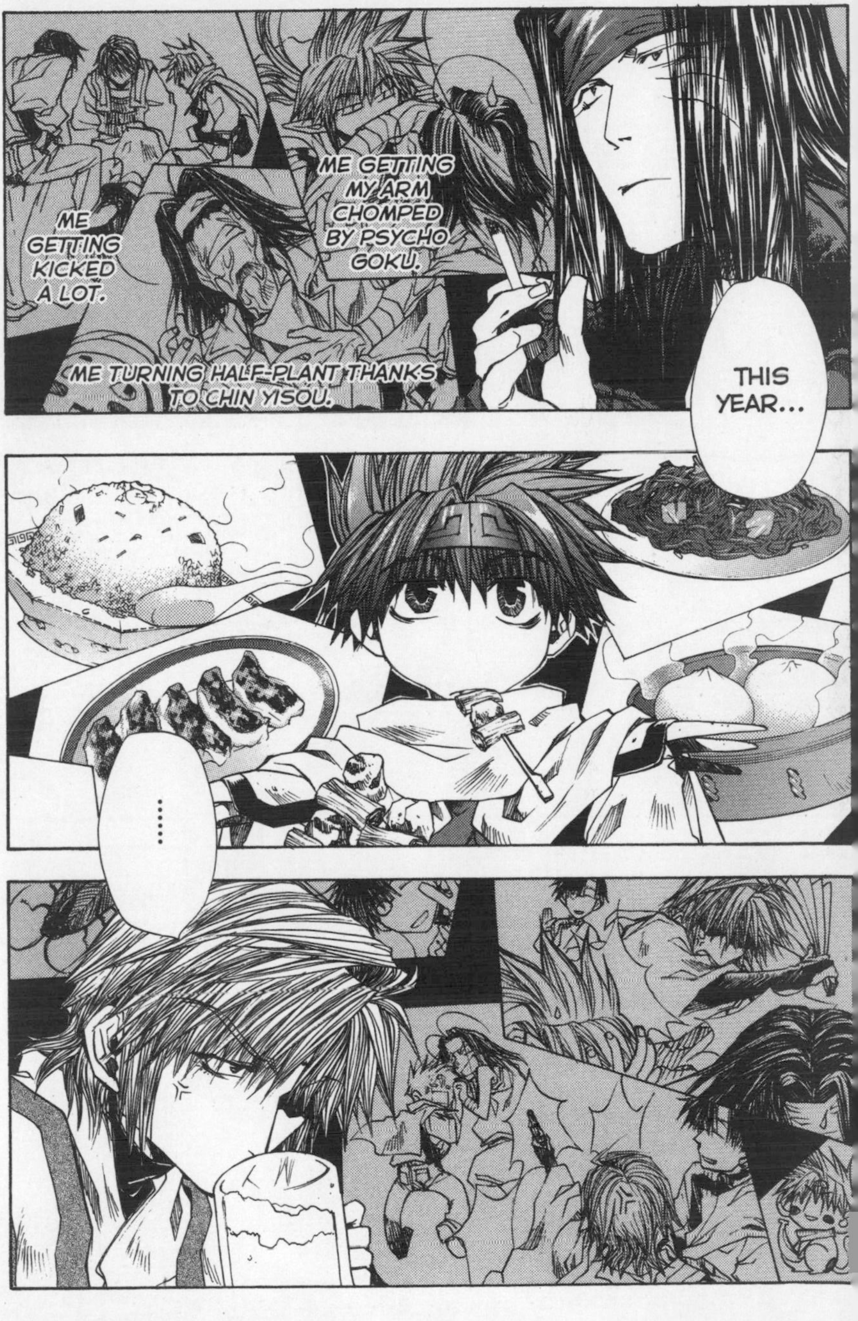
ME GETTING MY ARM CHOMPED BY PSYCHO GOKU.
ME GETTING KICKED A LOT.
ME TURNING HALF-PLANT THANKS TO CHIN YISOU.
THIS YEAR...
......

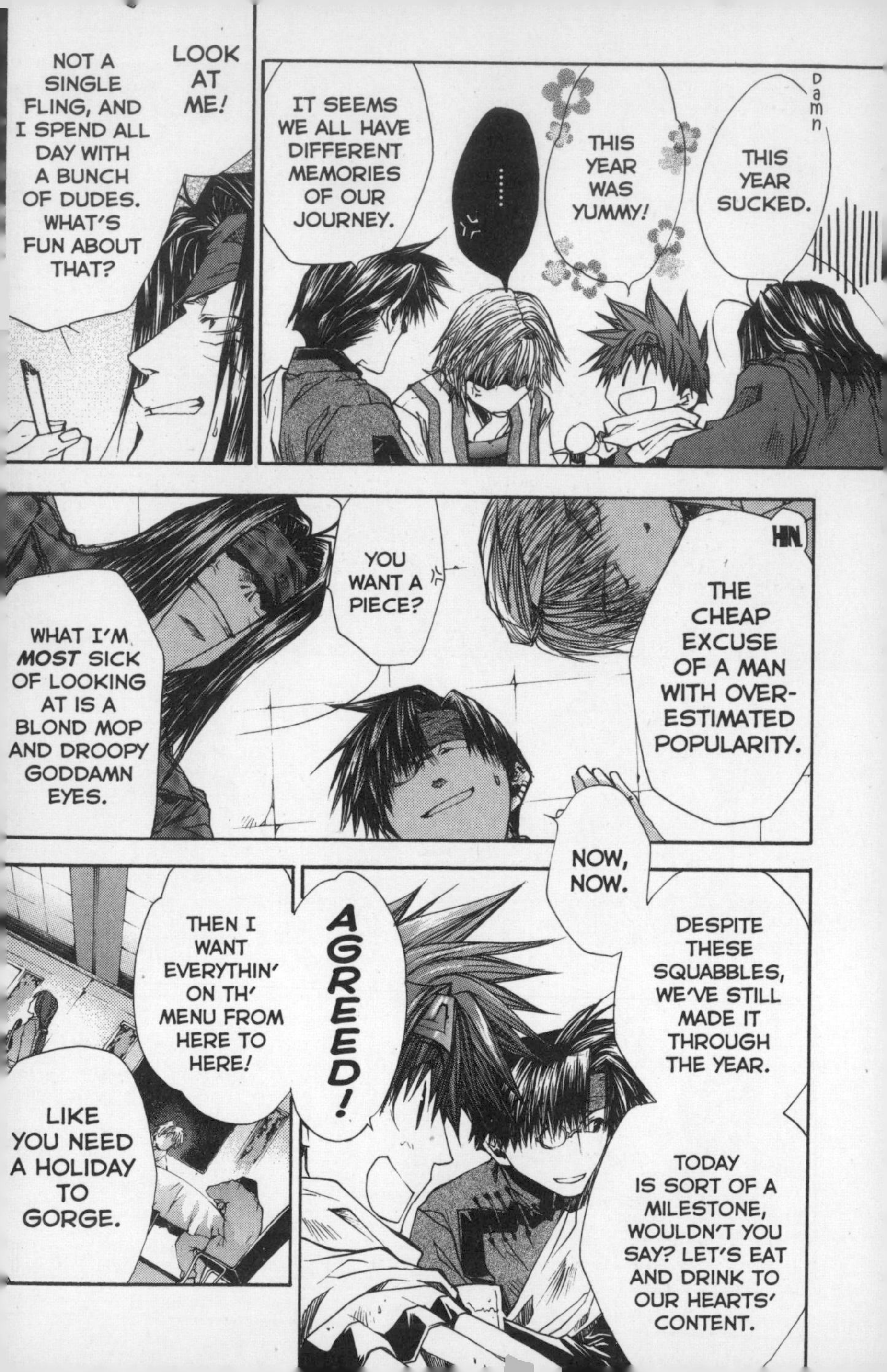
Damn
THIS YEAR SUCKED.
THIS YEAR WAS YUMMY!
......
IT SEEMS WE ALL HAVE DIFFERENT MEMORIES OF OUR JOURNEY.
LOOK AT ME!
NOT A SINGLE FLING, AND I SPEND ALL DAY WITH A BUNCH OF DUDES. WHAT'S FUN ABOUT THAT?
HN
THE CHEAP EXCUSE OF A MAN WITH OVER-ESTIMATED POPULARITY.
YOU WANT A PIECE?
WHAT I'M *MOST* SICK OF LOOKING AT IS A BLOND MOP AND DROOPY GODDAMN EYES.
NOW, NOW.
DESPITE THESE SQUABBLES, WE'VE STILL MADE IT THROUGH THE YEAR.
TODAY IS SORT OF A MILESTONE, WOULDN'T YOU SAY? LET'S EAT AND DRINK TO OUR HEARTS' CONTENT.
AGREED!
THEN I WANT EVERYTHIN' ON TH' MENU FROM HERE TO HERE!
LIKE YOU NEED A HOLIDAY TO GORGE.

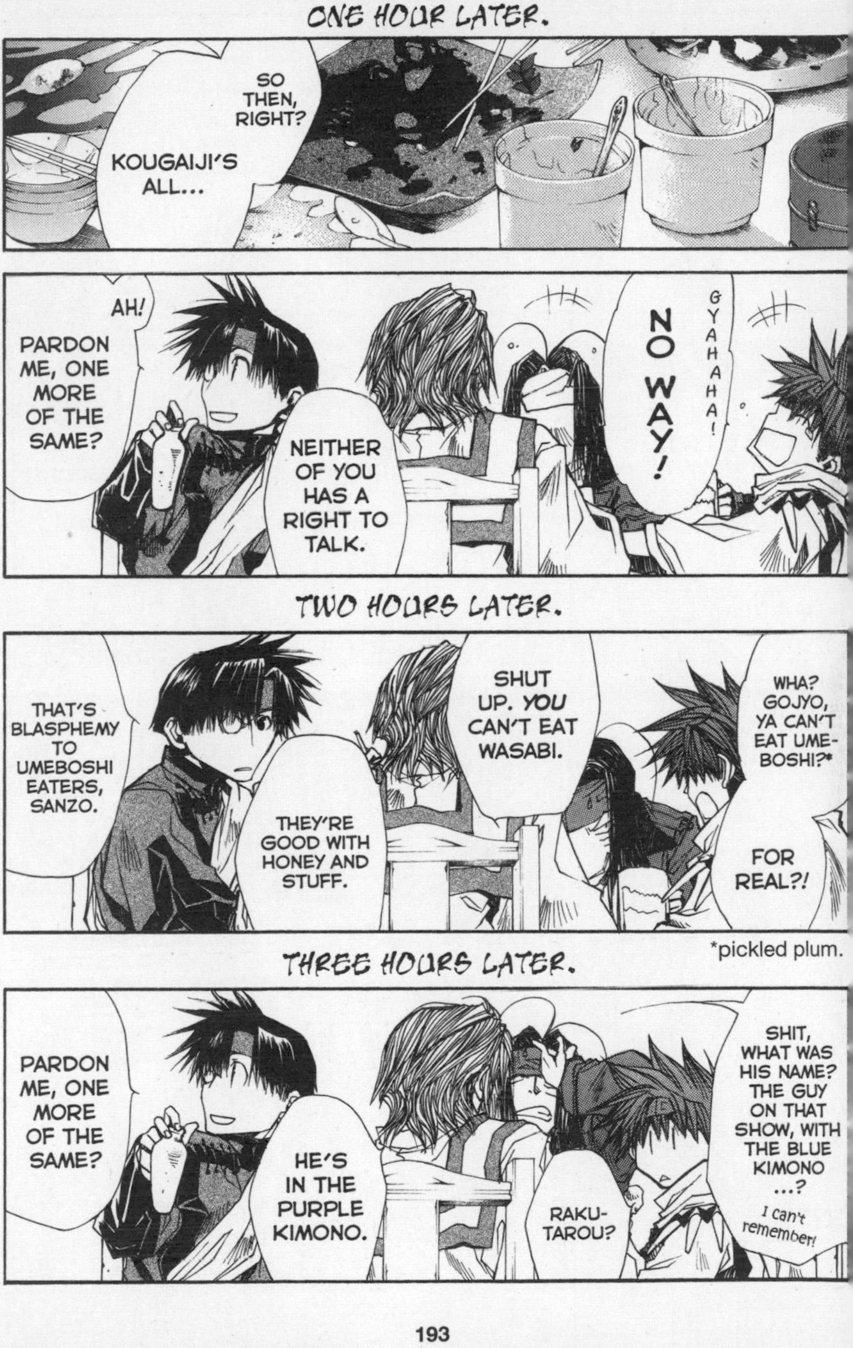
ONE HOUR LATER.
SO THEN, RIGHT?
KOUGAIJI'S ALL...
GYAHAHA!
NO WAY!
NEITHER OF YOU HAS A RIGHT TO TALK.
AH!
PARDON ME, ONE MORE OF THE SAME?
TWO HOURS LATER.
WHA? GOJYO, YA CAN'T EAT UME-BOSHI?*
FOR REAL?!
SHUT UP. *YOU* CAN'T EAT WASABI.
THEY'RE GOOD WITH HONEY AND STUFF.
THAT'S BLASPHEMY TO UMEBOSHI EATERS, SANZO.
*pickled plum.
THREE HOURS LATER.
SHIT, WHAT WAS HIS NAME? THE GUY ON THAT SHOW, WITH THE BLUE KIMONO ...?
I can't remember!
RAKU-TAROU?
HE'S IN THE PURPLE KIMONO.
PARDON ME, ONE MORE OF THE SAME?

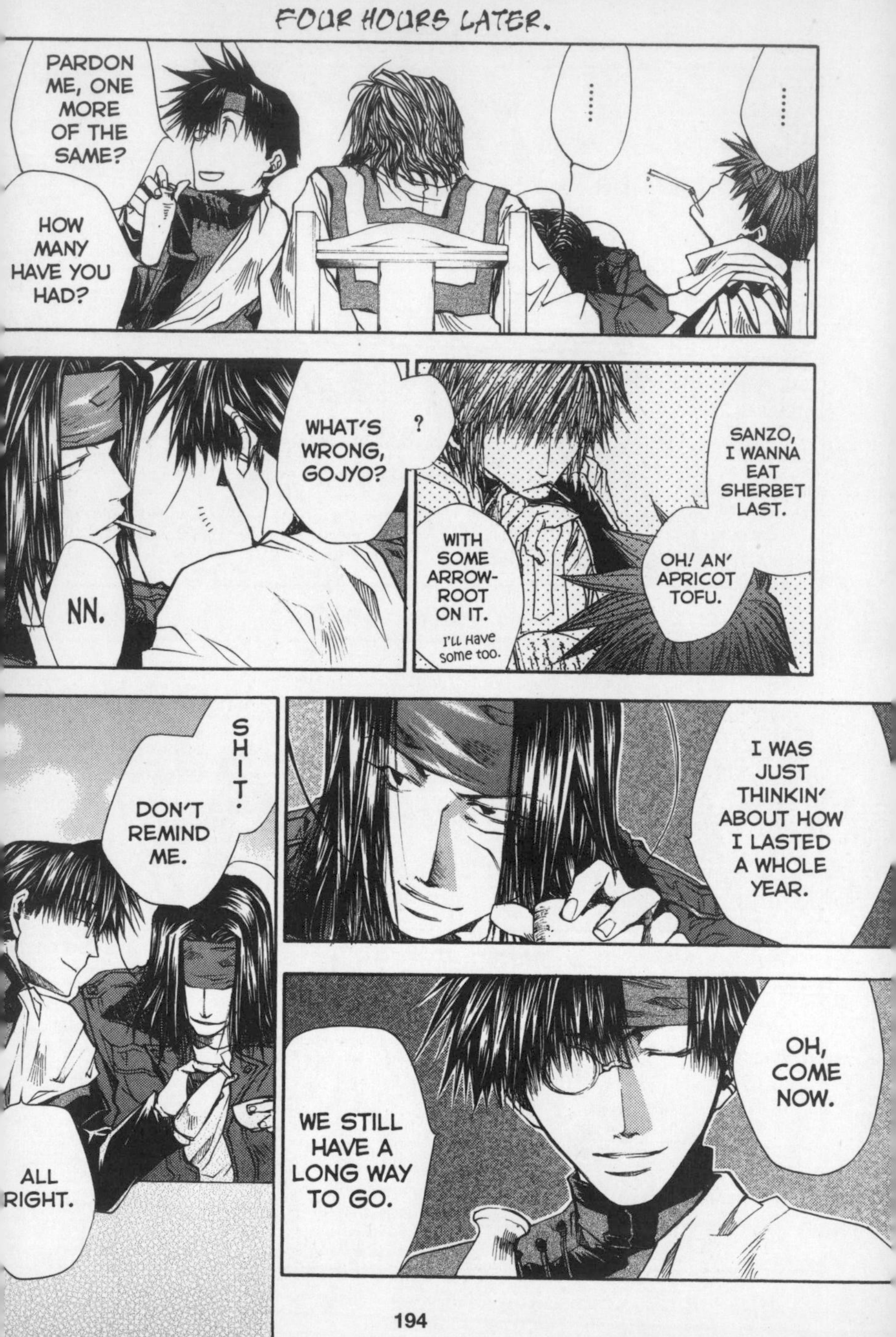
FOUR HOURS LATER.
......
......
PARDON ME, ONE MORE OF THE SAME?
HOW MANY HAVE YOU HAD?
SANZO, I WANNA EAT SHERBET LAST.
OH! AN' APRICOT TOFU.
WITH SOME ARROW-ROOT ON IT.
I'LL Have some too.
?
WHAT'S WRONG, GOJYO?
NN.
I WAS JUST THINKIN' ABOUT HOW I LASTED A WHOLE YEAR.
OH, COME NOW.
WE STILL HAVE A LONG WAY TO GO.
SHIT.
DON'T REMIND ME.
ALL RIGHT.

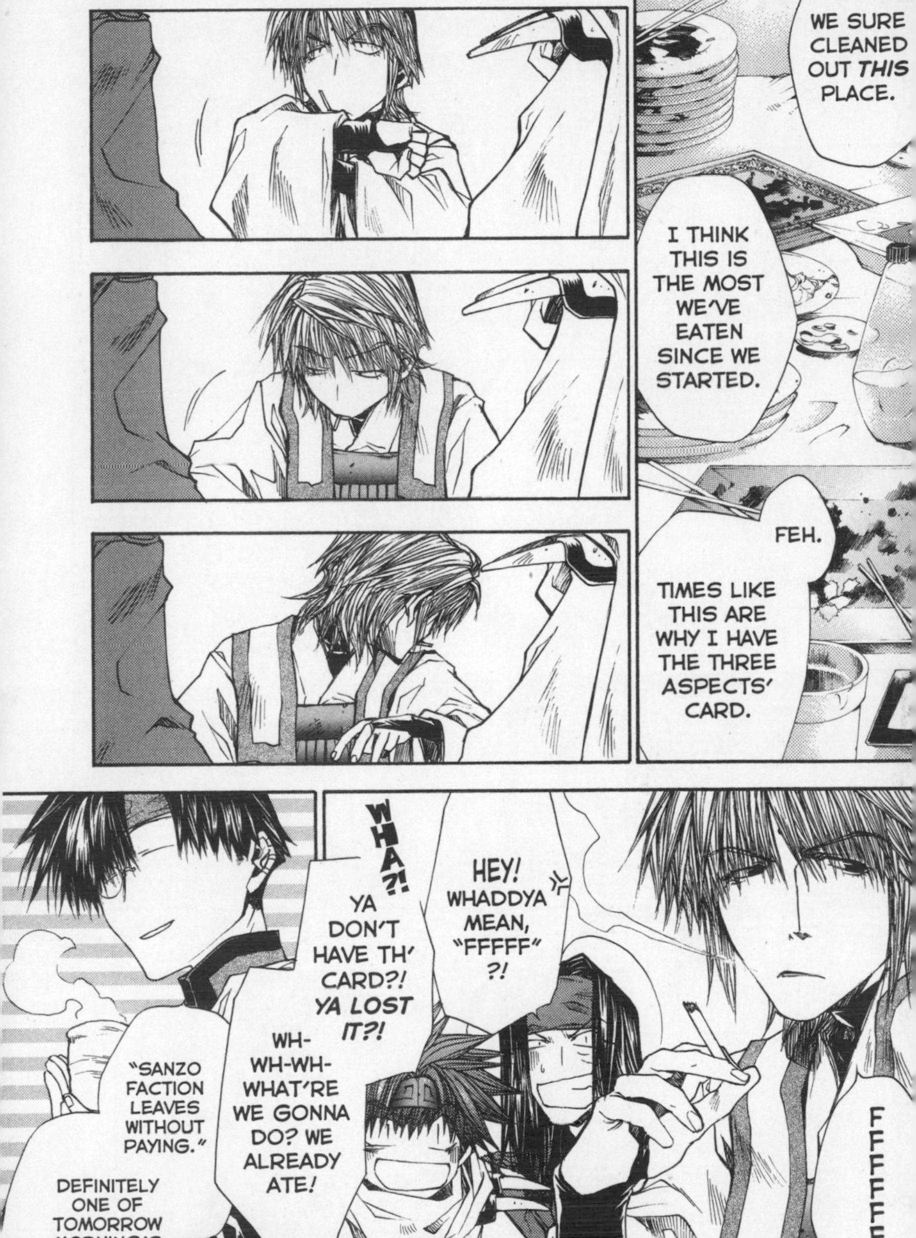
WE SURE CLEANED OUT *THIS* PLACE.
I THINK THIS IS THE MOST WE'VE EATEN SINCE WE STARTED.
FEH.
TIMES LIKE THIS ARE WHY I HAVE THE THREE ASPECTS' CARD.
FFFFFF...
HEY! WHADDYA MEAN, "FFFFF"?!
WHA?!
YA DON'T HAVE TH' CARD?! *YA LOST IT?!*
WH-WH-WH-WHAT'RE WE GONNA DO? WE ALREADY ATE!
"SANZO FACTION LEAVES WITHOUT PAYING."
DEFINITELY ONE OF TOMORROW MORNING'S HEADLINES.

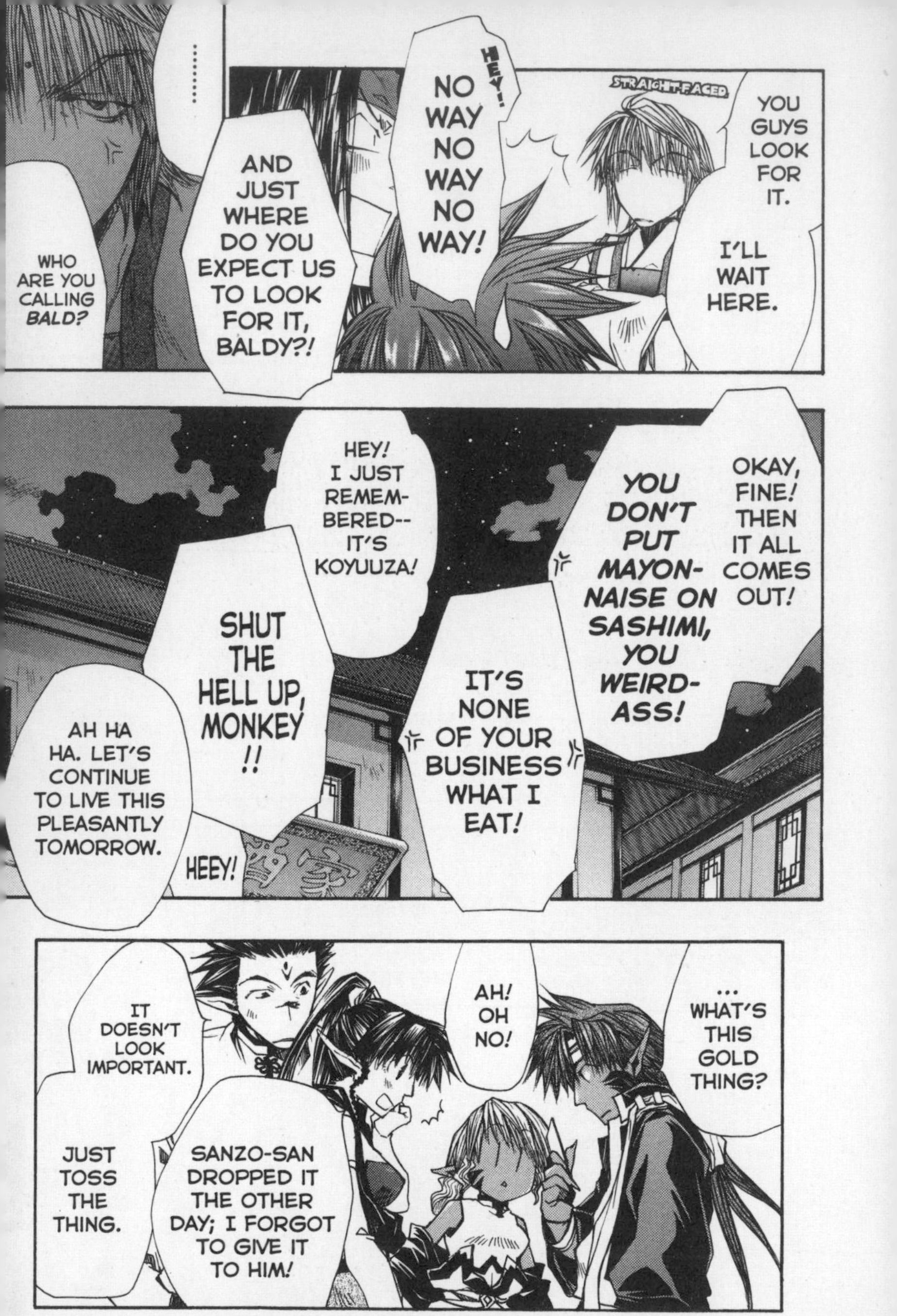
STRAIGHT-FACED
YOU GUYS LOOK FOR IT.
I'LL WAIT HERE.
HEY!
NO WAY NO WAY NO WAY!
AND JUST WHERE DO YOU EXPECT US TO LOOK FOR IT, BALDY?!
......
WHO ARE YOU CALLING *BALD?*
OKAY, FINE! THEN IT ALL COMES OUT!
YOU DON'T PUT MAYONNAISE ON SASHIMI, YOU WEIRD-ASS!
IT'S NONE OF YOUR BUSINESS WHAT I EAT!
HEY! I JUST REMEMBERED-- IT'S KOYUUZA!
SHUT THE HELL UP, MONKEY!!
HEEY!
AH HA HA. LET'S CONTINUE TO LIVE THIS PLEASANTLY TOMORROW.
... WHAT'S THIS GOLD THING?
AH! OH NO!
SANZO-SAN DROPPED IT THE OTHER DAY; I FORGOT TO GIVE IT TO HIM!
IT DOESN'T LOOK IMPORTANT.
JUST TOSS THE THING.

SAIYUKI RELOAD 3 THE END

SAIYUKI RELOAD
PRODUCTION STAFF

ORIGINAL WORKS
KAZUYA MINEKURA

ASSISTANT WORKS
KATSUYA SEINO
YUZU MIZUTANI
RIE TAHARA
TAKANO

EDITOR
YOUSUKE SUGINO

ISSAISHA

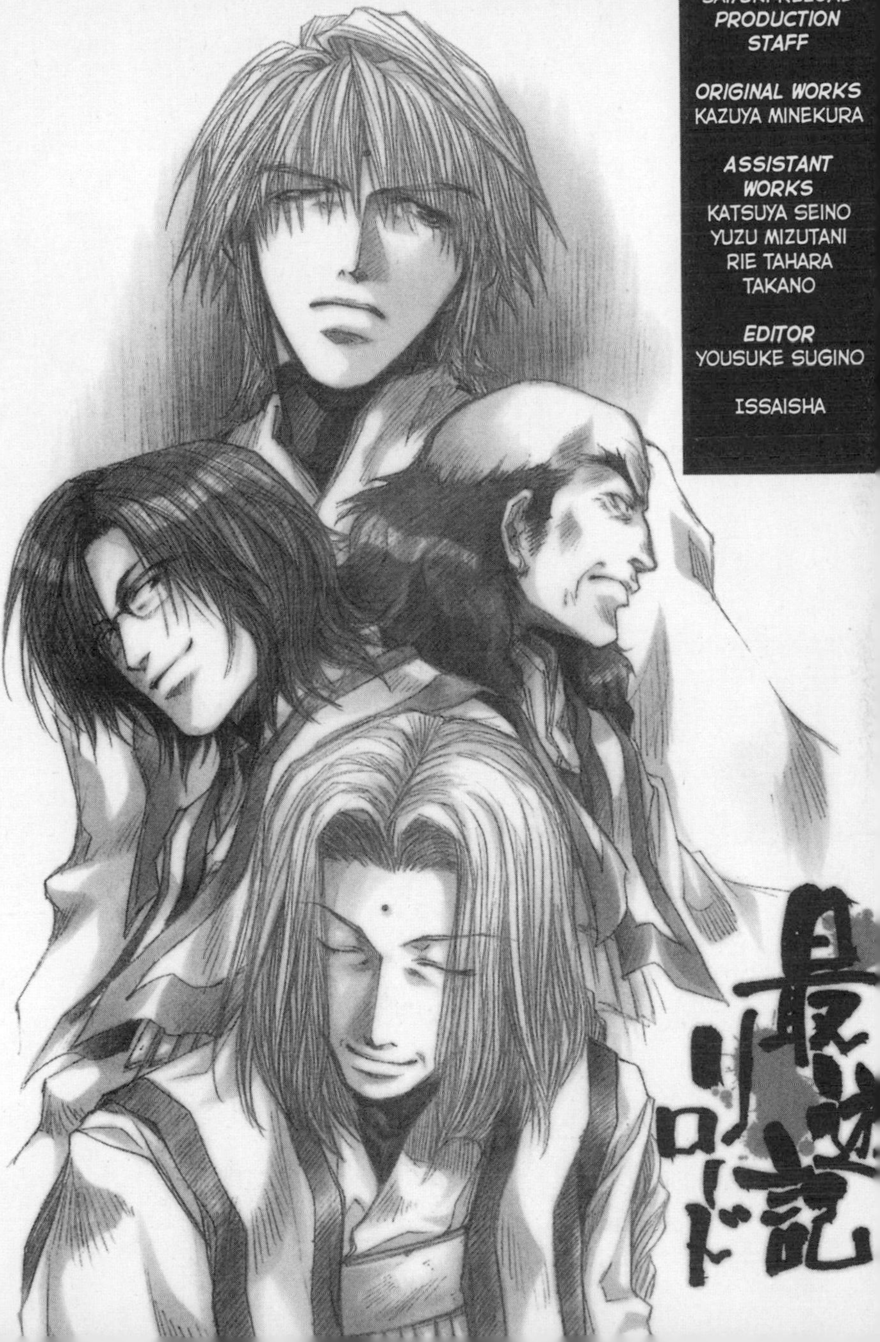
最遊記
リロード

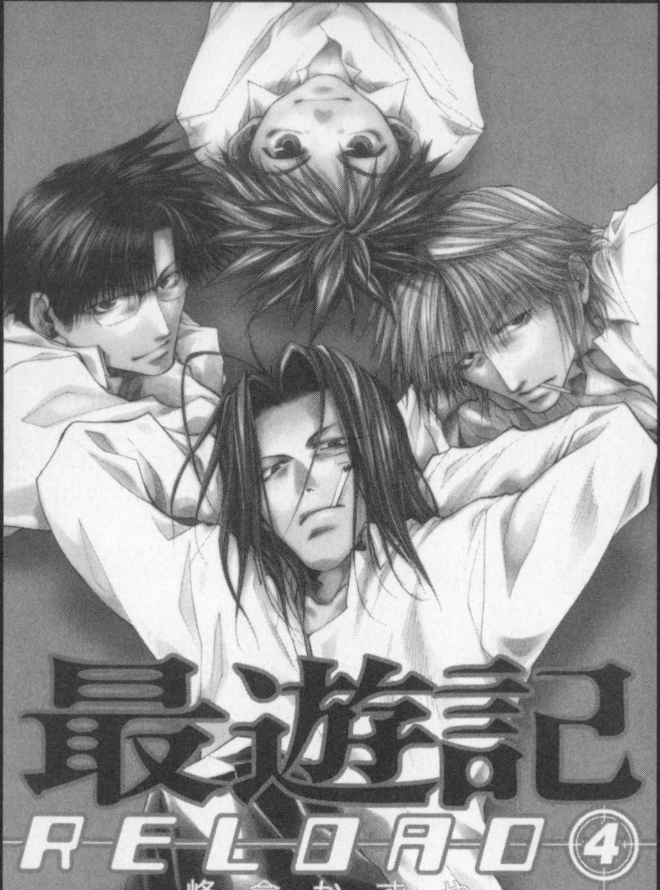
最遊記
RELOAD 4
峰倉かずや
KAZUYA MINEKURA

New troubles and new characters are introduced in this exciting installment of Saiyuki Reload! Sanzo and Goku become even closer while Hakkai and Gojyo's friendship is tested. As the fearsome foursome continue on in their latest adventure, what will happen when they are faced with a new kind of enemy?

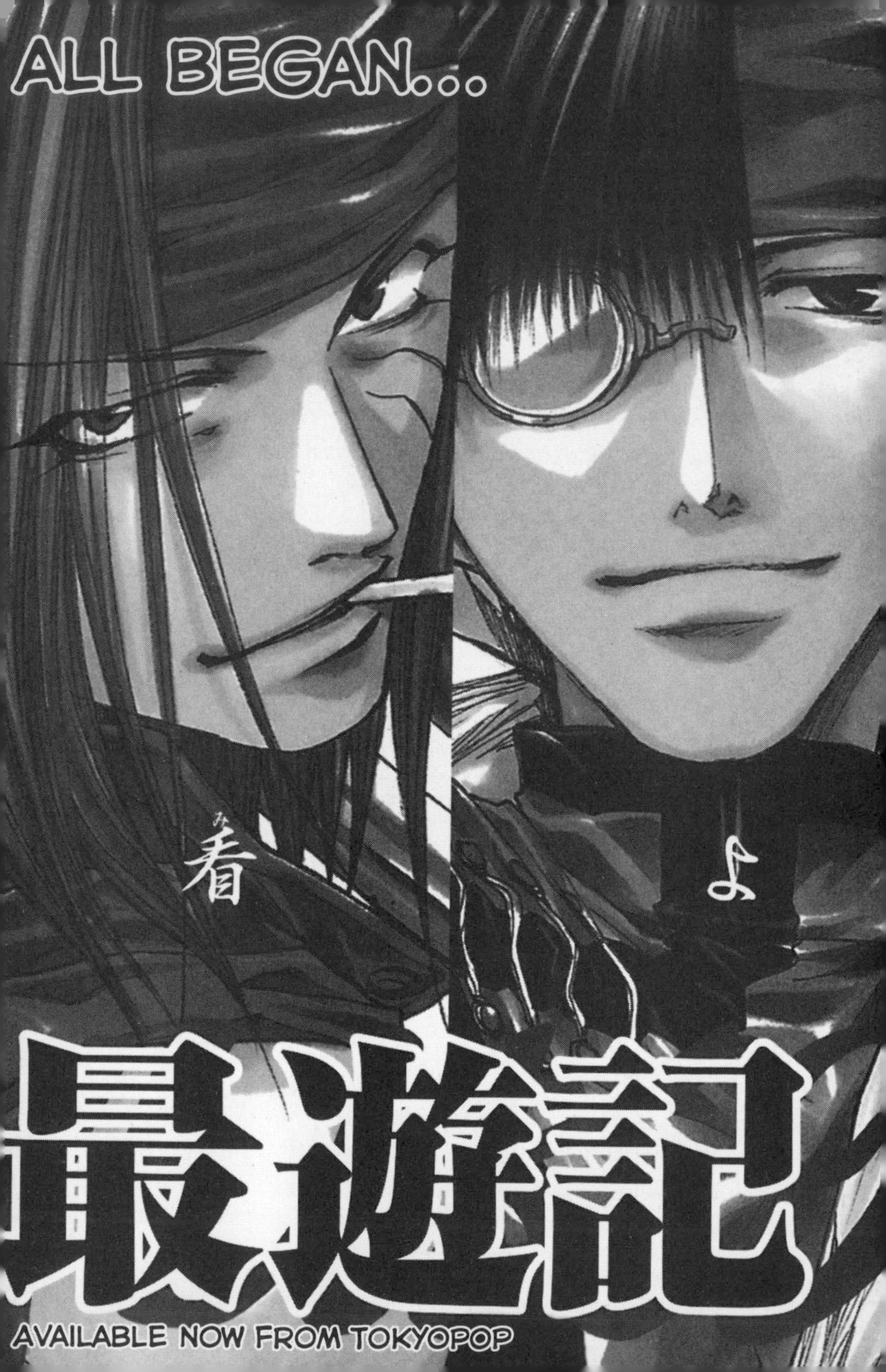
ALL BEGAN...
最遊記
AVAILABLE NOW FROM TOKYOPOP

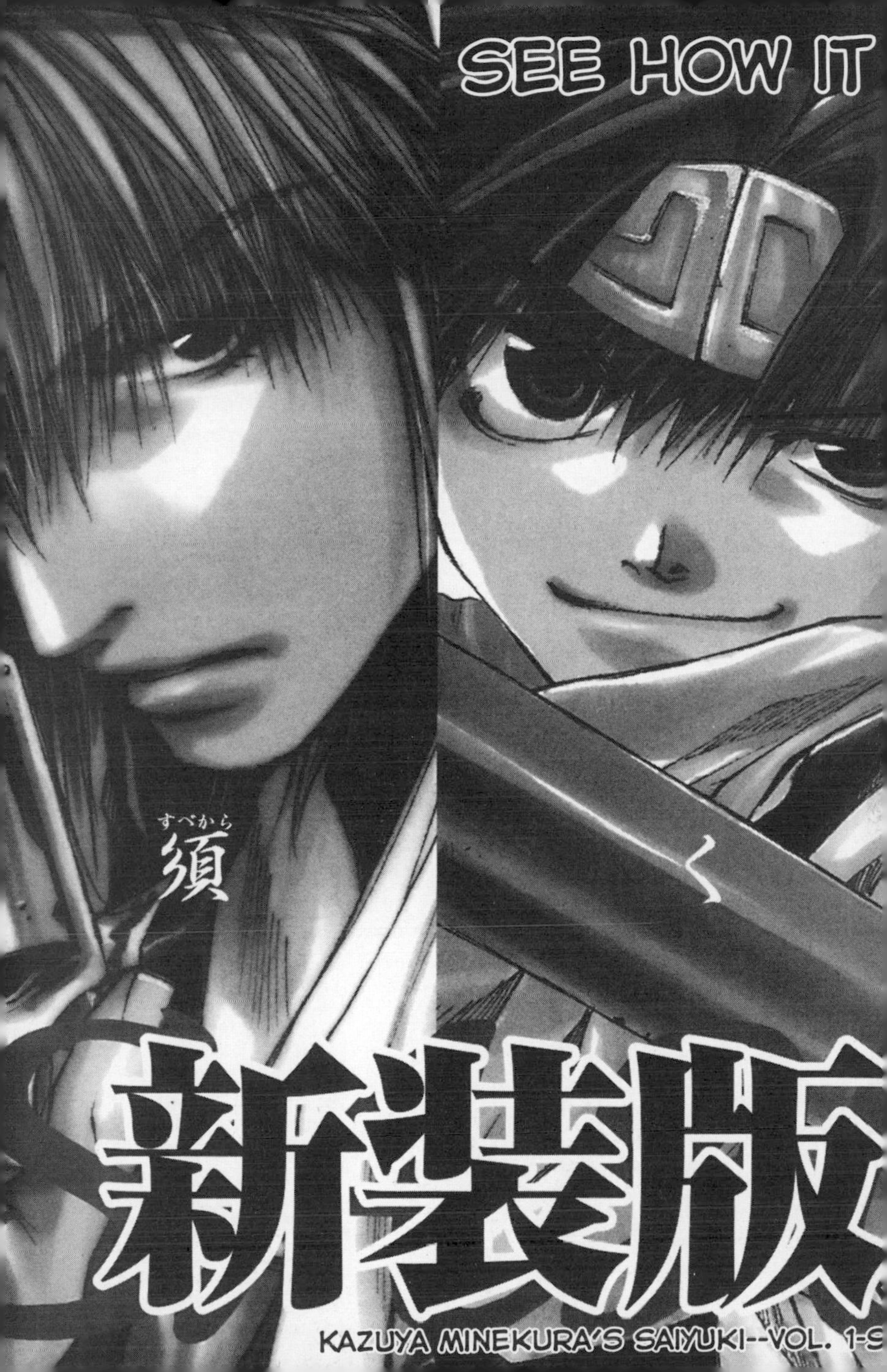
SEE HOW IT
すべから
須
新装版
KAZUYA MINEKURA'S SAIYUKI--VOL. 1-9

SOUND EFFECT CHART

THE FOLLOWING IS A LIST OF THE SOUND EFFECTS USED IN *SAIYUKI*. EACH SOUND IS LABELED BY PAGE AND PANEL NUMBER, SEPARATED BY A PERIOD. THE FIRST DESCRIPTION (IN BOLD) IS THE PHONETIC READING OF THE JAPANESE, AND IS FOLLOWED BY THE EQUIVALENT ENGLISH SOUND OR A DESCRIPTION.

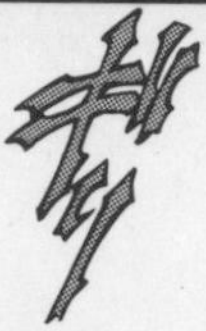

GIRI!

THIS USEFUL SOUND EFFECT HAS A COUPLE OF FUNCTIONS: IT CAN BE EITHER THE SOUND OF GRINDING TEETH OR TWO COMBATANTS STRUGGLING AGAINST EACH OTHER.

9.1	DOGOO!!: CRASH
9.2	PISHA: PTUI
10.3	ZA!: WHDD
10.4	BAN: BAM
12.1	OO: VOOM
12.3	BA!: BAM
13.1	GOGAA!: GAWHAM
13.3	ZUZAZAA!!: SKID
14.4	ZEE!x2: GASP
14.4	HAA: HUFF
16.1	PAN!: SLAP
17.2	DOSA.: THUD
18.1	ZA!: WHDD
18.2	PIKU: TWITCH
20.5	GUGOO: SNORE
23.1	OOO: HOWLING WIND
23.2	ZA!: WHDD
23.5	JA!!: RUSH
24.1	GOO!...: RUMBLE
24.3	DON!!: BOOM
24.4	BIRIx2: RIP
24.5	ZA!!: WHDD
25.3	DO!: BAM
25.4	GAUN!: BANG
25.5	GAUN!: BANG
26.1	GAUNX2: BANG
26.3	OOOO: HOWLING WIND
27.5	GO!: WHAM
28.1	ZAZA!: SKID
28.6	GO!...: ROAR
29.5	DOGOO!: KAWHAM
30.4	GACHA: CHAK
32.3	CHA!!!: AIM
32.6	GI!: CLENCH
33.1	DON!!: BOOM
33.3	OO: HOWLING WIND
34.1	OO...: HOWLING WIND
35.1	GAKII!: CLANG
35.4	ZA!: WHDD
35.5	ZA!: WHDD
36.1	ZA!.: WHDD
37.3	ZA!: WHDD

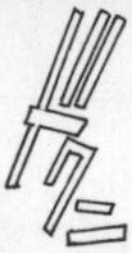

DOKUN!

IN MOST MANGA, A PLEASANT LITTLE "DOKI DOKI" IS THE PREFERRED SOUND FOR HEART-BEATS, BUT IN *SAIYUKI*, THEY NEEDED TO KICK IT UP A NOTCH. "DOKUN" IS THE SOUND OF A PARTICULARLY STRONG HEART-BEAT, USUALLY RESERVED FOR MOMENTS OF EXTREME SHOCK OR DEMONIC TRANSFORMATION.

37.4	GAKII!!: CLANG
38.3	GAKII: CLANG
38.5	BAAN: WHACK
39.1	ZA!: WHDD
39.3	GO: ONNG
39.4	DOON!!: BOOM
40.1	HYU!...: SWISH
40.2	GI: TANG
41.1	GO!!: WHACK
42.2	DOSAA: KATHUD
46.1	DOSAA: KATHUD

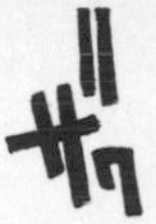

ZAWA!

NO ONE REALLY CARES WHAT ALL THOSE EXTRAS IN THE BACKGROUND ARE SAYING, RIGHT? THAT'S WHY MANGA-KA USE THIS HANDY SOUND EFFECT TO INDICATE BACKGROUND CHATTER. YOU'LL SEE IT HOVERING OVER CROWDED CITY STREETS OR CLASSROOMS THROUGHOUT MANGA. IT CAN ALSO BE USED TO INDICATE THE SOUND OF WIND BLOWING THROUGH THE LEAVES OF A TREE. AIN'T THAT SWEET?

47.6	YURA...: REEL
48.1	DA!!!: DASH
48.3	GAKII!: CLANG
49.3	OOO...: HOWLING WIND
49.5	GO...: ONNG
50.1	DON!: BOOM
51.3	OOO: HOWLING WIND
52.1	BAKII!!: CRASH
52.2	GO...: RUMBLE
52.3	DON!!!: BOOM
52.4	GARAx3: CRUMBLE
53.1	DOBON!!: GASPLOSH
53.2	BUWAx3: BLOOP
53.3	ZAPAA!: PLASH
54.1	ZAAA...: WHDD
57.2	DO!x3: BUMP
58.1	BURORORORO...: ENGINE RUMBLING
61.1	OO: HOWLING WIND
62.5	GASHAA!: CRASH
63.3	PARIN!: CRAK
63.4	GASHAA!!: CRASH
68.2	GASHAN!: CLATTER
68.4	GISHI!: CREAK
69.5	GYAA!: KAW
70.1	GYAAx2: KAW
70.1	BASAx3: FLAP
70.3	OOO..N: HOWLING WIND
77.1	PON.: CLAP
79.4	GAA!!!: KAW
81.5	DA!: DASH
82.1	BATAx3: SCRAMBLE
83.7	PIRA!: CRINKLE
87.5	ZA!x3: RUSTLE
87.6	ZA...: RUSTLE
90.2	ZA!x3: RUSTLE
91.3	ZAWA!...: MURMUR
92.3	ZAWA!...: MURMUR
94.2	DAN!!: DASH
94.4	BI!...: GRAB
94.6	GO: KA-
95.1	DAN!!: WHAM
96.1	HYU...: WHOOSH
96.2	PASHII!: GRAB
103.3	ZASHU.: SLASH
104.4	OOO: HOWLING WIND
104.5	DA!: DASH
105.3	GYAA!: KAW
108.1	BASAx2: FLAP
111.1	GOOO...: ROAR
111.3	DAN!!: BAM
111.4	OOO: HOWLING WIND
115.2	ZA!x2: WHDD

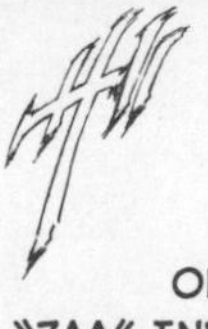

ZAA!

YOU'LL SEE THIS ONE A LOT IN *SAIYUKI*. "ZAA" INDICATES A DRAMATIC APPEARANCE. IF YOU WANT TO MAKE A LASTING IMPRESSION, ALWAYS COME IN WITH A COOL POSE AND A BIG "ZAA!"

152.1 KAAAN!!: GONG
152.2 KAAN: GONG
152.2 KAAAN: GONG
152.5 DON!: BAM
154[redacted] DON!: BAM
154.7 PATATAN: PLIP
155.3 GOBO!: COUGH
155.4 ZURU...: SLIDE
155[redacted] DOSAA: KATHUD
159.1 DAN!: WHAM
159.3 GO!!: THWOCK
159.4 ZUZAZAA!: SKID
159.5 GAGII: GAG
160.3 DON!: BOOM
162.3 GAUNx3: BANG
163.3 GAUN!!: BANG
164[redacted] BAAN!!: SLAM
166.1 ZAWA!: MURMUR
171.1 GASA!: RUSTLE
172.1 GASA!: RUSTLE
172.3 ZAA!..: WHOOSH
174[redacted] KERO: UNFAZED
175.2 JARA!: JANGLE
176.6 BUCHI!: SNAP
176.7 HIKU: TWITCH
177.1 GOCHI!: WHOCK
177.5 ZA!: WHDD
178.3 ZA!: WHDD
178[redacted] JAKI: KACHAK
178.6 TON!: BOUND
179.1 DA!!!: DASH
179.4 HYU...: WHOOSH
179[redacted] PAAN!!: WHANG
180.1 GOPAA!!: KAWHACK
180.2 SUTA!: TAP
180.4 TO!: CHOP
180.5 HYU...: WHOOSH
180.6 DO!: THUNK
181.1 BATAx3: SCRAMBLE
181.4 HETA!: SLUMP
181.6 GURUGYAA...: STOMACH GRUMBLE
182.5 GUSHI!: SNIFF
185.5 ZA!.: WHDD
185[redacted] NIHE.: GRIN
186.1 TA!: DASH
189.1 PATAN: CLAP
190.1 GACHOON: CLINK
190[redacted]4 GO!: WHAP
19[redacted] SHIRE!: SHRUG

115.4 JAN!!: JANGLE
118.2 BASA!: FLUTTER
121.1 OOO: HOWLING WIND
121.3 GII...: CREAK
123.1 ZUZAZAA!: SKID
123.2 BA!: BAM
123.3 ZA....: WHDD
123.4 BA!!!: BAM
123.6 GO: WHOCK
124.2 GUI!: YANK
124.7 GU!: GRAB

はっ HAH!

THIS IS ONE OF THE MOST COMMON SOUNDS YOU'LL SEE IN MANGA. IT'S USED TO INDICATE SURPRISE AND IS USUALLY EQUIVALENT TO "GASP!" "H" ISN'T NECESSARILY VOCALIZED, THOUGH.

125.1 DON: BOOM
125.3 ZUSHAA!!: SPLUT
125.5 KATAx3: SHAKE
126.1 SAWA...: RUSTLE
126.7 DON!x3: BOOM
127.1 GABA!!!: BOLT
128.3 ZAAA!: GUSH
131.4 ZAZAA!...: RUSTLE
132.3 GIGII...: CREAK
133.2 HOOx3: HOOT
136.2 ZAZAA: SPLASH
136.5 ZAZA!: SPLASH
136.6 GURA...: STAGGER
138.4 BA!: BAM
139.1 JAKI!: KACHAK
139.4 BATAx3: SCRAMBLE
142.4 PUHAA: HWAA
143.4 PASHI!: CATCH
146.2 DON!: BOOM
146.4 KO!: CRAK
146.5 GOTOO: THUMP
148.6 GUI!: GRAB
149.5 JA!: RATTLE
149.6 GICHI!: TENSE
150.3 PACHI!: CRACKLE

TOKYOPOP SHOP

that I'm not like other people...

Dear Diary,
I'm starting to feel

STOP!

This is the back of the book.
You wouldn't want to spoil a great ending!

This book is printed "manga-style," in the authentic Japanese right-to-left format. Since none of the artwork has been flipped or altered, readers get to experience the story just as the creator intended. You've been asking for it, so TOKYOPOP® delivered: authentic, hot-off-the-press, and far more fun!

DIRECTIONS

If this is your first time reading manga-style, here's a quick guide to help you understand how it works.

It's easy... just start in the top right panel and follow the numbers. Have fun, and look for more 100% authentic manga from TOKYOPOP®!